CISTERCIAN STUDIES SERIES: NUMBER ONE-HUNDRED SIXTEEN

SPIRITUAL DIRECTION IN THE EARLY CHRISTIAN EAST

by

Irénée Hausherr

Foreword by

Bishop Kallistos [Ware] of Diokleia

Translated by

Anthony P. Gythiel

Cistercian Publications
Kalamazoo, Michigan
1990

A translation of *Direction spirituelle en orient autrefois*. Orientalia Christiana Analecta, 144. Rome: Pontificium Institutum Orientalium Studiorum, 1955.

The foreword, 'The Spiritual Father in Saint John Climacus and Saint Symeon the New Theologian', was first published in *Studia Patristica XVIII/2* (Kalamazoo:Cistercian Publications-Leuven:Peeters, 1990) and is used here by permission of the Oxford Patristics Conference and Bishop Kallistos [Ware].

Available in Britain from Cassell/Mowbray pc
Artillery House Artillery Row London SW1P 1RT

Available elsewhere (including Canada) from
Cistercian Publications (Distribution)
Saint Joseph's Abbey Spencer, MA 01562

*The work of Cistercian Publications is made possible in part
by support from Western Michigan University to
The Institute of Cistercian Studies*

The translator and editors express their appreciation to
The Office of Research and Sponsored Programs at
The Wichita State University, Kansas
for a translator's grant which made this work possible.

Library of Congress Cataloguing-in-Publication Data
Hausherr, Irénée, 1891-1978
   [Direction spirituelle en Orient autrefois. English]
   Spiritual direction in the ancient christian east / by Irénée Hausherr; translated by Anthony P. Gythiel
   p.   cm. — (Cistercian studies series ; no 116)
   Translation of: Direction spirituelle en orient autrefois.
   Bibliography: p. 365
   ISBN 0-87907-416-7. — ISBN (invalid) 0-87907-516-6 (pbk.)
   1. Spiritual direction. 2. Orthodox Eastern Church—Doctrines. 3. Eastern churches—Doctrines. 4. Catholic Church—Oriental rites—doctrines. I. Title. II. Series
BX382.5.H3813 1989
253.5 —dc19
                                                                    88-38626
                                                                    CIP

Printed in the United States of America

CONTENTS

FOREWORD
THE SPIRITUAL FATHER IN SAINT JOHN CLIMACUS AND SAINT SYMEON THE NEW THEOLOGIAN

Bishop Kallistos [Ware] of Diokleia

'WHAT IS MORE TO BE DESIRED', asks Saint Theodore the Studite (759-826), 'than a true father—a father-in-God?'[1] This personal relationship between the spiritual father or elder—*gerōn* in Greek, *starets* in Slavonic—and his child in God is of crucial importance for any understanding of the Christian East. There are in a sense two forms of apostolic succession within the life of the Church. First there is the visible succession of the hierarchy, the unbroken series of bishops in different cities, to which Saint Irenaeus appealed at the end of the second century. Alongside this, largely hidden, existing on a 'charismatic' rather than an official level, there is secondly the apostolic succession of the spiritual fathers and mothers in each generation of the Church—the succession of the saints, stretching from the apostolic age to our own day, which Saint Symeon the New Theologian termed the 'golden chain'.[2] The two types of succession overlap, for a bishop may also be a spiritual father and a saint. The first type has as its chief centres the great primatial and metropolitan sees such as Rome, Constantinople, Alexandria, Moscow, or Canterbury. The chief

centres of the second vary from one generation to another, and
are usually certain remote hermitages in the desert or the
forest: Nitria and Scetis in the late fourth century, Gaza in the
early sixth, Sarov, Optino and Spruce Island, Alaska, in the
nineteenth. Both types of succession are essential for the true
functioning of the Body of Christ, and it is through their
interaction that the life of the Church on earth is
accomplished.

The ministry of the spiritual father is already foreshadowed
in the New Testament: 'Though you have countless guides in
Christ, you do not have many fathers. For I became your
father in Christ Jesus through the Gospel' (I Cor 4:15).[3] Here
Saint Paul makes an emphatic distinction between the 'guide'
or 'pedagogue' (*paedagogos*), in a broader sense, and the 'father':
the Corinthians have many 'pedagogues' but only a single
father, only one who has 'regenerated' them into the new life
in Christ Jesus, and who is thus uniquely entitled to say, 'I
have begotten you' (*ego umas egennesa*). Obviously Paul's ministry is not identical with that of the elder in later Eastern
spirituality: Paul was a preacher of the word, an itinerant
missionary, and not a director of souls working in a monastic
milieu. But at the same time there are striking parallels between Paul and the monastic elder. Paul feels a continuing
responsibility for those whom he has 'begotten' or 'initiated'
into the Christian life, a direct involvement in their subsequent struggles. Shifting from a paternal to a maternal image,
he writes to the Galatians: 'My little children, with whom I
am in travail until Christ be formed in you!' (Gal 4:19). As this
text makes clear, his commission does not come to an end with
their initial conversion, but he goes on caring and suffering for
them as a parent throughout the long process of development
during which Christ is being 'formed' within them. He does
not simply preach the word to them, but he bears their burdens, making their joys and sorrows his own: 'If anyone is
weak, do I not share his weakness? If anyone is made to
stumble, does not my heart blaze with indignation?' (2 Cor
11:29). He helps his children in Christ precisely because he is

willing to share himself with them, identifying his own life with theirs. All this is true also of the spiritual father at a later date. Dostoevsky's description of the *starets* may be applied exactly to the ministry of Saint Paul: like the elder, the apostle is one who 'takes your soul and your will into his soul and will'.[4] The ministry of the elder to his spiritual children is foreshadowed also in Alexandria during the second and third centuries. The teacher's role, as understood by Saint Pantaenus, Saint Clement and Origen, was by no means limited to instruction in the narrow academic sense, to the bare transmission of facts. The teacher was also a spiritual guide to his pupils, a living model and exemplar, providing them not only with information but with an all-embracing personal relationship. Origen's life of asceticism and prayer formed an integral part of his vocation as teacher.[5] Significantly Clement begins the *Stromateis* by likening the master-disciple relationship to that between parent and child, and he mentions that catechists in Alexandria were called 'father'.[6] There are important parallels here in classical philosophy[7] and Rabbinic Judaism.[8] The figure of the elder or spiritual father, of which Paul and Origen serve in some measure as precursors, occupies a decisive place in Eastern monastic life from the fourth century onwards. The 'founder' of Egyptian monasticism, Saint Antony (*c.* 251-356), provides in his own person a standard and norm for later generations. To appreciate how a true *gerōn* lives and acts, we need look no further than Saint Athanasius' biography[9] or the stories told by Palladius about the old man's dealings with Eulogius and Paul the Simple.[10] The centrality of spiritual fatherhood is likewise underlined in the sayings attributed to Antony at the start of the *Apophthegmata*:

> I know of monks who fell after much toil and lapsed into madness, because they trusted in their own work and neglected the commandment that says: 'Ask your father, and he will tell you' (Deut 32:7).

> . . . So far as possible, the monk should in full trust
> ask the elders how many steps to take and how many
> drops of water to drink in his cell, in case he is making
> some mistake in these matters.[11]

Although they offer no abstract definition of what the *geron* is,
the *Apophthegmata* remain up to the present the most important single source for the practice of spiritual direction in the
Christian East. The impression that they give is confirmed, in
a yet more vivid and first-hand manner, by the correspondence of two sixth-century spiritual fathers in Southern Palestine, Barsanuphius and John of Gaza: the questions put to
them and their answers survive in a remarkably detailed
form.[12]

The tradition of spiritual fatherhood or motherhood—for
this is a ministry also exercised by women[13]—retained its full
significance throughout the Byzantine era, while from Byzantium it spread to the Slav Orthodox world. To take but one
example out of many, the following advice is given in a text
from Kievan Russia, the *Admonition of the Father to his Son*
(?eleventh century):

> I show you, my son, true refuges—monasteries, the
> houses of the saints: have recourse to them and they will
> comfort you; shed your sorrows before them and you will
> be gladdened: for they are sons of sorrowlessness and
> know how to comfort you, sorrowing one. . . . In the
> city where you are living or in other neighbouring towns
> seek a God-fearing man—and serve him with all your
> strength. Having found such a man, you need grieve no
> more; you have found the key to the Kingdom of Heaven;
> adhere to him with soul and body; observe his life, his
> walking, sitting, looking, eating, and examine all his hab-
> its; first of all, my son, keep his words, do not let one of
> them fall to the ground; they are more precious than
> pearls—the words of the saints.[14]

It is noteworthy in this passage that the *starets* assists his disciple not by words of counsel alone but by the pattern of his entire life: ' . . . observe his life, his walking, sitting, looking, eating . . .'. As in the case of Origen at Alexandria, what he offers is not so much instruction as a personal relationship.

The relationship remains as significant in modern Orthodoxy as ever it was in the past. Spiritual fatherhood—as exemplified, for instance, by Saint Seraphim of Sarov or the elders of Optino[15]—provides the true key to nineteenth-century Russian church life; and the chief reason for the unexpected revival of Greek monasticism on Mount Athos in the last twenty years lies precisely in the presence there of elders able to supply the kind of charismatic guidance that Saint Antony provided in fourth-century Egypt. The Athonite houses which today attract novices are those with an abbot or other monk able to act as a true father in the Spirit.[16]

The *Apophthegmata* and numerous other texts, especially lives of the saints, indicate with many details *how* in practice the spiritual father fulfills his task. But it is less easy to find in Patristic sources an analysis of *what* in principle constitutes the essence of spiritual fatherhood. The matter is, however, discussed notably in two texts: the letter of Saint John Climacus (?579-?649), abbot of Sinai, entitled *To the Shepherd (Ad Pastorem)*,[17] sometimes treated as the thirty-first step in the *Ladder of Divine Ascent*; and the first letter of Saint Symeon the New Theologian (949-1022), abbot of Saint Mamas in Constantinople, entitled *On Confession*.[18] Both authors also make many references to spiritual fatherhood elsewhere in their writings, confirming what is said in these two letters. The points of similarity between the two texts are so striking as to exclude mere coincidence. Although Symeon, following his usual practice, does not quote any earlier Fathers in his letter *On Confession*, there can be little doubt that he is drawing directly upon Climacus, whose *Ladder* was certainly known to him.[19] I am encouraged to examine with some care the parallels between Climacus' letter *To the Shepherd* and Symeon's *On Confession* because, to the best of my knowledge, no one has so far attempted to do this in a systematic fashion. Somewhat surprisingly Dr. V. Ch. Christophoridis, in his valuable monograph specially devoted to Symeon's teaching on spiritual fatherhood, fails to note the close dependence.[20]

Although neither Climacus nor Symeon provides a systematic list of characteristics, the spiritual father is in fact described by both authors chiefly in five ways. He is seen as doctor, counsellor, intercessor, mediator, and sponsor.

1. *Doctor (iatros)*. This is the dominant 'model' for the spiritual father in Climacus and Symeon, and indeed in Eastern Christian literature generally from the fourth century onwards. Athanasius describes Antony as 'a doctor given by God to Egypt';[21] Gregory of Nazianzus[22] and John Chrysostom[23] use similar language about the pastoral work of the priest or bishop. The Council *in Trullo* (AD 692) refers to the sinner as a 'sick man'; sinfulness is a 'disease', while the confessor is the one who applies 'healing' for the 'illness'.[24]

Such exactly is the approach also of Climacus and of Symeon. In his treatise *To the Shepherd* Climacus develops the medical analogy at length. The spiritual father is a 'doctor', who cares for the 'sick man', using 'plasters, razors, eye-salves, potions, sponges, remedies against nausea, instruments for blood-letting and cauterization, ointments, sleeping draughts, the knife, bandages'. The 'penance' (*epitimion*) that he imposes is not a punishment but a healing remedy, a 'cauterization' that he administers 'in a compassionate way as an aid to repentance'.[25] The spiritual doctor can only help if the patient is completely honest, 'baring his wound with entire trust'.[26] Symeon uses the same medical language. 'Seek out a compassionate and merciful doctor', he enjoins in the letter *On Confession*;[27] 'let us run at once to the spiritual doctor'.[28] To confess our sins is to spit out the poison within us; and the penances (*epitimia*) that the confessor prescribes are, as in Climacus, not a punishment but a remedy or antidote (*antipharmakon*) against the poison.[29]

It is to be noted that neither Climacus nor Symeon—nor, indeed, the Eastern Christian tradition in general—envisages the confessor or spiritual father primarily as a judge, passing sentence and imposing penalties. He is on the contrary what in medieval England would have been styled a 'ghostly leech', a spiritual healer or physician. It is true that Symeon refers to the spiritual father's power to bind and loose, which may be taken to imply a measure of juridical authority;[30] but in Climacus this aspect is less evident, while even in Symeon it is not in any way the dominant 'model'. In both of them the main images are not legalistic but therapeutic;[31] confession is like going to a hospital rather than a court of law; the penance is not so much a punishment as a tonic to assist the patient in his recovery. Moreover, what the spiritual child reveals to his father are not only his sins but more generally his 'thoughts' (*logismoi*), long before they have led to outward acts—even those thoughts that are seemingly harmless and innocent.[32] The medical care of the elder embraces not just the transgressions but the entire inner life of the patient; the treatment is prophylactic rather than retrospective.

2. *Counsellor (sumboulos)*. Most obviously, although not exclusively, the spiritual father heals by his *words*, by his advice or counsel. In the *Apophthegmata* what the disciple or visitor says to the *abba* is commonly, 'Speak a word to me' (*eipe moi rhēma*),[33] or else, more specifically, 'Speak a word to us, how can we be saved?'[34] The word of the spiritual father is a word of power, saving and regenerating. Accordingly Climacus in the letter *To the Shepherd* describes the spiritual father as a 'teacher' (*didaskalos*) who heals through his *logos*.[35] He recognizes, however, that the elder may perhaps suffer from diffidence and find himself unable, face to face, to put his advice in words; in that case, says Climacus, let him write it down.[36] Symeon likewise speaks of the confessor as a 'teacher'[37] and a 'good counsellor who by his shrewd advice suggests in an appropriate manner ways of repentance'.[38] While healing by his speech, the spiritual father may also heal by his silence, that is, simply by virtue of his presence. When Saint Antony of Egypt asked a monk who came to see him regularly why he never put any questions to him, the other replied, 'It is enough

for me just to look at you, father.'[39] Saint Symeon the New
Theologian recounts of his own spiritual father, Saint Symeon
the Studite or 'the Pious' (*ho Eulabes*) (917-986/7), that he used
to spend the whole day in the company of his disciples, 'and
he helped many of them simply by his appearance'.[40] But
Climacus warns the elder against the danger of keeping silent
too much: it is his duty also to speak.[41]

3. *Intercessor (presbeutēs)*. The spiritual father heals, not by
his words of counsel only, but also and more fundamentally
by his prayers. In the *Apophthegmata* the visitor says to the
holy man, not merely 'Speak a word to me', but 'Pray for
me'.[42] I recall a visit made by a friend of mine, an American,
to a contemporary elder on Mount Athos. At the end of the
conversation my friend said to him, 'May I write to you sometimes to ask for advice?' 'No,' the monk replied, 'don't write;
but I will pray for you.' The American felt this as a rejection
and went away saddened. But another monk, who had over-
heard the conversation, said to him later: 'You ought to be
very happy that the *geronta* promised to pray for you; he
doesn't say that to everyone. His advice is good, but his
prayers are far, far better.' The intercessory prayer of the
spiritual father for his children is a master-theme constantly
recurring in the answers of Barsanuphius and John: 'Night
and day I am praying for you unceasingly to God.'[43]

Faithful to the Gaza tradition, Climacus states in the first
definition that he gives of the 'shepherd':

> A shepherd is pre-eminently one who has the power to
> seek out the lost spiritual sheep and to set them on the
> right path, by means of his guilelessness, his zeal and his
> *prayer*.[44]

The monk, says Climacus elsewhere, has, as a 'helmet of salvation', the 'protection given by his superior through
prayer'.[45] The obedient monk, even if he raises the dead, will
think that it is the intercession of his spiritual father which has
enabled him to do this.[46]

As before, Symeon agrees closely with Climacus. The function of the spiritual father, he says, is to win God's favor for his children 'through his prayer and intercession';[47] he is an 'intercessor'.[48] Visiting his own elder, Symeon the Studite, the New Theologian greets him with the words: 'Pray for me . . . that through you I may find mercy.'[49] In the account that the younger Symeon gives of his first vision of the divine light, he records that he saw, standing close to the uncreated radiance, the figure of his spiritual father; and this made him realize 'how greatly the intercession of that holy man had assisted him'.[50] The spiritual father's intercession continues even after his death.[51] But the relationship is reciprocal, for the spiritual father in his turn needs the prayers of his children.[52]

4. *Mediator (mesitēs)*. Pursuing further this conception of the intercessory function of the spiritual father, both Climacus and Symeon describe him as an 'intermediary' or 'mediator': he does not simply pray for his children, but through his intercession he *reconciles* them to God. So Climacus, at the very start of the *Ladder*, likens the spiritual father to a new Moses, mediating with God on our behalf against the invisible Amalek (cf. Exod 17:11-13):

All of us who wish to depart from Egypt and to escape Pharaoh certainly need some Moses, as a mediator with God, yet below God, who will stand on our behalf between action and contemplation and lift up his hands to God, so that those under his guidance may cross the sea of sins and overthrow the Amalek of the passions.[53]

Climacus is careful to say 'a mediator with God, yet *below God*' or '*after God*' (*meta Theon*). He does not lose sight of the fact that, in the full and strict sense, there is only one mediator between God and man—Jesus Christ the *Theanthropos* (cf. 1 Tim 2:5); the mediation of the spiritual father is secondary to that of Christ and dependent upon it.[54]

To the Shepherd develops this idea of mediation. The 'superior' or spiritual father is the friend of the king; because he has free access to the royal presence, he can plead with boldness on behalf of others:

> Just as those who behold the king's face and have made him their friend can if they wish reconcile any of the king's servants—and also strangers and even his enemies—and enable them to enjoy his glory, so it is also with the saints.[55]

From this Climacus draws the startling conclusion that a sin against one's spiritual father is graver than a sin against God:

> Do not be shocked by what I am going to say . . . . It is better to sin against God rather than to sin against our father. For if God is angry with us, our guide can reconcile him to us; but if our guide is roused against us, we have no one to make propitiation on our behalf.[56]

The spiritual father's mediation works in both directions: in the Godward direction, through his intercession he represents his children before the throne of heaven; in the manward direction he represents God to his children, so that his instructions have the value of the word of God. As an Alexandrian monk said to Climacus during the latter's visit to Egypt: 'I thought of the shepherd as the image of Christ. I thought of the command [that he gave me] as coming not from him but from God.'[57]

Since the spiritual father is the intermediary who has free access to the royal presence and so is able to introduce others to the Great King, it follows that no one should dare to assume the ministry of eldership unless he possesses personal experience of God. This is the basic and essential qualification of the spiritual father: direct inspiration by the Holy Spirit. 'Believe me, my child Zacharias,' says Abba Moses in the *Apophtheg-mata*, 'I saw the Holy Spirit descending upon you, and that is why I am compelled to question you.'[58] Saint Seraphim of Sarov (1759-1833) insists in similar terms upon the need for the *starets* to possess direct experience of the Spirit—for him to be, as it were, *transparent:* 'I give only what God tells me to give. I believe the first word that comes to me to be inspired by the Holy Spirit . . . God directs my words.' And he adds: 'Were I to give an answer out of my own judgement'—and, we may add, *a fortiori* an abstract answer copied from books— ' . . . then I would make a mistake.'[59] Such also is the standpoint of Barsanuphius: when called upon to give guidance, the spiritual father prays inwardly, 'Lord, whatever you wish for the salvation of this person's soul, entrust it to me so that I may speak it to him; then I shall speak your word and not my own.'[60]

The cardinal importance of direct, personal experience is precisely what Climacus underlines at the outset of his letter *To the Shepherd:*

> A genuine teacher is one who has received directly from God himself the tablet of spiritual knowledge inscribed by his divine finger, that is, by the active working of illumination, and who has no need of any other books. It is as unseemly for a teacher to copy out other people's writings, as it is for a painter to reproduce the work of someone else.[61]

No one can be a true elder at second hand; he needs to speak of what he has seen and felt for himself. If he is to be an instrument of reconciliation on behalf of others, he must first have 'reconciled God to himself'.[62]

In all this Symeon follows Climacus exactly. Quoting Hebrews 5:1-3,[63] he applies the title *mesitēs* to the spiritual father, whom he sees as an intermediary introducing the sinner into God's presence:

> In his desire to be forgiven his debts, a man seeks for a mediator and helper to this end; for, weighed down as he is by many degrading sins, he cannot shamelessly approach alone.[64] He will certainly seek out a mediator and

> friend of God, who is capable of restoring him as he was
> before, and of reconciling him with God the Father . . . .
> There is no other way of being reconciled to God, except
> through the mediation of a holy man who is a friend and
> servant of Christ, and through fleeing from evil.[65] As
> mediator, standing in God's presence face to face,
> through his prayer and intercession before God he wins
> on your behalf the gracious favor of the Deity.[66]

Here, as in Climacus, the spiritual father is the king's friend,
who can therefore gain the royal favor on behalf of others.
Such a man, adds Symeon, is not easily found.[67] Just as
Climacus insists that the spiritual father is a mediator only in a
secondary sense, 'after God', so Symeon likewise teaches that
Christ is 'the first mediator and sponsor (*mesitēs kai egguētēs*) of
our nature, offering it to his own God and Father'; our Lord
then entrusted the task of 'mediation and sponsorship' to the
apostles, and they in turn conferred it upon others, but it is
Christ who remains the unique source.[68]

Once more as in Climacus, the mediation works in both
directions: the spiritual father not only represents us to God
but equally represents God to us. He is a living ikon of Christ,
and we are to accept his counsel as coming directly from the
Lord:

> Looking at him and speaking to him as if he were Christ
> in person, you should honor him and learn from him
> what is to your profit.[69] He who has acquired explicit
> faith in his father according to God, when looking at him
> thinks that he is looking at Christ; when in his presence or
> following him, he firmly believes that he is in Christ's
> presence or following Christ.[70]

The corollary to this notion of mediation, for Symeon as for
Climacus, is that none can act as intermediary unless he is
himself a friend of the king; none can be a true spiritual father
unless he has acquired, in a direct and conscious manner,

personal experience of the Holy Spirit. The need for palpable, experiential awareness of the indwelling Paraclete is a dominant theme in all Symeon's writings:

> Do not say, It is impossible to receive the divine Spirit.
> Do not say, It is possible to be saved without him,
> Do not say, One can participate in him without
>   knowing it (*agnostos*)
> Do not say, God does not appear to men.
> Do not say, Men do not see the divine light,
> Or else, This is impossible in the present time.
> It is never impossible, my friends;
> It is certainly possible for anyone who wishes.[71]

Symeon composed a special treatise, attacking 'those who think that they have the Holy Spirit within themselves in an unconscious manner, but who do not feel his energy at all'.[72] It is not enough, Symeon maintains, to claim, 'I have received Christ and the Spirit in baptism', but each of us must become *consciously aware* of the baptismal grace already present and at work in his or her heart:

> If those who 'are baptized into Christ put on Christ as a garment' (Gal 3:27), what is this garment that they 'put on'? God. Then should not he who has put on God as a garment be aware spiritually and see what he has put on? One whose body is naked feels when he puts on clothes and sees what his robe is like; and should not he whose soul is naked feel God's presence when he has put on God?[73]

Applying this general teaching about personal experience to the specific situation of the spiritual father, Symeon insists that nobody should presume to embark upon such a ministry unless he has 'received the grace of the Spirit consciously and knowingly, becoming thereby taught by God'.[74] Direct experience of the Spirit is the one indispensable qualification for the spiritual father's ministry:

> Do not seek to be mediators on behalf of others until you have yourselves been filled with the Holy Spirit, and until

until you have come to know the King of all through the
conscious experience of your soul.[75]

Lacking this personal experience, we cannot act as mediators
on behalf of others, since we ourselves require someone else to
mediate on our own behalf.[76]

While stressing in this way the need for personal experience, never for one moment does Symeon isolate the attainment of such experience from the practice of the Christian life
as a whole, according to the pattern of Holy Scripture. He
would surely have found astonishing the theory advanced by
Aldous Huxley that the direct awareness of transcendent reality can be achieved simply through the use of drugs.[77] On the
contrary, there is in his view only one way to acquire conscious experience of the Spirit, and that is to practice the
virtues, to overcome the passions, and so to gain *apatheia*,
'passionlessness' or 'dispassion'.[78] Of course Symeon regards
experience of the Spirit, and the vision of divine light, as a free
and unmerited gift of God, not to be earned by human effort,
and he never ceases to reflect on his own unworthiness to
receive any such gift. But at the same time there is for him no
mysticism without asceticism, no *theoria* without *praxis*.
Claims to 'experience', if divorced from the profession of the
true faith and the pursuit of the 'active life', would have appeared in his eyes nothing but a diabolic delusion.

Symeon then proceeds to draw out the full implications of
this insistence upon personal experience. Priests, and even
bishops and patriarchs, who lack such experience of the Spirit
have no right to act as spiritual fathers, and no power to
pronounce absolution and to bind and loose; on the other
hand, lay monks, not in priestly orders, provided that they
possess this conscious experience, are fully entitled to hear
confessions and to exercise the ministry of binding and loos-
ing.[79] He appeals to the example of his own elder, Symeon the
Studite, who was not ordained.[80] While this is not a question
that John Climacus discusses explicitly, in fact he nowhere
specifies or implies that the spiritual father must be a priest.

There is, moreover, no evidence that he was himself ordained, and yet he certainly exercised the ministry of fatherhood and direction.

Here Symeon's letter *On Confession* raises, in a particular form, an issue that recurs constantly in religious history: the relationship between priest and prophet, between the hierarchy and the holy man, between the Church as 'institution' and the Church as 'charismatic event'. The right of lay persons to bind and loose had been a matter for dispute in the Church long before this, in Africa during 251-2, when the confessors in the recent persecution claimed the authority to reconcile the *lapsi*, while Saint Cyprian maintained that this could be done only by the hierarchy.

Symeon does not in fact allude to this precedent. He is making two connected assertions, the first positive and the second negative:

(1)   Persons not in priestly orders—or at any rate monks who are not ordained—have the right to bind and loose, provided that they possess conscious experience of the Spirit.

(2)   Ordained persons who lack this experience have no right to bind and loose.

For the first or positive contention, it is in fact possible to cite much supporting evidence in the history of Eastern Christian monasticism, from the fourth century up to the present day. Many of the leading elders in the Egyptian desert, including Antony himself, were never ordained; Barsanuphius and John of Gaza, so far as is known, were not priests. One of the best known *startsi* in the recent history of Athos, Saint Silvan (1866-1938) of the Russian monastery of Saint Panteleimon, was a lay monk;[81] so also is the Greek Father Paisios (living formerly near Stavronikita, and now close to Karyes), respected as a *geronta* throughout the Holy Mountain today. To explain this practice of lay confession, modern writers, both Orthodox and non-Orthodox, sometimes make a distinction between spiritual counselling in the broader sense—the disclosure of 'thoughts'—where the minister may be a lay monk, and in women's communities a nun, and the sacrament of penance strictly understood—the absolution of sins—which can be ministered only by priests.[82] But Symeon himself does not employ such a distinction: 'Pour lui la confession constituait un tout indivisible, un acte charismatique.'[83]

What is, however, more controversial is Symeon's second or negative thesis. Pressed to its logical conclusions, his argument appears to make the validity of the sacraments dependent on the sanctity of the minister, and thus comes perilously close to Donatism. In defense of Symeon it may be said that, in the letter *On Confession* and elsewhere, he is speaking pastorally rather than juridically, in moral rather than dogmatic terms. He is making, not primarily an abstract statement about sacramental validity, but a personal appeal to the priests and bishops in the Church of his own time. Do not be too quick, he is saying to them, to assume the ministry of spiritual fatherhood; perhaps God has not called you to it. Although Symeon actually says, 'You *cannot* bind or loose', surely his true meaning is, 'You *should* not take upon yourselves this task unless called directly by the Spirit.' His letter is to be understood, not as a systematic discussion of doctrine, but as a prophetic warning.

It is significant that Symeon was never censured or condemned for the opinions expressed in his text *On Confession*. When he was found guilty and sentenced to exile by the Holy Synod of Constantinople in 1009, the charge against him was the liturgical *cultus* that he was rendering, without ecclesiastical sanction, to his spiritual father, now dead, Saint Symeon the Studite. In any case, the Synod's sentence was revoked soon afterwards, and Symeon was declared innocent. It is true that, implicit in the conflict between him and Stephen the Syncellus, there was undoubtedly the question of confession to lay monks: Stephen considered that Symeon was dangerously undermining the prerogatives of the priesthood. But in his case against the New Theologian he preferred not to press that particular charge, presumably considering that a condemnation could more easily be secured over the question of the liturgical *cultus;* and so the issue of lay confession was not

brought clearly into the open. Symeon's standpoint in the letter
On Confession, even though many Orthodox disagree with it,
remains nevertheless a tenable view for an Orthodox to up-
hold.[84]

Setting aside this controverted topic, let us recall the basic
point about spiritual paternity that Symeon is here concerned
to make: the father in Christ is a mediator, reconciling his
children to God.

5. *Sponsor (anadochos)*. Healer, teacher, man of prayer—the
spiritual father is all these things, and yet he is also something
more. Fifthly and finally, for both Climacus and Symeon he is
an *anadochos*. Linked with *anadechesthai*, to take upon oneself, to
undertake, *anadochos* denotes somebody who assumes responsibility or provides security for another, standing surety for his
obligations. The term is applied to Christ as the redeemer of
our souls,[85] to the godparent at a baptism,[86] or to the sponsor at
a monastic profession.[87] In this way it is also used to indicate
the spiritual father. As mediator after the likeness of Christ, he
does not merely pray for his children, but takes on his shoulders
the weight of their temptations and guilt.[88] He is, in the Pauline
phraseology, a burden-bearer: 'Bear one another's burdens and
so fulfil the law of Christ' (Gal 6:2). This idea of burden-bearing
is to be found in the *Apophthegmata*: 'Confess your sin to me and
I will carry it', says Abba Lot to a brother who cannot find
peace in his conscience.[89] It is particularly emphasized by the
sixth-century Gaza school; thus Barsanuphius writes to one of
his spiritual children:

> After Jesus Christ, I have spread out my wings over you
> until this day, and I am bearing your burdens and of-
> fences. . . . I have seen and covered everything, just as
> God sees and covers our sins. . . . See, I give you a com-
> mandment for your salvation; and, if you keep it, I will
> take upon myself the sentence of condemnation that is
> against you, and by the grace of Christ I will not abandon
> you either in this age or in the age to come . . . . I have

taken from you the weight and burden and debt; and see, you have become a new man, free from guilt and pure.[90]

In this as in other ways the abbot of Sinai shows himself a faithful adherent to the Gaza tradition.

More than once in his text *To the Shepherd* Climacus applies the term *anadochos* to the spiritual father.[91] It is the elder's vocation, he says, 'to take upon himself (*anadexasthai*) the burden of the one under obedience to him'.[92] 'Let your father', he writes elsewhere, 'be the one who is able and willing to labor with you in bearing the burden of your sins.'[93] The influence of Galatians 6:2 is manifest. Like Barsanuphius, Climacus believes that this burden-bearing extends beyond the present life into the age to come. At the Last Judgement the elder will answer for his disciple's sins, and so the disciple can face death free from anxiety, 'knowing with certainty that, when it is time to go, not he but his spiritual director will be called to render an account'.[94] The evident corollary to all this, even though Climacus does not explicitly spell it out, is that each of us should be extremely careful before assuming the ministry of spiritual fatherhood: we may be taking upon ourselves far more than we realize!

Thus, as a mediator representing Christ to us, the spiritual father is more particularly an image or ikon of Christ the Good Shepherd, who carried the lost sheep on his shoulders and laid down his life for the flock. As a 'true shepherd' after the likeness of the 'Great Shepherd', the elder expresses above all the quality of sacrificial love:

> It is love that shows who is the true shepherd; for by reason of love the Great Shepherd was crucified.[95] Sponsorship (*anadochē*) in the proper sense is a laying-down of one's own soul on behalf of the soul of one's neighbour in all matters.[96]

Without this burden-bearing and self-sacrifice, no one can be an *anadochos* or spiritual father. Climacus provides an illustration of such sponsorship in action. For twenty years a monk had been troubled by unspeakable and blasphemous thoughts, and despite all his efforts in fasting and keeping vigil he could obtain no relief. Eventually he wrote the passion down on a piece of paper and gave it to a 'holy man', prostrating himself before him on the ground and not daring to look up. After reading what was on the piece of paper, the old man smiled, made the monk stand up, and said to him: 'Child, you put your hand on my neck . . . Let this sin be on my neck . . . . From now on, ignore it.' At once the brother was set free from the thoughts of blasphemy.[97] There is a close parallel to this in the *Life* of Saint Ioannikios the Great (*c.* 754-*c.* 846). The saint told a young nun, troubled by impure desires, to lay her hand on his neck: 'Place your hand on my neck, child . . . . By the power of Christ, my daughter, let the warfare of the temptation that has afflicted you until now pass over to me.' At once she was freed from the temptation. But in this instance it is emphasized that Ioannikios was immediately attacked, 'as with fiery arrows', by the passions that had been assailing her.[98] Once more the moral is clear: the 'way of exchange' or of 'substituted love', to use the phrase of Charles Williams, is a serious matter, and none should embark on such a path who is not prepared to lay down his own life for the sake of others. The gesture occurring in both these stories, whereby the penitent places his or her hand upon the neck of the spiritual father, is found in ancient rituals for confession.[99]

Here, as elsewhere, Symeon's letter *On Confession* contains the same terminology and ideas as are found in Climacus. According to the New Theologian, the spiritual father is 'a man of God who becomes sponsor (*anadochos*) for the debt of others'; he 'assumes responsibility (*anadexetai*) for the sins of the other and answers on his behalf', although it is presumed that the person himself will be genuinely repentant.[100] Along with *apatheia*, 'dispassion', an essential characteristic of the spiritual father is *sympatheia*, 'compassion', in the full sense of suffering with and for others. This quality is prominent in Symeon's portrait of his own elder, Symeon the Studite: 'There were no limits to his compassion'.[101] Through *sym-*

patheia the spiritual father can 'make his own' the joys and sufferings of others (*idiopoieisthai . . . ta allotria*).[102]

Thus for Symeon, as for Climacus, compassionate and sacrificial love is an essential characteristic of the true elder. Symeon himself felt so closely bound to his spiritual children that he regarded his own salvation as inseparable from theirs. 'I saw a man', he writes, alluding to himself in the third person (cf. 2 Cor 12:2),

> . . . who longed so intensely for the salvation of his brethren, that he often prayed to God the lover of humankind with scalding tears and all his soul, that either they might be saved or else he might be condemned with them. Modelling his attitude on God and also on Moses (cf. Exod 32:32), he absolutely refused to be saved alone. Spiritually bound to them by a holy love in the Holy Spirit, he did not want to enter the kingdom of heaven itself if that meant he would be separated from them.[103]

Barsanuphius offered the same prayer:

> O Master, either bring my children with me into your kingdom, or else wipe me also out of your book.[104]

If such are the qualities required of the spiritual father in his fivefold role as doctor, counsellor, intercessor, mediator and sponsor, we may well be tempted to ask with Saint Paul, 'Who is sufficient for these things?' (2 Cor 2:16). The Patristic sources agree with us in this. Nothing, says Saint Gregory of Nazianzus, is so difficult as to direct others: it is 'the art of arts and science of sciences'.[105] The answer must be that no one would dare to assume such a ministry, did he not feel compelled to it by love for others. Even so, it should not be he that takes the first step, but he awaits a specific call from God. This comes in various ways. Sometimes, as with the *startsi* of Optino, an elder before his death chooses one of his spiritual children to take his place. On other occasions the initiative comes from the disciples: in search of guidance, people approach a recluse or hermit; at first he gives them no answer, telling them to go to others for counsel;[106] but eventually the moment arrives when he accepts their requests for help as an indication of the divine will and stops sending them away. In this fashion it is the spiritual children who disclose the elder's vocation to himself. That is what happened, for example, to Saint Antony of Egypt and Saint Seraphim of Sarov.

Enough has been said to indicate the striking parallels between Climacus and Symeon in their characterization of the spiritual father. There are also differences of emphasis: Climacus uses in particular the image of the shepherd and the sheep, as the title of his treatise indicates; the idea is present in Symeon,[107] but is much less accentuated. Climacus also speaks of the elder as 'guide' (*hodēgos*), 'director' (*kubernētēs*) and 'superior' (*proestos*), terms which are not prominent in Symeon's treatment. The New Theologian makes more use of the image of the father begetting children,[108] or even of the mother conceiving and bearing them.[109] He also thinks of the spiritual father as an apostle,[110] an idea not found in Climacus. In general, however, there is a remarkably close correspondence between the two authors, alike in vocabulary and thought; and this is particularly evident in the use by both of them of the categories 'doctor', 'mediator' and 'sponsor'. The freshness and vivacity with which Symeon writes should not blind us to the truth that, in his letter *On Confession* as elsewhere, he bears witness not only to his personal experience but equally to the long tradition of which he is the heir.

NOTES

Published originally in *Studia Patristica* XVIII/2. Papers of the 1983 Oxford Patristics Conference (Kalamazoo: Cistercian Publications - Leuven: Peeters, 1990) 299-316. Reused by permission.

1. *Ep*. i. 2 (*PG* 99: 909B). The basic study on spiritual fatherhood is still the work translated here, Irénée Hausherr, SJ, *Direction spirituelle en orient autrefois*, *Orientalia Christiana Analecta* 144 (Rome, 1955). See also H. Dörries, 'The Place of Confession in Ancient Monasticism', *Studia Patristica* v, Texte und Untersuchungen 80 (Berlin, 1962) pp. 284-311; K. Ware, 'The

Spiritual Father in Orthodox Christianity', in K.G. Culligan, O.C.D. (ed.), *Spiritual Direction: Contemporary Readings* (Locust Valley, 1983) pp. 20-40.

2. *Cap.* [*Theological, Gnostic and Practical Chapters*] iii. 4. References to Symeon are made, wherever possible (i.e., except in the case of the *Letters*), to the *SCh* [*Sources Chrétiennes*] edition; in the case of works other than *Cap.*, the line of the *SCh* text is given.

3. On this text see P. Gutierrez, *La paternité spirituelle selon Saint Paul* (Paris, 1968); M. Saillard. '"C'est moi qui, par Évangile, vous ai enfantés dans le Christ Jésus" (1 Co 4.15)', *Recherches de science religieuse* 56 (1968) pp. 5-41. Both authors are at pains to argue that Paul's words should not be discounted as mere metaphor: he is describing a 'réalité ontologique' (Gutierrez, p. 172); 'la paternité spirituelle de Paul est bien plus qu'une image émouvante' (Saillard, p. 5).

4. *The Brothers Karamazov*, i. 5; Eng. trans. by D. Magarshack, (Penguin Classics, Harmondsworth, 1958), vol. i. p. 28.

5. Eusebius, *Hist. Eccl.* VI. iii. 8-12.

6. *Strom.* I.1.2 (*GCS*, p. 3, line 15).

7. For example, Iamblichus, *De Vit. Pyth.* 31. 198 (the father-child relationship among the Pythagoreans); *ibid.*, 35. 250 (Epaminondas calls his teacher Lysis 'father').

8. Cf. Babylonian Talmud, *Sanhedrin* 19b: 'When a man teaches the son of another the Torah, Scripture treats him as if he had begotten him.'

9. Note especially *Vit. Ant.* 81 (*PG* 26:957A): 'He was beloved by all, and all desired to have him as their father.' The title 'father' was applied equally to Pachomius: cf. L.Th. Lefort, *Les vies coptes de saint Pachôme* (Louvain, 1943) pp. 3. 55, 211; P. Deseille, *L'esprit du monachisme pachômien* (Bellefontaine, 1973) pp. vii-xix.

10. *Hist. Laus.* 21 and 22 (Butler, pp. 65, 19-68, 12; 70, 7-74, 20).

11. Alphabetical collection, Antony 37 and 38 (*PG* 65: 88B).

12. *Erotapokriseis:* Greek text, ed. Nicodemus of the Holy Mountain (reissued S. Schoinas, Volos, 1960); critical ed. and Eng. trans. of Letters 1-124 by D.J. Chitty, *Patrologia Orientalis* 31. 3 (Paris, 1966); French trans. of the whole collection by L. Regnault and P. Lemaire, *Barsanuphe et Jean de Gaza, Correspondance* (Solesmes, 1972).

13. In the alphabetical collection of the *Apophthegmata* (*PG* 65), in addition to 127 'abbas' there are also three 'ammas' or spiritual mothers, Theodora, Sarah, and Syncletica. For the title 'amma', cf. Palladius, *Hist. Laus.* 34 and 59 (Butler, pp. 99, 18; 153, 8: see app. crit. and p. 180); *Apophthegmata*, alphabetical collection, Sarapion 1 (*PG* 65: 416B). Around the year 1200 the monk Isaias even composed a complete *Meterikon* or 'Sayings of the Mothers', parallel to the *Paterikon* or 'Sayings of the Fathers': cf. Hausherr, *Direction spirituelle*, pp. 266-7 [below, pp. 282-83].

14. Cited in G.P. Fedotov, *The Russian Religious Mind*, vol. i, *Kievan Christianity, the Tenth to the Thirteenth Centuries* (Cambridge, Mass., 1966) p. 215.

15. Cf. I. Gorainoff, *Seraphim de Sarov* (Bellefontaine, 1973); V. Zander, *St Seraphim of Sarov* (London, 1975); Macarius of Optino, *Russian Letters of Direction 1834-1860*, ed. I. de Beausobre (London, 1944); J.B. Dunlop, *Staretz Amvrosy, Model for Dostoevsky's Staretz Zossima* (Belmont, Mass., 1972).

16. Cf. K. Ware, 'Wolves and Monks: Life on the Holy Mountain Today', *Sobornost incorporating Eastern Churches Review* v. 2 (1983) pp. 56-68.

17. *PG* 88: 1165-1208; Eng. trans. by Archimandrite Lazarus (Moore),

The Ladder of Divine Ascent (Holy Transfiguration Monastery, Boston, Mass. 1978) pp. 231-50.

18. Critical text in K. Holl, *Enthusiasmus and Bussgewalt beim griechischen Mönchtum. Eine Studie zu Symeon dem neuen Theologen* (Leipzig, 1898) pp. 110-27. A revised critical edition is to appear, with Symeon's other letters, in *SCh*. Doubts have sometimes been expressed about the authorship of the letter *On Confession:* cf. B. Englezakis, 'A Note on Tradition and Personal Experience in Symeon the New Theologian', *Eastern Churches Review* vi (1974) pp. 88-89. Englezakis refers to J. Gouillard, 'Constantin Chrysomallos sous le masque de Syméon le Nouveau Théologien', *Travaux et Mémoires* 5 (1973) pp. 313-27; but Gouillard is concerned here with the *Discourses* attributed to Symeon (which have long been regarded as suspect), and not with the letter *On Confession [Ep.* i]. On Symeon and Chrysomallos, see also J. Gouillard, 'Quatre procès de mystiques à Byzance (vers 960-1143). Inspiration et autorité, *Revue des Études Byzantines* 36 (1978) pp. 5-81, especially pp. 24-39; on p. 35, n. 45, *Ep.* i is treated by Gouillard as an authentic work of Symeon.

Ep. i appears occasionally in the manuscript tradition as a work of Saint John of Damascus. When included among Symeon's writings, it often occupies in the manuscripts a place somewhat apart from his other works. But this in itself is not a sufficient reason to question its authenticity. The opinions expressed in it can in fact be paralleled from Symeon's other works.

19. See Nicetas Stethatos, *Vita Sym. Jun.* 6 (ed. 1. Hausherr, *Orientalia Christiana* xii, no. 45 [Rome, 1928] p. 12). The *Ladder* (but not *To the Shepherd*) is twice cited explicitly in Symeon's *Cathecheses:* cf. *Cat.* iv. 540; xxx. 141. But, although Symeon was widely read in earlier Patristic works, only very occasionally does he cite his authorities by name. In the letter *On Confession*, he appeals to Scripture (*Ep.* i. 2; p. 110, 15) and in general terms to the 'inspired Fathers' (*Ep.* i. 11; p. 120, 1), but without mentioning any specific Father.

20. In *He pneumatiki patrotes kata Symeon ton Neon Theologon* (Thessaloniki, 1977) [henceforward cited as 'Christophoridis'], a few similarities with Climacus are noted in passing, but only on peripheral matters. There is no reference to the parallels in B. Krivochéine, *Dans la lumière du Christ: Saint Syméon le Nouveau Théologien 949-1022, Vie - Spiritualité - Doctrine* (Chevetogne, 1980) [henceforward 'Krivochéine']: spiritual fatherhood is discussed on pp. 94-106, 131-47. Both authors quote freely from the letter *On Confession*, treating it as a genuine work of Symeon. Likewise nothing is said about the parallels in Holl, *Enthusiasmus and Bussgewalt*, or in H. Graef, 'The Spiritual Director in the Thought of Symeon the New Theologian', in P. Granfield and J.A. Jungmann (edd.), *Kyriakon. Festschrift Johannes Quasten*, vol. ii (Münster Westf., 1970) pp. 608-14. W. Völker gives more attention to Symeon's use of Climacus: see *Scala Paradisi: Eine Studie zu Johannes Climacus und zugleich eine Vorstudie zu Symeon dem Neuen Theologen* (Wiesbaden, 1968) pp. 27-51, and *Praxis und Theoria bei Symeon dem Neuen Theologen: Ein Beitrag zur Byzantinischen Mystik* (Wiesbaden, 1974) pp. 111-29, especially p. 119, n. 1, and p. 125, n. 1; but even so he notes only a few points of similarity, and does not make a specific comparison between Climacus' *Ad Past.* and Symeon's *Ep.* i.

21. *Vit. Ant.* 87 (*PG* 26: 965A). For similar imagery in Pachomian sources, see the Greek *Vita Prima* 132 (Halkin, p. 83, 23).

22. *Or.* ii. 16 and 28 (*PG* 35: 425A, 437A).

23. *De sac.* i. 9 (*PG* 48: 630); cf. *Vita Phocae* 1 (*PG* 50:699).
24. Canon 102: G.A. Rallis and M. Potlis, *Syntagma tōn theiōn kai ierōn kanonōn*, vol. ii (Athens, 1852) p. 549. Compare the exhortation to the penitent in the Russian rite of confession: 'Take care, then, lest having come to the doctor's you depart unhealed': cf. *Service Book of the Holy Orthodox-Catholic Apostolic (Greco-Russian) Church*, ed. I.F. Hapgood (Boston/New York, 1906) p. 289.
25. *Ad Past.* 2 (1168D-1169C).
26. *Ad Past.* 7 (1184AB). For further uses of medical language, see *Ad Past.* 1 (1165B); 5 (1177A); 7 (1181C); 13 (1196C); *Scala* 4 (*PG* 88: 697A, 716A); 5 (776C), etc.
27. *Ep.* i. 5 (p. 114, 21-22).
28. *Ep.* i. 6 (p. 115, 26).
29. *Ep.* i. 6 (p. 116, 2). Further instances of medical imagery: *Ep.* i. 7 (p. 117, 9-14); *Cat.* xviii. 469-70; xx. 198; and above all *Ethical Treatise* [*Eth.*] vi. 269-328.
30. *Ep.* i. 1 (p. 110, 4-5), etc. Sin is a debt for which payment will be demanded: *Ep.* i. 3 (p. 111, 12-21); i. 5 (p. 114, 17-20). For the spiritual father as judge, see *Eth.* vi. 427.
31. Cf. K. Ware, 'The Orthodox Experience of Repentance', *Sobornost incorporating Eastern Churches Review* ii, 1 (1980) pp. 22-26.
32. On the receiving of *logismoi* by the spiritual father, see Climacus, *Scala* 4 (701CD); Symeon, *Ep.* i. 9 (p. 118, 24); i. 17 (p. 127, 13-14); *Eth.* v. 524; vi. 75-76; *Hymn* iv. 27-28.
33. Alphabetical collection, Ammonas 1; Poemen 69, 111; Sisoes 45 (*PG* 65; 120A, 337C, 349C, 405B), *et passim*.
34. Antony 19 (*PG* 65: 81B).
35. *Ad. Past.* 1 (1165B); 2 (1169AB); cf. *Scala* 4 (704D). See A. Louf, 'La parole au-delà de la Liturgie', *Collectanea Cisterciensia* 31 (1969) pp. 165-94, esp. pp. 188-9.
36. *Ad. Past.* 6 (1180A).
37. *Cap.* i. 55 and 59; *Cat.* vii. 8; *Ep.* iii. 647-8, in Christophoridis, p. 29; *Ep.* iv. 212-14, in Christophoridis, p. 25.
38. *Ep.* i. 7 (p. 117, 1-2).
39. *Apophthegmata*, alphabetical collection, Antony 27 (*PG* 65: 84D); cf. Poemen 173 (364BC).
40. *Cat.* xvi. 34.
41. *Ad Past.* 6 (1177C).
42. *Apophthegmata*, alphabetical collection, Antony 16; Macarius of Egypt 33; Felix 1 (*PG* 65: 79C, 277C, 433D), etc.
43. *Erotap.* 17; cf. 27, 144 (Regnault, 217), 208 (Regnault, 113), 507.
44. *Ad Past.* 1 (1165B).
45. *Scala* 4 (677D); cf. 15 (893B).
46. *Scala* 4 (705D-708A).
47. *Ep.* i. 7 (p. 117, 3-5).
48. *Cat.* xxxv (*Euch.* i). 74-75; cf. *Cap.* i. 84.
49. *Cat.* xvi. 62-63.
50. *Cat.* xxii. 105-6 (Symeon is speaking of himself in the third person). Cf. *Cat.* xxviii. 276-8; xxxii. 89; *Cap.* i. 84; *Hymn* xviii. 176, 207; xxxii. 4; lv. 82.
51. *Cat.* xx. 155-7. Cf. the words of Saint Seraphim of Sarov to the nuns in his charge at Diveyevo, shortly before his death: Gorainoff, (op. cit. note 15), pp. 133-4; Zander, op. cit., p. 112.

52. *Cat.* xii. 22.

53. *Scala* 1 (633D-636A). For the spiritual father as a new Moses, cf. Symeon, *Hymn* xviii. 124-221.

54. For the phrase *meta Theon*, cf. Lefort, (note 9), pp. 55, 211: Pachomius is 'father *after God*' to his monks; ps.-Basil, *Const. asc.* 20 (*PG* 31: 1389D): the true father is God; after God, the abbot is father.

55. *Ad Past.* 3 (1172D).

56. *Scala* 4 (725D-728A).

57. *Scala* 4 (692B).

58. Alphabetical collection, Zacharias 3 (*PG* 65: 180B).

59. Zander (note) 15), pp. 32-33

60. *Erotap.* 577.

61. *Ad Past.* 1 (1165B). On the need for direct experience, cf. *Scala* 25 (988AB); 28 (1140C).

62. *Ad Past.* 11 (1188B).

63. *Ep.* i. 11 (p. 120, 12-15): not an exact quotation from Hebrews, for the word *mesitēs* has in fact been added.

64. *Cat.* xxxv (*Euch.* 1), 251-5.

65. *Ep.* i. 5 (p. 115, 9-11 and 19-21).

66. *Ep.* i. 7 (p. 117, 3-5). For further uses of the term *mesites* see *Cat.* xxxv (*Euch.* i). 74; *Ep.* iii. 554-6, in Christophoridis, p. 29.

67. *Ep.* i. 7 (p. 117, 14-15).

68. *Ep.* iii. 550-64, in Christophoridis, p. 116.

69. *Cat.* xx. 60-62.

70. *Cap.* i. 28. Cf. *Cat.* iii. 216; v. 882-3; xx. 60-186; *Eth.* vii. 435-45; *Ep.* iii, *passim*.

71. *Hymn.* xxvii. 125-32.

72. *Eth.* v, title.

73. *Eth.* v. 60-65. Cf. B. Krivochéine, *SCh* 96 (Paris, 1963) pp. 151-4. Symeon does not, however, altogether identify the *reality* of grace with the *conscious experience* of grace, but sometimes allows for the possibility that divine grace may be at work inside our heart without our conscious knowledge (see *Cap.* iii. 76-77) In this way he avoids what Hausherr regards as the 'fundamental error' of Messalianism: 'L'erreur fondamentale et la logique du Messalianisme', *Orientalia Christiana Periodica* i (1935) pp. 336-8; reprinted in *Études de spiritualité orientale, Orientalia Christiana Analecta* 183 (Rome, 1969) pp. 72-74.

74. *Eth.* i. 12. 469-70.

75. *Ep.* i. 10 (p. 119, 4-7). Cf. *Cat.* xxviii. 344-53; *Eth.* vi. 413-28.

76. *Ep.* i. 10 (p. 119, 11-12).

77. Cf. *The Doors of Perception* (London, 1954); shrewdly criticized by R.C. Zaehner, *Mysticism Sacred and Profane* (Oxford, 1957) pp. 1-29.

78. On the need for *apatheia* in the spiritual father, see Climacus, *Ad Past.* 11 (1185D); Symeon, *Ep.* i. 1 (p. 110, 11); *Eth.* xi. 703-25.

79. *Ep.* i. 11 (pp. 119, 24 - 120, 12); i. 13-14 (pp. 122,9 - 124,21). Cf. *Cat.* xxxiii. 37-41; *Eth.* iii. 590-99.

80. *Ep.* i. 16 (p. 127, 6-7).

81. For his life and writings, see Archimandrite Sophrony, *The Undistorted Image* (London, 1958); revised ed. in 2 vol., *The Monk of Mount Athos* (London, 1973); *Wisdom from Mount Athos* (London, 1974).

82. See Christophoridis, pp. 56-57, 123.

83. Krivochéine, p. 147.

84. For a typical statement, denying to lay monks the right to bind and

I

INTRODUCTION

AN ENTRY IN the *Dictionnaire d'archéologie chrétienne et de liturgie* (Paris, 1903 sq.) states—unexpectedly—that 'Among the many subjects worthy of study, that of spiritual direction in early christianity has not yet been made.'[1] This book endeavors to set forth the theological and psychological principles that governed the *praxis* of spiritual direction in the ancient christian East.

Let us delineate our inquiry more precisely. The term 'spiritual direction' is here understood in the narrow sense it has indeed acquired during the past centuries. It could have a wider sense incorporating the powers of the church hierarchy: the *potestas ordinis* (power of orders) and the *potestas jurisdictionis* (power of jurisdiction). *In itself*, the function of the spiritual director is independent of the power of orders. The latter being two-fold (teaching and governance), it must be made clear that since all church teaching and governance is ultimately directed at the very goal of the christian life, it could be called spiritual direction. In practice, however, one does not apply this term to the public exercise of teaching or of jurisdiction. It will be reserved for the relationships between *one* master, informed and experienced in the ways of the spirit, and *one* disciple who wishes to profit from such knowledge and experience.

We will therefore not be concerned with such documents as Gregory of Nazianzen's long oration *Apologeticus de Fuga*, a true pastoral treatise for the use of bishops and priests in caring for souls. The doctrine of spiritual direction will be gathered only from passages in which the Theologian describes the infinite variety of individuals and the need to adapt oneself to each. This personal character of direction is often stressed by the great spiritual writers, either implicitly—the letters of Saint Nilus of Ancyra, Isidore of Pelusium and especially Saint Barsanuphius apply to specific situations—or explicitly. For instance, while commenting on Mt 24:25, 'Who then is the faithful and wise servant, whom his lord has made ruler over his household to give them meat in due season?' Origen notes that 'given the great number of christians, one ought to exercise great caution not to impart the reasonable and spiritual food to companions of any quality whatsoever and to whom one should not; for there are some who are in greater need of moral edification for the betterment of their life, than of knowledge and wisdom. To others, by contrast, one should not feel reluctant to expand higher things. To the one who is faithful and wise both the one and the other are difficult, but not impossible.'[2] Alongside the *Conferences* (*the Conlationes* of Cassian), the *Lives of the Fathers* (*Vitae Patrum*) clearly illustrates the practice of such personal direction. The Desert Fathers have, if not brought into being—and who knows?—then, at least, systematized this magnificent thing, the art of arts (*ars artium*), 'the divine art of healing another's wounds,' as Cassian said,[3] that 'declaimer well skilled in divine incantations' (*peritissimus carminum divinorum incantator*)[4]—in one word, the direction of souls.[5] Theodosius the Cenobiarch 'imitated Moses' authority to the best of his ability, while having recourse to God in order to discover how to direct (*oikonomeisthai*) everyone's conduct.'[6]

Granted that all the principles of morality must ultimately

be adapted to particular situations, there are weapons in the arsenal of spiritual warfare that are not fit for everyone—for example, the *antirrhesis* (the counter-statement) of which Saint Barsanuphius wrote: 'it is not fit for everyone but only for the powerful according to God, for those to whom the demons submit. If another practices it, they mock him because, as their inferior, he talks things over with them.' Likewise, *epitimesis* (the reproof of demons) belongs only to the great and to those who have the power. 'It is not the concern of us who are weak.'[7] It is the function of spiritual direction to apply this to particular situations. What is needed is a sure judgment which beginners could not command. Saint Poemen himself had to learn this lesson.

He asked Abba Joseph of Panepho, 'What would I do when the passions assail me? Should I resist them, or let them enter?' The old man answered, 'Let them enter, and fight against them.' Poemen returned to Scetis where he remained (as a hesychast). Now someone from Thebes came to Scetis and said to the brothers, 'I asked Abba Joseph, 'When a passion draws near, should I oppose it or allow it to enter?' He answered me, 'Absolutely do not let the passions enter, but cut them off at once.' When Abba Poemen learned that Abba Joseph had spoken to the Theban in such a manner, he arose, went to see him in Panepho, and said, 'Abba, I confided my thoughts to you; and you have said one thing to me, and another to the Theban.' The old man replied, 'Do you not know that I love you?' He answered, 'Certainly.'—'And did you not say, speak to me as you would speak to yourself?' 'Indeed,' Poemen replied. Then the old man said, 'When the passions enter and you give and receive blows while contending with them, they will make you stronger. Surely, I spoke to you as to myself. But there are others who should not let the passions draw nigh: they must cut them off instantly.'[8]

There is no need to cite other passages. We are only delineating our subject-matter. The rest of the text will show us this individualized direction of souls.

This book is addressed to western Christians interested in the East:[9] its main intention is to make them breathe the spirit which animated the great spiritual masters of the past. To reach this goal, the most efficient way, it seems to me, is to hear the Fathers themselves speak as often as possible. Their sayings (*rhēmata*) still retain something of their old flavor and force. Would it be unrealistic to expect that, God willing, they may contribute to bring us *sōtēria*—the psychic well-being, the health of the soul, the search for which formed them and the experience of which they formulated? To those who know, this essay is addressed only as an encouragement to do better, in the hope of preserving—or reestablishing—'the unity of the spirit by the peace that binds you together' (Eph 4:3).

In the East, the person we call 'spiritual director' has been characterized in various ways. First and above all, as 'spiritual father,' or just 'father' or *abbas* (fem. *ammas*). Then, depending on the various aspects of his function, as *gerōn* (*senior*, old man), *presbyteros* (elder), since he normally was advanced in years or at least older; as *didascalos*, since he had to teach; *diorthōtēs* (one who sets right), *paideutēs* (teacher), *aleiptēs* (trainer). Especially among cenobites they used *prostatēs* (leader), *epistatēs* (master) and *ephestos* (director). Still other terms were also used.[10]

Of all these names, the most important, the one used most frequently, the only one that explains everything and stresses what is essential is *father*, with or without the adjective *spiritual*. The fact that the adjective can remain presupposed does not imply that the quality it expresses is of secondary importance, even less that the name 'father' is merely a metaphor whose epithet determines its meaning and limits our understanding. *Spiritual father* does not simply mean director of things spiritual. The phrase 'spiritual direction' is insufficient when applied to the christian East. Does it suffice elsewhere? Indeed, it is not in the least a matter of supplying the type of information a tour guide or travel bureau may give to the traveler unable to find his way through the train timetable. It is not even a matter of giving elementary moral instruction, even when applied to the particulars. This point needs to be developed.

One should clearly differentiate the master (*ho didaskalos*, *sensu stricto*) from the 'pedagogue' (*paidagōgos*). Clement of Alexandria deceives us a little and offends the Lord a bit by calling him 'a pedagogue'. The New Testament does not use the term, though Saint Paul does, and even there the term has a negative connotation. The term refers to 'a slave whose job it was to take the children to school' (Bailly); a tutor himself, his function made him feared, as attested by numerous ancient, and even fairly recent, texts. It is not by chance that the Spanish proverb '*la letra con la sangre entra*' (learning comes from blood) is not unlike the Russian saying, '*bez palki net nauki*' (no knowledge without the rod). 'In Greece and Rome, the more reliable slaves to whom parents entrusted their children to escort, supervise, and discipline them . . . were called *pedagogues*. In 1 Cor 4:15, Saint Paul dubs all other teachers pedagogues; himself he calls father of the Corinthians, because he gave them supernatural life.'[11] Even the term *didaskalos* (teacher), and the function it implies among the Greeks, does not really prefigure the role of the spiritual father: it is too clearly intellectual for that. We know that Socrates refused the title: 'I was never anyone's teacher'.[12] What he wanted to do was not to teach, but to be useful (*ophelein*), to perform the good.[13] If in later schools of philosophy, there is anything that resembles direction (not spiritual but moral), it will be found only later, particularly among the Stoics and the Neo-Platonists. Diels has made an entire list of such directors of conscience,[14] the most eminent of whom was perhaps Plotinus. 'Plotinus has indeed the profile of a director of conscience. He possesses that intelligent goodness which would let itself be duped, that openheartedness tempered by reason. One ought not to forget that in Roman times personalized direction which concerned itself even with the day-by-day details of life, was the great occupation of the philosopher; his professional activity was subordinated to this task.'[15] Moreover, and contrary to what was said earlier, Antiquity fully recognized the role of older people—*senes, seniores, gerontes*—as counselors to the young. Cicero became the spokesman of this axiom: '*Est igitur adolescentis maiores natu vereri, exque e his deligere optimos et probatissimos, quorum consilio et auctoritate nitatur; ineuntis enim aetatis inscitia senum constituenda at regenda prudentia est. . . . Senibus autem labores corporis minuendi, exercitationes animi augendae videntur; danda vero opera, ut et amicos et juventutem et maxime rempublicam consilio et prudentia quam plurimum adjuvent*' (*De Officiis*, I. XXXIV. 122 sq.). ('A young man should respect his elders and choose the best and most tested of them so as to rely on their advice and judgment. Indeed, the inexperience of youth needs the wisdom of old age as its ruler and guide. . . . The duty of the old is to spare their physical efforts and to give increasing exercise to their minds. Their particular aim should be to give the maximum help to their friends, young people and the state by offering them wise advise' (*On Moral Obligation*.)[16] More succinctly, Theophylactus of Bulgaria would write eleven centuries later: 'spiritual realities are the opposite of carnal things; in life the young man is useful, an old man unprofitable; in things spiritual, when advanced age has arrived, eminence is more manifest.'[17] It is this conviction which led to the advice of Saint Basil to also take age into consideration when choosing his community leaders: 'for what is older in the nature of men is somehow more worthy of respect.'[18] What we find here is not so much custom as universal human facts, though disastrous exceptions have occurred.[19]

Among the Hebrews, one notes that Joshua was Moses' 'servant', as later, among the Desert Fathers, the disciple-novice would often be entitled 'his elder's servant'. In the eremitical life, monastic obedience consisted in submission to the spiritual father.[20] *Kathezesthai en hypotagē patros pneumatikos* (to remain in submission to a spiritual father) would become the classical expression for such a condition. For example,

John of Thebaid, disciple of Abba Ammoes, 'persevered for twelve years serving the old man in his illness.'[21] Elijah and Elisha, Elisha and Gehazi, and others mentioned in the Old Testament, may have contributed through their example to give a definite form to the image of the master and the disciple, even that of the spiritual father and child. Did Elisha not address this heart-rending cry to Elijah, 'My father, my father?' Anyone who wants to pursue this parallelism may do sot; it is not part of this study. Meanwhile, let us mention that certain Old Testament words—even more than ancient Hebrew institutions—have probably influenced the theory and practice of spiritual direction among the Fathers, one utterance in particular. Saint Antony says, 'I have known monks who fell away after many labours and lost their mind, for they had put their hope in their own works. In their delusion, they did not obey the commandment that states, "Ask your father, let him teach you".'[22]

More than the ancient prophets, it is the rabbis of later Judaism whom one could compare to spiritual fathers.[23]

NOTES

1. Ed. Dom Cabrol and Dom Leclercq, vol. IV, part I, col. 1170-72.
2. *In Matthaeum commentariorum series* 16; PG 13:1697D-98A; GCS 11, ed. E. Klostermann (1933) 142, 19ff.
3. *Conference* 18.17.
4. PL 49:1124A.
5. Jean Bremond, *Les Pères du désert*, vol. I (Paris, 1927), Coll. *Les moralistes chrétiens*, Introd., p. xiv.
6. Theodore of Petra, *Vita Theodosii*, Usener, p. 88, 2ff.
7. Barsanuphius, *Epist.* 301; ed. Nicodemus the Hagiorite (Venice, 1816) 159.
8. *Apophthegmata Patrum*, *Alph.*, Joseph Panephysis, n.3; PG 75:228D-30A.
9. Among eastern Christians, the Russians are practically the only ones who have dealt with the subject of spiritual direction—and even so, not extensively. Several books which, according to their titles, seem to deal with spiritual guidance, limit themselves to sacramental confession. The most important of these is by Sergei J. Smirnov, *Duchovnyi otec v drevnei vostocnoij Cerkvi (Istorija duchovničestva na vostoke)* [*The Spiritual Father in the Ancient Christian Church*],(Sergiev Posad, 1906); cfr *ViVr* 14, 399-442. Smirnov made use of the work by A. J. Soloviev, *Starčestvo po učeniju svjatych otčev i asketov* [*The Office of Starets According to the Teachings of the Saintly Fathers and Ascetics*],

(Semipalatinsk, 1900): 'A collection of texts not always appropriate to the subject, since the author works exclusively with translations,' as Smirnov remarks on p. 7, n. 2. However, Smirnov himself understands by the term 'spiritual director' one's 'confessor,' except in the opening chapter, to which we will refer on several occasions. Much earlier, Nicodemus the Hagiorite had dealt with the duties of the spiritual father in his *Biblion psychōphelestaton* [*A Book Most Profitable to the Soul*], (Venice, 1794). The title of the book's third edition (Venice, 1818) is *Exomologetarion* [*Manual of Confession*]. The only aim of this book, which went through numerous editions, appearing even in Turkish, is to teach how to administer the sacrament of confession properly. Nicodemus too equates the spiritual director with the confessor. However, things are different in Igor Smolitsch, *Leben und Lehren der Startzen* (*Life and Teaching of the Startzy*), Vienna, 1936 [2nd ed., Cologne-Olten, n.d. (1952?)] which really deals with 'Old Men' in the spiritual sense of the term. Indeed, Smolitsch deals with 'Spiritual Guidance in Ancient Ascetism' (pp. 24-37).

10. See S. J. Smirnov, vol. I, p. 7.

11. F. Zorell, *Lexicon graecum Novi Testamenti* (2nd ed., 1931) s.v. *paedagogos*. Cfr Origen, *Comment. in Joan.* I, VII (9); Preuschen, p. 11, 26-12, 7.

12. *Apology* 33a.

13. There is a literary genre of *narrationes animae utiles* (stories profiting the soul), *psychōpheleis*.

14. *Doxogr. Gr. Proleg.*, p. 82, n. 2.

15. Emile Bréhier, *Plotin, Ennéades*, Introd., p. ix.

16. Trans. John Higginbotham (Berkeley: University of California Press, 1967).

17. *Enarratio in Evangelium Joannis*, ch. 21, 15-19; PG 124: 309Dff.

18. *Sermo asceticus* I, n. 3; PG 31: 876A.

19. On spiritual guidance in classical Antiquity, see the article by Edouard des Places, 'Direction spirituelle,' I, in *DSAM*, vol. 3 (Paris, 1957) col. 1002-8.

20. See, for example, *Apophthegmata Patrum*, *Alph.*, Macarius, n. 1 (PG 65:257C); Joseph of Thebes; Isaac, priest of the Cells, n. 1-2 (233); Isidore, priest of Nitria, n. 1 (233-36); Sisoes, n. 7 (393), and so forth.

21. *Ibid.*, John of Thebes, 241C = CS 59:109.

22. *Ibid.*, Antony 37; PG 65:88G = CS 59:8-9. Cfr. Deut 32, 7.

23. See K. H. Rengstorf's articles *Didascalos* and *Mathetes* B2 in Gerhard Kittel, *Theological Dictionary of the New Testament*, trans. Geoffrey W. Bromiley (Grand Rapids: Eerdmans, 1967) p. 427: 'Apart from the formal relation of teacher and pupil, the OT, unlike the classical Greek world and Hellenism, had no master-disciple relation. Whether among the prophets or the scribes, we seek in vain for anything corresponding to it.' For the opposite view, see L. Duerr, 'Heilige Vaterschaft im antiken Orient,' in *Festgabe Ildefons Herwegen* (Münster i-W., 1938) pp. 1-20.

II

THE SPIRITUAL FATHER

DESPITE THE ANALOGIES we could easily draw from every time and place—direction (instruction, institutions, education) being of necessity based upon the mere succession of generations—spiritual direction has its own physionomy which radically distinguishes it from everything it is not.

1. FATHER

The *spiritual father* is not a rabbi who explains or applies Torah; he is neither a *mufti*, a specialist of *fatwa* (legal advice), nor a canonist who resolves a moral problem. He is a *father*, and to understand his role one should first study the christian meaning of this term. An eleventh-century Muslim will set us on our way. Struck by the esteem in which christians held their 'fathers,' he explained this in his own way. 'With them, the title "father" is the greatest honor to be found in their teaching. Indeed, the principles of their religion are based doctors, however, whom they honor greatly, deduced the christian principles from rules given orally by Christ and the Apostles. The Christians commemorate the role which they fulfilled.'[1] Here we find an acceptable fact: the title 'father' is the greatest honor recognized among Christians. We should, however, refute or correct the explanation, because the follower of the Koran who created it viewed things his own way, as one of the 'people of a book' (*ahl Kitab*). In fact, in Christianity, the great honor of being called Father derives from something entirely different from the simple codification of past oral teaching or the mere exegesis of a written law; it deals with true, not just legal or metaphoric, fatherhood. Such fatherhood is characteristic not only of the great doctors we are used to reading in the *Patrology* but also and equally with them of saints who did not leave a single written line, and of others who left only a few which are not always remarkable, or even authentic. Whether it be a Saint Gregory the Theologian or a Saint Arsenius, or even a fourteenth-century holy man, those who published their writings or composed their panegyric used exactly the same formula: *tou hosiou* (or *tou en hagiois*) *patros hēmōn tou deina* (the wondrous deeds of our saintly father) (our saintly mother) so and so. Far from viewing the Desert Fathers as inferior to the great hierarchs, on account of their lack of culture, they are often placed above them. One should psalmodize, an ancient writer states, by understanding the psalms, 'not in the manner of an exegete like Basil or John (Chrysostom), but spiritually, according to the interpretation of the Fathers. That is, one should apply them to one's own life and work and passions . . .'[2] Without utilizing such an upside-down order, Saint Dorotheos warns against the temptation of pride which consists in recognizing only the authority of the most famous Fathers.[3]

Our use of the title 'father' may mislead us, even if recent Greeks (e.g. K.L. Logothetes in his work *La philosophie des Pères et du moyen âge*[4]) follow it through unconscious *mimēsis*. The eastern tradition does not recognize the, indeed highly uncertain, time limit we impose on the 'patristic' age. It is true that we too continue to greet some of our own contemporaries as father, whether they are priests, as in England, or, elsewhere, religious and priests. Like the title 'sister' and 'mother' given to nuns, this custom goes back, by an uninterrupted tradition, to a venerable antiquity. Over the centuries, however, these terms have lost some of their value, like sacred vessels gradually lose their shine, the result of being held in priestly hands or of being rubbed by those of sacristans. Since then, one has had recourse to various epithets such as 'Reverend, Very Reverend,' and so forth—though such expedients only helped to accelerate the process of externalization and banalization by stressing the official aspect of such a nomenclature and titles. We call the former 'Fathers' for a chronological reason, and those of our present-day 'Reverend Fathers' for no reason at all, except to distinguish them from those we in French call 'Monsieur l'Abbé' (Father). And yet, Father and *Abbé*, *Pater et Abbas*, have precisely the same meaning.

But this meaning is such that it must fade as its spirit weakens. The name 'father' is to be understood in a realistic, mystical sense which those who used it outside Christianity did not and could not have given it, and which we ourselves cannot give it except by internalizing the profound theology with which the ancients accepted it. For instance, when Marcus Aurelius[5] differentiates between what he received from Antoninus, his adoptive father (*para tou patros*), and from Annius, his natural father, his 'progenitor' (*ara tou gennēsastos*);[6] or Theodore of Studios makes a distinction between the one he usually calls his father, Saint Platon, and Photinus (the husband of his mother, '*ho gennēsas*'),[7] the difference is not merely nominal. In eastern hagiography we constantly find that spiritual generation is more excellent than natural generation. To draw the reader's attention from now on to this basic concept, let us immediately give an especially striking example. Toward the end of the tenth century a certain Arsenius entered the monastery of Saint Mamas in Constantinople. One day his mother came to the monastery door to see him— an opportunity for the following solemn (in our view, too solemn) declaration: 'From now one, I am dead to the world. How could I move backwards? How should I want to see the woman who brought me forth in the flesh? I have a father according to the spirit, from whom I daily receive the very pure milk of divine grace, I mean my father in God. He is also my mother since he had begotten me in the Spirit, and he warms me in his womb like a new-born babe.'[8] The person who penned these lines took this idea so seriously that he applied the words of Ben Sira, 'It is in his children that a father will be known', to this spiritual begetting.[9]

Father and child (*teknon*):[10] to understand the profound meaning of such correlatives, one should recall how christian usage employed them. God is our Father and we are God's children, through the Holy Spirit—the Spirit of the Father and of the Son, the paternal and filial Spirit, the Spirit of Fatherhood and the Spirit of Sonship (*hyiotēs*), the sanctifying Spirit who sanctifies us precisely by making us sons of God through participation in the divine nature which he imparts to us, through the second birth of which he is the Author, through union with the Father's well-beloved Son he gives to us: realities all, or rather aspects of the one and same divine reality by virtue of which the Spirit says in us, by letting us say, 'Abba, Father.' When Saint Paul writes to his 'children' that he 'must go through the pain of giving birth to you all over again, until Christ is formed in you,'[11] he knows that he is referring to real fatherhood, an active participation in the Fatherhood of God.[12] Every fatherhood, even in the natural order, but especially spiritual fatherhood; every motherhood, to begin with that of the Most Blessed Virgin Mary and the Church *quae est mater nostra* ('which is our mother')[13] justifies its name through an ontological reference to the Father of our Lord Jesus Christ.[14] We should also take into consideration that this spiritual fruitfulness does not occur without pain. The Church was born on Calvary, from the Lord's pierced side, and anyone who is called to transmit the life of the Spirit will not be able to do it except by agreeing, together with Saint Paul, to suffer in order to make up all that is still to be undergone by Christ for the sake of his body, the Church (Gal. 1:24). For the time being, let us examine this reality in itself, without taking historic conditions into account.

Christian antiquity has handed down the name 'father' advisedly. Why is it that the Semitic term *abbas* passed into Greek, Coptic, Armenian, Georgian, Latin, and from there into all the languages spoken in christendom?

Richard Reitzenstein[15] believes that this use can be explained through sustained exchange (*lebhaften Austausch*) between Egypt and Syria. In consequence, a purely linguistic phenomenon. But why did such 'exchange' never take place in the opposite direction, from Coptic to Syriac, and from there to all countries, since Egyptian monasticism had, after all, greater influence upon Syrian monasticism than the reverse? To suppose that reading the New Testament had something to do with the diffusion of the Semitic term would not be rash, since the term is found in several places.[16] Furthermore, the monks did memorize the entire New Testament, and the *Our Father* gave them ample opportunity to think of this 'Abba-Pater.' In the New Testament, however, 'Abba' is found only as it applies to God, the Father of Jesus Christ and our Father; it is uttered by your Lord Jesus Christ or it is the Holy Spirit who makes us say it. Is man not impious, not arrogant to let this term be applied to him, especially when the Lord gave this explicit warning: 'You must call no one on earth your father, since you have only one Father, and he is in heaven.'[17] If such prohibitions did not prevent certain very godly christians from calling mere mortals 'Father' or 'Abba' (or Père Abbé), it is because—far from viewing this habit as an act of disobedience to the Lord's admonition—they advisedly saw in it homage to the one fatherhood of God, just as we do not disregard the solemn declaration of Christ, 'There is one alone who is good',[18] when we recognize goodness in human beings. Created goodness praises the one source of all goodness. The word father or mother in connection with a benefit received glorifies God the Father knowingly or unknowingly (*sive sciens*, *sive nesciens*): 'all that is good . . . comes down from the Father of all light.'[19]

This, however, it an *a priori* insight, a logical deduction rather than an historical conclusion. We would like to know whether such a concept did indeed govern the evolution of the term *abbas*. The clearest text to be found on the subject is late and western, the well-known second chapter of the *Rule of Saint Benedict*. Let us cite it nonetheless, as we quoted another text earlier, so that it brightens the road like a far-away beacon toward which we are moving: 'To be worthy of the task of governing a monastery, the abbot must always remember what his title signifies and act as a superior should. He is believed to hold the place of Christ in the monastery, since he is addressed by a title of Christ, as the Apostle indicates: You have received the spirit of adoption of sons by which we exclaim, abba, father.'[20]

A gloss could be made about the fact that the name 'father' is used as a title of Christ (*pronomen Christi*). But this is undoubtedly a type of *hypallagē* (transferred epithet): the word *Christi* takes the place of *Dei*. Dom Cuthbert Butler seems not to have paid attention to this; at any rate, he adds no note to the text. In his Letter 61, Evagrius Ponticus exhorts his correspondents: 'Therefore, since you are fathers, imitate Christ your father.' And in the Syrian *Book of Degrees* we read, 'Thus we should say in our prayer, "Lord Jesus, free us from evil and fashion us according to your will. Our Father who are in heaven, blessed Jesus Christ! Set us free from temptations and form us according to your will."'[21] It is true that 'the saint who wanted to remain anonymous' (Preface) inclined towards Sabellian Modalism, according to the editor. Gerhard Kittel's *Theological Dictionary of the New Testament*, s.v. *Abbas*, alludes only briefly to the liturgical usage of this term in early Christianity. However, the closing remark of this article is worthy of note: 'Jewish usage shows how this Father-child relationship to God far surpasses any possibilities of intimacy assumed in Judaism, introducing indeed something which wholly new.'[22] Within its own category, the spiritual father-spiritual child relationship will likewise be something entirely new.[23]

R. Reitzenstein[24] states that 'the title *pater* is found in the cult of Isis at Delos, in the Phrygian mystery communities, in the Mithras cult, among the worshipers of the god most high (*theos hypsistos*) and elsewhere.' This, together with other data found in the *Theological Dictionary of the New Testament*, s.v. *pater* (vol. V, pp. 945-859), unquestionably proves that the concept and the desire for a fatherhood of a religious character is found outside Christianity, perhaps also that this is a universal human aspiration. Indeed, while studying the inscriptions on Egyptian sarcophagi, someone has recently been able to write: 'The dead person is transformed into a child in order to enjoy the solicitude of father and mother. Here we undoubtedly find the reason for such representation: the universal desire to be a child, to be surrounded by the care the dead find desirable.'[25] This, however, does not prove that the concept of fatherhood is the same everywhere, or that christian revelation does not give an original and more satisfying answer to that universal desire; nor, consequently, that the Christians, especially the monks, borrowed their vocabulary, still less the doctrine, of spiritual fatherhood from pagan sources. Karl Heussi, who knows Reitzenstein's theory, would at this point (and others) prefer to link the institution of monasticism to the charisms of the early Church, especially the 'charismatic didascalia'[26] known from *Acts* and *The Doctrine of the Twelve Apostles*.[27] This hypothesis is still more plausible because it is new and does not conform in the least to previously accepted Protestant views on the origins of monasticism. Still, one would like to be able to follow the traces of such persistency and development through the ten or twelve generations separating the Desert Fathers from the 'prophets and pneumatics'[28] of Corinth and elsewhere.

Understandably, this would be difficult. One would have to see the Christians live, hear them converse with one another, photograph their interpersonal behavior, as we are able to do so well with the Desert Fathers. But the testimonies we have from that time certainly have other concerns besides satisfying our hunger for detail; an Ignatius, a Polycarp, a Clement had to assure the life, the harmony, the hierarchy of the churches. By contrast, what we grasp most clearly are the great principles of this life. The first generation of Christians lived in amazement at God's love for man. And their faith in this love is summarized especially in the name 'Father,' which is the proper title of the God of Jesus Christ. The *Letter to Diognetus* states explicitly that the first information a catechumen receives is 'knowledge of the father.'[29] Even before this anonymous author, Saint Clement of Rome had exhorted the Corinthians 'to fix their gaze on the Father'[30]; and Saint Ignatius of Antioch allowed the secret of his miraculous inner life to burst forth: 'There is in me no fire of love for material things; but only water living and speaking in me, and saying to me from within, *deuro pros ton patera*, come to the Father.'[31] What a profound meditation about the fatherhood of God one could make from the writings of the Apostolic Fathers! It was not only the first object of their faith chronologically; ontologically and logically, it was the fountainhead of all things for them.

Yet, and perhaps for this very reason, we still do not find any explicit reference to this shared fatherhood by virtue of which the title 'father' would later be given, for example, to bishops. With the Apostolic Fathers, the term *pater* always refers to 'the one father,'[32] except in the case of Abraham, Jacob, and other ancestors of the people of God.[33] This is because Ignatius, like Clement and Saint Paul before him, is preoccupied with unity. 'Hasten all to come together as to one temple of God, as to one altar, to one Jesus Christ, who came forth from the one Father.'[34] Though the name 'father' is not given to them, the bishops seem invested with all the qualities and powers which eventually were to cause it to be given to them. Rather than calling them fathers, Saint Ignatius does more: in his usual manner, he condenses in an admirable formula the concept that will forever justify such a designation. To the Magnesians, he writes: 'It is not right to presume on the youthfulness of your bishop. You ought to respect him as fully as you respect the authority of God the Father. Your holy presbyters, I know, have not taken unfair advantage of his apparent youthfulness, but in their godly wisdom have deferred to him—nay, rather not so much to him as to the Father of Jesus Christ, who is everybody's bishop.'[35] A few lines further down, Ignatius calls God the Father 'the invisible bishop' (*episkopon aoraton*—here one obviously pays attention to the etymological meaning of *episkopos*, 'overseer,' from the verb *episkopeō*), while distinguishing him from *the bishop who is seen*. We also read, 'Everyone should respect the deacons as they would Jesus Christ, just as they respect the bishop as representing the Father'.[36] 'All be obedient to the bishop, as Jesus Christ was obedient to the Father.'[37] We constantly hear the fatherhood of God mentioned in connection with the bishop. We see from this that it is not correct to say that 'The reason why the designations *pater* and *papa* are given to the bishops hardly needs to be explained: as the leader of the community, the bishop is compared to the father of the household.'[38]

The *Didascalia Apostolorum (The Teaching of the Twelve Apostles)* should be mentioned next; the bishop must be holy because he represents God himself.[39] 'He is your father, after God, having regenerated you to (divine) sonship through water and the spirit.'[40] 'Let the lay person therefore honor the good shepherd; let one love and fear him as a father, a lord and master. Likewise, let the bishop love the lay people as children, hatching and keeping them warm with his eager love, as if they were eggs that will be chicks; or carrying them in his arms like fledglings, to make birds of them.'[41] 'Through your bishop, O man, God makes you his child; son, recognize the right hand, your mother: love her. Honor the one who has become, after God, your father.'[42] In the Latin *Didascalia* we read, 'Love him who has become, after God, your father and your mother' (*Et ama eum qui post Deum pater tuus et mater tua est*). The following lines express a concept that will often be found in later times: 'If the word of God, while referring to parents according to the flesh, declares, "Honor your father and your mother, that your days may be long", how much more, with respect to spiritual parents, will the Word not exhort you to honor them like benefactors and intercessors with God—those who by water have regenerated you, who have filled you with the Holy Spirit, reared you with the Word as with milk, bred you with doctrine, strengthened you with admonition, deemed you worthy to partake of the precious body and blood of salvation, loosed your sins and made you partake of the Holy Eucharist, who made you partakers and joint heirs of God.'[43] Clearly, all these texts presuppose that the bishop himself administers the sacraments, especially baptism, which conferring the quality of a child of God upon the one baptized, makes the one who baptizes 'a father, after God'.

In the sections added to the *Didascalia*, the *Apostolic Constitutions* entrust the administration of baptism to the priest. 'Neither a priest nor a deacon (must) ordain from the laity into the clergy; but the priest (is) only to teach, to baptize, to bless the people. The deacon is to serve the bishop and the priests (this is what being a deacon means); he is not to perform other offices' (III. 20. 2). This is a logical, though tacit, acknowledgment that the priest is to be called father and be honored as such.

These texts, which come from the third century, came to be viewed as authentic 'Apostolic Constitutions' and became as authoritative as Sacred Scripture, to which we find them juxtaposed.[44]

During the fourth century, Amphilochius of Iconium, without citing the *Apostolic Constitutions*, appropriates and expresses the same concepts, though not without polemic intent:[45] the church is 'the mother'; the priest who baptizes, 'the father.'

It is self-evident that apostates are insane: they injure everyone through their divorce. They call the father who begot them a whoremaster, and view the mother as a prostitute. They do not observe God's commandment that says, 'Whosoever shall revile his father or his mother, shall die the death.' One could perhaps say, 'I mock my parents in the flesh!' Even in this you do evil . . . One could say a great deal about respect and awe for parents; but . . . let us see whether they at least honor their spiritual parents. And then, who is the spiritual father? After God, certainly the priest who baptized you. For it is written: 'it was I who begot you in Christ Jesus by preaching the good News'[46]; and, "Here I am with the children whom God has given me'[47]; and for the attention of those who had fallen away, 'my children! I must go through the pain of giving birth to you all over again, until Christ is formed in you.'[48] We wish that this be accomplished in all those people. The mother who nourished them is unquestionably the Church.[49]

We must stop here as far as the attribution of the name *Father* to bishops is concerned; to pursue things further would lead us away from the subject. One may consult the opening pages of various *Patrologies*, or the article by E. Amman, 'Pères de l'église' in the *Dictionnaire de théologie catholique*, vol. 12 (Paris, 1933) pp. 1192-1215. Indeed, the evolution of this usage, along dogmatic and hierarchical lines, had led to the concept of the Church Father, though it contained many other possibilities.

Of them, one became a reality with the Desert Fathers. They seem to appear suddenly in the *Apophthegmata Patrum* (*Sayings of the Fathers*) and the *Vitae Patrum* (*Lives of the Fathers*), surrounded by the radiance of their spiritual fatherhood. At any rate, the vocabulary presents itself as fixed from the beginning: they are called 'Father' (*Pater*, or *Abba*) in such a way that the collections of their deeds and sayings has always been known as *Paterika*. For this term the learned J.G. Cotelier[50] refers to 'Rosweyde's Prolegomena to the Lives of the Fathers' (*Rossveydus Prolegomenis ad Vitas Patrum*). The latter [51] starts by quoting the exposition of Pope Gelasius to the Council of

Rome in 494[52]: 'We receive with honor the lives of the Fathers, of Paul, Antony, Hilarion and of all the other hermits, which the blessed Jerome wrote down.' What is to be remembered from this text is that Gelasius I saw no difficulty in the fact that the title Father had been given to hermits; one needed not be in clerical orders to receive such honor. An observation all the more necessary since the same Rosweyde[53] cites a protestation by S. Jerome.[54] One should read these lines, because they clearly illustrate what is of interest to us here, the link between the name Father or Abba and the fatherhood of God: 'Since *Abba*, Father, is used in Hebrew and Syriac and the Lord warns in the Gospel that no one is to be called father except God, I do not know by whose authority we either should call others by this name in monasteries, or should acquiesce to being called so ourselves. Certainly, the one who said not to swear at all commanded this. If we do not take an oath, let us not call anyone father. Should we understand the reference to 'Father' differently, we will be compelled to think differently about oaths.'[55] Some have doubted the authenticity of these lines.[56] Nonetheless, they are certainly in the style of Saint Jerome. They can only be adjacent to the places and times when the custom they censure arose; after the *Rule of Saint Benedict* (which only records the manifestly pre-existing title *Abba*), we could not understand even a Westerner dreaming of making such a censure. At any rate, it comes from a Westerner. If it is Saint Jerome—and there is no serious reason to doubt this—he corrected himself a few years later by writing in his commentary on Mt 23:8:

No one is to be called either Master or Father, except God the Father and our Lord Jesus Christ. Father, because all things proceed from him. Master, because all things exist through him; or because we have become reconciled to God through the dispensation of his flesh. It is asked why the Apostle may have called himself the praeceptor of the human race; or why, in the vernacular, they call each other Fathers, especially in the monasteries of Palestine and Egypt. This is the answer: it is one thing to be a father and master by nature, and quite another, by way of speaking (*indulgentia*). If we call a human being 'father,' we honor his age; we do not point out the creator of our life. One is called master through one's association with the true Master. To be more precise: in the same manner as the one God and the one son by nature does not hold it against others that they be called gods through adoption, and sons, so does the one Father and Master not hold it against others that they be called Fathers or Masters improperly (*abusive*).'[57]

This text, written somewhat hastily by Saint Jerome, deserves a detailed analysis. Let us note at least l) that the Latin adverb *abusive* does not have the meaning of the English 'abusively,' just as the verb *abuti* does not always mean 'to misuse.' *Abuti* means 'to consume entirely,' or 'to use in a derivative sense, improperly.' Origen, or his translator Rufinus, explains this very well: 'the word 'God' is used properly (*principaliter*) for the one by 'whom are all things and in whom are all things'; secondly, and so to speak improperly (*abusive*), Scripture describes as gods those 'to whom the word of God came,' as the Saviour confirms in the Gospel; in the third place, not improperly, but falsely (*jam non abusive, sed falso*), demons are called 'the gods of the nations'.[58] 2) This broad usage of the term Abba (*Abbas*) or Father (*Pater*) has the same justification as the word Master (*Magister*). It is not by nature that a creature is father or master, but *indulgentia*, by taking such terms in a less strict sense, and also *consortio*, through participation, not by essence. In summary, this is the same as saying that only God is (*ontos*) all that he is, and that we only 'are' in a derivative, analogical sense. In a *Letter to Eustochius*,[59] Saint Jerome was to make a mere note about 'Macarius, Pambo, Isidore, and the rest of those whom they call Fathers' (*Macarius vero, et Pambo, et Isidorus, et caeteri, quos Patres vocant*).

But let us leave the Latin writers; the usage of which we speak became so solidly rooted among them that, instead of being shaken by Jerome's quibble, one of them preferred to attribute it to 'a certain quarrelsome monk.'[60] The Easterners do not seem to have questioned the legitimacy of their custom. Even commentators on Matthew 23 do not express the least apprehension or admonition in this regard. They knew too well that the literal sense can be a 'misconstruction' (*un contre-sens*), especially if one 'dissects' [61] Scripture into isolated passages. For Origen, the passage into which the prohibition of Mt 23:8 is inserted refutes the vanity of the Pharisees. It is true that vanity can be found even in the Church of Christ; here too there are those who love 'the best chairs' (*cathedras primas*) and who, to obtain them, try first

to become deacons, but not as Scripture would have them[62]; next, they seek to take away the best offices of those who are called priests. Not satisfied with this, some arrange to be called bishop by the people, that is, Rabbi—whereas they should understand that a bishop should be irreproachable and possess the other qualities (enumerated in 1 Tm), so that even if he is not called a bishop by men he nonetheless is a bishop before God. The one who has these qualities mentioned by Saint Paul *is* a bishop before God, even if he is not a bishop in human eyes, even if he did not arrive at this rank through human ordination.

Reading these lines makes us think of certain personalities who came after Origen and of certain conflicts caused by the 'spirituals.' Let us also read the comparison that follows:

Someone who has studied the art of medicine and is able to heal like a physician is a physician; even if the sick do not lend him their bodies, he *is* a physician. A helmsman is one who has learned the art of steering and who is able to use it as he should; even if one gives him the helm of the ship, he *is* a helmsman.[63]

This too was soon to find its application.

If in Origen's day bishops received the title father 'through human ordination,' why would people not also give it to certain bishops, priests, and deacons on account of their qualities, virtues, and inner gifts? Accordingly, the same Origen gives us some principles that were to lead straight to this conclusion.

> To demonstrate that we have a double line of fathers, we use Ps. 44 which states, 'Listen, O daughter, and see, and turn your ear; forget your people and your father's house!' . . . We said a while ago that the devil had been our father before God became our father. We assent to the Catholic Epistle of Saint John where it is written, 'The one who does sin is from the devil.'[64] As often as we sin, so many times are we born from the devil. Unfortunate is the one who is always born from the devil. On the contrary, greatly blessed is the one who is always born of God. I will not say that the just one is born from God only once: the just man is born from God always, according to each good deed. God engenders the just one in each of these. If then the Lord is always generated from the Father, so are you always born of God (if you have the spirit of sonship), with each good work, each of your thoughts. And thus born, you will be continually born a son of God in Jesus Christ.'[65]

This concept of continued generation establishes the possibility of an eternal participation in the fatherhood of God. There is not only baptism,[66] and the sacraments, but also all spiritual growth and education. Those who will have such good deeds performed, or who will inspire them according to the spirit of sonship, will be called spiritual fathers *abusive*, that is , analogically. In the long series of deeds which are like so many steps towards the perfection of the child of God, there is one which plays a special, even essential, role, namely the entry into the monastic life. Its importance emerges from the esteem in which the Byzantines and the Easterners held the religious profession. Saint John Chrysostom does not express an individual but rather a universally held conviction when he demonstrates, first in passing,[67] then *ex professo*,[68] the pre-eminence of the monk and of the 'true and christian philosophy' above every human dignity, whether royal of imperial. If some Byzantines viewed the monastic profession as a second baptism,[69] this was above all a somewhat simplistic way of affirming its high purifying and sanctifying value, and also of establishing between a novice and the elder who admits him the same father-son relationship as exists between the baptizer and the one baptized. And even if sacramental theory collapses, the value of sanctification remains, and with it spiritual fatherhood.

'Having freed a widow from the dungheap of the present life (that is, gold),' Saint Stephen the Younger 'gave her the holy habit, and changed her name to Ann. Thus he became her father in the Lord and her God-father (*anadochos*, sponsor at baptism). At once he sent her to the monastery below (of Saint Auxentius); he recommended her to the venerable and holy prefect of the monastery, having exhorted this worthy human being to become the patronness for the salvation of her soul.'[70] Ann was and remained his 'spiritual daughter.'[71] She called him 'an educator profiting the soul, the guide of my salvation.'[72]

It is this fatherhood which is expressed by the name Father or Abba the ascetics gave to their spiritual director—a fatherhood accomplished actually or potentially. A fatherhood in fact. Saint Theodore of Tabennisi states that Saint Pachomius 'is father to us all, after God.'[73] 'After God, Pachomius was their father.'[74] What is said here about Pachomius is expressed in general terms in the *Monastic Constitutions* attributed to Saint Basil: 'As God, who is and wants to be called Father of all, demands an undiminished obedience from his servants, so, among men, does the spiritual father (require obedience) . . .'[75] In the chapter about family relationships we read, 'The Father of all is the one who guides all along the spiritual path.' The mention of spiritual fatherhood is often linked to the memory of one's reception into the religious or spiritual life. Saint Gregory of Nyssa writes to Letoius, Bishop of Melitine, 'Do not forget to offer God the customary prayers for me. As a grateful son, you owe (old age) the provisions[76] of your prayers, according to the commandment which orders us to honor our parents. . . .'[77] We do not know the historical event to which Saint Gregory refers: baptism, monastic profession ordination to the priesthood, episcopal consecration. All this establishes a fatherhood and a sonship, as, in general, does everything that brings one close to God.[78] 'The one through whom we have been led to God' is our father. 'The one who has brought forth according to God,'[79] that is, to the perfect life, is a spiritual father. A father or mother according to nature can become a son or daughter to the child. Thus 'the one who according to the flesh had brought forth' Saint Theodosius, 'was engendered according to Christ by her child.'[80] Thus it is that, according to Barlaam's prophecy, Joseph achieves this 'innovation' (*to kainotaton*), becoming his father's progenitor, and giving a spiritual regeneration to the one who had brought him forth in the flesh.[81] What is more, according to Saint Gregory of Nyssa, everyone can become his own father, spiritually: 'In a certain manner, we become our own father when, through a good disposition of our soul, we shall have formed and engendered ourselves and have brought ourselves to the light. We do this when we receive God in ourselves, thereby becoming the sons of God and sons of virtue, and sons of the Most High'.[82] On the other hand, we bring ourselves forth prematurely and make ourselves imperfect and sterile[83] when, according to the Apostle, the 'form of Christ' (*hē tou Christou morphē*)[84] has not been developed. For it is necessary, he says, for the man of God to be perfect and whole.[85] The person in whom the condition of his nature has been realized is entirely perfect. Consequently, if one has made himself a son of God through virtue, having accepted the power of a noble birth,[86] he knows the appointed time of this happy birth; he rightly rejoices, according to the Gospel, because a man has been born into the world.'[87] It is indeed impossible to push the logic of the principle that governs the doctrine of spiritual fatherhood any further. The one who 'leads towards God' is a father, according to the Spirit, according to God, according to Christ. And this fatherhood is pre-eminent above all other in the world because it produces 'a regeneration that in all truth is more divine.'[88]

Regeneration may equally well be called motherhood, not merely because it can be achieved by a spiritual *mother*, but on account of a fullness that belongs only to her. Saint Symeon the Stylite (the Elder), having thrown himself at the feet of an old man (*senior*) who 'had interrogated him like God,' said, 'You are my father and my mother the instructor of my good deeds, my guide toward the kingdom of God. You have acquired my soul which was sinking into perdition . . .'[89] There is no lack of examples of women who 'having left the world, serve(d) God with the children they brought forth according to Christ.'[90]

One can be a physician without practicing medicine; know the art of steering without actually doing navigation, Origen said. The number of 'spirituals' greatly surpasses the number of spiritual *fathers*, at least hopefully. The ancients called these available spiritual directors *Abbas* (fem. *Ammas*) or they used words which in every language translate the terms used to designate father and mother. R. Reitzenstein correctly states that '*Pater*, like *Abbas*, is a title for the perfect.'[91] Only later did the term Abbas become a synonym for 'monk'; and what makes some people today say 'Monsignore' to simple *frati* when they want to worm themselves into their good graces, undoubtedly results from the same phenomenon. J. Pargoire[92] writes: 'Mr Lombard would have us believe that the word *abbas* means something else, besides "monk"? It is true that this word, in the sense of *hegumen*, is found in the writings of certain ancient authors like Dorotheos and certain jurists or canonists who were inspired by the Justinian Code or the *Novellae* ('New Laws'), sources that are Latin in language or at least in inspiration. But aside from these, and especially with the ninth-century authors, chroniclers and biographers, such a meaning cannot be applied at all. In these texts, the word *abbas* must be understood in terms of religious in general. The *abbades* of Byzantium were the *frati* of Naples.'[93] In its precision, this criticism is the mark of an unusual competence.[94] *Abbas* in the Benedictine sense of Right Reverend Father Abbot is indeed very rare; and I wonder whether this sense, even in exceptional cases, might not be secondary, the primary meaning remaining that of 'spiritual.' Examples where the title *abbas* has a hierarchical-administrative meaning only lead one strongly to suspect a Latin influence.

To follow the purely Byzantine evolution of the term, one should begin by establishing its original definition at the time of Saint Antony and the first monks. 'One day abba Antony received a letter from Emperor Constantius, inviting him to come to Constantinople; and he wondered what he should do. Then he says to abba Paul, his disciple, 'Should I make the journey?' Paul replied, 'If you leave, you will be called Antony; if you stay, abba Antony.'[95] Likewise, the archbishop Theophilus of Alexandria qualified as abba[96]: *ho autos Abbas Theophilus ho archiepiskopos*, which Pelagius, in the sixth century, translated as: *Venit aliquando sanctae memoriae Theophilus episcopus* . . . (one day Theophilus of blessed memory came to the mountain of Nitria . . .·[97]. In the *Apophthegmata Patrum*, the title abba is a title of honor given spontaneously to a monk or churchman by those who believed they had been able to detect in him special signs of holiness. We will make the same observation for other documents, but one should take care to remember that in saints' lives the biographer often gives his hero titles which he earned only later. Thus Saint Sabas is called *abbas* from his youth[98]; a little further down,[99] we learn that Saint Euthymius himself gave the young Sabbas the surname *'paidariogerōn,'* which is more or less the equivalent of 'young abba.' In the *Life of Saint Stephen the Younger,*·written at the beginning of the ninth century, the iconoclast Emperor Leo, who did not like monks, called them *abbas* with a touch of

ironic respect.[100] In Dorotheos, *abba* retains its ancient nuance
of 'a monk advanced in perfection; if it is occasionally also
used to designate the superior, this is not by virtue of the word
itself as is the case with the Latins, but because the superior
happens indeed to be a saint: Seridos, Barsanuphius, or John
the Prophet.[101]

In short, one should always take into account both context
and environment. In the *Apophthegmata Patrum* the name abba
appears almost always to have been given advisedly, with full
consciousness of its spiritual meaning. Those whose saying
and deeds deserve to be handed down to posterity are *abbas*.
The Preface to the *Alphabetical Collection* also calls them 'the
saintly and blessed fathers, the holy elders.'[102] Even there,
however, one is not always sure that politeness did not play a
great role in this, especially in the case of ecclesiastics who
were not monks, such as the *papa* of Alexandria (see above,
p.27) or *abba* Gregory the Theologian.[103] There is even 'the
abba of the mountain of Nitria,'[104] and 'the abba of the monastery (which) the blessed Epiphanius had in Palestine'[105]: two
'directors'? Yet 'a certain Eulogius, priest and great ascetic,'
was denied this title, despite his protracted fasts, because he
had been 'glorified by men,' and did not know *krypta ergasia*
(secret occupations), the need to hide one's ascetic perfor-
mances.[106] The farther removed we are from heroic times, the
more emptied ancient words are of their fulness, in the monastic vocabulary as in any other. In the *Life of Saint John the
Almsgiver*, to a woman saved from a life of prostitution by a
monk's devotion, who had adopted a foundling, one of those
spiteful people who see evil everywhere ironically says, '*Alethōs
kalon abbadopoulon egennēsas*' (Indeed, you have brought forth a
beautiful abba-offspring).[107]

Whatever the case with the word abba and its changing
fortunes, the term spiritual father has always kept its essential
original meaning, at least among ascetics, either because of the
adjective which often accompanied it or simply because it was
clearer than the other, or because, unlike the other, it evoked
the concept of spiritual child. When the hagiographers write,

'The life of our saintly father so and so,' they know that their saint, precisely because he was a saint, had the necessary qualities to bring forth disciples to the spiritual life, to rear them and guide them to perfection.

The authors who have commented (summarily) upon the term *Pater* at the opening of their *Patrologies* have long conveyed to one another a sentence from Saint Irenaeus: '*Que enim ab alioque edoctus est verbo, filius docentis dicitur, et ille eius pater*' (Indeed, when one has been instructed by someone's words, he is called the instructor's son, and the other is called his father).[108] This may be followed by a few words of Clement of Alexandria at the opening of Book I of his *Stromata* (*Miscellanies*): 'Children are the offspring of our bodies, but words are the progeny of the soul. Hence we call those who have instructed us father . . .'[109] The motivation Clement gives does not seem particularly profound. We will return to him shortly. As for Saint Irenaeus, it is not in the passage quoted that we should look for his best doctrine, but in others which we will cite. H. du Manoir adds still another text, taken from a letter of Alexander of Jerusalem to Origen.[110] The passage can easily be mistranslated. It does not read, 'We know those blessed Fathers who trod the road before us,' as if the name Father had already passed into custom, but 'We know that the blessed ones who trod the path before us are Fathers.'

It would be a serious error to conclude from such texts that the word used, father, is but a trite metaphor. A person can be a professor, and a very good one, but that does not make him a spiritual father; it does not even prove that he can become one, at least in the judgment of the Easterners. R. Reitzenstein has found a short formula that expresses their view perfectly: 'Only someone who has become spiritual can be a spiritual father.'[111] The essential, the indispensable, condition for becoming someone's spiritual father is to first be spiritual oneself. There is good reason to insist on this concept; it dominates our entire subject.

2. 'SPIRITUAL'

We would perhaps do better to transcribe the Greek *pneu-matikōs*, for it is not automatically certain that the Latin has the same significance. Even the Greek includes gradations of meaning ranging from its bad sense, an heretical exaggeration, to its weakened and almost secularized use.

Like many others, the concept 'spiritual' has its history, but here we cannot possibly expound it in detail. What is important for us to know is not so much the vicissitudes of this history as its invariables. It is not a matter of describing the various aberrations or of summarizing all the discussions; rather, we will attempt to understand their lasting results. We can only indicate rapidly how this concept gradually took shape from its beginnings, to stop at its fixed definition, if there is one.

Far from going back to the Stoic *pneuma*,[1] we shall not dwell even on Sacred Scripture,[2] for in all this there is hardly any question of personalized spiritual direction.[3] We need only point out the scriptural passages which had the most influence upon it. In addition to those cited earlier, the line which spiritual men would claim most readily is Mt 10:20: 'It is not you who will speak; the Spirit of your Father will be speaking in you.'[4] Spiritual direction is done above all through the word, according to the perpetual demand of the disciples in the *Sayings of the Fathers*, 'Give me a word for my salvation.' And also, 'Anyone who listens to you, listens to me.'[5] The 'you' refers to the Apostles; those who lead 'the apostolic life,' in the original meaning of this term, are spiritual men. We may quickly pass over the period that follows, since spiritual direction hardly appears there.[6] 'As far as we can tell, nowhere do the leaders of the community exercise an individual *cure of soul*.' The great concern is the sanctification of the community as a whole. Clearly, this does not mean that the Apostles and those who replaced them took no interest in the perfection of each of their christians, but only that their letters, the only testimony we have, do not often inform us about this aspect of their apostolate.

The concept 'spiritual' begins to appear ambiguous when the gnostics spread their tripartite division of humanity into material men (*hylikoi*), animate (*psychikoi*), and spiritual men (*pneumatikoi*). Such division contained a two-fold error: 1) the spiritual as well as the material men are such from birth and definitively, that is, the former have no need of salvation, the latter cannot be saved; 2) the essential, formal element of 'spirituality' is *gnōsis*. The reaction of the orthodox to these two points is known especially from Saint Irenaeus. Here is his definition of the spiritual man: 'The union of flesh and spirit, receiving the Spirit of God, brings about the spiritual man' (*animae et carnis adunatio assumens spiritum Dei, spirit[u]alem hominem perficit.*'[7] But the great contribution of the saintly doctor of orthodoxy, at this point, is to have definitively established the primacy of love and to have eliminated the concept of the spiritual man 'by nature': 'This is the principal function of love: (to be) more valuable than knowledge, more glorious than prophecy, super-eminent also above all other charismata.'[8] Immediately after this famous declaration, Saint Irenaeus adds a chapter to demonstrate 'that the Church not only possesses charity, but that the Spirit of God rests on her.' The proof of perfect love is martyrdom. There is indeed a true divine *gnōsis*, that of the Apostles; it essentially differs from the one that puffs up, causes one to fall away from charity, and inspires in those who have it the pretense of being perfect. It is better and more profitable to be unlettered (*idiōta*), unlearned, and yet to achieve union with God through love.[9] The surest sign of 'spirituality' is martyrdom: the flesh is weak, the Spirit strong.

If, therefore, one adds the readiness of the Spirit like a stimulus to the weakness of the flesh, it necessarily follows that what is strong will prevail over what is weak, so that the infirmity of the flesh is absorbed by the Spirit, and such a person cannot in that case be carnal, but is spiritual, because of the communion of the Spirit. In such manner the martyrs bear their witness and hold death in contempt, not after the infirmity of the flesh, but because of the readiness of the Spirit. Once the weakness of the flesh is absorbed, it presents the Spirit as strong.'[10]

Beyond martyrdom, 'the spirit of God is preserved through faith and a pure way of life' (*dia tēs pisteōs kai tēs agnes anastrophēs syntērein to Pneuma tou Theou*).

Subordinated to the great gift of God which is love, are the charisms of which Saint Paul speaks, and which still existed at the time of Saint Ireneaus. Of these, the most important, as was true for the Apostle, is prophecy.[11] 'We have listened to many brothers, in the church, who had prophetic gifts, and were speaking all kinds of languages through the Spirit, bringing to light the hidden things of men for the benefit of men, and unfolding the mysteries of God. These the Apostle calls 'spiritual.' They are spiritual through the participation of the Spirit. . . .'[12] More than the others, this free gift of God,[13] under its two-fold aspect—knowledge of the mysteries of God (which came to be called theology), and the searching of the heart (*cardiognōsis*)—all of this given 'for the benefit' (*ad utilitatem*), to enable the spiritual man to become a spiritual father. It is not by accident that, centuries later, the title *prophet* would be added to the name of great directors of souls such as Zeno the Prophet,[14] in the fifth century; and, in the sixth, John the Prophet, Barsanuphius' *alter ego*, from whom we still have a collection of letters of direction. Whatever might be the case for other charisms, this one cannot occur without charity. 'The persons who have the pledge of the Spirit and are not enslaved to the lusts of the flesh, but submit themselves to the Spirit and live rationally, . . . these the Apostle rightly calls spiritual because the Spirit of God dwells in them.'[15]

One more idea from Irenaeus deserves our attention: 'Paradise, into which the Apostle Paul was taken up, and where he heard words ineffable, has been prepared for the just and for bearers of the spirit. . . '.[16] And also: 'Just as the wild olive tree bears fruit as if it had been transplanted to the king's garden, so human beings will be spiritual and, as it were, transplanted into the Paradise of God, if through faith they make progress toward the good, receive the Spirit of God, and bring forth the fruit thereof.'[17] Freed from all millenarianism, this thought may have contributed to letting the *Apophtheg-mata Seniorum* be called the *Paradisus Patrum*; the very title of this book bears witness to confidence in the *spiritual* gifts of the Fathers.

As for the remaining epochs, a careful study would reveal that this faith affirmed itself in the same proportion as the extraordinary charisms seemed to become rare. We should, in fact, make a distinction between two things which more than one scholar has confused: essential spirituality and its subsidiary mainfestations. Recent western scholasticism did not introduce the difference between *gratiae gratum fa-cientes* (sanctifying graces) and *gratiae gratis datae* (freely bestowed graces). This had been confirmed, more or less explicitly, from the beginning,[18] and was articulated more and more as the doctrine of the discernment of spirits was being developed, to a high degree on account of heresies such as Montanism.[19] Gradually, too, people formed clearer ideas about the hierarchy of charisms: those which to the eyes of many were the most impressive, such as thaumaturgy—while they always played a certain role in the evaluation of holiness—were nonetheless not as highly regarded by theologians and ascetics as others that were more inward and less spectacular. The *fama miraculorum* does not seem to have been of great importance in the sometimes anxious search for a spiritual father.

Scholars like R. Reitzenstein have not been sufficiently preoccupied with the evolution of precision in concepts, and this is why their all-too-general description of the 'pneumatic' is often wrong. The term 'enthusiasm', so greatly honored by K. Holl,[20] contains a confusion which the Easterners had long ago overcome. Holl's great error is recognized today: 'Following Daillé, K. Holl has attempted to show the existence of a power of the keys held by lay people, and W. Völker admits this in Origen; but after Poschman's study it is no longer possible to hold that position.'[21] This rebuttal to a thesis which has not been too successful frees us from insisting more upon it here.

The defeat of Montanism disentangled the concept of 'the spiritual' from ecstasy, this 'enthusiastic' element. 'The most characteristic, the most certain, the most specific, and also the most important sign of the influence exercised by Montanism' is that it 'forced the Church to acquire a clearer understanding of prophecy, its proper nature, its psychological conditions, and also to determine the place which it should be assigned in the organism of the Church.'[22] The 'New Prophecy,' as it styled itself,[23] almost discredited prophecy itself. Saint Irenaeus[24] had already warned against an integration that ran the risk of excluding prophecy from the Church under the pretext of eliminating pseudo-prophecy. This danger was avoided. However, 'from then on prophecies were made without ecstasy,' as Harnack says.[25] When de Labriolle adds[26] 'In truth, prophecies were hardly ever made,' this holds true for prophecy in the narrow sense of predicting future events. But the two main elements of this charism, knowledge of the mysteries of God and scrutinizing the heart, never disappeared, according to Irenaeus. We will see more than one example of this. In relation to spiritual direction, they are the most important. Even the others never ceased completely, and were to enjoy a renewed popularity with Messalianism.

Meanwhile, Clement of Alexandria and Origen were instrumental, for their part, in according honor to 'spiritual' persons. Clement uses the term much less than he does *gnostic*. The 'true gnostic' according to Clement will undoubtedly always be discussed in detail—despite W. Völker's weighty volume,[27] which has already produced many followers and a few critics. On what is essential, agreement has been reached on the following points:

Whatever the exaggerations, deviations, illusions, and unrealities which sober authors claim to detect in the doctrine of *gnōsis* and in the portrait of the gnostic according to Clement, it is wrong to say, without more ado, that he subordinates love to gnōsis, as a means to an end.

> The gnostic is one who is in the image and likeness of God.[28] He imitates God as far as he is capable; he neglects none of the things that contribute to this potential likeness [but is] chaste, self-restrained, living justly, ruling over the passions. . . .
> These three things our gnostic claims as his own: first, contemplation; second, obeying the commandments; third, forming good persons. Indeed, when these three meet together, they make the gnostic.[29]
> The gnostic prays to God at every hour, even in thought, having become intimate, united to God through love. First, let him ask forgiveness of sins; then, that he may sin no more; and further, that he may perform the good and understand the dispensation of the entire creation made by God, so that, having become pure in heart, he may be initiated into the beatific vision.'[30]

The gnostic so resembles the spiritual man that he could be mistaken for one through his moral perfection, the insights he has, the zeal he shows for the good of souls, and also, through his prayer and union with God.[31] Yet, try as one might, no exegesis, no 'harmonizing' will ever suppress the Clementine originalities which clearly differentiate his ideal of perfection from that of the monks, to the point that the monks would certainly not have recognized *their* spiritual men in the portraits of the gnostic after his own heart so obligingly drawn by Clement. It is the gnostic's duty to work at leading others to the *gnōsis* he himself possesses. But by this, Clement understands chiefly teaching, as he himself practiced it in his career as educator and lecturer, and not so much direction as we view it here and as the ascetics and their spiritual fathers understood it. It is not surprising that the prototype of all the manuscripts of the *Protreptikos* (*Exhortation to the Greeks*) and the

Paedagōgos (*The Tutor*), *Parisiensis graec.* 451, was written not by a monk for fellow monks but by the notary Baanes for the great scholar Arethas, Bishop of Caesarea. Monks though they were, they had better things to do than occupy themselves with Clement.

Origen is found to be more on their side, if only in their shared practical concerns. The *pneuma* is essentially active: it is acquired through practice (*praxis*). One perceives its presence through its operations. Through it, above all, one becomes 'diacritical', that is, able to discern spirits. This is essential. When 'most of the uncommon charisms have disappeared,'[32] this *diakrisis* remains, and constitutes one of the higher degrees of the perfect life. Not the highest degree, since 'the essence of the spiritual life is that uninterrupted non-proprietary attitude towards things which makes the soul rest in what she has already acquired and keeps her in a state of readiness to receive further gifts. It will be noticed that this brings us back to Origen's idea of the created spirit as a being perpetually advancing towards the good.'[33] Discernment is always necessary, but especially from the moment the angel of darkness, in despair of not being able to succeed through crude temptations, disguises himself into an angel of light. It is the special prerogative of the spiritual man to judge and to discern, according to words of Saint Paul often cited by Origen.[34]

> Indeed, temptation is likely to be found in visions. Sometimes the angel of iniquity transfigures itself into an angel of light. And thus one should be on one's guard and act cautiously (in order to discern with knowledge the type of visions). When the soul has progressed to the point where it begins to have discernment of visions, it will be proved to be spiritual if it knows how to discern them all. Accordingly, this is why discernment of spirits is mentioned among the spiritual gifts as a gift of the Spirit.[35]

Of the three Persons, the Father operates in all creatures; the Son in all rational creatures; the Holy Spirit only in the saints.[36]

Through such agreement, the working of the power of God the Father and the Son extends without distinction to every creature; but we discover that participation in the Holy Spirit is found only in the saints. . . . Creatures draw their existence from God the Father; their reason from the Word; their holiness from the Holy Spirit.'[37]

Thus one becomes spiritual through this participation of the Holy Spirit. This is holiness, and the mark of this spirituality and holiness is *diakrisis*. 'The doctrine of the discerning of spirits . . . is one of the chief elements Origen developed in the spiritual life. The Fathers of the Desert inherited the doctrine from him.'[38] It is even more important for us to form a clear concept of the spiritual man according to the Desert Fathers and the ascetics because they, more than anyone else, have given spiritual direction the classical form it has in the East. Karl Heussi has applied himself to this.[39] He insists particularly on what is *unheimlich* (sinister) in the spiritual fathers, disquieting, vaguely terrifying; he would gladly say *satanic*, to use a truly modern term. And all this on the basis of the following little story:

At first, abba Ammoes says to abba Isaiah, 'How do you see me now?' He replies, 'Like an angel, father.' Later on, he says, 'At this time, how do you see me?' Isaiah answers, 'Like Satan; although you have quoted a good word to me it is like steel.'[40]

Heussi concludes, 'The more intimately the disciple knew his abba, the more *unheimlich he appears*.'[41] This immense general inference rests on a very slender base. It is true that subsequently the gift of performing miracles was included among the disquieting realities, and that the 'supernatural knowledge' which the great Antony, abba Moses, Ammonas, and Paul the Simple showed under certain circumstances was ascribed to thaumaturgy. But what about the power of intercession (*Gebetskraft*)? We must now, or never, show that we are worthy of the clearsightedness of the Fathers by avoiding confusion in what they very clearly distinguished. That they believed in miracles is self-evident. Yet they did not ascribe all the wonders they worked or witnessed to 'miracle.' Saint Antony trusted visions only reluctantly[42]; and as for the second sight he enjoyed, he viewed it as the natural prerogative of a recovered spiritual purity. 'As for me, I believe that, when a soul is perfectly pure and made steadfast according to nature, it can become clearsighted,, and is able to see more and futher than the demons.'[43] As for miracles, Saint Athanasius notes explicitly that, 'Antony healed, not as one commanding, but by praying and by calling on the name of Christ, so that it was evident to all that not he, but the Lord, was the doer, who, through Antony, showed his love for humankind and healed the suffering.'[44] How then can anyone write sentences like this without any qualifiers: 'What is most typical [about the miracles worked by the Fathers] is that they result, almost without exception, from a magical view of reality.'[45] It would have been fairer to recall the teaching of philosophers-theologians no one would dream of taxing with a belief in magic, such as Gregory of Nyssa who explains how the *dioratikon tēs psychēs* (keen vision of the soul) is developed through moral purification.[46] One should also take into account faith in Divine Providence: even today there are many people who believe in the efficacy of prayer without any need to detract from the laws of nature. The imagination of the anchorites was struck by the unexpected manner in which they sometimes escaped the all-too-real dangers of the desert; we need not have the slightest understanding of this to find reason for irony in it. And when those who narrated these facts exagerrated their swiftness or the picturesque by introducing fantastic characters, this folkloristic or 'mystic' element does not yet prove that the hermits confused the marvellous with the spiritual, or made the former a necessary element of the latter. K. Heussi himself admits that 'the visionary element of piety is not stressed as much as one would at first be inclined to suppose. Also, when it comes to visions, we should ask in which cases we are dealing with accounts of visions that were in fact experienced, and in which stories the vision exists only on paper, merely as a literary form given to fixed religious concepts.'[47]

All things considered, while duly recognizing the element of the marvellous in the *Lives of the Fathers*, we should recognize that the concept of the spiritual does not essentially depend upon it. When R. Reitzenstein tells us that 'the psychic is a human being, nothing more; the spirit-bearer is no longer "human,"'[48] some justification for this phrasing is found in the *Apophthegmata*,[49] but 'evidently that does not mean that the spirit-bearer has ceased being a man; but only that he should no longer live as one, but (should live) through the Spirit.'[50] What is much more important than miraculous deeds is life. The great law is expressed in less than ten syllables by abba Longinus, '*dos haima kai labe pneuma*' (give blood, and receive spirit.).[51] 'Spirituality' is acquired through 'the martyrdom of conscience;' in other words, through 'the contest of faith and through great, intense asceticism,'[52] and by following the way which the Fathers taught ceaselessly, according to Evagrius Ponticus. 'Faith, O children, is made firm by fear of God, and the latter by continence, which is rendered immovable by patience and hope; from these is born *apatheia*, whose offspring is love. Love is the entrance to natural cognition, which is succeeded by theology, and the supreme beatitude.'[53] This is 'the way one becomes spiritual,' to use Reitzenstein's expression.[54] At no point are miracles even mentioned. Nonetheless, the same Evagrius actually inserts short sequences of *Apophthegmata Patrum* into several of his writings, where apparently miraculous deeds are found nonetheless. But Evagrius only reports these to recommend imitation of the heroic perseverance of these 'spiritual brothers.'[55]

Was it different for Cassian, of whom, as Reitzenstein says, we are able to draw a portrait of the spiritual man better than of anyone else?[56] Without repeating Reitzenstein's statement in detail, let us at least note that 1) the opposition between spiritual men and the hierarchy, which was evident to the scholars of half a century ago, is actually denied by their present-day successors. 'Always to speak of a so-called conflict between the charismatics and the hierarchy is a typically modern misunderstanding. Functionaries too possess the Spirit, and spiritual men teach by virtue of the traditional apostolic truth.'[57] The same author maintains that this is equally true of the second century: 'A conflict between those who held official positions and free peddlers of orthodox doctrines is nowhere to be found.'[58] This also holds true for the centuries that follow. 2) As for the extraordinary phenomena of the life of prayer, we can accept what von Campenhausen says (with respect to Montanism): 'The manifestations of enthusiasm—inspirations, trances, and visions—are generally relegated to the borderlands of the church, the domain of heresy, until such time as monasticism gives them a new home and the possibility of a structured development,'[59]—provided we insist on the adjective *structured* and understand by this a return to theological order and church discipline. Cassian does indeed speak of *apostolicarum signa virtutum* (signs of apostolic virtue),[60] but he invokes these only as evidence of the faith of the Fathers, or as supplementary proof supporting a verdict they had pronounced.[61] After all, the essential reason for their authority lies in the fact that they 'treated all things with judgment and discretion of spirit rather than with obstinacy of mind' (*universa judicio potius ac discretione spiritus quam animi obstinatione gesserunt*)·[62] I believe, moreover, that miracles are generally attributed only after the death of their real or alleged authors. As long as they lived in the world, they were horrified at giving the appearance of being miracle workers; at no price did they want people to turn to them, as to spiritual men, led by trust in a reputation of this type. 'Have you seen anything here?' Saint Arsenius asked a brother who had come to observe his ecstasy; he responded in the consultation only after the other had assured him that he had not seen anything.[63] The second generation of Desert Fathers already recognized that they were inferior to the first; and they attributed miracles only to them.[64] The farther removed one is from the ancients, the more their reputation grows: 'Think of the illustrious Fathers; how, ignorant as they were—abba Paul the Simple, abba Pambo, abba Apollo, and the other God-bearing Fathers—they even raised the dead, worked great wonders, and received powers against the demons. . . .'[65] The intention of such *laudationes temporis acti* (praises of bygone days) is not to cause a desire to work wonders, but to make one feel regret, to re-discover the former simplicity and humility. Miraculous deeds are mentioned only as signs of approval given by God to the great monastic ancestors' *politeia* (way of living). Their 'spirituality' derives from something entirely different: the asceticism and the purification caused by it, the death of the passions and the cultivation of virtues, especially charity which embraces all of them. 'How is it that the ascetics of our day do not receive grace after the manner of the ancients, despite their toil?' Answer: 'Charity was then supreme, and everyone drew his neighbor on high; whereas now charity has become cold, and everyone pulls the neighbor down. This is why we do not deserve the grace of God.'[66] In this, we may confidently state, lies the keynote of the concept 'spiritual'; it is valid at all times, though the supporting harmonics, depending on the era, assume a tonality that is persistent but never predominant. All things considered, this invasion of the primary by the secondary is not most noticeable in early times, except in Montanism and later in Messalianism. These two forms of the eternal tendency towards pseudo-mystical empiricism purified the religious atmosphere in the end, through reaction, and they made a renaissance of false mysticism more difficult. We have only to observe the horrified reaction with which Byzantines and Syriacs of every confession from Saint Ephrem to the Palamites spoke of the Euchites. The history of the significance of the marvellous among eastern Christians remains to be written. In reading the *Lives of the Saints*, one gets the impression that the marvellous, the extraordinary, and the unusual become more and more important as one moves farther from ancient times.

Whatever the variations, we may give the following definition of 'the spiritual', in conformity with the classical ideas of the East: a spiritual person is someone in whom, because of the mortification of the passions and the *apatheia* (dispassion) which results from it, charity has brought about the knowledge (*gnōsis*) of things divine and the *diacrisis* of things human, so that one is able to guide others in the ways of God, without danger to self. These are the ones who were originally called *Abbas*. In a word, the spiritual persons are the perfect, as far as one can admit the existence of perfect human beings. If, with Diadochus of Photice or John Climacus, one does not admit this, one should also not apply the term gnostic or pneumatic to any ascetic.[67] Diadochus avoids it, as does the *Historia Monachorum*.[68] The only ones who are truly perfect are those who have been 'consumed by martyrdom'; as Clement of Alexandria already explains, these are the people who have accomplished a perfect work of charity.[69] The others are perfect to the degree that they come near them through some sort of ascetic death and mystic resurrection. "If, beginning with this life, one could die in the midst of work, one would then entirely become the house of the Holy Spirit since, before dying, such a person has already been raised up, as happened to Saint Paul himself and to all those who have struggled or are struggling to perfection against sin."[70] What characterizes such men is 'spiritual charity', a curious expression of Diadochus,[71] taken over by Saint Maximus the Confessor. In Diadochus, its synonyms are 'holy charity,'[72] 'perfect charity.'[73] Holy, perfect, spiritual it *is*, since it bestows or presupposes the likeness of charity-God, which the other virtues do not have.[74] Hence we understand that it is rare, if it is ever actualized in this life. For Saint Maximus, it only exists in those who have eliminated every trace of self-love (*philautia*) from their being.[75]

In considering all these expressions, and many others which could easily be assembled, we arrive at the conclusion that there was little variation among the orthodox with respect to the concept they had of 'the spiritual'; there was even no variation about what was essential. Even those who seem to stress accessory things too much strongly maintain the distinction between what is primary—holiness—and what is secondary, the signs that occasionally accompany it. Nicetas Stethatos and his entire school exaggerate the link between these two, but they never confuse them. Nicetas deals with them separately, in two successive questions, 'What is the aim of the virtuous life?' and 'What is the sign of perfection?' We have to quote the answer to the second question because Saint Symeon the New Theologian, whose ideas it expresses, will often be referred to in the pages that follow.

> The sign of perfection, thanks to which we recognize the perfect man, fully mature with the fulness of Christ,[76] and entirely possessed by the Spirit, is the unerring knowledge of God, from which, bestowed from on high by the Holy Spirit, flows the word of superior wisdom, from which derives the aptitude to function as a theologian; to scrutinize the depths of God,[77] to utter good words from the heart[78] in the midst of the assembly; to resolve the difficulties of the parables, riddles and concealed words of the Spirit, from which follow foresight and the foretelling of things to come. From (*gnosis*) are derived revelations, visions when one is awake or asleep; also derived from it are ecstasy of the mind, the understanding of the hidden beauty of the kingdom of heaven, the discovery of the mysteries of God, the desire to be united to Christ and to mix with the powers on high, the longing to taste the good things reserved for the saints, and the contemplation of the divine light of the glory of God, according to the sacred verse, 'Happy the pure in heart; they shall see God.'[79]

If, according to this very explicit text, the marks of holiness are all of a mystical nature—supernatural knowledge, revelations, prophecies—it still remains true that they are not given on account of holiness itself. The danger of mistaking the second-ary function for what is essential has always existed, especially when what is secondary is rather spectacular, while that which is primary tries to remain hidden from the eyes of men, condi-tioned as it is by humility. If Nicetas and his school have stressed the phenomena of conscience too much, we should remember that they do not represent all of Byzantine spir-ituality. Even in Symeon's day—around the year 1000—a work as sedate as the Suda gives us the following description of the spiritual man, one of which the average byzantine theolo-gian would approve:

When someone does something that is pleasing to God, he is called spiritual. He is not described after the soul (psy-chic), but according to another and much greater honor, the activity of the Spirit. Indeed, the soul is insufficient if it is not helped by the Spirit. And as the person who becomes a slave to the flesh is called carnal, so the Apostle Paul calls psychic the person who leaves things to human reasoning, and does not receive the influence of the Spirit. Also, when we practice virtue, we are called spiritual; when we stumble and do something that is contrary, he[80] calls us earth according to base nature.[81]

Such explanations indicate at least the path through which one becomes spiritual. They neglect the charismatic aspect a little too much. Traditional doctrine is situated between two exag-gerations. Everyone is spiritual according to the degree of his participation in the Holy Spirit, that is, according to one's degree of holiness.[82] We will try to determine through which signs the degree required for spiritual fatherhood may be recognized.

NOTES

1. FATHER

1. Mohammed Al-Birouni, *Les fêtes des Melkites*, Kanoun I, POr X, p. 298, ed. R. Griveau. For spiritual guidance among the Muslims, see M.

Palacios, 'El Islam cristianizado,' and 'Šādiliēs y Alumbrados,' in *Al Andalūs*, 10 (1945) 141-44; 155-56; 261-66.

2. Cfr Ernest A. Wallis Budge, *The Paradise of the Holy Fathers*, vol. 2 (1907) 306.

3. *Doctrina* II. 4; PG 88:1644C-45A. [Available English translation, Eric P. Wheeler, *Dorotheos of Gaza: Discourses and Sayings*, Cistercian Studies 33 (Kalamazoo, 1977).—ed.]

4. Athens 1930-1934.

5. *Meditations* I.16.

6. I.2.

7. See Irénée Hausherr, 'Saint Theodore Studite,' in *Orientalia Christiana* 6 (Rome, 1926) 4-5.

8. Cfr Irénée Hausherr and G. Horn, eds. and trans., *Un grand mystique byzantin. La Vie de S. Syméon le Nouveau Théologien par Nicetas Stethatos*, *Orientalia Christiana* 12 (Rome, 1928) 61.

9. Eccl 11:30.

10. See, for example, *Didache* 3, 1. 2. 4. 5. 6; 4, 1; 5, 2, and so forth.

11. Gal 4:19. Cfr Hans von Campenhausen, *Kirchliches Amt und geistliche Vollmacht in den ersten drei Jahrhunderten* (Tübingen, 1953) 48-51.

12. Cfr Eph 3:14-15.

13. Gal 4:26.

14. Eph 3:15.

15. *Historia Monachorum und Historia Lausiaca. Eine Studie zur Geschichte des Mönchtums und der frühchristlichen Begriffe Gnostiker und Pneumatiker* (Göttingen: Vandenbroeck-Ruprecht, 1916) p. 210, n. 1.

16. Mk 14:36; Rom 8:15, Gal 4:6.

17. Mt 23:9.

18. Mt 19:17.

19. Jm 1:17.

20. Trans. Timothy Fry. *RB 1980. The Rule of Saint Benedict: in Latin and English with Notes* (Collegeville, 1981) 171-72.

21. *Liber Graduum, Sermo* XXIX. 19; Kmosko, p. 858, 6-12.

22. Vol. I (1976) 6, trans. W. Bromiley.

23. See Saint Angela Merici, 'Quanto piu sarate unite, tanto piu Jesu Christo sara in mezzo de voi a fozza de Padre e buon pastore.' *Testamento Spirituale*, Legato 10 , Vatican Arch., B 150, fol. 953ff.

24. *Hellenistische Mysterien-religionen* (3rd ed.) 40.

25. E. Otto, *Sprüche auf altägyptischen Särgen*, ZDMG 102 (1952) 193.

26. Spiritual direction is linked somehow to prophecy, if one considers the latter's characteristics: knowledge of the future, knowing the will of God in concrete situations, *cardiognosis* (knowledge of the heart), the gift of words. (Cfr K. Müller, *Kirchengeschichte* I/1 (1941) 95; the thaumaturgy mentioned there plays no necessary role in direction).

27. Karl Heussi, *Der Ursprung des Mönchtums* (1936) 166.

28. I Cor 14:37.

29. *Epistola ad Diognetum* X. 1.

30. I *Clem.* XIX. 2. Trans. Kirsopp Lake, *The Apostolic Fathers* (Cambridge, Mass.: Harvard University Press, 1959) 43.

31. *To the Romans* 7. 2; trans. K. Lake.

32. *To the Magnesians* 7; trans. Lake.

33. In the stadium, it is the mob of pagans and Jews (living in Smyrna) who shouted to Saint Polycarp: 'This is . . . the father of the Christians.' *Martyrium Polycarpi* XII. 2.

34. *To the Magnesians* VII. 2; trans. Lake.
35. *Ibid.*, III. 1; trans. Cyril C. Richardson, *Early Christian Fathers*, vol. I (Philadelphia: Westminster Press, 1953) 95.
36. Cfr *To the Trallians* III. 1.
37. *To the Smyrnaeans* VIII. 1.
38. H. du Manoir, 'L'argumentation patristique dans la controverse nestorienne,' in *RSR* 15 (1935) 444.
39. II. ll. 1; cfr II. 16-20.
40. II. 26. 4.
41. II. 20. 2.
42. II. 33. 1.
43. II. 33. 2; cfr II. 34. 5; VII. 31. 2.
44. See the *Testimonia Veterum*, ed. Franz Xavier Funk, vol. 2 (Paderborn, 1905) 1-39.
45. On Amphilochius of Iconium's use of the *Didascalia Apostolorum*, see G. Ficker, *Amphilochiana*, vol. 1 (Leipzig, 1906) 180-84.
46. I Cor 4:15.
47. Heb 2:13; Is 8:18.
48. Gal 4:19.
49. G. Ficker, vol. 1: p. 33, 7-34, 9; *DSAM*, vol. 1, col. 544; cfr Joseph C. Plumpe, *Mater Ecclesia. An Inquiry into the Concept of the Church as Mother in Early Christianity* (Washington, 1943); reviewed by Christine Mohrmann in *VC* 2 (1948) 57-58. Hans von Campenhausen, *Kirchliches Amt und geistliche Vollmacht in den ersten drei Jahrhunderten* (Tübingen, 1953) 263.
50. *Ecclesiae Graecae Monumenta*, vol. 1 (Paris, 1977) col. 794C.
51. PL 73:13A.
52. *Gratiani Decreta, distinctio* 15, *cap. Sancta romana Ecclesia*: 'Vitas Patrum, Pauli, Antonii, Hilarionis, et omnium eremitarum, quas tamen vir beatus scripsit Hieronymus, cum omni honore suscipimus.'
53. PL 73:18B.
54. *In Epistolam ad Galatas* II; PL 26: 374B.
55. 'Cum autem Abba, pater, Hebraeo Syroque sermone dicatur, et dominus noster in Evangelio praecipiat nullum Patrem vocandum nisi Deum, nescio qua licentia in monasteriis vel vocemus hoc nomine alios, vel vocari nos acquiescamus. Et certe Ipse praecepit hoc qui dixerat non esse jurandum. Si non juramus, ne Patrem quempiam nominemus. Si de Patre interpretabimur aliter, et de jurando aliter sentire cogemur.' PL 73: 18B.
56. Sixtus of Sienna, *Bibliotheca Sanctorum* 1. VI, annot. 279.
57. 'Nec magister, nec pater vocandus est alius, nisi Deus pater et Dominus noster Jesus Christus. Pater, quia ex Ipso sunt omnia. Magister, quia per Ipsum omnia: vel quoniam per dispensationem carnis Ejus, omnes reconciliati sumus Deo. Quaeritur quare adversum hoc praeceptum, doctorem gentium Apostolus se esse dixerit (II Cor: v; Coloss. 1); aut quomodo vulgato sermone, maxime in Palaestinae et Aegypti monasteriis se invicem Patres vocant? Quod sic solvitur: Aliud esse natura patrem vel magistrum, aliud indulgentia. Nos si hominem patrem vocamus, honorem aetati deferimus, non auctorem nostrae ostendimus vitae. Magister quoque dicitur ex consortio veri magistri. Et ne infinita replicem, quomodo unus per naturam Deus et unus Filius, non praejudicat caeteris ne per adoptionem dii vocentur, et filii: ita et unus et Pater et Magister, non praejudicat aliis, ut abusive appellentur patres et magistri.' PL 26: 169BC.
58. Ps 96:5; Origen, *In Cant. Prol.* PG 13: 70BC. See also, *Thesaurus Linguae Latinae*, s.v. *Abusive*.

59. *Epistola* XII. 33; PL 22: 48.

60. Sixtus of Sienna, *loc cit.*

61. Cfr Saint John Chrysostom, *In illud, Domine, non est in homine via ejus* (Jer. 10:23); PG 56: 156B.

62. Cfr I Tim 3, 8, 9ff.

63. Origen, *In Matthaeum Commentariorum Series*; PG 13:161BC.

64. I Jn 3:8.

65. Origen, *In Jeremiam Homilia* IX. 4; PG 13: 356Cff.

66. 'Godfathers' and '-mothers' are called that way for the same reason; cfr D. Sherwin-Bailey, *Sponsors at Baptism and Confirmation* (London, 1953).

67. *Adversus Oppugnatores Vitae Monasticae* II. 6; PG 47: 341.

68. *Comparatio . . . Regis cum Monacho*; PG 47: 387-92.

69. See Karl Holl, *Enthusiasmus und Bußgewalt beim griechischen Mönchtum* (Leipzig, 1898) 205ff.

70. *Vita S. Stephani Junioris*; PG 100: 1108A.

71. *pneumatikē thugatēr*; cfr col. 1128A, 1129D.

72. Col. 1129B.

73. E. Amelineau, *Histoire de S. Pachome et de ses communautés*. Annales du Musee Guimet XVII (1889) 249; cfr pp. 252, 273.

74. L. Th. Lefort, *Les Vies coptes de S. Pachôme* (Louvain, 1943) 3, 20ff. [See e.g. Greek Life, 29: 'our great father Pachomius'; CS 45:316—ed.]

75. *Constitutiones Monasticae* XIX; PG 31: 1388B.

76. *Gērokomia*, the care of old people, old age pension.

77. Gregory of Nyssa, *Epistola Canonica*; PG 45: 236B.

78. H. Usener, *Der heilige Theodosius*, p. 98. 26ff.

79. *Ibid.*, p. 46. 22; 47. 9.

80. *Vie de S. Theodose par Pierre*, ed. Usener, p. 7, 5ff and ch. 35, p. 321.

81. *Vita Barlaam et Joasaph*, ch. 16, ed. Boissonade, p. 134.

82. Cfr Jn 1:12.

83. *hypēnemious*, like a wind-egg; by copying the Greek, the Latin translator came up with *subventaneus*.

84. Cfr Gal 4:19.

85. Cfr 2 Tim 3:17.

86. Cfr Jn 1:12.

87. Cfr Jn 16:1; Gregory of Nyssa, *In Ecclesiasten. Homilia* VI; PG 44: 704A.

88. See the *Typikon of Our Lady of Mercy of Stroumitza*, ed. L. Petit, Izvestia de l'Institut archéologique russe de Constantinople VI (1500) p. 73.

89. *Vita Sancti Simeonis Stylitae*, ch. 1, PL 73: 325C.

90. *Vita S. Theodosii*, ed. Usener, p. 41.9-12.

91. *Historia Monachorum und Historia Lausiaca*, p. 41.

92. In a review of A. Lombard, *Constantin V, empereur des Romains* (Paris, 1902).

93. *ViVr* 11 (1904) 163.

94. Cfr du Cange, s.v. *abbas*.

95. *Alph.*, Antony n. 31; PG 65: 197D (CS 59:8).

96. *Alph.*, Theoph, n. 2; PG 65: 197D (CS 59:81).

97. *Vitae Patrum* V, Bk XV, n. 42.

98. *Vita Sancti Sabae*, by Cyril of Scythopolis, n. 9; Cotelier, p. 230; Schwartz, p. 92.[Translated by R.M. Price, *History of the Monks of Palestine*, Cistercian Studies Series, 114 (Kalamazoo, 1990)].

99. N. 11, Cotelier, p. 233A; Schwartz, p. 94.

100. *Vita S. Stephani Junioris*, *Analecta Graeca* (Paris, 1688) 442. 472; PG 100: 1112B, 1236B.

101. See, for example, *Doctrina* IV, n. 9; PG 88: 1669A where these three saints are named.

102. Cotelier I: 338ff; cfr Jacques Dupont, 'Le nom d'Abbé chez les solitaires d'Egypte,' *VS* 77 (August, 1947) 216-30.

103. Cotelier I, p. 410. (Note: 'Basil the Great,' p. 401ff does not receive this title.) Cfr John Moschus, *Pratum spirituale*, ch. 31.

104. *Alph.*, Theophilus n. 1; PG 65: 197D=CS 59:80.

105. *Alph.*, Epiphanius n. 3; PG 65: 163C=CS 59:57.

106. *Alph.*, Elogius, priest=CS 59:61.

107. *Vita Sancti Joannis Eleemosynarii*, ch. 43, p. 88, 1ff, ed. Gelzer. Cfr PG 93: 1653C.

108. *Contra Haereses* IV. 41. 2; PG 7: 1115B.

109. *Stromatum Liber* I. l. 3; PG 8: 688B; ed. Staehlin, vol. 2, p. 3, 15ff.

110. *RSR* 25 (1935) 443. Cfr Eusebius, *Historia Ecclesiastica*, IV. 14. 8 (Paris, 1911) 197.

111. 'Pneumatikos pater anderer kann nur sein, wer pneumatikos geworden ist,' in *Historia Monachorum und Historia Lausiaca* (Göttingen, 1916) 195.

2. 'SPIRITUAL'

1. See Gerard Verbeke, *L'évolution de la doctrine du Pneuma, du stoïcisme à Saint Augustin* (Paris-Louvain, 1945).

2. See André-Jean Festugière, 'La division corps-âme-esprit de I Thess. 5:23,' Excursus B in *L'idéal religieux des Grecs et l'Évangile*, coll. Études bibliques (Paris, 1932) 196-220.

3. Cfr F. Büchsel, *Der Geist Gottes im Neuen Testament* (Gütersloh, 1926). H. Leisegang, *Pneuma hagion* (Leipzig, 1922). P. Gaechter, 'Zum Pneumabegriff des hl. Paulus,' in *ZKTh* 53 (1929) 345-408.

4. See, for example, Saint Barsanuphius, *Letter* 795, p. 360, ed. Nicodemus the Hagiorite.

5. Lk 10:16.

6. See Hans von Campenhausen, *Kirchliches Amt*, pp. 145, 148, 151.

7. *Contra haereses* V. 81 1; PG 7: 1142B; ed. W. W. Harvey, *Sancti Irenaei Episcopi Lugdunensis Libros Quinque Adversus Haereses* vol 2 (Cambridge, 1957) p. 340.

8. 'Praecipuum dilectionis munus, quod est pretiosius quam agnitio, gloriosius autem quam prophetia, omnibus reliquis charismatibus supereminens.' *Adv. Haer.* IV 53. 2; Harvey, vol. 2, p. 263.

9. *Adv. Haer.* II. 39; Harvey, vol. 1: 345.

10. *Adv. Haer.* V. 9. 2, PG 7: 1144C-45A; Harvey, vol. 2: 342-43.

11. Cfr 1 Cor 14:1ff.

12. *Adv. Haer.* V. 6. 1, PG 7: 1137B; Harvey, vol. 2: 334.

13. Cfr *Adv. Haer.* I, 7. 3; PG 7: 516B; Harvey, vol. 1: 120.

14. See the *Vie Syriaque de Pierre l'Ibérien*, ed. Richard Raabe (Leipzig, 1895) 47, 49, and so forth.

15. *Adv. Haer.* V. 8. 2; PG 7: 1142B; Harvey, vol. 2: 340.

16. *Adv. Haer.* V. 5. 1; Harvey, 2: 331.

17. *Ibid.*, ch. 10; 1:345.

18. Cfr 1 Cor 13:1ff.

19. See Pierre de Labriolle, *La crise montaniste* (Paris, 1913) 562ff.

20. *Enthusiasmus und Bußgewalt beim griechischen Mönchtum* (Leipzig, 1898).

21. Hans von Campenhausen, *Kirchliches Amt*, p. 287, n. 1. Cfr Karl Holl, p. 234ff; Bernhard Poschmann, *Poenitentia secunda. Die kirchliche Buße im ältesten Christentum bis Cyprian und Origenes* (Bonn, 1940) 462ff; Walter Völker, *Der wahre Gnostiker nach Clemens Alexandrinus*, *TU* 57 (Berlin, 1952) 172.

22. Pierre de Labriolle, *La crise montaniste* (Paris, 1913) 555; *Id.*, *Les sources de l'histoire du montanisme: textes grecs, latins, syriaques* (Paris, 1913) 175.

23. Eusebius, *Historia Ecclesiastica* V. 16. 4; PG 20: 465A.

24. At least if the emendation of *Adv. Haer.* III. 11. 9, ed. Sagnard, *SCh* (Paris, 1952) 202, 28ff—generally accepted today—is correct.

25. *Die Lehre der zwölf Apostel*, *TU* 2 (1884) 128, n. 38.

26. *La crise*, p. 547.

27. *Der wahre Gnostiker nach Clemens Alexandrinus*, *TU* 57 (1952).

28. *Strom.* II. 19. 97; PG 8: 1040B; *GCS* 2, ed. Otto Staehlin (Leipzig, 1906) 166.

29. *Strom.* II. 10. 46; PG 8: 981B; Staehlin, vol. 2:137.

30. *Strom.* VI. 12. 102; PG 9: 324A; Staehlin, vol. 2:137.

31. Cfr, for example, *Strom.* V. 25, Staehlin, vol. 2, p. 341ff. '*pneumatikon gar kai gnōstikon oiden ton tou hagiou pneumatos mathētēn.*'

32. Origen, *In Proverbia*, ch. 1; PG 13: 25A.

33. Jean Daniélou, *Origène* (1948). *Origen*, trans. Walter Mitchell (New York, 1955) 304.

34. I Cor 2:15; see, for example, *In Numeros, homilia* 1. 1; W. Baehrens, p. 9; *In Libr. Jud. hom.* 8. 4, p. 513, etc.

35. *In Num. hom.* 271. 11; Baehrens, p. 272.

36. Cfr *Peri Archon* I. 3. 5, Koetschau, p. 56.

37. *Ibid.*, n. 7, p. 59; n. 8, p. 61.

38. Jean Daniélou, *Origène*, trans. Mitchell, p. 300.

39. *Der Ursprung des Mönchtums* (Tübingen, 1936) 171-86.

40. *Alph.*, Ammoes n. 2; PG 65: 125D=CS 59:30.

41. Heussi, p. 171.

42. *Alph.*, Antony n. 2= CS 59:2.

43. *Vita S. Antonii* n. 34; PG 26: 893B; cfr *DSAM.* vol. 2, col. 1857; *Vie de S. Antoine le Jeune* (d. 865), n. 4, b.

44. *Vita Antonii*, n. 84; PG 26: 961A. *Life of Saint Antony*, trans. Mary E. Keenan, *The Fathers of the Church*, vol. 4 (Washington, 1952) 208.

45. Heussi, p. 173.

46. *De Virginitate* X; PG 46: 360Cff; Werner Jaeger, 288ff.

47. *Loc. cit.*, p. 178.

48. *Die hellenistische Mysterien-religionen* (3rd ed., 1927) 341. Cfr Origen, *Comment. in Joan.* vol. 1. 3: '*Ambrosie, alēthōs Theou anthrōpe kai en Christō anthrōpe, kai speudōn einai pneumatikos, ouketi anthrōpos.*' 'O Ambrosius, a true man of God, a man in Christ, eagerly seeking to be spiritual, and no longer a man.' PG 14: 24D.

49. For example, in the declaration of Saint Melania, who had come to Rome in the hope of seeing Saint Arsenius: 'I trust in God that I shall see him, for I have not come to see a man (our city is filled with them!): I have come to see a prophet.' *Alph.*, Arsenius, n. 28; PG 65: 96D = CS 59:13.

50. Hans von Campenhausen, *Kirchliches Amt* (1953) 69, n. 1.

51. *Alph.*, Longinus n. 5 = CS 59:123.

52. *Vita Antonii* n. 47; PG 26: 912B.

53. Evagrius, *Capita Practica ad Anatolium*; PG 4: 1221BC.
54. *Historica Monachorum und Historia Lausiaca*, p. 147.
55. See *De Oratione*, chs. 106-12. [English translation, J. E. Bamberger, *Evagrius Ponticus: Praktikos and Chapters on Prayer*, Cistercian Studies 4 (Kalamazoo, 1978).—ed.]
56. Richard Reitzenstein, *Historia Monachorum*, p. 114.
57. Hans von Campenhausen, *Kirchliches Amt*, p. 185.
58. *Ibid.*, p. 214.
59. *Ibid.*, p. 209.
60. *Conference* 17. 23. Note: why does R. Reitzenstein quote the Greek *sēmeia tou apostolou?* Moreover, see Saint Athanasius, *Epostola ad Dracontium*: '*Oidamen kai sēmeia poiountas episkopous monachous de mē poiountas.*' 'We know bishops who work wonders, as well as monks who do not.' PG 25: 533A.
61. *Conf.* 21. 10.
62. *Ibid.*, 17. 23.
63. *Alph.*, Arsenius n. 27 = CS 59:13.
64. *Ibid.*, Macarius n. 2 = CS 59:125-26.
65. Paul Evergetinos, *Synagogè* II, ch. 34, p. 41.
66. *Vitae Patrum* III, n. 181, PL 73: 799B; V, XVII, n. 19, col. 976BC; VII, XXVIII, n. 4, col. 1050C.
67. See Edouard des Places in *SCh* n. 5, p. 29.
68. Reitzenstein, p. 115.
69. *Strom.* IV; PG 8: 1228B.
70. Diadochus of Photice, end of ch. 82.
71. Ch. 20, Weis-Liebersdorf, p. 128, 11ff; ch. 89, p. 127.4.
72. P. 128. 6.
73. P. 126. 8.
74. Ch. 89.
75. See Irénée Hausherr, *Philautie. De la tendresse pour soi à la charité, selon Saint Maxime le Confesseur* (Rome, 1952).
76. Eph 4:13.
77. I Cor 2:10.
78. Ps 44:2.
79. Mt 5:8. Nicetas Stethatos, 'Logos par demande et résponse,' in *Orientalia Christiana* 12 (1928) xxiv.
80. Saint Paul? Cfr I Cor 15:47.
81. Suidas, *Lexicon*, s.v. *psychikos*, ed. Ada Adler, vol. 4, p. 853.
82. See, for example, *Amphiloque d'Iconium*, ed. Ficker, p. 38ff.

III

THE QUALITIES NEEDED TO BE A SPIRITUAL FATHER

1. MORAL QUALITIES

'SOMEONE WHO HAS NOT received the baptism of the Spirit has not been born to the spiritual life; in the order of grace, he does not exist, is incapable of anything, especially of bringing forth spiritual children, not having been engendered himself.'[1] Symeon the New Theologian understands the 'baptism of the Spirit' in his own fashion; aside from this, he merely echoes the tradition when he calls for 'spirituality' in anyone who believes he is called to the role of spiritual father. Nothing is more difficult than exercising this office; it is the *technē technōn kai epistēmē epistēmōn* (the art of arts, and the science of sciences)—a definition which was that of philosophy, but became that of the *regimen animarum* (guidance of souls.)[2] C. Weyman[3] has described the semantic evolution necessitated by a profound ideological revolution. Now that the true philosophy—the quest and possession of true wisdom—has passed to the Christians, especially to those among them who plan to do everything and to sacrifice all things in order to become good Christians, the science and art of guiding them to this supreme goal will take precedence over every other art and science.[4] Gustave Bardy has described the history of this term up to Eusebius of Caesarea. 'This church historian is especially interesting because with him, the word "philosophy" is commonly used with the two meanings we have just pointed out in Clement: doctrine, and the christian or, more precisely, the ascetic life. At the time Eusebius wrote, the true Christian no longer was the person who lived in the world while observing the principles of the Gospel as well as he could: it already was the one who withdrew from the world to live the eremitical life, so that there was no longer any difference between the philosopher and the ascetic . . .' Bardy concludes his article by saying, 'It would not be without interest to pursue the history whose beginnings we have tried to sketch.' For our purposes, a few indications will suffice. In his first *Irenic Oration*, Gregory Nazianzen indentifies the life of the monks with *di' ergōn philosophia* (philosophy through action),[5] the exercises and activities of which he readily enumerates.[6] Human governance, even within the boundaries of natural law, is noble but also very difficult; 'how much harder it is to rule them according to our principles, which are founded on the law of God and lead to God; the greater the sublimity and the dignity, the greater also the danger in the eyes of the prudent, judicious men.'[7] To confront the dangers of such an elevated office, one would have to possess all the virtues and have no failing—an impossibility. 'But let us admit that there is someone who is free from vice and has reached the height of virtue; I do not see what knowledge or power would justify his assuming such an office. In truth, the guidance of human beings, the most diverse and variable of creatures, seems to me to be the art of arts and the science of sciences.'[8] To account for this, let us think of medicine: how difficult it is to study and practice it. And yet, our profession is still more demanding, 'because of the nature of the subject (which is the soul), because of the power of the knowledge (which it applies), and because of the goal its activity pursues.'[9]

Thus the art of arts and science of sciences is still philosophy, except that its definition has changed. Now it no longer is the pursuit of totally human wisdom, but the monastic life, in so far as it takes the best way to approach God. *Philosophein = pros ton anō bion metharmosthētai* (to practice philosophy is to exchange the human life for the celestial (angelic, divine) life[10]—an enterprise which is certainly very noble but thereby also very difficult.[11] It means to imitate the life of Elijah and John, *tōn panu philosophōn* (famous philosophers).[12] The ascetics are the philosophers, and monasteries are *tēs philosophias phrontistēria* (training schools of philosophy).[13]

This philosophy must be taught: it is impossible even to study and practices it without paying attention to the lessons and examples of a teacher who has mastered this art of arts. It is important for us to see what the great masters of eastern spirituality have to say about this. With impressive unanimity, they call for a perfect preparation before allowing anyone to deal with direction. Saint Nilus warns us that 'of all things, the care of souls is the most difficult,' and he proves this in detail.[14]

Every art needs time, and great study toward a successful accomplishment. Only the art of arts is practiced without having learned it. Someone who is unacquainted with agriculture would not dare practice it, nor would the uninstructed practice medicine. The latter is culpable because he brings no aid to the sick, and he may add a more serious disease; the former will reduce excellent land to wild and neglected ground. But someone utterly unlearned in the work of God will dare to teach it, as if it were easier than the rest; and the thing most difficult to handle is viewed by many as being a snap. Saint Paul says that he by no means understands it, but they declare that they know all about it, who do not even know that they do not know. The monastic life has therefore fallen into contempt, and those who undertake it are ridiculed by everyone. Certainly, who would not ridicule someone who yesterday carried water in a tavern, but is viewed today as a master of virtue surrounded by a retinue of disciples? Or someone who has returned from villainy in the morning, proudly advancing toward the market place at night with a crowd of disciples? If they were truly convinced that leading others to piety is difficult work and that such toil entails danger, they would decline this occupation as being too much for them. But since indeed they do not know this, they believe that it is glorious to rule over somebody, and they easily fall into the deep pit. They are of the opinion that leaping into this furnace is easy. They arouse laughter in those who know the life they led yesterday, and the indignation of God, at such temerity.

The author then appeals to the frightening example of Eli the high priest, whom nothing could save from the wrath of God, and to the maledictions uttered by Christ against the scribes and pharisees: 'You who travel over sea and land to make a single proselyte, and when you have him you make him twice as fit for hell as you are'[15]. By contrast, Job had to teach the impromptu spiritual masters with what care one's children are to be purified.[16] Then there are those who 'not knowing how to discern even the most manifest sins, because their reasoning is clouded by the dust raised by their struggle against the passions, undertake the oversight and direction of others, before they have even healed their own passions and could therefore not guide others, out of victory, in subduing them.'[17] The rest continues in this vein for long chapters (24-36ff.), citing Jonah, Abimelech, Gideon, and others. 'But all such things they neither see, nor do they listen when others talk about them; they only respect their own convictions, and impose slave labor upon their brothers as if they had bought them at the market place. They find glory in ruling over a great number. There is even rivalry: no one wants to be followed by a smaller number of attendants than others have. Thereby they display the character of hucksters instead of teachers.'[18] Nothing is easier than commanding with words. One should teach through deeds; anyone who does not do this proves that he holds leadership not for the good of others, but for his own gratification. This is not how Saint Paul or the Lord Jesus Christ himself acted.[19] Furthermore, with respect to faults, one should not fall into weakness and commit the error of complacency. 'Let no one suppose that this thing (direction) is a pretext for relaxation and amusement; the work of guiding souls is the most difficult of all.'[20] Moreover, while aspiring to purify others, one may become impure oneself.[21] And what great knowledge is needed to reveal all the enemy's ruses to others!

> I do not say these things to dissuade from directing others or to prevent the guidance of certain young people on the path of piety; but, in the first place, to exhort them to acquire a habit of virtue that is equal to the magnitude of the task. Let them not apply themselves to it without preparation, or calculate that these things are going to be pleasant: the submission of one's disciples and the applause of those on the outside, while, through false reasoning, taking no notice of the danger that follows close. Let them not turn instruments of war into implements for agriculture before peace has been established. Truly, it is honorable to improve others after all the passions have been subdued, when the enemy no longer moves and weapons are no longer appropriate or necessary.[22]

As long as the passions exercise their tyranny and the war against the physical senses continues, it is not proper to drop one's weapons; one should have them in hand incessantly, and so forth.

Saint Nilus wrote for cenobites. Those who lived in lavras or hesychasts, Saint Nilus warned that no one should rush to direct others before subduing one's own carnal and psychic passions.[23] We hear the same admonition on the womens' side, from Saint Syncletica: 'For someone who has not undertaken the practical life, it is a dangerous thing to begin teaching. Indeed, just as anyone who has a house which is tumbling down would bring destruction to his guests by receiving them, so would those destroy the persons coming to them if they have not strengthened themselves earlier.'[24] Unfortunately, this is a frequent temptation, against which Evagrius had already warned in his *Antirrheticus* and, as is proper, in the chapter on vainglory. It is this latter that whispers to the monk to go into the world at the wrong time in order to make disciples, brothers and sisters (n. 1), to aspire to the priesthood without thinking of the danger it brings with it (n. 3), to teach both religious and worldly people before having acquired health of soul (n. 9), to imagine that one is the supervisor of one's brothers (n. 10). Vainglory suggests the idea of putting oneself at the head of others to lead them to the knowledge of Christ (n, 13). During the night, vainglory makes me dream that I am a pastor of souls; during the day it explains the dream to me by saying, 'you will become a priest: they will soon come to ordain you' (n. 26). It is another vainglorious idea to want to give lessons to others before arriving at a perfect observance of God's commandments (n. 29); it is vainglory 'that encourages us to get away from the master before reaching health of soul or true gnosis' (n. 41).[25]

Reading such admonitions must unquestionably have had a salutary effect on the best. More than one may have felt an invincible reluctance to the very idea of guiding others, since in order to consent to this, one had to believe that one had arrived where others were asking to be led, and that one possessed the qualities of a spiritual man to such a degree and in such a manner that the disciple, by merely visiting the master, would contract them, so to speak, by contagion.

Even so, we have only viewed these qualities in their totality. We should examine them one by one, at least the ones the Byzantines deemed most necessary to the exercise of spiritual direction. There are intellectual and administrative qualities that are not contained in the concept 'spiritual.' This concept is to be analyzed more closely: we should describe its constituent elements in greater detail.

The first is charity. In the general sense of inward love of God and neighbor, charity is the same as perfection and indeed spirituality itself. No one gives but what he has. How could someone pretend to lead others to God while being removed from him oneself? 'No one,' then, 'comes near God except through charity.' This formulation itself, coined by James of Sarug,[26] merely repeats what no Christian, since Irenaeus, has doubted. Holiness consists in being God's neighbor through charity (*dia tēs agapēs plēsion genesthai tou Theou*); and all spiritual direction consists in bringing another close to God through charity. 'God is charity, and the one who possesses charity possesses God.'[27] Other complementary graces such as the gift of words are certainly needed to lead another to this supreme goal, but such graces too are linked to charity, as someone competent in this has already told us in reply to the question: 'How is it that the ascetics of our day do not receive grace after the manner of the ancients, despite their toil?' The answer: 'Charity was then supreme, and everyone drew his neighbor on high; whereas now charity has become cold, and everyone pulls the neighbor down. This is why we do not deserve the grace of God.'[28]

We must view charity especially as it relates to our special neighbors, the spiritual children in one's care. Once such a relationship has been agreed upon, even before we have the right to accept it, what forms will charity have to take, which virtues will the practice of spiritual direction especially require?

First, it is beyond question that it is charity or the reputation of charity that attracts disciples, not only average sinners seeking a remedy for their ills, but the saints themselves.

One day a brother from abba Poemen's neighborhood went abroad to visit an anchorite, for many came to see him because of his charity. The brother talked to him about abba Poemen and his virtue. The anchorite wanted to meet him. Some time after the brother had returned to Egypt, the anchorite, in turn, arrived there. The brother had told him where he lived. When he saw him, the brother was surprised and very pleased. The anchorite said to him: 'Please would you be so kind as to take me to abba Poemen.' So he led him to the old man and introduced him, saying: 'This is a great man, of profound charity; and he is greatly honored in his country.'[29]

In like manner, people flocked to Saint Antony, despite his repeated flights—a remote prefiguration of the attraction the crowds felt toward the *Startsy*.

> Antony was like a physician God had given to Egypt. For who came to him in grief and did not return rejoicing? Or who drew near him, mourning his dead and did not at once put off his sorrow? Who arrived angry and did not turn his aggravation into friendship? What poor man in low spirits met him who, after hearing and seeing him, did not scorn wealth to find consolation in his poverty? What discouraged monk did not become stronger after speaking with him? What young man having come to the mountain to see Antony did not renounce pleasure at once to love temperance? Who when tempted by the demon came to him and did not find rest? Who arrived harassed by [evil] thoughts and did not find peace of mind?[30]

The context indicates that the reason for such attraction was not thaumaturgy but, on one hand, a charity that made Antony feel the pain of others as if he himself had been the 'patient' (*ton paschonta*) and, on the other, the discernment (*diacrisis*) that gave him experience in prescribing the appropriate remedy for each.[31] *Charity and discernment* are pre-eminent qualities of a spiritual father.

The reputation of being holy unquestionably played an important role in such attraction. More precisely, the certainty that identifies charity with holiness had influenced people for so long that they instinctively felt that one could expect total charity from a saint, and that a truly charitable person could be nothing but a saint. Nonetheless, it is one or the other of these two aspects of a same reality that stands out more, depending on one's temperament and life history. One may appear more holy than kind—for instance, Saint Arsenius with his blunt answers, and the Arsenii are legion in the East. Another shows himself to be so amiable that one goes to him without thinking too much about being a saint, for example, Saint Antony. Both can become excellent spiritual directors, provided the austerity of the first does not lack goodness and the gentleness of the latter is not deprived of energy—in one word, on condition that their varied aptitudes are in the service of God in souls with an equal benevolence.

'Love is the law in all its fulness.'[32] Diadochus of Photice quotes this Pauline maxim while adding one little word that makes it peremptory and excludes further discussion on the subject: '*Plērōma gar apax nomou he agapē* (Once for all, charity is the full measure of the law)'.[33] 'The sound of these words is brief,' Saint Syncletica concluded, 'but their power is immense. All spiritual profit depends on them. . . . Therefore, any useful thing [God's] people might say according to the grace of the Spirit proceeds from charity and ends in charity. . . .'[34] Since Gnosticism, there is no longer any hesitation about this among catholics or in any christian sect. 'Love is the perfection of the believer.'[35] 'Apart from love, there is no perfection according to faith.'[36] 'Without charity, there is not one single virtue.'[37] Without charity, the virtues are merely an illusion, Isaiah the Monophysite said.[38] The Nestorian Isaac of Nineveh [of Syria], contemplative that he was, greatly stressed the mental and intellectual aspect of perfection. Nonetheless, he has some very clear lines about charity: 'The sign of having reached perfection is this: if a man were to be condemned ten times a day out of love for his neighbors, he would find that this is not enough.'[39] In their psychological value, such sentences are subject to caution, but the doctrine is impeccable. The Christians farthest removed from the center, the Ethiopians, did not think differently from the rest of Christianity on the pre-eminence of charity.[40]

The spiritual father's charity is demonstrated in many ways: patience, clemency, or a benevolent severity. As long as each 'senior' had only one disciple, the difficulty was undoubtedly less, but still real, depending on the character of each. We must admit that the law which burdened the disciple, the revelation of thoughts (*exagoreusis*), was enough to impose a heavy burden on the master. So and so returned eleven times on end, and 'the old man did not sadden him, but told him what was useful for the benefit of his soul.'[41] A spiritual father is 'the one who encourages the brothers.'[42] 'This was the work of the monks of Scetis: to give heart to those who were in conflict.'[43]

Abba Isidore, priest of Scetis, paid particular attention to this: 'If anyone had a brother who was ill, faint-hearted, or insolent, and wanted to drive him out, Isidore said, "Bring him to me." Accepting him, he cured the brother's soul through patience.'[44] Some examples seem to push patience to the point of indifference:

They said about a certain old man that he had a little boy living with him. Seeing him doing some work that was not profitable, he told him once. 'Don't do that.' The boy did not obey him. When the old man saw this, he removed all care from his thought, and let the boy do as he liked. The boy then closed the door of the room where the bread was stored, and let the old man go hungry for three days. The old did not say, 'Where are you?' or 'What are you doing out there?' The old man had a neighbor; when he saw that the boy was late in bringing food, he made a little porridge and gave it to him through the wall. He asked him to eat, saying, 'What is that brother doing outside for so long?' 'In truth, the old man replied, 'he will return when he has time.'[45]

A man from Scetis, very austere in body but not very strong in the science of thoughts, came to ask abba John Colobos (John the Dwarf) about forgetfulness. Having received an answer, he returned to his cell and forgot what abba John had said to him. He went back to ask him again, heard the answer once more, and left. When he arrived at his own cell, he had forgotten it again. Subsequently, he went many times, returned, and was overcome by forgetfulness. Later, he met the old man and said to him, 'You know, abba, I have once again forgotten what you told me, but I did not come back to you.' Abba John told him, 'Go and light a lamp.' He lit it. 'Bring more lamps and light them from the first.' He did so. Abba John then said to him, 'Has the first lamp been defrauded because others were lit from it?' He said, 'No.' 'Well,' abba John said, 'so it is with John; all of Scetis may come to me, and they would take nothing away from the grace of Christ (*var.* the love of Christ). Therefore, whenever you want to come, come without hesitation.' Finally, thanks to the patience of the one and the other, God delivered the man from Scetis from forgetfulness.[46]

How heavy must the burden sometimes have been for those hegumens who, because of a plurality of offices—that of superior and spiritual father—were under obligation daily to hear the intimate thoughts of all their people. Let us listen to the sighs of Saint Theodore of Studion:

Unhappy and unworthy that I am, I had to assume the care of governing you. For your salvation I have to deliver my frail soul, even shed my blood. According to the words of the Lord, this is the special function of the good and true shepherd. Struggles arise from this, and sadness, and anxieties, preoccupations, sleeplessness, and despondency. Besieged on all sides and unable to do everything myself, I take refuge in God, the Friend of humankind, asking and imploring him not to become irritated by this lack of courage and energy to the point of removing his powerful hand from the affairs of our salvation. Thanks to your charity and the purity of your faith, he continues to protect and guard all of you for the praise and glory of his majesty. Thanks to you, he is compelled to save even the sinner I am. Truthfully, to guide rational souls and to support such a great multitude is a heavy burden.[47]

Also, my brothers, fathers, and children, to have to talk to you on every occasion, to admonish and exhort you is hard work for me, a merciless struggle, for if shepherds of flocks take upon themselves watchings and worries . . . how much more should we sinners—who, without merit on our part, have received the obligation of governing the sheep of Christ, which you are,—keep the eye of the soul awake and make use of the word, as a shepherd uses his flute, to remind you of what is profitable or an obligation, while never ceasing to take great pains, discomfort, and distress to provide you with bodily and spiritual food.[48]

What can one say when some get lost, despite full solicitude? The laments uttered by one true spiritual father move us even today. Take note of Eulalius and Petronius, two inconstant brothers who joined together to find the sad courage to run away.

My children and brothers, how could I not weep over and be afflicted by their ruination? How could I not shed tears of pity because they have wilted in shame at the moment that should have been one of harvest? They fell victim to the frost, like the leaves that fall from trees. A sad spectacle indeed: such toil, weariness, and struggle— if they endured all this—lost in a moment, and they became the devil's prey. Ah! What blindness! Who would not lament such unfortunates? Who would not cry over them, so deserving of tears? As for me, who had to account for them, I understand that I may have omitted something I should have done or said on their behalf. But—to speak in the same manner again—what had to be done to the vine that I did not do? To the best of my weak power, after bringing them forth spiritually and educating them, I warned them, exhorted, sustained, advised, and threatened them. Sometimes I imposed penance on them. I do not even mention the rest: consoling them in hours of trial, being patient during days of laxity, carrying the burden of their revelation of thoughts (*exagoreusis*), lovingly curing their ills, nourishing them like a father, teaching them as beloved children. . . .

What is frightening is that the hegumen has no right to rejoice when these spiritual children leave him more leisure time because they come to him less frequently: 'These days, I feel great sorrow, an unbearable sorrow indeed, relating to you. It appears that there is a slackening of *exagoreusis*, this great means of salvation. If I could see that you have become better because of this, I would rejoice at having been freed from an irksome task, for it is no mean toil to cure another's ills. But as I see the opposite change, I seek the reason for it. . . .'[49] Thus the spiritual father is trapped on all sides: he can escape anxiety only when his sons eagerly walk along the path of perfection, where he has to guide them. But then, the joy is still purer when the idea of taking even the slightest credit in this work of God (*opus Dei*) does not occur to him: it is *chara chairō* (joy unmixed, because entirely detached).[50]

A patience akin to gentleness: the most exquisite form of charity. 'Holy people'—at least those who like to view themselves that way without admitting it—have a zeal for perfection that is ready to explode at the sight of another's weaknesses. The *Lives of the Fathers* do not favor such a disposition. They borrowed[51] a passage from Cassian[52]—one we should reread.

One day, an old man whom I knew well, received the visit of a young monk, not one of the most slothful. He had come to him hoping to make progress and be healed of his ills. When he had admitted simply to being troubled by the spurs of the flesh and the spirit of fornication—believing that he would find in the old man's prayer a consolation for his troubles and a remedy for his wounds—the old man rebuked him with most bitter words, calling him, 'miserable, dishonorable, undeserving of being a monk, that he could be agitated by such a vice, such concupiscence'.

He wounded him with his vituperations to such a degree that he left the cell, a prey to dark despair and lethal sadness. When, oppressed by such grief, he was plunged in deep thought—not about a remedy for his passion but on how to satisfy the passion he had conceived—Apollo, the most trusted of the old men, came to meet him. From the gloominess of his face, he guessed the trouble and the vehemence of the assault that was taking place silently in his heart. The other monk could give no answer to the old man's gentle prodding. Seeing more and more that the other vainly wanted to conceal in silence the reasons of a sadness so deep that he could not hide it from his face, he began to inquire more intently about the causes for such grief. Encircled by this, the young monk began to confess that he was on his way to the village to return to the world after leaving the monastery, and to marry a wife since, according to the statement of that old man, he could not be a monk and had not been able to curb the stings of the flesh and seek a remedy to his temptation.

The old man Apollo began to touch him caressingly, with friendly consolation, stating that he too was daily agitated by such temptations and pricks of desire. He told him that he ought not therefore to give in to despair, and should not wonder about the ferocity of the assault, which would be overcome not so much by toil and exertion as by the grace and mercy of the Lord. He asked for a delay of one day, and begged the monk to return to his cell. As fast as he could, Apollo went back to the monastery of the above-mentioned old man.

As he was drawing near, he stretched out his hands and began to pray with tears, 'Lord, who are the one upright judge of our hidden strengths, and of human weakness the secret healer, turn the temptation from this young man to that old one, that he may learn to condescend to the infirmity of those in toil, and have compassion with the frailty of youth, at least in his old age.'

And on ending his prayer with sighs, he saw a hideous Ethiopian standing in front of the old man's cell, throwing fiery javelins at him. Wounded by these immediately, the old man came out of his cell, running to and fro, like a lunatic or a drunk. Going in and out, unable to stay, he began to proceed along the same road the young monk had taken earlier. When abba Apollo saw him behaving like a man gone out of his senses and driven by some Furies, he understood that the devil's fiery dart he had seen thrown at him had struck his heart, and had worked disorder in his mind and confusion in his senses through its intolerable heat. 'Whither are you hurrying,' he said, 'or what diseases disturb you so as to forget the gravity of old age and compel you to run here and there so rapidly?' Because he, confounded by a shameful secret and because of the reproach of his conscience, believed that the passion in his heart had been discovered, he dared give no answer to the one who questioned him. 'Return to your cell,' Apollo said, 'and finally understand that either you have been ignored by the devil or he scorned you. He did not count you among the number of those whose progress and zeal cause him to wage daily war against them. After so many years spent in your [monastic profession], you could not, I shall not say repel, but even postpone, for one day the dart he directed at you.

'The Lord allowed you to be wounded by it, so that in your old age you would learn to pity another's weakness, and you might know from your example and experience

how to condescend to the frailty of your younger brother.
After receiving a young monk oppressed by an assault of
the devil, not only did you not offer consolation, but you
delivered him into the enemy's hands to be miserably
devoured by him, cast down in pernicious despair. That
he was not swallowed up is not due to you. The enemy,
who up till now has scorned an attack on you, would not
have assaulted him with such a vehement attack if, in his
envy of future progress, he had not made haste to rush in
ahead and with fiery darts overthrow the virtue he discovered in him. Learn from your own admonitory example to feel pity for the afflicted, and not to frighten those
who are endangered through pernicious despair. Do not
wound him with harsh words, but restore him instead
with kind consolation. According to the precept of Sol-
omon the Wise, "Do not fail to free those who are being
led away to death, and to save those about to be killed."[53]
After the example of our Lord, do not break the crushed
reed, nor put out the smoldering wick.[54] Ask the Lord for
the grace by which you may sing with confidence and in
truth, "The Lord has given me a disciple's tongue. So
that I may know how to sustain the wearied."[55] No one
would be able to endure the enemy's ambushes or to
extinguish or repress the carnal passions which burn in us
with a somehow natural flame, did the grace of God not
sustain our weakness and protect and fortify it. And
therefore, inasmuch as the salutary purposes by which
the Lord wanted to free the young man from pernicious
passion and to instruct you about the vehemence of the
assault and the desire to have compassion have been
fulfilled, let us join our prayers to ask the Lord that he
may order the sting which he deigned to inflict on you for
your good to be removed—"For he who wounds is he
who heals the sore, and the hand that hurts is the hand
that heals."[56] "He gives death and life, brings down to
Sheol and draws up."[57] May he quench the fiery darts
with which he allowed you to be pierced, at my behest.'

At the single prayer of the old man, the Lord removed the temptation with the same speed with which he had permitted it. Through this vivid experiment he taught not only that we should not upbraid someone whose faults have been disclosed, but that we should not despise the sorrow of someone who suffers only lightly.[58]

Abba Poemen briefly announced the rule to be followed:

If a man should have committed a sin and does not deny it, saying, 'I have sinned', do not berate him, because you will break the resolution of his soul. If you want to say, 'Do not be sad; but from now on be watchful', you awaken his soul to repentance.[58]

If need be, one should 'lay down one's life [soul] for one's brother', as did the brother whose companion has fallen into fornication and refused to return to the desert, through discouragement. Whereupon, 'the other, wanting to regain him, began to say, "this also happened to me; when I was separated from you, I too fell into fornication. But let us go and do penance together with great toil, and God will pardon us sinners. . . ." Thus they submitted themselves to the penance the elders had imposed upon them. Only, the one did penance not for himself, but for the other brother, as though he himself had sinned [in the same manner].'[59]

The two elements of this kindness, humility and charity, are often found in the most famous spiritual fathers. The person who humbles himself before them by telling them the least glorious aspects and secrets of his soul does not have to be afraid of being humiliated, in addition, by the display of their perfection. Saint Theodore of Studion, to return to him, 'disregards the need to appear virtuous; on the contrary, while speaking of specific temptations against chastity, he states that he speaks about them from experience. The monks, under obligation to give an account of their secret thoughts, would certainly not have to be afraid that, by showing him their miseries, they would feel like a foil to his virtues. Experience had taught him the art of compassion, and this without a shadow of humiliating condescension. He views himself as the least of men, "not because of humility," he says, "which I do not have, but simply because it is true."[60]

In order to awaken in the other the trust that will lead him to open up, the spiritual father must be a saint and call himself a sinner. The two are but one: 'Abba Matoes said, 'the closer a man comes to God, the more he sees himself as a sinner. Upon seeing God, the prophet Isaiah called himself wretched, a man of unclean lips.'[61] Abba Hybistion, gloriously unknown, had discouraged a brother through his incomprehension; abba Poemen, called the Shepherd through autonomasia, mended things with a marvellous word: 'What do you want? The impulses of abba Hybistion are in heaven with the angels; you and I are prey to fornication. But let a monk be assured that he will not die of controlling his stomach and his tongue and remaining in solitude.'[62] Another young monk, tormented by lust, rose in the night and went to an old man. He told him his thought, and the old man consoled him. But the demon gave the novice no rest, and he returned frequently to his spiritual father. Far from showing impatience or sadness, he asked him to come back each time the demon troubled him. Finally, 'the brother said to the old man, "show an act of kindness, father, and speak a word to me." And the old man said to him, "Believe me, my son, if God would allow the thoughts by which my soul is agitated to be transferred to you, you would not be able to bear them, but would sink to the ground." While the ancient was speaking, the goad of lust quieted, because of the other's very great humility.'[63]

Another axiom: 'It is not possible for a man to be recalled from his purpose through harshness, because one demon does not drive out another. Rather, you will bring the lost one back through benevolence, for our God draws man to himself through counsel.'[64] Saint Antony had already approved this method as the mark of a true psychiatrist. A cenobite who had been accused of something took refuge with abba Antony; but his brothers came 'to take care of him' through vituperation. 'Just in time, abba Paphnutius, called Big-head (*Kephalas*), was there, and told this parable: "I saw on the bank of a stream a man who had fallen into the mud up to his knees; some men came to give him a hand, but they plunged him down up to his neck." The abba Antony told the cenobites, while speaking about abba Paphnutius, "Here is a man who can care for souls and save them."'[65]

It is clear that there had to be a limit to such indulgence, especially in the cenobium, when the common good was at stake. Saint Pachomius, who owed his conversion to the mercy practiced by Christians,[66] and who heard an angel say, 'The Lord's will is that you minister to the human race and . . . reconcile them to him',[67] was demanding with his monks for this very reason, and even more with those who were dearest to him. 'O God, you commanded us to love our neighbors as ourselves. Look upon these souls, take pity on them and fill them with awe, so as to fear you and to know what monastic life is, in order that they, like the other brothers, may place their hope in you.' But for those who kept on dissenting, he did not want to relax the regulations. He preferred to let them go rather than allow them to live according to their whims.[68] Saint Theodore, Pachomius' favorite disciple, never realized, for seven years, that in rank he came immediately after the father; but one day, the thought (that he should be Pachomius' successor) came to him, because 'old fathers and the heads of the monasteries' made it very clear to him. He admitted this to abba Pachomius, who said, before all the hegumens of the monasteries, 'Very well. You no longer have authority over anything. Depart by yourself, and ask the Lord to forgive you.' He condemned him to an *epitimia* (punishment) of seclusion that lasted two years, 'in tears and great pain', though the 'senior brothers' did 'not consider what had happened a sin but merely the thought . . . that he was after Pachomius in rank.'[69] It was Petronius whom Pachomius chose as his successor.[70]

Saint Basil, more humane and more psychological, was not

therefore more indulgent about sins, whatever they might be. He recommended mercy and forbearance for the sinner, 'not by passing sins over in silence but by supporting with gentleness those who are recalcitrant, by applying the remedy with all clemency and moderation.' For every disease the appropriate cure should be found, and for this reason the superior 'must be watchful, in the present; foresee the future; be able to contend with those who are strong; bear the infirmities of the weak; do and say everything to bring to perfection those who are with him.'[71] These principles from the *Detailed Rules* found their application in the *Short Rules*. 'What agreement should those who want to live together according to God demand from one another?' The response is clear and altogether evangelical. 'The one which Christ offered to anyone who came to him, "If anyone wants to be a follower of mine, let him renounce himself and take up his cross and follow me."'[72] 'The meaning of each of these propositions is explained in a special question';[73] and we know how strongly Saint Basil understood the gospel doctrine of renunciation, here and elsewhere. The aim of the common life is to live by these, and the members of a community 'must demand strict observance of them from one another.' It is not surprising that most of the 313 *Short Rules* present the details of this total renunciation almost exclusively, and the ways of having the cenobites practice it. 'How shall we convert someone who sins; and how should one treat someone who does not convert?'[74] 'When someone harasses the brothers for even the slightest sins, saying, "You must do penance", he is a person without mercy who destroys love'. And numerous other problems of this type, always resolved in the same spirit.

Since the Lord has determined that not one dot, not one little stroke, shall disappear from the Law until its purpose is fulfilled,[75] and since he declared that for every unfounded word men utter they will answer on judgment day,[76] nothing should be disdained as being little. 'The one who holds something in contempt shall be held in contempt by it.'[77] Moreover, which sin would one dare call little ever since the Apostle said, 'by disobeying the Law, you bring God into contempt'?[78] If sin is the sting of death, not this or that sin, but sin generally, indeterminately, the person who keeps silent about it, not the person who disproves of it, is without mercy, just like the person who leaves poison from a venomous beast in the wound, and not the other who takes it out. It is the former who subverts charity. For it is written, 'the man who fails to use the stick hates his son; the man who is free with his correction loves him.'[79]

This answer to Question IV of the *Short Rules* exempts us from insisting on it.

Nothing would be more incorrect than to confuse the spiritual father's indulgence, even the most unflagging indulgence, for his children's frailties, with weakness or the cowardice that would not dare to speak freely. If one had to adduce traits of firmness, apparently even of harshness, the choice would only be too great. Instead of transcribing numerous anecdotes, let us first specify two rules in order to interpret correctly such small facts. One should distinguish the past from the present; a given story which apparently pushes condescendence to an extreme conceals a profound experience, almost a ruse.

Catalogues of *epitimies* provide numerous examples of severity for past faults. It is not the function of the spiritual father to apply such lists. He knows how quickly God forgives the person who asks for forgiveness[80]; and how he is 'the guardian of divine love towards humanity', as Gregory of Nazianzus expresses it.[81] Consequently, rather than being hypnotized by the past, he is concerned with the future; and this inspires in him a preoccupation with raising the disciple's courage: 'Such was the task of the monks of Scetis: to inspire fervor in those who are in the conflict.' Their slogan could have been formulated by the three words that end the first treatise of S. John Chrysostom *To the Fallen Theodore* (*Ad Theodorum lapsum*), '*monon mē apognēs*,' 'provided you do not despair, do not become disheartened. I will not stop repeating this every time I speak to you, wherever I see you; and I will not cease to have others repeat it. If you listen to me, you will not need other remedies.'[82] Worst of all is 'despair that destroys the confidence of those who have fallen.'[83] Furthermore, can one ask for a greater effort from someone who has given proof of his frailty than someone who insists on getting up and starting to walk again? Is there a more authentic heroism than the one taught by abba Sisoes in very simple words:

> A brother asked abba Sisoes, saying, 'What shall I do, abba, for I have fallen?' The old man answered, 'Get up again.' The brother says, 'I got up and I fell again.' The old man continued, 'Get up again and again.' The brother asked, 'Till when?' The old man answered, 'Until you have been seized either by virtue or by sin.'[84]

Sayings of this type abound, as do many others that surprise us with paradoxical appearances which can be explained by the aim of assuring perseverance.

And then, a given answer which seems to be inspired by laxity or minimalism if one considers it superficially, takes on an entirely different meaning in the eyes of the 'Ancients' who are great psychologists, especially the recommendation to remain in one's cell, without doing anything, if need be.[85] Such a *sententia* on the subject has taken on an axiomatic value, however surprising it may seem. 'Remain in your cell, and it will teach you everything.' Who said this first? No one will ever know, and it is not important. The fact remains that the most famous of the Fathers, consulted in turn—Moses, Macarius, Paphnutius, John Colobos (the Dwarf), Arsenius, and then 'Saint Isaac of Syria'—accepted it and found it indisputable.[86] There is only one anonymous grump who indulged in a jest against it: 'Such a person spends a hundred years in his cell, and does not even learn how one should sit.'[87] It is hardly necessary to warn that the reference was to the hermit cells in the desert. The axiom would probably not be applicable to 'rooms' in our sense, with all the things we have in them to distract us. But in the fourth and fifth century, in a monastic colony, the austere Arsenius could agree unhesitatingly with the opinion of the not less austere John the Dwarf: 'Don't pray at all, just sit in your cell.'[88] He knew what courage, what heroic endurance was needed to tolerate the demon of *acedia* or *taedium cordis* (weariness of heart),[89] the most oppressive of all,[90] whose specialty it is to cause people to take a dislike to stability in one place. All things considered, this commonplace advice to stay in the cell, even without working or praying, concealed a fearsome demand under a conciliatory appearance, and the conviction that the fight itself against the 'noonday demon' would, sooner or later, and more often sooner than later, lead the monk who observed it spontaneously to perform this prayer or that work which was not imposed upon him.[91]

Such treatment, however, remains the exception, and perhaps its only value is against the temptation to throw the helve after the hatchet. In every other case, the Fathers were not afraid of speaking out loud and clear, while attuning their forcefulness to everyone's strength. As always, Saint Antony sets the tone: 'A brother said to abba Antony, "Pray for me." The old man said to him, "I will not pity you nor will God, unless you perform the work and pray to God."'[92] Let us not forget that the same Antony is the great herald of discretion! It is he who taught not to bend the bow so far that it would break.[93] Discretion, in the language of the Fathers, does not mean mediocrity, or even the 'right mean' in Aristotelian language. The clear understanding of spirits often demands energetic, even violent, efforts, especially at the beginning. This is why directors of novice souls generously use words such as *biazesthai* (do violence to) so frequent in the *Spiritual Homilies* of Pseudo-Macarius, which are addressed to beginners. A certain Zacharias even ventures the opinion that '*to eauton biazesthai eis panta, outos estin ho monachos,*' 'he is a monk who does himself violence in everything.'[94] It is true that he only utters this opinion after being asked twice, and he says it to abba Macarius, whose spiritual child he is.

The austerity of the spiritual father in giving direction could depend on several factors: the doctrine itself, the generosity of the disciple, or, by contrast, his incorrectibility. The last-named is the most rare; it would easily contradict the manganimity of which we spoke. There are, however, desperate cases, not in themselves or before God, but in the eyes of the persons involved. When the ineffectiveness of such a master-disciple relationship has been sufficiently established, good sense demands that it be discontinued. Saint Barsanuphius was unquestionably of this opinion when he wrote to someone who had persistently consulted him: 'You ask me questions. Let go of your own will and your mania for justifying yourself, or I will let you go! If you do not work at de-centering your will, even if your heart is not in it, what profit is there to your questions?'[95] In the cenobia, this type of ultimatum must have been more frequent because there the incentive of the common good is added to that of uselessness.

More frequently, the severity of the spiritual father simply depends on the freedom with which he applies traditional ascetic doctrine, or what he views as such. We shall find many examples of this in the letters of the same Barsanuphius, or in those of Saint Nilus, without, as always, taking into account the *Vitae Patrum*. Saint Arsenius thought he was simply uttering a truth from experience when he said, 'One hour of sleep is enough for a monk if he deserves to be called a fighter.'[96] As did abba Achilles when he upbraided abba Isaiah for taking a mouthful of water on the pretext that a dry throat would not allow him to swallow his bread and salt. Nonetheless, abba Isaiah was no weakling, but a future celebrity of Scetis. And yet abba Achilles, perhaps even because of this, strongly took him to task. 'Come and see Isaiah swallowing broth. If you want to eat broth, go to Egypt.'[97] One should compare this anecdote to the first apophthegm of Isaiah himself who had, in turn, become a spiritual father: 'Nothing is as useful to a beginner as an insult. The beginner who bears insults is like a tree that is watered every day.'[98]

Worse than insults, deserved or not, is systematic coldness, or at least what appears like it.

> Young John the Theban, a disciple of abba Ammonas, took care of this ailing old man for twelve years. Though the old man saw him toiling, he never said a kind or gentle word to him. But when he died, in the presence of the other men, he took his hand and said three times, 'Be saved. Be saved. Be saved.' Then he assigned him to the old men, saying, 'this is not a man, but an angel.'[99]

Ammonas had undoubtedly acted that way advisedly, for the novice's greater spiritual profit. Examples of such more or less intentional severity abound. *The Lives of the Saints* often let us witness such austere paternal education, the slogan of which appears to be the same as that of God the Father: 'I am the one who reproves and disciplines all those he loves.'[100] For the ancients, *paideusis* (instruction) did not come without powerful discipline. Pachomius had experienced it under his abba, Palamon[101]; he used it in turn with his favorite disciple, Theodore, more than with anyone else, as we have seen.[102] In the *Life* of Symeon the New Theologian, we read how he molded the one he was to appoint hegumen in his place, Arsenius:'[103] 'Once blessed Symeon had launched Arsenius in the arena of virtue and had found him to be obedient in everything, he never stopped providing occasions for profit to this thirst for progress. At one time, he put him to work with the mules; at another time, in the kitchen; at still other times, at carrying water. He finally made him get used to the most menial tasks,'[104] without omitting insults and humiliations in front of the community he was destined to rule. Saint Sabas had already acted that way with one of the most famous monks of his lavra, bishop John the Hesychast.[105] There are many other examples.

In order for such treatment to be possible without committing a breach of discretion, it was necessary for several persons to be present: a master who wanted nothing but his disciple's spiritual good, and a disciple who had perfect faith in his spiritual father, which presupposed an uncommon strength of soul in the one and the other. The great art consisted above all in judging the trials against everyone's endurance; the great charity, in using every means gradually to develop such endurance. The story of Saint Dosithee and his novice master Saint Dorotheos seems to have been written explicitly to make us see this indulgent, patient, strong, loving yet demanding education through which an extremely delicate adolescent was led, almost imperceptibly, to a life of austerity befitting a monk.

When mealtime had come, Dorotheos said to him, 'Eat your fill. Just tell me what you eat.' And Dosithee came back, saying, 'I have eaten a [loaf of] bread and a half.' Now, the bread weighed four pounds. Dorotheos asked him, 'Are you all right, Dosithee?' He replied, 'Yes, Master, I feel fine.' He said, 'Are you hungry?' The other answered, 'No, Master, I am not hungry.' Then he told him, 'Well, from now on, eat one of the loaves and a quarter of the other;[106] as for the other quarter, divide it in two, eat half of it, but leave the other half.' This he did. Dorotheos then said to him, 'Dosithee, are you hungry?' He replied, 'Yes, Master, a little.' After a few days, Dorotheos asked him again, 'How are things, Dosithee? Are you still hungry?' He replied, 'No, Master, thanks to prayer, things are going fine.' Then he said, 'Well, now reserve the other half of the quarter.' He did so. Again, after a few days, Dorotheos asked him, 'How are you doing now? Are you hungry?' He answered, 'Things are going well, Master.' Then he said to him, 'Divide the other quarter in two, eat half of it, and leave the other half.' This he did. And with the help of God, little by little, he went from six pounds [of bread] to eight ounces; for, even in eating, there are habits to be formed.[107]

We have not cited this story as a good example of discretion; the young director of conscience Saint Dorotheos was perhaps a little bit too hasty (he had pointed out to Saint Barsanuphius that he felt incapable of being in charge of someone). Young Dosithee died of phthisis after five years of monastic life, despite the mitigations he enjoyed and which some rigorists had complained about.[108] At any rate, this story and the entire biography of Dosithee illustrates both the firmness of the guidance he received and the director's desire not to impose anything that would have been beyond the physical and moral strength of this exceptional novice.

2. INTELLECTUAL QUALITIES

The most precious asset of the spiritual person, with respect to direction, is the virtue or the gift of God called, in Greek, *diakrisis*. It might be better to retain this word, which means 'discernment' and 'discretion' (in the sense of the ability to make distinctions). Spiritual direction is merely the discernment of spirits put into practice for the profit of those being directed. Talent is needed for spiritual direction to be called the *science of sciences* and the *art of arts*.

For the early christian community, let us simply refer to Hans von Campenhausen's *Kirchliches Amt* (p. 202ff.) though here there is no question yet of spiritual direction in the specific, that is, individual, sense. Beginning with Antony, the doctrine of *diakrisis* is seen very clearly, whether in Antony himself or in Saint Athanasius. We should note from the outset that it is a 'charism' of the Spirit. This notwithstanding, 'much prayer and asceticism is needed'[1] to receive it and make use of it. 'What is remarkable in Antony's ascesis is that, having received the gift of discerning spirits, as I have said, he recognized their movements at once and was not ignorant of the speed and the impetus of each one. Not only was he not deceived by them, but to those who were troubled by them he taught how they could avoid their stratagems, thereby exposing their powerlessness and tricks. Thus each one, as if anointed with oil by him, came down to the arena, having received confidence against the devil and his demons.'[2]

The requirement for *diakrisis* needed to direct those who *ex hypothesi* do not have it, is based on the dangers one may risk without it in the course of asceticism. Everyone knows Cassian's forceful pages on the subject.

> I remember the time during my childhood years in that part of the Thebaid where blessed Antony lived. Some old men had come to him to inquire about perfection. The conference lasted from the hour of Vespers till daybreak; the question (of the usefulness of *diakrisis*) took up most of the night. For a very long time they asked which virtue, which observance, would keep the monk unharmed from the demon's snares and deceptions and would lead him on a straight path with sure step to the height of perfection. Everyone gave his opinion as he understood the matter. Some said that *diakrisis* would be found in an eagerness for fasting and vigils whereby the mind, become spiritualized and having acquired purity of heart and body, would be more easily united with God. Others posited detachment and contempt for all things, through which the mind, inwardly free, would arrive with God more quickly, there being nothing to hold it back. Others thought that what was needed was withdrawal (*anachōrēsis*), the remoteness and the secret of the desert where one could be more familiar with God and more intimately united to him. Some opted for charity, that is, the work of hospitality since the Lord has especially promised to give the Kingdom of Heaven for this: 'Come you whom my Father has blessed, take for your heritage the Kingdom prepared for you since the foundation of the world. For I was hungry and you gave me food; I was thirsty and you gave me drink,' and so forth.[3] And when in this fashion they had determined that through different virtues a more certain access to God

would be provided, and most of the night had been taken up by this inquiry, blessed Antony finally concluded: 'All these things of which you have spoken are necessary and useful to those who are thirsting for God and desirous to reach him. But countless falls and the experiences of many do not in the least allow us to give the main award to these. For time and again some who gave themselves to strict fasting and vigils, who withdrew into solitude admirably, pursued such sensory deprivation that they would not allow even one day's food or a single coin to remain with them, fulfilling the duties of hospitality with great devotion, we have seen fall into delusion unexpectedly, so that they could not bring the work they had undertaken to an appropriate ending, but brought their exalted fervor and praiseworthy mode of life to an abominable conclusion. We will be able to recognize clearly the virtue that is most apt to lead us to God, if we probe the reason for their delusion and fall with greater care. While the works of the above mentioned virtues abounded in them, discernment alone was lacking and did not permit such deeds to last to the end. Another reason for this fall cannot be discovered, except that, as they had not been educated by the ancients at all, they could not find the way of discernment which, avoiding excesses on either side, teaches the monk to walk on the royal road and does not allow him to turn to the right, in foolish pride and exaggerated zeal which overstep the bound of moderation, or, to the left, to slackness and vices, and on the pretext of ruling the body, into lazy and deadly indifference. In the gospel, discernment is called the eye and the lamp of the body, according to the Saviour's statement: 'The lamp of the body is the eye. It follows that if your eye is sound, your whole body will be filled with light. But if your eye is diseased, then your whole body will be all darkness.'⁴ Indeed, the eye discerns all a person's thoughts and actions, viewing and examining all the things we have to do. If the eye is not sound, that is, if it is not strengthened by sure judgment and knowledge or is deluded by error and proud opinions, it darkens our entire body, that is, the sharpness of the mind and our activities; we will be surrounded by the blindness of vice and the darkness of passion. 'If, then, the light inside is darkness,' he says, 'what darkness that will be!'[5] No one doubts that when the judgment of our heart goes wrong and is overcome by the night of ignorance, our thoughts and deeds, which originate from the deliberations of discernment, will be enveloped by the still greater darkness of sins.[6]

How many have gone off the track because they lacked this indispensable virtue! 'How pernicious it is not to have the grace of discernment, which is demonstrated by the fall and experiences of several!'[7]—in addition to those mentioned by Cassian, there are Saul and Abraham in the Old Testament; during the days of monasticism, Hero, who after fifty years of an heroically austere life welcomed Satan like an angel of light and who, at the command of the deceiver, threw himself into a well[8]; or the anonymous monk who died of hunger, having convinced himself he would eat only food offered by the Lord himself;[9] also the other whose name Cassian does not give because he was still alive, but who, to compete with Abraham in generosity, would have killed his own son had the boy not promptly run away; finally, the monk from Mesopotamia who, after surpassing in ascetism every monk living in the area, ended up by going over to Judaism by being circumcised. We could add not a few others, such as the man from Sinai of whom Antiochus writes in his *Pandectes*.[10]

Because of the dangers that threaten superiors as well as subordinates when *diakrisis* is lacking, 'it is necessary that those who are to be promoted to the care of souls have an understanding of things human and divine, and know how to discern the movements of psychic and somatic powers; and they must also possess the other qualities consequent on these. We must search out such guides and submit to them, for fear that the divine word of Christ, "if the blind lead the blind, both shall fall into the ditch,' might become true of us."[11] How much harm can a director who lacks discretion not do to others, unless a diacritic intervenes in time!

> Someone had lapsed into grave sin. Touched by repentance, he went to tell a certain old man. He did not tell him the deed he had done, but merely the thought that had come to him: 'Such a thought has occurred to me; is there salvation for me?' The other replied, 'You have lost your soul.' On hearing this, the brother said, 'If I have lost my soul, I might as well return to the world.' While on his way, however, the thought occurred to him to visit abba Silvanus, who was a great diacritic, in order to make his suggestion known to him. When he arrived at his place, he did not tell him his deed either but only his thought, as he had done to the other man. But the Father started by citing passages from Holy Scripture to him to show that thoughts alone do not carry a definitive condemnation with them. Such declarations comforted the brother's soul; he regained confidence, and admitted his deed. Like a good physician, the old man formed the soul according to Scripture, and indicated to him that there is a penance for those who return to God for good. Later, my abba met this Father, who told him what had happened to this brother: 'the one who had despaired and was on the verge to returning to the world, now shines like a star among the brothers.' The Moral: I have told you this so that we would see that there is danger, and great danger, in confiding one's thoughts (that is, the direction of one's soul) to men without *diakrisis*.[12]

In the matter of direction, the gift of *diakrisis* so greatly surpasses all the others that it may be worth all of them; and especially that it may be the *equivalent of a dispensation of age* and of knowledge. 'An old man had a good disciple. But in a fit of ill humor he chased him away with his sheepskin robe.

The brother remained sitting outside. When the old man opened the door, he found him sitting there. Then [the old man] performed a *metania* and said to him, '*Father*, your humility and patience have overcome my ill humor. Enter. From now on, you are the old man and the father; and I am the young man and the disciple.'[13] One of the most famous examples of precocity is that of Saint Theodore, disciple of Saint Pachomius. It is told briefly in the *First Greek Life*, [14] more extensively in the *Paralipomena*,[15] and in a rather prolix manner in the *Second Greek Life*.[16] It is this last redaction which Paul Evergetinos transcribed.[17] Theodore had entered the monastery at the age of fourteen; he had hardly had the chance to study, and, scarcely twenty, he received from Pachomius an order to speak in his place before the plenary assembly of monks gathered to hear the habitual exhortation of their 'Father in the Lord.' Some older monks refused to listen to this novice (*archarios*) and withdrew to their cell. This earned them another strong sermon from Pachomius on the pride they had shown. It is evident that in cases of this type, the authority of a respected elder always intervened to guarantee the meritorious nature of such early promotions.

This intervention is based on the clearsightedness of the old man, perhaps even on a revelation he will have received: 'One day, abba Moses said to abba Zacharias, "Tell me what I should do?" At these words, he threw himself at his feet, saying, "You are asking me, Father?" The old man said, "Believe me, Zacharias, my son; I have seen the Holy Spirit descending on you, and I am compelled to ask you."' The young man did not press his request; the *sententia* he uttered could well be doctrine he had learned from his master now become disciple: 'Then Zacharias removed the cowl from his head, put it under his feet and trampled on it, saying, "If a man is not trampled underfoot in the same manner, he cannot become a monk."'[18] Everyone can obtain this charism; at least, no human condition is excluded out of hand. A former slave at Scetis had become a *diakritikos sphodra*, experienced in discernment.[19] Even a dissolute past does not rule out the possibility of reaching the heights, despite the bad habits one has acquired which are so difficult to overcome. A certain Silvanus 'had lived in impurity' to such degree that Pachomius accepted him only with this reservation, 'If he does not do penance, I will chase him away.' The young man's resolution not having lasted long, 'our father . . . informed him that he would chase him from the brothers. Overcome by the pleadings of the guilty one, he tried one last avenue: he gave him to an old brother named Psanamon. 'Here is your father after God; do everything he does. . . .' The hard struggle against the tyranny of old enticements is described at length. But finally, Pachomius had the joy of announcing victory to the brothers: 'I want to let you know about the miracle God has worked among us. There is someone in your midst who has converted and has become a new man, through a second birth, so that by the fruits of the Holy Spirit, he has acquired perfect purity of heart . . .; because of the purity of his intentions in his whole behavior, the Holy Spirit has filled him from the nails of his toes to the hairs on his head. There is not one among you who resembles him, but he resembles me. . . .' The special spiritual father Pachomius had given to Silvanus then heard a voice telling him: 'At one time, you were his father; but now, because of the progress he has made thanks to the Lord, he is higher than you are: he is your father.'[20]

Diakrisis also dispenses with knowledge, whether secular or sacred. Deacon Theodosius, to judge from the long letter Saint Nilus wrote him, was a learned man, devoted to the reading of religious books, possessing 'encyclopedic knowledge', but the saint praises him above all because he was not ashamed of 'conversing with uneducated monks, joyfully receiving from them food for the salvation of his soul.'[21] Saint Arsenius, the most cultivated man in the desert, did not hesitate to consult the Egyptians about his *logismoi* (thoughts). To someone who was surprised at this and said to him, 'Abba Arsenius, how is it that you who are versed so well in Latin and Greek learning can ask this peasant about your thoughts?' he said, 'Indeed, I know the Latin and Greek disciplines, but I have not yet learned the alphabet of this peasant.'[22] As he says elsewhere, this is because 'we get nothing from our secular education, but these Egyptians have acquired the virtues through their ascetic labors.'[23]

The most famous of the spiritual fathers owe their reputation, not to their studies, but to their life and to the gifts this life earned them from God, in fourth-century Scetis as well as in nineteenth-century Russia. Even if they knew letters, their biographers took care either to minimize or to pass over this in silence, or, at any rate, to show that such human knowledge hardly deserved mention at all, since it has nothing to do with their heroes' infused knowledge. For it is understood that 'discourses about faith and the reading of dogmatic books dry up . . .,'[24] while only purity gives access to true knowledge, as many examples show. Secular knowledge and even 'simple knowledge' of things divine have no value in matters of a spiritual order; here, only knowledge received from God at the price of purity of soul is valid.[25] This distinction between two types of knowledge, and the high even excessive, esteem for spiritual and charismatic knowledge represents one of the dominant characteristics of the eastern monastic mentality, from the beginnings to our day. The ideal is the 'apostolic life,' and we should remember that the Princes of the Apostles, Peter and John, are characterized as *agrammatoi* (without learning) and *idiōtai* (illiterate men).[26]

Knowledge is not a recommendation, unless it comes directly and only from the Holy Spirit as a reward for ascetic purifications and toil. Regarding this point, the eastern mystics would not accept the opinion of Saint Teresa,[27] or at least they would define in their own terms the *letrado* (learned person) who never misleads. Acquired knowledge is not enough. 'There are some who seemed to have renounced the world but have no concern for purity of heart or the uprooting of vices and passions from their soul; their one desire is to see one of the holy Fathers, to hear some words from him, and then to repeat these, boasting that they have learned them from so and so. And if they perhaps acquire a little knowledge by listening, they immediately want to become instructors, and to teach not what they have done but what they have heard and seen; and they despise the others. They aspire to the priesthood, and try to mix with the clergy, not knowing that there is less blame in not wanting to teach when one is strong in virtue than in teaching about virtue when one is in the grip of passions and vice.'[28]

There was real rivalry in calling oneself *idiōta*. Cyril of Scythopolis, who is after all the best byzantine hagiographer, claims this title.[29] By doing the same, Leontius of Neapolis was not afraid of disgracing his episcopal dignity, [30] and on it goes to Agapios Landos, the most frequently edited of all those who wrote in Greek after the evangelists and who, in *The Salvation of Sinners*, his most widely diffused book, declared[31]: 'I, the unworthy one . . ., who am a sinner, an unlearned man (*agrammatos*). The greatest byzantine theologian (if we can call a fourth-century writer byzantine), Saint Maximus the Confessor, believed that he was telling the truth when he stated, among other self-deprecating things, that he was *idioteiạ syntethrammenos*. This can be mistranslated as 'having always lived separately'[32] or as 'I did not stay in the schools,'[33] but the correct translation, 'I was educated by ignorance' makes a liar of the biographer, who does not mention anything so implausible but states that this son of noble and rich parents 'visited professors and applied himself to all the liberal disciplines.'[34] Maximus liked this expression, moreover, since he repeats it, no doubt unconsciously,[35] and accuses himself of *amathia* (stupidity) [36] *agnoia* (ignorance),[37] calls himself *apaideutos* (uneducated),[38] and so forth. Statements of this type occur so frequently and so insistently that the conclusion is imperative: Saint Maximus viewed the knowledge acquired by studying as worthless and nonexistent or at least as entirely negligible in the realm of the Spirit. True knowledge is acquired by purity of soul and mind.[39] When the mind is pure, it is sometimes God himself who invades and teaches it; sometimes the Holy Powers (angels) who suggest good, beautiful things to him; at other

times, natural contemplation.[40] 'The function of applied philosophy, namely asceticism,' then, 'is to purify the mind with
a view to natural contemplation which, in turn, leads to theological mystagogy.'[41] Despite his encyclopedic studies, Maximus the Confessor can in all sincerity call himself *idiōteiā*
syntethrammenos; as long as he does not think he is a saint he
must, according to the logic of his ideas, call himself *idiōtes*
through the life he has led. In this respect, he remains the
disciple of Evagrius Ponticus, or rather the representative of
the entire Eastern tradition formulated by Evagrius as follows:
'The knowledge of Christ needs not a dialectical soul, but a
seeing soul; knowledge due to study one can possess even
without being pure. Contemplation belongs only to those who
are pure.'[42] Although Gregory the Theologian was a true
scholar, he does not owe his title to this erudition; and then
there is a new theologian, Symeon of Saint Mamas, and he,
theologēsas agrammatos, was at the same time a theologian and
unlettered,[43] and equal to the Apostles, because of each of
these qualities.[44] The anonymous Syrian who wrote the *Book
of Degrees* summarized this doctrine in a sharp formula: 'the
idiōtae whom God has chosen were ignorant of earthy, but
wise in heavenly things, according to what is written,[45] "even
though I knew no numbers, I shall enter your mighty house,
O Lord." That is, because I have rejected the wisdom of the
earth, I will acquire the wisdom of heaven.'[46] This is exactly
what Daniel of Raithu says about John the Scholastic (the one
we call John Climacus or John of the Ladder, the author of
another *Book of Degrees*), in a text which unfortunately is not
very critical but the sense of which is clear from the context:
'John the Scholastic too had been initiated into the "cycle of
wisdom" (all literary and scientific disciplines), but he possessed something which was much better, an *ouranios idiōteia*
(heavenly private life), whose disciple he professed to be'.[47]
Elias of Crete says the same thing more simply in a passage of
his *vaegrandis commentarius* (little notebook) cited by Raderus.[48]
'Though he excelled in every type of human knowledge, he
lived in the manner of the unlettered (*idiōtas*)—in a word, like

a rustic, a man without culture—out of humility in the love of God, knowing full well that what the world views as stupid God has chosen to confound the wise. . . .'

From the distinction between acquired and infused knowledge, it seems that sometimes only scorn for the first remains. The most fanatic of the monks over whom Eulogios Kourilas was the chief overseer obstinately maintained that 'knowledge is a diabolical invention'.[49] These modern dissenters undoubtedly view themselves as the faithful heirs of their great ancestors; in this respect, they can irrefutably claim numerous texts and examples. But they take these in perhaps a too literal sense. The history of the relationships between knowledge in the Aristotelian sense and knowledge in the mystical sense remains to be written, especially for the East.

Meanwhile, the low esteem for mere knowledge which we detect at all periods did not prevent certain ancient masters from practicing experimental psychology, even psychoanalysis, in the distinct service of *diakrisis*. Origen, Evagrius Ponticus (or Saint Nilus), Diadochus of Photice, even Macarius—to name but the most original—would greatly deserve the attention of the psychiatrist curious about the history of his specialty. These, no less than the others, view discernment as a gift of God, but they understand better than the others that God's gifts do not free us from working hard with our human faculties. Once more we must be satisfied with drawing attention to this subject which would demand patient research before being presented in detail, and especially in a synthesis-summary each word of which would represent the result of long analyses. Nevertheless, let us indicate the leading concepts.

First, these psychologists certainly knew the existence of the subconscious. 'Numerous passions are hidden in our soul, but they escape notice. They are revealed when a temptation comes upon us.'[50] Saint Maximus calls this subconscious presence *anergēsia* (inefficaciousness).[51] Let us even boldly add that, in this matter, the 'demonism' of the Fathers accentuates the depth of their psychological insights. Lower than the psychic elements, even those which are not noticed, is a force, or rather, a series of forces—formidable ones! Moderns undoubtedly refuse to call these obscure powers demons or spirits. But a change of names essentially neither suppresses nor transforms the reality. Our ancient psychologists too used more neutral terms, such as *logismos* (thought) or *prosbolē* (attack). Some even went so far as to say, or had the devil himself say, that he is not needed. At any rate, the devil for them was not a *daemon ex machina* whose intervention excused them from reflexion. They cleverly risked assessing the psychology of their demons, indicating what they have in common and the specific traits of each[52]; observing their procedures, their succession, their interferences, affinities or incompatibilities; the warning signs that allowed them to be tracked, the effects of their presence, and so forth. And when all this is done, they may in passing say that 'it is impossible to describe all the deceptions of the demons or to enumerate the mischievous skills they use in the service of evil.'[53] It is true that Evagrius was prevented by shame (*aischynomai*) from describing all the things he had learned from experience and observation; he was afraid 'of offending the simple souls who would read this'. In those days, psychology did not feel it was excused from respect for persons. It was not viewed as an end in itself, but was only intended the good of souls. Moreover, it is not in the chapter on *libido* that this psychologist is afraid of saying too much, as one would suppose. To what we have transcribed, he adds, 'Concerning the spirit of impurity, hear the demon's cunning. . . .' Besides, whatever the suggestion is that rises to the consciousness, one should deconstruct it carefully into its elements in order not to lose one's head by seeing evil where there is none. Furthermore, one should distinguish between psychic zones: human or animal, rational or affective.[54] Also, one should examine whether the cause of such a psychic reaction has an outer physical or a moral, inward character. There are many other observations which we would need only to express in terms of modern psychology to make very worthy of attention.

Even the trouble these ascetics went through to establish the list of the eight evil thoughts does not deserve the disdain of modern psychology in the least. By putting the most corporeal passions at the beginning, Evagrius followed a theory of which he would not have to be ashamed in modern times. He recognizes the somatic origin of the two primordial instincts which he calls gluttony and wantonness, which are but a deviation (a 'mis-use') of the personal and of the generic will-to-live. And when Saint Maximus taught that every passion, even the most cerebral, like vainglory and pride, were based upon an attachment of an affective order to something material, this psychogenesis is not lacking in depth. Also remarkable is the attempt to reduce the psychic multiplicity—in his *Antirrheticus* Evagrius enumerates hundreds of various 'suggestions'—first, eight *logismoi*, then the three chief ones, and finally everything to the unity called *philautia* (self-love). To our psychologists-ascetics, analysis and synthesis go hand in glove, and together these must cooperate to achieve *diakrisis*, the seeing clearly into oneself; to the discernment of spirits, to make one follow the straight road of the right mean; and to discretion in one's works.

It goes without saying that the psychology of the ancients is deficient in certain points, chiefly because of the excessive confidence they had in free will. Mental pathology in particular still had progress to make, as is shown by the story about the incorrigible thief we read in Saint Dorotheos.

I shall tell you the story of someone who had a passion that was to become a habit. Hear a story worthy of tears. When I was at the cenobium, the brothers, I know not why entertained themselves by revealing their thoughts to me. On the advice of the elders, the abbot even agreed and laid this ministry on me. One day, one of the brothers came to me, saying, 'Forgive me, I beg you, and pray for me. I steal food secretly, and eat it.' I asked him, 'Why do you do this?' He said, 'I do not get enough from the brothers' meal, and I cannot ask for more.' I say to

him, 'Why don't you talk about this to the abbot?' He
replies, 'I am ashamed.' I say, 'Do you want me to go
myself?' He says, 'As you wish, Father.' I went and told
this to the abbot who said to me, 'Have the charity to be
concerned about him, as you see fit.' I took him with me
and told the cellarer, the other being present, 'Do me a
favor. Each time this brother comes to you, no matter
what the hour, give him everything he wants, and do not
impede him.' The cellarer listened and said to me, 'You
order this; I will do it.' The brother did so for a few days;
then he returned to me, saying, 'Forgive me, Father, but
I have begun to steal again.' I said to him, 'Why? Does
the cellarer not give you what you want?' 'He does give
me my supplies, everything I want, but I feel shame
before him.' I said, 'Are you ashamed with me?' He replied, 'No.' I said to him, 'When you want something,
come and take it from me, and steal no longer.' I was then
in charge of the infirmary. The brother thus came to me
and received everything he wanted. Nonetheless, after a
few days, he began stealing again. He came to me in
tears, saying, 'I have begun to steal again.' I said, 'Why,
my brother? Do I not give you what you want?' He said,
'You do.' I said to him, 'Why do you steal?' He replied,
'Forgive me, I do not know why. I simply steal.' Then I
said to him, 'Seriously, what do you do with what you
steal?' He said, 'I give it to the donkey.' And it was
discovered that the brother had stolen beans, dates, figs,
onions—everything he could find; and he hid these
things under his mattress or elsewhere. Finally, not
knowing what to do with these things, and seeing that
they had begun to spoil, he gave them to the animals or
threw them away.[55]

Had the word kleptomania existed, it would have done
Dorotheos and his monk at least the service of making this
poor man's case seem less tragic. But it would not have suppressed either the psychological problem or the correctness of

the proposition we had to prove, the terrible force of a habit that has become a second nature.[56]

These few observations must suffice, in the hope that specialists in psychoanalysis will undertake a professional study of their monk-predecessors. If it comes to this, they will have to pay attention above all to Evagrius—without forgetting that he became the psychologist of the desert only because he lived among psychologists in the desert—and then to Saint Diadochus, Saint Nilus, Saint Barsanuphius and John, and Maximus the Confessor. I do not know whether it would be of great interest to push the research further, since, in this case as in everything else, the initiators come first and then the repetitive bores follow.

There were *degrees in the gift of diakrisis*; consequently, there was a hierarchy among the spiritual fathers. The *diakritikos* could at the same time be a *dioratikos*, one who had the gift of insight, even of *kardiognōsis* (knowledge of the heart). Crowds flocked to the one who had such a reputation—not only in the East but more in the East—because the phenomenon was more frequent and more appreciated; and even more among the Russians in recent centuries than among the Greeks. Nonetheless, we can detect or catch a glimpse of it since ancient times. Even when alive, Saint Antony attracted numerous disciples, Saint Athanasius tells us,[57] before he became the great ideal of the monks over the centuries. In the *Vitae Patrum* there are anonymous ascetics of whom one occasionally reports an apophthegm; but there are above all a few great personalities whose activity, as directors, was extended more widely: Macarius of Egypt, Sisoes, and especially Poemen, whose name means 'the Shepherd'. Despite the law which prohibited the opening of one's soul to several persons, since one had to have absolute faith in one's spiritual director, some appealed to higher authorities. Thus an inhabitant of the Thebaid who did not know which to prefer, eremitism or cenobitism, went to find Paphnutius, John, and Arsenius successively.[58]

Diorasis, spiritual insight, is like seeing through the screens that stop the gaze of the common mortal, some type of psychic radioscopy.[59] Is it a gift of God entirely or also, at least in part, the natural result of purification? Saint Antony appears to lean toward the second opinion: 'As for me, I believe that, when a soul is perfectly pure and made steadfast according to nature, it can become clear-sighted, and is able to see more and further than the demons.'[60] But this is more a case of far-seeing (tele-vision) than of *cardiognosis*. The latter, which is a divine prerogative[61] can only be God's gift in man; it is given only to the saints, and then, it seems, not to all, but unequally to some and not to others. In the *Apophthegmata Patrum* we see abba Joseph who, before being interrogated by unknown visitors, reacts by carefully setting the stage before responding to the question they had planned to ask him.[62] In the *Lives* of Saint Pachomius, it almost seems that *cardiognosis* replaces *exagoreusis* (revelation of thoughts). At any rate, it is often mentioned. Saint Pachomius possessed it, and tells us that it is a gift of God.[63] The same is true of Saint Theodore; concerning all this we are provided with a long demonstration from Sacred Scripture about the following problem, whether it is possible 'for a man to see the hearts of men.'[64] The answer is evidently affirmative, on the strength of numerous examples taken from the Old and New Testament. The ending of this treatise excluded every attempt to explain this charism through physiognomy: 'Faith (and all that is inward) is seen in the heart, not physically on facial features.' There must have been differences of opinion on this. A given hagiographer had no scruples about resorting to the forbidden explanation. 'Saint Euthymius,' Cyril of Scythopolis writes, 'perceived psychic phenomena by looking at somatic phenomena.'[65] Saint Paul, called The Simple, 'had this grace too. Merely by looking at the physiognomy of those who entered church, he formed a clear idea of whether their thoughts were good or evil.' Did we not have the rest, we could consider this merely the talent of a physiognomist. But Paul did not see just the expression on the face. He also saw radiant angels who accompanied those whose face was joyful, and 'on either side of one who was dark and dusky all over the body, demons pulling him toward them, having put a rope through his nostrils, while his holy angel followed from afar, sad and mourning.'[66] The problem remains: could others besides Paul the Simple have seen the radiant faces of the ones and the frowning faces of the others and been able to infer something about the state of their soul without seeing either angels or demons? Holy Scripture, while affirming that feelings are reflected in the face,[67] warns against the habit of judging people by their expression.[68] Whatever the case may be for this debate, all the Easterners agree in linking clearsightedness to purity, either through a natural link or, more frequently, thanks to a special intervention of God. Passions harm the *dioratikon tēs psychēs* (the soul's clearsightedness) and prevent it from exercising its perspicuity, as Saint Gregory of Nyssa explains *ex professo* in *De virginitate*. And this is why only saints enjoy the gift of *diorasis*, vision through either space or matter, and of *proorasis*, vision through time.

A few examples. One of the most curious, let us even say most comic (the author will be grateful to us!) is the one found in the *Life* of Symeon Salos by Leontius of Neapolis. This fool (*salos*), this madman, (*exōchos*) shows himself all the more resourceful as his madness is feigned (*prospoioumenos mōrian dia Christon*), but also aimed at rescuing people from vice. He was especially interested in the fate of prostitutes. 'If ever one of those who were thought to be his girlfriends had sinned, he saw in his mind that she had fornicated.' The remedies he then used, which are not at the disposal of all spiritual fathers, do not concern us for the moment. Close to Emesa lived a certain *protocomes* (first overseer)[69] who said, after he heard people talk about Symeon's life, 'If I see him I will find out whether his mind has really left him or whether he acts the fool'. When he had come to town, he met him by chance; one of those he cared for was carrying him, while the other kept flogging him. The *protocomes* was immediately scandalized; and thinking to himself, he said in Syriac, 'Does the Devil himself not admit that this pseudo-abba fornicates with them?'

At once, Symeon Salos came to the *protocomes* who was standing a stone throw away. He slapped him, pulled off his
clothes, began to dance, and said, 'Come hither! Vile man!
Amuse yourself! There is no fraud in this!' The other understood that he had seen what was in the heart.'[70]

The unusual clientele of this holy man was perhaps inclined
to dissembling, which made such cardiognosis particularly
desirable. We rediscover these elements in the life of another
'Fool for Christ,' but more developed, as is fitting; the imitators readily fell into caricature. Andrew Salos arrived at
knowledge of the heart by assisting at battles between angels
and demons without the knowledge of those whose salvation
was at stake.[71] More frequently, the 'dioratic charism' is simply mentioned to typify a fact which cannot be explained
otherwise, as in the *Life* of Saint Stephen the Younger[72] and
the *Life* of Saint Paul of Latros.[73] A document where we see
this at work rather well is the *Life* of Saint Antony the Younger.[74] In it there is an entire line of dioratics who transmit the
Spirit to one another, as Elijah did to Elisha.[75] A palestinian
christian named John, of Herculean physical strength, had
become a leader of bandits (*archilēstēs*), while not giving up the
habit of making an annual pilgrimage to the Holy Places.
After knocking out an unbeatable ethiopian champion boxer,
he himself was knocked down by the grace of God, and entered the lavra of Saint Sabas. There, together with the monastic habit, he was given a very discerning old man (*di-
oratikōtaton*) as director (*epistatēn*), to be guided by him and
from him to learn prowess in the ascetic *palaestrum* (wrestling
ground). He succeeded so well in this that his 'former physical
strength was eclipsed by his soul's prowess in virtue'.[76] But
one day or rather, one night, his old athletic instincts were
awakened when six thieves came to ransack the spiritual father's cell. The former bandit was the first to notice this. He
ran after them at once, overtook them, and seized five of them
with one single armful to bring them back to the monastery,
while he immobilized the sixth by laying him on his back and
putting a heavy stone on his sternum. Only, upon his return

and before he even had a chance to mention his exploit, his 'abba' hailed him with words that showed he had seen everything in spirit. Whereupon, 'stupefied at the saint's far-seeing (*prognōsis*),' John promised not to do this again.

After a ten year struggle against self, the former boxing champion was, in turn, to 'arrive at the measure and the stature of the fulness of Christ,[77] and to move from the second rank to the first which consists in seeing what is to be done, on your own,' which allowed him to begin the life of a hesychast.[78] Soon the people came flooding to him. 'The old man was (not only a thaumaturge, but) also *prooratic*, having acquired simplicity of character and purity of heart to the highest degree.' As proof there is the story of a Jew 'deprived of sight,'[79] but learned in the teachings of Torah, and who attempted to impose upon his naivete and simplicity of thought. 'The saint, *foreseeing in spirit* that the Jew would believe in Christ, tells him, "I am a man who has been a robber and a great sinner, except that I have never killed a Christian. I was never initiated into Sacred Scripture, and I cannot answer your questions. But what I say to you is according to the truth: if within forty days, you have not recovered your sight, I will become a Jew. But if you find your eyesight again, you will believe in Christ."' The prediction came true. Here, the gift of diorasis is not at the service of spiritual direction properly speaking. But one day, the charismatic bandit-boxer would have a disciple, the real hero of the story, another John who will change his name to Antony at his religious profession. At the request of his parents, this John had since childhood been admitted into the company of a saintly hesychast,[80] who was not long in making a detailed prediction of the extraordinary career that awaited him, so that the entire life of Saint Antony the Younger unfolds under the sign of the *proorasis* of his father in God. Even when, intoxicated by success, the spiritual child was about to forget his father and go wrong by getting married,[81] 'the God of anticipating knowledge, The One who before the birth of man had predetermined everything that is not in our power, revealed from on high to John, hesychast on the mountains of Palestine, what would happen to his son. Moved by the Spirit who spoke in him, he wrote him a letter and had a monk take it to him. The monk presented himself with these words: 'Abba John, the ex-bandit sends me to you'.[82] Here is what the letter said: 'My child, you have forgotten my words, the ones you heard when you were in the land of your fathers. You have come to forget what my lowliness has told you. Do you not know that you are mortal and that before too long you will depart this life? What good is it to create vain worries for yourself, to embarrass yourself through easy things that hold you captive? You are not predestined to rule a woman. The time which I predicted to you . . . has been accomplished. It is absolutely imperative that from now on you walk the path of the monks.'

The 'old man's prognostic words' plunged the disciple at once into 'divine compunction'.[83] With the help of a 'faithful servant named Theodore', he had a 'Syracusan Banquet' served to his intimates, and when, thanks to his courtesy, everyone was plunged into a 'solid Bacchic narcosis', he ran away and was given the name Antony, along with the monastic tonsure. Needless to add that from then on, the main hero of this story was his father's equal in charismatic gifts.

Such are the main qualities needed to exercise the function of spiritual father. All of them can be reduced to 'spirituality'. There is, however, one quality which can be lacking in even the most authentically spiritual man. One should be able to express correct ideas, and for a purpose; one should be able to exteriorize the inner dispositions of charity, tenderness, patience, and paternal courage, and to put them into play according to circumstances. Not all the saints have the talent which Saint Athanasius attributes to Saint Antony as a prerogative, and which he seems to put on the same level as thaumaturgy. 'Through him, the Lord healed many sick, and cleansed others from demons. Likewise, the Lord had given him the grace of language, so that he consoled many who were afflicted, and brought others who were at enmity to friendship, exhorting all not to value anything in the world higher than the love of Christ.'[84] The charism of *diakrisis* would remain useless, at least for others, unless the gift of words were added to it—words that are clear, precise, effective, and nuanced: 'All rejoiced when Antony was speaking; in some, the love of virtue was increased; in others, sluggishness was driven out; the self-conceit of others departed. All were convinced that the devil's snares were to be despised, and they were amazed at the grace the Lord had given Antony of discerning spirits.'[85] In ancient style, one could say that the two charisms that make the perfect father are *diakrisis* and prophecy: *didaskalos apostolikos kai prophētikos genomenos* (he was born an apostolic and prophetic teacher), as the *Martyrdom of Polycarp* has it.[86] These two things, however, do not necessarily go together in the same man or at all times. 'It is an excellent thing always to wait, in faith and through an active charity, for the illumination that leads one to speak. Indeed, nothing is so destitute as a thought about God that philosophizes outside of God.'[87] After this wise observation, Diadochus observes that the very abundance of light, and not only its lack, may inhibit speech. This is what we find with more than one famous Father. And how should one move, without a more or less long preparation, from this 'perfect prayer' where one has lost even the sense of one's existence,[88] to human discourse, even pious and charitable? 'Two brothers once came to abba Pambo,' to ask him about their respective practices.

> After they had questioned him a long time, he gave no answer. When they left after four days, they were comforted by clerics with these words, 'Do not be distressed, brothers. God will reward you. It is the old man's habit not to speak readily until God inspires him.' So they went to the old man and said to him, 'Abba, pray for us.' He said, 'Do you want to go away?' And they said, 'Yes'. Then he answered them, while writing on the ground.[89]

This anecdote has passed into the *Vitae Patrum* in a long chapter entitled *On Discretion*.[90] Indeed, should the spiritual father not also discern the time and the moment at which he is able to speak profitably, according to God?[91]

To this aspect of direction is linked the habit, which became law, of not speaking, even of the things of God, until the other had asked a question. Evagrius received this lesson at the beginning of his stay in the desert: 'When you go to someone, do not speak before the other asks you a question. . . .' Evagrius so marvelled at this that he said, 'Believe me, I have read many books, but I have never discovered such learning.'[92] How can we be certain that God invites us to speak, as long as no one asks us? Discernment also lets us see the subjects about which we can discourse: the psychology of the passions does not require the same strength of mind as questions related to theology.[93] It also happens that words fail the old man, or that he does not think he has to speak because the petitioner does not deserve an answer which he is not prepared to put into practice.

> Some brothers, accompanied by worldly men, went to abba Felix [who manifestly does not belong to the first generation of Desert Fathers], and asked him to speak a word to them. But the old man kept silent. After they had asked him a long time, he said, 'You want to hear a word?' They say, 'Yes indeed, abba.' The old man said to them, 'Nowadays there are no more words. When the brothers asked the old men and they did what was made known to them, God provided the manner of speaking. But now, because some ask and do not carry out what they hear, God took the grace of the word away from old men. They find nothing to say, because there is no one to perform what is said.' On hearing these words, the brothers sighed and said, 'Pray for us, abba.'[94]

Generally, however, the old men replied at once when asked. They knew this was the duty of charity, and they viewed the fact that others asked them as a sign of God's will.

3. HIERARCHICAL QUALIFICATIONS

1) Must one be a priest?
2) Must one be an hegumen?

There are differences of opinion, controversies, sometimes fights over both points.

1. *Must one be a priest?* The most emphatic document concerning this problem is the famous letter of Pseudo-Dionysius to Demophilus the monk, a vehement formal demand to keep to the role which has been assigned to each one, in conformity with the entire structure of the celestial and ecclesiastic hierarchies. 'The fact that the monk does not bend the knees and does not have Scripture put on his head, but stands behind the priest who recites the *epiklesis* (invocation), indicates that it does not belong to the monastic order to lead others; but that the monk, remaining by himself in a state of holy and solitary life, must follow the priests, and be led by them, as one of their servants, to the divine knowledge of the mysteries in which he participates.'[1] The Greek *tēn monachikēn taxin ouk einai prosagōgikēn heterōn* is perhaps not as clear as the Latin version in Migne, *ordinis monastici non esse, alios adducere* (To lead others is not the function of the monastic order). The reference is not necessarily to spiritual direction, but surely only to the powers of holy orders and to the sacraments. Indeed, one should make a careful distinction between two types of confession, the accusation of sins with a view to absolution, and the 'revelation of thoughts' with a view to direction to be received. The documents do not distinguish these two well enough; both are referred to by the same names: *exagoreusis* (revelation of thoughts), *dechesthai logismous* (to receive thoughts), and others. To determine the meaning of such terms, one should pay considerable attention to the context. For not having done this, some scholars of fifty years ago have made grave errors, as is recognized by their present-day successors. K. Holl, in particular, erred in an all too hasty work which only certain 'orthodox' keep calling 'a lovely book', but about which Martin Jugie correctly wrote twenty-

five years ago: 'To be read with caution. He exaggerates the abuse of which we speak more than is reasonable and arbitrarily attributes its origin to the primitive enthusiasm of the beginning church, about which liberal Protestants have said such amazing things.'[2] Twenty years later, the Protestant Hans von Campenhausen fully justified this judgment, without knowing it.[3] There have undoubtedly been Easterners, especially Byzantines, who have claimed, in opposition to the tradition of their church, the power 'to bind and loose' for spiritual men whether they were priests or not. But they are the exception. They were wrong, as, in the opposite sense, those would be wrong who forbid non-priests, both men and women, from exercising spiritual fatherhood and motherhood, which is what the direction of souls aspiring to perfection truly is. The sacrament of forgiveness and the art of moral education or re-education are two distinct realities, separable, and in fact quite frequently, if not most frequently, separated. To classify as usurers all lay people, monks or not, who devote themselves to leading others on the path of spiritual progress is not good methodology. One would have to prove that they gave sacramental absolution. Thus, to give only one example among many, at the time when all discussions about the minister of the sacrament had been closed, Saint Germanos the Hagiorite (d. about 1336) chose several spiritual fathers, but it is to the hieromonk Pezos that he went to receive absolution.[4]

The most flagrant exception to this rule of the Eastern church is the teaching of Symeon the New Theologian, not only in the letter sometimes attributed to Saint John Damascene,[5] where he explains and defends his thesis *ex professo*, but more than once throughout his numerous writings. Besides, Symeon sees the practical problem very clearly: 'By the grace of God, to protect myself and my listeners from a double precipice: either to bury the talent received, or to interpret divine truths in an unworthy fashion. . . .'[6] He does not deny that the power of binding and unbinding had passed from Christ to the apostles, and from the apostles to the bishops and priests; but he also states that the latter can no

longer exercise it because of their moral corruption. To reconcile someone with the holiness of God, one must be holy
oneself; to impart the Holy Spirit one must have the Spirit
oneself through purity of life. The monks actually fulfill these
conditions, and only those who live in conformity with their
profession, not the ones who *gegonasi monachoi pampan
amonachoi* (as monks have become quite unmonklike.)[7] However, one should not think that this theory has had great success in the East. M. Lequien, OP, writes admirably: 'The older
masters of the spiritual life not only did not know but would
indeed have disapproved of the evil habit whereby monks,
who would not have been priests, would reconcile sinners
after hearing their confession. . . . My opinion about the author of the *Epistle* is that he was neither Syrian nor Palestinian,
but was from the other region which is subject to the Patriarch
of Byzantium, because it is not evident from any discovered
document that Eastern Christians, Catholics as well as
Nestorians and Jacobites, would have tolerated such a distur-
bance of church order, while from the documents which have
been produced . . . we are certain that it was stronger among
the Greeks and the Asians.'[8]

Among the Byzantines themselves, before and after the
time of Symeon the New Theologian, there were apparently
not many monks who were carried away by such infringe-
ments. At any rate, this is much more an historical than a
doctrinal problem. Symeon himself seems to have released his
theory more to justify his own deceased spiritual father, Symeon called *Eulabēs* (the Pious), monk of Studion, than to avail
himself of it. He even praises his father for having 'wisely
decided that Symeon should also receive the ordination which
men confer,' and at the end of the sentence he speaks of 'the
great desire for this which the Holy Spirit had inspired in him
for a long time.' The majority of the texts which seem to
affirm or pre-suppose the power to absolve among monk non-
priests can be explained by the very widespread, recommended custom of consultation with regards to 'thoughts' (*logismoi*). One should not forget what theology teaches even

today: venial sins can be forgiven without recourse to the sacrament of penance. What the 'spiritual children' asked of their fathers in God was not the removal of a past sin through an act of authority, but the means to avoid it better in the future. Their role was more psychological than theological or canonical. In the *Dictionnaire de théologie catholique*, III, col. 935, T. Ortolan says of venial sins: 'One can mention some without the others, or mention them in a general manner, since a numerical accusation is not imposed. In practice, it is better to mention them in detail, so as to engender greater sorrow for them, and to receive pardon of them more completely'. The statement would be valid among Easterners only by means of a transformation that would let one view the problem no longer from the point of view of guilt but from that of the soul's progressive purification as a source of good or evil deeds. We will speak about this later in connection with the duties of the disciple toward the spiritual father.

Having made the distinction between the sacrament of the remission of sin and the ministry of counseling, one should also note that holding hierarchical rank, the priesthood, is not enough to make someone a 'spiritual father' in the sense of confessor. On this point the Greek church has for a long time exercised a control at least as rigorous, in principle, as the Latin church. The exercise of the power of Orders, with regard to the sacrament of confession, often remains subject to the granting of a personal authorization; of an *entalma* (a command) or *entalteria grammata* (a written mandate).[9] Through this regulation, the church sought the good of the faithful, by preventing such an important ministry to be exercised by the unworthy or the inept. This is a point on which Dionysius the Areopagite agrees with Origen: the priest loses the right which his dignity conferred, if he is *aphotistos* (unenlightened).[10] Furthermore, without being concerned with either Dionysius or Origen, the christian people of Byzantium, for matters of conscience, instinctively preferred to address themselves to monks after the iconoclast crisis, during which the secular clergy had shown itself to be less firm than the others. During the twelfth century, John of Antioch clearly states that 'for forty years, since the time [of Copronymus] until now, the order of monks has been honored and exalted by the faithful to such a degree that confession and avowal of sins, absolution and penances (*epitimias*) have been transferred to the monks.'[11] The result of this was a type of monopoly in the monks' favor (or burden) to such an extent that Balsamon felt the need to state that the reconciliation of sinners belongs to all priests in general, and not only to hieromonks; even though, in fact, 'patriarchs and bishops do not charge priests who are not monks to receive confessions.'[12] Balsamon, Patriarch of Antioch, revolts against this fact: it is an injustice (*adikon*). Furthermore, it happens that monks hear people's confessions without being priests.[13]

It is up to canonists to treat this problem *ex professo* and in detail. What we have said is enough to indicate that the exercise of spiritual fatherhood, far from having been taken away from the monks or contested, almost became their exclusive prerogative, even with regard to penitential jurisdiction. Finally, however, everything was set in order: everyone recognized that to give valid absolution one needed to have priesthood and, in addition, the approval of the bishop. For the spiritual direction that was independent of the sacrament monks, nuns, and lay persons continued to ask for it from the *gerontes*, old men they considered spiritual men, and in fact these were almost always monks.

2. Here a new question arises, at least for the cenobites: who is to be a spiritual father? Does this office not *by right belong to the hegumen*?

One finds documents that go in both directions. The first, above all, in the theoretical works, the *Typika*; the second especially in saints' lives which describe the practice. This too would be a study for the canonists to make, one we can only outline tentatively, for lack of preparatory studies. Cenobitism contained seeds of both tendencies. The non-existence of superiors among the Desert Fathers established the right, even the necessity, for everyone to choose a spiritual director for himself. On the other hand, the strongly inculcated duty to obey 'the old man' once he had been selected gave him an authority which later, in organized communities, could only belong to the hegumen. Advocates of the one system and the other could therefore claim ancient authorities. What is important, above all, is to see what Saint Pachomius and Saint Basil thought about this and what they did.

In the case of Saint Pachomius, we are better acquainted with the hierarchical organization of his communities than with the doctrine and practice of spiritual direction. Even on the level of spirituality, he seems to have counted on the personal relationships between subjects and their superiors. More specifically, both the *Vitae Pachomii* and the *Praecepta et Instituta* hardly ever mention the obligatory revelation of thoughts to the superior or to others he would have appointed to replace him. The natural or supernatural *cardiognosis* of Saint Pachomius or Saint Theodore seems sometimes to be sufficient for this.[14] Given the great number of monks, there evidently could be no question of 'our holy father'[15] listening to each one individually. He entrusted the monks to several 'housemasters.' But their powers were carefully limited: 'The housemaster and his second shall have the authority to compel brothers to penance only for individual sins either in the house *synaxis* (gathering) or in the major *synaxis* of all the brothers.'[16] The next paragraph, it is true, speaks of '*paenitentia recipienda*' but this one example is not clear enough for us to understand it in the sense of the classical *dechesthai logismous*, that is, to receive overtures of the soul in secret. The reference here is almost certainly to the simple fact of presiding over the ceremony of penitence. These housemasters and their seconds are often seriously warned to show the brothers 'all solicitude'.[17] They must 'warn the irregular, console the discouraged, support the weak, show themselves patient with everyone,'[18] according to the recommendation of Saint Paul.[19] The subordinates, on their part, must 'submit to the father in full obedience, without murmuring or various excuses, bringing simplicity of soul to good works.'[20] But in these texts into which others were later to insert passages about the 'revelation of thoughts,' we do not make so much as an allusion to it.[21] *Exagoreusis*, confession, and other terms meaning this are completely missing; when it is a matter of 'giving an account', the reference is to manufactured objects, at the annual general chapter,[22] or at the 'terrible tribunal of the Saviour.'[23] By contrast, other terms play an important role: *commonere* (forcibly to remind), *corripere* (to reprove), *corrigere* (to correct), *disciplina* (discipline), above all *increpare* (to rebuke), *neglegentia* (negligence), *ordo* (order), *poenitentiam agere* (to do penance), which never means 'opening up the conscience,' but ordinarily 'to perform a *metania*,'[24] followed at once by an *increpatio* (rebuke), or the performance of public[25] correction.[26] Found still more frequently are the words *praepositus* (superior), *pater monasterii* (father of the monastery), *domus* (house), and *princeps monasterii* (the head of the monastery).

Evidently, Pachomius and his successors counted more on the zeal of superiors than on the good will of individuals. Let those who are responsible be able to say with Jesus Christ, 'Father, not one of those you gave me have I lost.'[27] Was it easy to trust everyone when the conditions for admission to the monastery had been reduced to a minimum? 'Both in the various rules attributed to Pachomius and in the *Lives* of the Saints we have found only two reasons for non-admission to the houses of the Order: first, a previously guilty life, when circumstances would not allow subjecting the applicant to the supervision Pachomius wanted in such a case . . .; then, lack of freedom in the person presenting himself, his not being able to run his own life. Of those who did not belong to the one case or the other, only a serious desire to observe the rules was demanded.'[28] One could count even less on personal dispositions as the postulant was admitted to the brothers' community after only a few days, without a novitiate. 'In early cenobitism, the absence of the novitiate,[29] regrettable as it was , was nonetheless corrected by the preliminary admission test,[30] by the power the superior had simply to dismiss a religious whose conduct was not edifying and, above all, by the special supervision and the extraordinary exercises to which the saint submitted those about whose virtues he had reasons to be distrustful.'[31] 'Special supervision': this applies to all pachomian monks, if we add to it the numerous instructions—twice a week by the housemasters, three times by the 'father of the monastery' to the assembly of the monks—to prevent faults, and the still more numerous 'public corrections' created to suppress them. Dom Amand has stated it very well: '[primitive cenobitism] was secured because of the master's eye and the vigilant solicitude of the colleagues . . . for those to whom the austere seduction of duty and the intransigent demands of conscience were insufficient—the overwhelming majority, no doubt.'[32] 'The organization of these immense human ants' nests has evidently nothing to do with the "family ideal" of Basil and of Benedict, but makes one think rather of the discipline of the barracks and comes close to a fairly rigid military system.'[33]

On Saint Basil, Humbertclaude has a rather long chapter on 'Spiritual Direction'.[34] 'There were in the monastery a certain number of monks who possessed the charism of the direction of souls, and were recognized as such by the competent authorities. These monks made up some type of distinct group, that of the *proestōtes* or *presbyteroi* (aged men).'[35] Whether these were priests in the canonical sense, as Humbertclaude attempts to show,[36] or 'elders' in the broader sense, as seems more likely, the fact remains that Saint Basil added some helpers to the superior, both to control him and to help him with his task. One of the things they did has special reference to the practice of *exagoreusis*. This 'presbyterate' enabled the elders to receive manifestations of soul and to fix penances. 'This last task is probably the one that occupied them most, for if the brothers were not allowed to keep any of their thoughts to themselves, the spiritual guides must frequently have had to receive visits from them. They listened to every confidence, revealed to them the ruses of Satan, and finally prescribed a line of conduct.'[37] 'Basil leaves the religious the freedom to choose his director from those who have fulfilled the required conditions (according to the superior's judgment!). Meanwhile, such a precaution came to be viewed as not useful for young boys. The special competencies their age demands, the usefulness of a specialized education, caused all of them to be entrusted to some type of novice master. Also, they are less complicated than grown-ups and have less difficulty in opening up to the first person who comes along.' 'Their simplicity and the absence of rationalizing at their age not yet accustomed to lying, will easily show the secrets of the soul.'[38]

Such wise legislation could have been imposed, it seems, on all founders of monasteries. In reality, in the *Typika* one detects a perpetual hesitation between two tendencies: one stressing the uniqueness of a spiritual father identified with the hegumen, the other, a freedom of choice generously or parsimoniously left to the individuals. For lack of certainty about the interdependence of these texts, we can only trace the curve of a continuing evolution; we must be satisfied with giving the reader a few samples of writings that waver between a law that cares little about psychology, and the breadth of a psychology that is less concerned with uniformity.

The *Typikon* of Saint Mamas[39] has a chapter, the twentieth, entitled: 'Of the confession of the brothers; and that all must have the hegumen as their spiritual father'. The text specifies: 'Even if the hegumen is not a priest, because he has been charged with direction by the ecumenical patriarch, he is able to apply the appropriate remedy to each weakness.' If need be, the text allows one to ask the hegumen's permission to go to confession to someone else, not of his own choosing but selected by the superior. 'But this, let us say at once, we have said with extreme condescension, since the traditions of the Fathers do not give the subjects any right whatsoever not to have their hegumen as their spiritual father.'[40] This text passed into other *Typika*. For example, that of the Most Holy Theotokos *tōn Hēliou Bōmōn*. At the monastery of the Pantokrator in Constantinople, the law is more detailed: 1) the hegumen must hear the *exagoreusis* of his monks twice a week;

2) he can ask for the help of others, priests or deacons, or brothers who are more 'pious' (*eulabeis*) and seem to be adept at receiving the manifestation of thoughts; 3) But all these will have power only for thoughts that are *eudialutoi* (capable of good resolution); the more serious must be confessed to the hegumen; 4) In all cases, the first confession, the one at the moment of tonsure, must be made to the hegumen, 'so that he has the means to know all his subjects and may proportion remedies suitable to each'. 5) Anyone who does not confess should, by rights, be chased from the monastery, though he is tolerated there in the hope of the improvement. Meanwhile, he is deprived of communion.[43] However, such accommodations do not abolish the principle stated explicitly a little further down, in the chapter entitled 'On the topic that all the brothers must do *exagoreusis* to the hegumen, and that no one among them is to have another spiritual father. . . .' But this chapter, of a violent forcefulness, derives from another tradition. It is found again, and this time without any contrast to the context, in the *Hypotypōsis* (Constitution) of the monastery of John the Baptist *tou phoberou* (inspiring fear).[44]

> The monks of the monastery must not confess to anyone aside from the hegumen. If, with respect to this, someone happens to lack flexibility and gentleness, and is so unyielding (*ateramon*, literally, unsoftened) and so indomitable that, attached to his own will, he does not want to confess to the superior but decides that another, and not he, will be his spiritual father, and pretends to reveal his thoughts to that one, let him be dismissed far away from our *mandra* (enclosed space, monastery). Let him be chased away at once. Let no one have either pity or compassion for him; he has estranged himself. Let him, according to his perverse decision—O God, your eyes see everything—this truly perverse and all too dangerous decision, let him go to the devil (*aposkorakizesthō*), far from the monastery. Let him be banished from it. Let him be an alien to our vocation and our community, our life and

company, as befits someone who has been the cause of uncommon disorder, trouble and calamity.[45]

This applies specifically to 'the first and great confession we are bound to make at the moment of tonsure to the superior, and not to another, so that he might know all his subjects and prepare for each the remedy he needs.'[46]

In a more even tone, and with more supporting arguments, the same law was decreed by the great Servant of the West, Gregory Pacourianus for his monastery of the Most Holy Mother of God in Petritzos (Bačhovo), Bulgaria.[47] The major reason is always that the superior must know 'everyone's secret thoughts as well as their deeds.' One should therefore not 'reveal these to someone else, but only to the superior.' Otherwise, self-will will reign! The one who refuses to open up to the hegumen will keep to himself or will surrender to preoccupations to his own taste. There will be no more father-son relationships. And from then on, the word of the Apostle will be fulfilled, 'if the unbelieving partner does not consent, let him separate'.[48] 'According to the parable of the fig tree, why do you make the soil unproductive[49] and do you impose vain labor on the farmer? . . . Let such a man therefore be removed, so that he does not become' a bad example to his brothers and contemporaries, a master of insubordination.' Saint Christodoulus, founder of the Monastery of Saint John the Theologian on Patmos, had earlier been the head of the monastery of Stylos on Mount Latros. Forced to leave, he bequeathed his powers to the monk Sabas, with this recommendation: 'It is your duty to see to it that they all declare their thoughts (*logismoi*) to you, and that they do not keep any thought hidden from you. Let anyone among the brothers who would not agree to have you as father in our stead and would not confess the thoughts that harass him, not be tolerated among the brothers. He will be seen as an outsider to this spiritual family (*zeuglē*), a stranger to the community of brothers.'[50] The same exclusivism is found in the *Typikon* of Our Lady of Aeria,[51] in a statement notable for its conciseness:

'We want the thoughts to be revealed to the hegumen and to him alone.' This *Typikon* finds a way to add a reason which should be mentioned, namely that allowing communion is the privilege of the hegumen.

One particular case still deserves our attention. It happens that the hegumen resigns, but remains at the monastery. Saint Plato did this and he continued to guide Saint Theodore the Studite; Symeon of Saint Mamas did likewise, and it seems that he remained the spiritual father of all his monks, while Arsenius, his successor, took care of the more material things. At least, this is suggested by the following text: 'From then on, his disciple Arsenius took over the administration of the cenobium, while the shepherd and master of all the monastery's inhabitants devoted himself to the solitary life, contemplating the reasons of creation; in such a manner the one would lead the flock and the other would support the leader by his prayers and would watch the hidden movements of the other brothers in order to lead them to what is better and more perfect.'[52]

These eleventh and twelfth-century texts would surely not have used such a style unless this legislation was running the risk of remaining a dead letter. Indeed, it too brings with it inconveniences which are perhaps no less serious than the ones it seeks to remedy. The great law decreed by the ancients—the anchorites—concerning the choice of a spiritual father was that the newcomer feel confident. Did the mere fact of having entered a monastery prove that such confidence existed, and especially that it would always last? Within the cenobitic life, Saint Basil proved his wisdom by leaving some of the freedom the eremites had in this matter. But the *Typika* are careful not to mention Basil on this point. Saint Theodore the Studite himself, who swears only by Saint Basil, seems on this point to have been more impressed by the need to know everyone than by the difficulty some may have had in opening up their soul to him. His 'father' was Saint Plato, his maternal uncle, whom he loved naturally and supernaturally, more than the 'husband of this mother.' But his psychology breaks down perhaps when he seems to think that everyone could have the same ease he had. The life of the byzantine cenobite was so dependent[53] on his spiritual father-hegumen that a misunderstanding with him would quite simply make things intolerable. They never ceased repeating, of course, that all this derives from the subject's self-will. But the very repetition of this idea, and the conviction with which it was viewed as a truth not open to discussion , after the fashion of a first principle, could exacerbate the malaise. Here we find one of the reasons, perhaps even the main one, for the instability so often found among eastern monks, a true inheritance of the desert. 'What would be typified by a Westerner as drifting (*gyrovagism*) is but the holy freedom to break with surroundings that would harm sanctification,' a contemporary Greek tells us.[54] The problem of the 'spiritual father' becomes complicated because of the problem of stability, or finds a solution in it. The other solution would have been, and has in fact sometimes been, the freedom within the monastery to entrust the care of one's soul to an 'elder'who is not the hegumen. Only, the elder is generally not authorized to take care of the one who freely comes to him, but is designated by name to take care of this particular individual. Saint Dorotheos told us that he was in charge of a kleptomaniac.[55] The *Hypotypōsis* of Saint Athanasius refers to facts of this type when, by reason of an old tradition and legislation of the saintly Fathers, it prescribes that the brothers must confide their thoughts and secret actions to the superior . . . 'or to the one the superior recognizes' for such office.[56] Would it not have been better openly to establish or re-establish the freedom of choosing among a number of spiritual fathers whose aptitude the superior had recognized, without ever imposing anyone in particular on a person? This is what the *Typikon* of the Monastery of Prodromos, close to Serras in Macedonia, did in 1324: 'I also desire that there be spiritual fathers in the monastery, so that, according to the tradition of the holy canons, the monk show his wounds to the one each will have chosen, to receive help appropriate to every type of wound from the spiritual physicians. The wounds are the *logismoi*. . . . It is therefore very useful to have the physician close at hand.'[57] M. Jugie, who has edited this document, proves that its author 'wants to proscribe forever the type of life we nowadays call idiorrhythmic.'[58] But the superiors' aversion to this 'cause of disorder, trouble, and damage' remained opposed to such an arrangement. Moreover, the ancient tradition of absolute dependence upon the spiritual father would make the division of spiritual from administrative responsibilities more difficult than in our age. Hence the conflicts between the hegumen and the spiritual father, such as the one related in the *Life of Symeon the New Theologian*.[59] Peter, the hegumen of the Studites, is not the monster of jealousy Nicetas Stethatos makes him out to be; not because he 'did his best to separate Symeon the novice from his master and to attract him to himself,' nor when confronted by the stubbornness or the devotion of the young man, 'he orders that the blessed one be chased from the monastery'. He merely tried to carry out a tradition which had become customary law, if not sanctioned by legal texts. Saint Theodore the Studite, the great ancestor, would no doubt have approved of this; he never ceased preaching the obligation of *exagoreusis* to his 'father, brothers, and children', because just as 'God knows everything, and nothing is hidden from his sight but all things are naked and unveiled before him, so must I (your hegumen and father) also know you.'[60] Theodore himself, stubbornly determined to maintain ancient customs, had to consent more than once to abandon his rights over a given monk in favor of the hegumen of another monastery where the fugitive had asked for admission.

And Theodore is a saint, one of the most admirable saints of Byzantium! What would happen when the hegumens forgot the obligations of their superiorship in order to accentuate the marks of their superiority? In no country of the world has this danger ever been chimerical. The recommendations of Symeon the New Theologian to his successor Arsenius undoubtedly deal with facts that are real and frequent, if not commonplace: 'May your blameless, upright life among your brothers and fathers be like a norm, a rule according to which the warpedness and the crookedness of others may be corrected. Do not be a friend of worldly vanities, or glory, or pleasure, or the table, or wine. Be neither a jester nor indecorous, nor greedy, nor angry, nor desirous of vainglory, nor insolent, nor resentful, and do not pay back evil for evil. . . . Do not turn to softness or to the pleasantness of the body; do not wrongly waste the wool and the fat of Christ's sheep by hoarding treasure more for yourself than for your brothers. For fear of what people might say, do not change any of the things that go with the monastery. Do not love frequent leaves on splendidly decked out mules accompanied by servants that precede and follow you.'[61]

Quoting the entire text would be worthwhile. After a careful reading, one understands the 'Satire against the Hegumens,' edited by Hennsseling and Pernot[62] a little better. There is a racy French translation of it by E. Jeanselme and L. Oeconomus.[63] The complaints of brother Hilarion against the hegumens will appear less outrageous if they are juxtaposed to the list of faults Symeon the New Theologian recommended his successor avoid. Moreover, from the year 1005, the date of Symeon's resignation, until the end of the twelfth century, the splendor of the hegumen may have grown more outrageous still, with great damage to monastic life. Under such conditions, how can one still speak of spiritual fatherhood?

Together with worldly abbots there were others whose dignity and prestige had been reduced to nothing by the *charisticarii* or abbots *per commendam*.[64] The decadence of the religious life derived from both abuses, and one of the first symptoms of this withering was seen in the governance of souls; the confidence of the subjects could not be given to superiors who had ceased to be fathers.

Even before, and also after [other inconveniences], every canon, every rule, every monastic command had been done away with. There no longer is any authority in the hegumens, nor respect, nor any other good. And the perversity of the *charisticarii* is not satisfied with such serious evils: it attacked what was most inviolate. It even distorted the sacred rite of monastic initiation. The sacred law of the monks prescribed indeed that the person who has just renounced the world be received by the head of the monastery and by the brothers; that he be tested for three years to see whether he is fit to be a monk; that, if he appears fit, he be tonsured and entered in the register of monks. If not, let him return whence he came. Once tonsured, the head entrusts him to a monk of a proven ascetic life and virtue to undergo, under his direction, the apprenticeship of this art of arts, this science of sciences which monastic philosophy is. He will only be given his own cell when the head judges him to be capable of taking care of himself in the affairs of salvation. This is the sacred canon and foundation, the principle and the root of a healthy religious life. But the malice which is itself without law abolishes this law, and sends the hegumen a written order couched in these terms: 'We have assigned so and so as a brother to such and such a monastery under your jurisdiction. Admit him, hegumen, tonsure him, and give him cells for his dwelling place and his pleasure. Let him receive everything the other brothers receive. Moreover, make a copy of our present ordinance and give to N. as a warranty.' This is how the most religious of the *charisticarii* acted. They do as they please, as if the hegumen did not exist. Since then all monastic life began to break adrift, even more in women's monasteries than in the others.[65]

Should the hegumen be the spiritual father? There is in this debate a question or at least an eternally practical problem: centralized government or the separation of powers? Until our day the two tendencies are maintained in the athonite monasteries: some are cenobitic, others idiorrhythmic. Idiorrhythm, then, derives a great deal, if not most, of its value from the freedom that was left to the monks to choose a spiritual father on their own. The latter ended by grouping their disciples around them. 'Of all of Germanus' spiritual fathers, only Malachy was an hegumen. At Vatopedi, the simple monk Sabas grouped numerous disciples around himself. At Caracallou, Pezos had his disciples, as Germanus would have them toward the end of his life.'[66] Now, not one of these heads of 'family' (the name given to such groupings) was an hegumen. It remains to be seen, but this is not our task, if and in what measure and for what reasons, motives of an inferior, material order became mixed with spiritual concerns. Actually, idiorrhythm, as solidly installed as it is, greatly depends on economic considerations. At any rate, the search for greater spiritual perfection no longer plays any role in it. The very name idiorrhythm horrified Saint Theodore, but he was not able to prevent it, and it finally became a system. To be successful, he would have had to find a solution to the conflict between the omnipotence of the hegumen and the demands of discretion and of charity in the governance of souls.

NOTES

1. MORAL QUALITIES

1. Irénée Hausherr and G. Horn, ed. and trans., *Un grand mystique byzantin. Vie de Syméon le Nouveau Théologien par Nicétas Stethatos*, *Orientalia Christiana* 12 (Rome, 1928) Introd., p. lxx.

2. See Überweg-Praechter, *Die Philosophie des Altertums* (12th ed., 1926) 5.

3. 'Die Wissenschaft der Wissenschaften,' in *Festgabe G. Freiherr von Hertling* (Freiburg in Br., 1913) 371-78.

4. See Gustave Bardy, "Philosophie" et '"philosophe" dans le vocabulaire chrétien des premiers siècles,' in *RAM* 25 (1949) 106ff.

5. *Oratio VI, Prima de Pace*; PG 35: 721ff.

6. Cfr *Oratio XXV, In laudem Heronis philosophi*; PG 35: 1198ff.

7. *Oratio II, Apologetica* n. 10; PG 35: 420A.

8. *Ibid.*, n. 16, col. 425A.

9. *Ibid.*, B.

10. Gregory Naz., *Oratio VII, In Laudem Caesarii fratris* IX; PG 35: 765B.

11. *Ibid.*

12. Greg. Naz., *In laudem Basilii* XXIX; PG 36: 536B.

13. See, for example, Theodoret, *Religiosa Historia* II; PG 82: 1308C, 1309D, 1313B, 1324D, 1325D, and others. [Trans. by R. M. Price, *A History*

of the Monks of Syria. The Religious History of Theodoret of Cyrrhus (Kalamazoo, Michigan: Cistercian Publications)—ed.]
    14. *Liber de monastica exercitatione*, chs. 21-22; PG 79: 748C-49B.
    15. Mt 23:15.
    16. Cfr Job 1:5.
    17. Nilus, *Liber de monastica exercitatione*, ch. 23; PG 79: 749C-52A.
    18. Ch. 24.
    19. Ch. 25.
    20. Ch. 27.
    22. Ch. 31, 760B.
    23. *Vita S. Sabae*, n. 39, ed. Jean-Baptiste Cotelier, *Ecclesiae*, vol. 3, p. 281A.
    24. *Vita Sanctae Syncleticae*, n. 79; PG 28: 1533B.
    25. Wilhelm Frankenberg, ed., *Evagrius Ponticus*, Abhandlungen der königlichen Gesellschaft der Wissenschaften zu Göttingen, Philol.-histor. Klasse, Neue Folge, Band 13, n. 2 (Berlin, 1912) 530-37.
    26. Ed. Paul Bedjan, vol. 1, p. 441.
    27. Saint Athanasius, *De Virginitate* 21; PG 28: 276Dff.
    28. *Vitae Patrum* V. XVI. 9, PL 73: 976; cfr III. 181, col. 799B; VII, XXV. 11. 4, col. 1050C. See above, p. 39.
    29. *Alph.*, Poemen n. 8 [CS 59:167].
    30. *Vita Antonii* 87; PG 26: 65AB.
    31. *Ibid.*, n. 88.
    32. Rom 13:10.
    33. Diadochus of Photice, ch. 89, ed. Edouard des Places, *SCh* 5.
    34. *Vita S. Syncleticae* XXII, ed. Jean-Baptiste Cotelier, vol. 1: p. 215.
    35. Clement of Alexandria, *Adumbrationes in Epistolam I Joannis*, ed. Otto Staehlin, vol. 3: p. 214, 21ff.
    36. *Ibid.*, p. 215, 6.
    37. *Vita S. Euthymii*, ed. Schwartz, p. 58, 6ff.
    38. *Nomizomenai*, Isaiah *Logos* 21, n. 9, ed. Augustinos, p. 131.
    39. Isaac of Ninevah, *De perfectione religiosa* 74, ed. Paul Bedjan, p. 508.
    40. See *Le Livre des mystères*, *POr* I, p. 80.
    41. *Vitae Patrum (De vitis patrum)* V. 5. 13, PL 73: 876CD.
    42. Amélineau, *Histoire de Pakhôme*, p. 49.
    43. *Alph*, John Colobos n. 18 [CS 59:90].
    44. *Vitae Patrum*, V (*Verba Seniorum*) ch. 16. n. 5, PL 73: 970C.
    45. *Vitae Patrum* V. 16. 15; PL 73: 972A.
    46. *Alph.*, John Colobos n. 18; *Vitae Patrum* V. 15.
    47. *Grande Catéchèse* Bk 2, 20, ed. Papadopoulos-Kerameus (Saint Petersburg, 1904) 248ff.
    48. *Ibid.*, 210ff; cfr 34, 248ff; 43, 307ff.
    49. *Petite Catéchèse* 133, ed. E. Auvray (Paris, 1891) 164.
    50. See *Grande Catéchèse* 34, 249.
    51. *Vitae Patrum* V. 5. 4, PL 73: 874:5.
    52. *Collatio* II. 13, PL 49: 544-7C.
    53. Prov 24:11 (LXX).
    54. Cfr Mt 12:20.
    55. Isaiah 50:4.
    56. Job 5:18 (LXX).
    57. 1 Kings 2:6-7.
    58. *Vitae Patrum* V. 10, 48; PL 73: 921C.

59. *Vitae Patrum*, V. 5. 27; PL 73: 880D.
60. Cfr Theodore the Studite, *Grande Catéchèse* 48, ed. Papadopoulos-Kerameus, p. 345; see Irénée Hausherr, *Saint Theodore Studite, Orientalia Christiana* 6 (Rome, 1926) 41.
61. *Vitae Patrum* V. 15. 28, PL 73: 959D. *Alph.*, Matoes n. 2; PG 65: 289C [CS 59:143]; for Dorotheos' fine commentary on this thought, see *Doctrina* II, 6; PG 88: 1645ff [Cfr *Dorotheos of Gaza: Discourses and Sayings*, trans. Eric P. Wheeler, Cistercian Studies Series n. 33 (Kalamazoo, 1977) 98-99.—ed.]
62. *Vitae Patrum* V. 5. 9; PL 73: 876A.
63. *Ibid.*, V. 5; PL 73: 876CD; cfr 9, 876A.
64. *Ibid.*, V. 5. 28; PL 73: 881A.
65. *Alph.*, Antony n. 29; PG 65: 85A.
66. *Vita* I. 4, ed. François Halkin, p. 3 [CS 45:300].
67. *Ibid.*, n. 23 [CS 45:311-312].
68. *Ibid.*, n. 38 [CS 45:324].
69. *Ibid.*, n. 106ff [CS 45:371-72] .
70. *Ibid.*, 114 [CS 45:379].
71. *Regulae fusius tractatae* 43; PG 31: 1028D-29.
72. *Regulae brevius tractatae* 2; PG 31: 1080Dff.
73. Undoubtedly, *Reg. fus. tract.*, 8, col. 933C-941A.
74. *Regula brev. tract.*, 3; PG 31: 1083B.
75. Mt 5:18.
76. Mt 12:36.
77. Prov 13:13 (LXX).
78. Rom 2:23.
79. Prov 13:24.
80. See *Alph.*, Poemen n. 12, 99; PG 65: 325A, 345C; Moses 16, 18; 288C; Sisoes 20, 36; 400AB, 404B, etc.
81. *Oratio* IV. *Contra Julianum* 1; PG 35: 593C.
82. *Ad Theodorum Lapsum* 1.19; PG 47: 308, *in fine*.
83. *Ibid.*, II. 5; col. 316.
84. *Alph.*, Sisoes n. 38; PG 65: 404C [CS 59:219-220]. *Vitae Patrum* 3, 103, PL 73: 780AB.
85. See *Vitae Patrum*, III, 106; PL 73: 780D.
86. See Irénée Hausherr, *Penthos. La doctrine de la componction dans l'Orient chrétien*, OrChrA (Rome, 1944) 93ff. [Trans. by Anselm Hufstader, *Penthos. The Doctrine of Compunction in the Christian East*. Cistercian Studies 53 (Kalamazoo, 1982). See also, Thomas Špidlík, *The Spirituality of the Christian East*, Cistercian Studies 79 (Kalamazoo, 1986) 193ff.—ed.]
87. Paul Evergetinos, *Synagogē* I, p. 151, col. 2.
88. *Alph.*, Paphnutius n. 5 [CS 59:203].
89. John Cassian, *De coenobiorum institutis* 10. 1, PL 49: 360C.
90. Evagrius, *De octo vitiosis cogitationibus ad Anatolium* (= *Praktikos*) 7; PG 40: 1273C. [English trans. by J. E. Bamberger, *Evagrius Ponticus: Praktikos and Chapters on Prayer*, Cistercian Studies 4 (Kalamazoo, 1978).—ed.]
91. Cfr *Vitae Patrum* V. 7, PL 73: 900BC; 34, 901C, etc.
92. *Alph.*, Antony n. 16; PG 65: 80C [CS 59:4].
93. *Ibid.*, n. 13, 80A [p.3].
94. *Ibid.*, Zachary n. 1, 180A [p.67].
95. *Biblos Barsanuphiou kai Joannou*, ed. Nicodemus the Hagiorite (Venice, 1816) *Letter* 236, pp. 127-28.

118   Spiritual Direction in the Early Christian East

96. *Alph.*, Arsenius n. 15; PG 65: 92A [CS 59:11].
97. *Alph.*, Achillas n. 3; PG 65: 124D [29].
98. *Alph.*, Isaiah n. 1; PG 65: 180D-1A [69]; *Vitae Patrum* III. 155; PL 73: 792C; V. 16, 970C. This apophthegm is perhaps not by the same Isaiah.
99. *Vitae Patrum* III. 155, PL 73: 792C; V. 16. 4, 970C.
100. Rev 3:19; Prov 3:12; Heb 12:6.
101. *Vita* I. 6, ed. François Halkin, pp. 4-5 [CS 45:301-302].
102. *Ibid.*, n. 106, p. 70 [371]; n. 114, p. 75 [378-79].
103. Irénée Hausherr and G. Horn, ed. and trans., *Vie de Syméon le Nouveau Théologien*, nn. 47-51, *Orientalia Christiana* 12 (Rome, 1928) 60-68.
104. *Ibid.*, n. 4.
105. *Vie de Saint Jean l'Hésychaste*, ed. E. Schwartz, 205ff.
106. In Greek, *ton arton* (with the article).
107. *Vie de Saint Dosithée*, ed. P. Brun, *Orientalia Christiana* 26 (Rome, 1932) 109.
108. *Ibid.*, 119.

2. INTELLECTUAL QUALITIES

1. *Vita Antonii* n. 22; PG 26: 876B.
2. *Ibid.*, n. 88; PG 28: 965B.
3. Mt 25:34-35.
4. Mt 6:22-23.
5. Mt 6:23.
6. John Cassian, *Collationes* II. 2; PL 49: 525-27.
7. *Ibid.* II. 10.
8. *Ibid.*, 5.
9. *Ibid.*, 6.
10. *Hom.* 84; PG 89: 1689D-90B.
11. *Lettre d'un preposé à un vieillard sage et diacritique* . . ., Dmitrievsky, *Opisanie* III. 1, p. 137; see the *Typikon* of the Most Holy Theotokos *Hēliou Bōmōn*, ch. 47, I, *ibid.*, p. 765.
12. Paul Evergetinos, *Synagogē* I, ch. 21 (Constantinople, 1861) 65ff.
13. *Alph.*, An abba of Rome n. 22 [CS 59:210].
14. *Vita*, 77, ed. François Halkin, p. 52 [CS 45:350-51; also trans.] by Apostolos N. Athanasakis, *The Life of Pachomius*, Society of Biblical Literature, Texts and Translations 7, Early Christian Literature Series 2 (Scholars Press, 1975).—ed.]
15. Halkin, n. 1, p. 122ff [CS 46:20-21].
16. N. 53, pp. 222-24.
17. *Synagogē* I, ch. 38, p. 131.
18. *Alph.*, Zachary n. 3 [CS 59:68].
19. *Alph.*, Mius n. 2 [150].
20. *Vie de Pakhôme*, Annales du Musée Guimet 17, pp. 518-33, *passim.* Cfr *Sancti Pachomii Vitae Graecae*, *Vita* I, n. 104ff [CS 45:368-70]. Halkin, p. 68ff: *Paralipomena* nn. 2-4, pp. 124-27 [CS 46:21-25].
21. S. Nilus, *Epistolarum Liber* III, 43; PG 79: 413A.
22. *Alph.*, Arsenius n. 6 [CS 59:10].
23. *Ibid.*, n. 5 [10].
24. Evergetinos, II, ch. 32, p. 104.
25. See *DSAM* (Paris, 1957) s.v. *contemplation*, col. 1802-05.
26. Acts 4:13.
27. *Vida*, ch. 5, Silverio de Santa Teresa I, p.28.

28. Rufinus Aquileiensis Presbyter, *Historia Monachorum seu liber de vitis Patrum*, PL 21: 397AB. Note that in E. Preuschen, *Palladius und Rufinus* there is no Greek text that corresponds to this passage. [English translation of Rufinus by Norman Russell, *Lives of the Desert Fathers*, Cistercian Studies 34 (Kalamazoo, 1980) 145-46.—ed.]

29. *Vie de S. Euthyme*, ed. Schwartz, p. 83, 24.

30. *Vie de S. Jean l'Aumônier*, ed. Gelzer, p. 3, 18ff.

31. Part Two, ch. 20 (edition of 1779) 283.

32. '*avendo vissuto sempre in disparte*,' R. Cantarella, *S. Massimo Confessore. La mistagogia ed altri scritti* (Florence, 1931) 125.

33. '*je n'ai pas étudié dans les écoles*,' anonymous translation, with a Foreword signed by M. L.-B. in *Ir* 13 (1930) 469.

34. *S. Maximi Confessoris Vita ac Certamen* 3; PG 90: 69C-72B.

35. '*alla kame ton idiōteią syntethrammenon sympsēron labein tōn egnōsmenōn soi kalos katēxiōsas*,' *Opuscula theologica et polemica*; PG 91: 12B.

36. *Epistolae* 19; PG 91: 593D.

37. *Tomus dogmaticus ad Marinum presbyterum*; PG 91: 229B.

38. *Opuscula theologica et polemica ad Domnum Marinum Cypri presbyterum*; PG 91: 133B.

39. See *Capitum de charitate centuria* III. 34. 35.; PG 90: 1027BC.

40. *De charitate* III. 94; PG 90: 1045BC.

41. See *Ambiguorum liber*; PG 91: 1241C.

42. Evagrius, *Cent.* IV. 90.

43. Irénée Hausherr and G. Horn, ed. and trans., *Vie de Syméon le Nouveau Théologien*, *Orientalia Christiana* 12 (Rome, 1928) n. 130, p. 186.

44. Cfr Acts 4:13.

45. Ps 71:15ff.

46. *Liber Graduum* 27. 5, Patrologie Syriaque vol. 3, ed. M. Kmosko (Paris, 1926) 777, 12-17.

47. *Isagogē ad Scalam Paradisi*; PG 88: 597B.

48. PG 88: 597, note (g) '*omnibus literarum disciplinis eruditus.*' On Elias of Crete, see *ibid.*, pp. 617-18.

49. E. Kourilas, *Historia tou Asketismou*, vol. I (Thessalonika, 1929) 54, note.

50. Evagrius, *Praktikos*, Cent. VI. 52, ed. W. Frankenberg, p. 393.

51. *Capita de charitate* 2. 40; PG 90: 997B.

52. S. Nilus, *De malignis cogitationibus* 2; PG 79: 1022ff.

53. *Ibid.*, ch. 16, col. 1217C.

54. *Ibid.*, 19-21, 1221-25.

55. Dorotheos, *Doctrina* XI. n. 8; PG 88: 1744C-1745B [See ch. XI, 'On Cutting off Passionate Desires,' in *Dorotheos of Gaza. Discourses and Sayings*, trans. Eric P. Wheeler, Cistercian Studies 33 (Kalamazoo, 1977)].

56. See *ibid.*, n. VII (1741D) and IX (1745B) [178-179].

57. *Vita Antonii* 14, 55.

58. *Alph.*, Paphnutius n. 5 [CS 59:203].

59. A prologue to the history of this charism may be found in *DSAM* vol. 2, col. 1856-58.

60. *Vita Antonii* 34; PG 16: 893B.

61. See Acts 1:24; 15:8.

62. *Alph.*, *De abbate Joseph in Panepho* n. 1 [CS 59:101-102]; cfr *Vitae Patrum* V, XIII, 1, PL 73: 943B-D.

63. *S. Pachomii Vitae Graecae, Vita* I, n. 112, ed. François Halkin, p. 73 [CS 45:376-77].
64. *Epistola Ammonis Episcopi* n. 16, Halkin, p. 105.
65. *Vita Euthymii.* ed. Schwartz, p. 45, 22ff.
66. *Vitae Patrum* III. 167, PL 73: 795D; V, XVIII. 20, col. 985C.

67. See, for example, Prov 15:13.
68. See, *e.g.*, 1 Sam 16:17; Ps 7:10.
69. See Palladius, *Historia Lausiaca*, ch. 64, 'De Protocomite,' PG 34: 1169B.
70. *Vita S. Symeonis Sali Confessoris* 7; PG 93: 1725C-28A.
71. Cfr *Vita S. Andreae Salis*, 14; PG 111: 74(-60B); see also ch. 8, n. 3, col. 697Bff; ch. 21, col. 812-32, etc.
72. *Vita Sancti Stephanis Junioris*; PG 100: 1105C.
73. Ed. Hippolyte Delehaye, n. 51, in Wieland, *Milet* III, p. 153, 38.
74. Ninth century; ed. Papadopoulos-Kerameus, *Pravosl. Palest. Sbornik* 19, 57, pp. 186-216.
75. *Ibid.*, n. 2, p. 187, 34.
76. *Ibid.*, n. 4, p. 189, 30ff.
77. See Eph 4:13.
78. Papadopoulos-Kerameus, n. 7, p. 191.
79. *apo Ommaton*, the editor Papadopoulos-Kerameus writes; and on p. 221, in the *Index Nominum Propriorum*, one finds *ommata oppidum* 191. Nonetheless, the translator, V. V. Latychef has understood correctly: 'deprived of eyesight'.
80. *Ibid.*, n. 9, p. 192.
81. *Ibid.*, n. 19, p. 200.
82. *Ibid.*, n. 20, p. 201.
83. N. 21.
84. *Vita Antonii* 14; PG 26: 865A.
85. *Ibid.*, 44, col. 908A.
86. *Martyrium Polycarpi* 16. 2.
87. Diadochus of Photice, *Capita centum de perfectione Spirituali*, 7.
88. Cfr Cassian, *Coll.* IX. 31.
89. *Alph.*, Pambo n. 2 [CS 59:196].
90. *De vitis patrum liber* V, 65, 'Venerunt aliquando duo fratres ad abbatem Pambo,' PL 73: 923C.
91. Cfr *Alph.*, Poemen n. 33 [CS 59:172].
92. *Vitae Patrum* V. 10, 19, PL 73: 915D.
93. Cfr *Alph.*, Poemen n. 8; PG 65: 324A [CS 59:167].
94. *Alph., De abbate Felice*; PG 65: 434CD.

3. HIERARCHICAL QUALIFICATIONS

1. *De ecclesiastica hierarchia* VI. 3. 1; PG 3: 533C.
2. '*Caute legendus est; plus aequo enim abusum de quo loquimur amplificat, ejusque originem arbitrario tribuit ille primitivo enthousiasmo nascentis Ecclesiae, de quo Protestantes liberales tam mira comminiscuntur.*' *Theologia dogmatica Christ. Orient.*, vol. 3 (1930) p. 365, n. 1.
3. See above, p. 34.
4. 'Vie de S. Germain l'Hagiorite par son contemporain le patriarche Philothée de Constantinople,' n. 11. 14. 24, ed. by Pierre Ioannou, in *AnBoll* 70 (1952) 35-115; see p. 47.

5. M. Lequien. *S. Joannis Damasceni opera*, vol. 1 (Paris 1712) 598-610; *Epistola de Confessione*; PG 95: 283-304.

6. Karl Holl, p. 111, 1-4.

7. *Ibid.*, p. 124, 10-1.

8. 'Vetustiores (Damasceno) vitae spiritualis magistros non solum ignorasse, verum et improbaturos potius fuisse pravum illum morem quo monachi, qui sacerdotes non essent, peccatores auditis confessionibus reconciliarent. . . . Mea itaque de auctore Epistolae opinio haec est, eum nec Syrum nec Palaestinum fuisse, sed alterius regionis quae Patriarchae Byzantino subesset: quia nullo aperto monumento constat, orientales christianos perturbationem hanc ordinis ecclesiastici tolerasse, tam Catholicos, quam Nestorianos et Jacobitas; cum ex testimoniis quae . . . allata sunt, certum habeamus eam invaluisse apud Graecos et Asianos.' PG 95: 282 *in fine*.

9. Samples can be found in Leunclavius, *Jus Greco-Romanum* (Frankfurt, 1596) vol. 1, p. 437: *entalma eis to genesthai patera pneumatikon*; Habert, *Archieratikon Liber Pontificalis Eccl. Gr.* (Paris, 1676) vol. 5, pp. 578-80; G. A. Rhalli and M. Potli, *Svntagma Can.* (Athens, 1855) 573-74; Hergenroether, *R^mo et Illmo D^no Antonio de Stahl . . . gratulatur . . . edito entalmate patrum spiritualium officium describente . . .* (Wircebergi, 1865). Cfr *RQH* (1893) 23.

10. Dionysius the Pseudo-Areopagite, *Epistola ad Demophilum*, paragr. II; PG 3: 1092B; for Origen, see Hans von Campenhausen, p. 287.

11. *Oratio de disciplina monastica et de monasteriis laicis non tradendis*; PG 132: 1128BC.

12. *dechesthai logismous*, Rhalli-Potli, II, p. 69ff.

13. *Loc. cit.*,9 (n.11) IV, p. 464; cfr Symeon of Thessalonika, *Dialogus contra omnes haereses, cap.* 249ff; PG 155: 468Aff.

14. See *Sancti Pachomii Vitae Graecae*, n. 112, ed. François Halkin (Brussels, 1932) 73; *Epistola Ammonis* n. 16-17; *ibid.*, 105-06, n. 20, 22, 24. [See also, Armand Veilleux, trans., *Pachomian Koinonia*, vol. 1, *The Life of Saint Pachomius*; vol. 2, *Pachomian Chronicles and Rules*; vol. 3, *Instructions, Letters and Other Writings*, Cistercian Studies 45, 46, 47 (Kalamazoo, 1980, 1981, 1982).—ed.]

15. *S. Orsiesii Liber* n. 10, *Pachomiana Latina*, ed. A. Boon, p. 115 [CS 47:178].

16. *S. Pachomii Praecepta et Leges* n. 5, B 44 k, p. 72 [CS 46:181].

17. *S Orsiesii Liber*, n. 13, ed. Boon, p. 116; cfr 13-18, pp. 116-20.

18. *Ibid..*, n. 15, p. 118 [CS 47:179].

19. Cfr I Thess 5:14.

20. *Orsiesii Liber*, n. 19, p. 121, 2-4 [184].

21. Nonetheless, see *Vita* I, n. 96.

22. *S. Pachomii Praecepta*, 27, Boon, p. 20.

23. *Orsiesii Liber*, n. 10, p. 114; cfr p. 115, 13 and 22, etc.

24. For example, *S. Pachomii Praecepta*, n. 31, p. 21.

25. '*Aget publice poenitentiam iuxta ordinem constitutum.*' 'He shall do penance openly according to the order of the monastery,' *Praecepta et Instituta* n. 11, p. 56ff.

26. *E.g.*, n. 125, p. 46.

27. *Orsiesii Liber*, n. 13, p. 117, 8; cfr Jn 18:9.

28. P. Ladeuze, *Étude sur le cénobitisme pakhômien* (Louvain-Paris, 1898) 279.

29. Ladeuze, p. 280-82.

30. How short, that probation!

31. Ladeuze, p. 282.

32. See David Amand, *L'ascèse monastique de Saint Basile* (Maredsous, 1948) 45-46.
33. *Ibid.*, p. 46.
34. *La doctrine ascétique de S. Basile de Cesarée* (Paris, 1932) 131-66.
35. P. 139.
36. Pp. 146-52.
37. P. 153.
38. P. 158; see *Regulae fusius tractatae* 15, n. 3; PG 31: 956A.
39. Paris MS, Greek Supplement 92, dated 1159-60.
40. See Dmitrievsky, *Opisanie* 3: p. 745ff.
41. *Ibid.*, p. 673.
42. Dmitrievskij, t. 3, vol. 1: p. 143.
43. *Ibid.*, I: pp. 621-24.
44. Papadopoulos-Kerameus, *Noctes Petropolitanae* (Saint Petersburg, 1913).
45. *Ibid.*, n. 36, p. 54.
46. *Ibid.*, n. 15, p. 27.
47. L. Petit, *Typikon de Grégoire Pacourianos pour le monastère de Petritzos (Bačkovo) en Bulgarie, Vyzantina Chronica*, Supplement to vol. 11 of *ViVr* (1904) ch. 13, p. 30ff.
48. 1 Cor 7:15, where the reference is to the pagan husband of a christian woman.
49. Lk 13:7.
50. Miklosisch-Mueller, *Acta et Diplomata* VI, p. 16ff.
51. *Ibid.*, V, p. 182, n. 2.
52. Irénée Hausherr, ed. and trans., *Vie de Syméon le Nouveau Théologien, Orientalia Christiana* 12 (Rome, 1928) n. 59, pp. 80-81.
53. See Theodore the Studite, *Epistola ad S. Platonem*; PG 99: 909C.
54. Pierre Ioannou, *AnBoll* 70 (1952) 44, n. 3.
55. See above, p. 89. It is to be noted that Dorotheos is addressed not as father or abba, but as *kuri*, which has no spiritual connotations. It merely is a polite term, even when children use it when addressing their father (see Antoine Hepites, *Dictionnaire grec-français*, s.v. *kures*). An old French translation by P. Du Mont has '*sire*'.
56. Ph. Meyer, *Die Haupturkunden für die Geschichte Athoskloster* (Leipzig, 1894) 139, 35ff. I may be wrong, but the context tells me that about 1020 *exagoreusis* had lost some of its psychological importance; the stress is on *kanonizesthai*.
57. Martin Jugie, *Le Typikon du monastère du Prodrome*, ch. 13, *ByzB* 12 (1937) 50.
58. *Ibid.*, p. 68, a note to p. 49.
59. By Nicetas Stethatos, ed. and trans. by Irénée Hausherr and G. Horn, *Orientalia Christiana* 12 (Rome, 1928) n. 21, p. 30ff.
60. *Grande Catéchèse*, ed. Papadopoulos-Kerameus, p. 177.
61. *Symeonis Junioris Oratio* XXIV; PG 120: 438AD. Cfr the *Vita* of Symeon by Nicetas Stethatos (see n. 59) nn. 61-63.
62. *Poèmes Prodromiques en grec vulgaire*, Verhandelingen der Koninklijke Akademie van Wetenschappen te Amsterdam, Afdeeling Letterkunde, Nieuwe Reeks, XI, n. 1 (1910).
63. *ByzB* 1 (1924) 321-39.
64. John of Antioch, *In Monasteriis don. laicis*, Jean-Baptiste Cotelier, *Ecclesiae*, vol. I, pp. 159-91, especially nn. XIV and XV.

IV

THE DUTIES OF THE SPIRITUAL FATHER

I T IS DIFFICULT TO DEAL separately with the qualities and duties of the spiritual father, though the two concepts are easily differentiated in practice. In practice, the exercise of duties is but the practical application of these qualities. Meanwhile, their application is governed by a very important principle, that of the aim to be followed, namely the disciple's spiritual growth. The qualities of the spiritual person must be real before they can be put in the service of another. The use of such qualities will be governed by the welfare of the disciple, depending on human situations which are infinitely variable. Such unceasing adaptation is possible only through the mediation of discernment which dictates to the spiritual father the various apparently contradictory attitudes he will have to accept and will not be able to accept unless he is equally disposed to gentleness and firmness, kindness and rigorousness, to relentless perspicuity and a highly compassionate willed blindness.

1. SHOULD ONE ACCEPT SUCH A ROLE?

The first sign of the charity, perhaps we should say the justice, of the spiritual person is not to refuse this role. Spiritual direction is a duty of the gnostic, as Origen indicated frequently.[1] Yet Origen's considerations reach far beyond the role of the spiritual father in the sense of the person honored by monasticism. They extend to the duty of teaching, an echo of Saint Paul's 'woe if I do not preach the Gospel'. The monks never took the initiative of teaching a *rhēma* (a word, a saying); they waited until it was asked of them,[2] reserving the right to answer or not depending on their conscience, their inspiration (or their mood?). Furthermore, they did not have to be afraid of letting a good chance to speak an edifying word pass by, so frequently did the disciples plague them with questions, and so strongly did everyone emphasize to them their obligation to ask questions.

We often witness an inner struggle between the fathers' charity and their humility. Humility with regard to their past and present state: how dare one think that one has arrived at the degree needed to guide another?

> Some brothers had gone to hear a word from abba Sisoes. He never said anything to them. He always said, 'Forgive me'. Seeing the little baskets [he had made], they said to his disciple Abraham, 'What do you do with these little baskets?' He answered, 'We sell them here and there.' On hearing this, the old man said, 'Even Sisoes eats now and then.' When they heard this, they acquired great profit for their souls. They went away joyfully, edified by his humility.[3]

This is the usual formula, 'Forgive me.' It is often accompanied by a justification: 'Forgive me,' the same Sisoes says, 'I am an uneducated man (*idiōta*).'[4] 'I prefer to be taught rather than to teach,' says another.[5] He discovered the shortest expression of a principle that had been universally accepted, if not practised. And is all this not one aspect of the supreme law: The beginning of salvation is to correct oneself?'[6]

At other times, what stopped the 'old men' when confronted with the prospect of having to assume the role of spiritual father was the fear of temptations against humility. In the *Lives of the Saints* there is no lack of examples of flight at being confronted with a multitude of disciples. Concern for other virtues and benefits of a spiritual order, especially love of silence (*hēsychia*), played a role in this. It is hard to tell which of the two triumphed more frequently in this debate of the soul—charity toward the neighbor, or humility, the sign of the love for God. This would be a very interesting history to write, since the struggle takes place in the depths of even the most saintly souls. All things considered, among the Easterners, it was refusal that usually gained the upper hand, or at least that almost always came first—as happened in the matter of clerical rank; is spiritual direction not a type of spiritual priesthood, according to the thinking of Origen we have set out? In which biography of holy priest or bishop is 'praiseworthy resistance' not mentioned? 'The humility of [Symeon the New Theologian's] heart persisted in his respectful fear of the priestly dignity, and thrust aside the burden of having to command, through a humility which was all to his praise and more perfect.'[7] The same is true for spiritual direction. the *Apopthegmata Patrum* (*Sayings of the Fathers*), it is true, give us almost no information here. Their very title, like that of the *Verba Seniorum* (*Words of the Elders*) warns us that here we should look only for examples in the opposite direction, of 'old men' who agreed to speak.

Besides, not infrequently they get out of having to speak through a stratagem described at length by Leontius of Neapolis in the preamble to the *Life of Saint Symeon Salos*:

Those who are anxious to have power over others through the authority of teaching should illustrate the doctrine they teach to others through their own life . . .; without which, while they first admonish, instruct, and

seek to lead others before having learned themselves and
before purifying themselves by observing the commandments, they forget to grieve over their own corpse, while
being distressed about another's. . . . The wise author of
the Acts of the Apostles writes about our true God and
Master: . . . Jesus had done and taught.[8] And Saint Paul
asks, 'Why not teach yourself as well as the others?'[9]
Since we, who carry around everywhere the passions of
sin, cannot propose our own life as an image and figure of
doctrine and deeds according to virtue, we may find good
sustenance in the deeds of others and in the toil they
suffered, one which does not perish but will lead our
souls to life eternal.[10]

Macarius of Egypt had already done so. When an old man
asked him to say a word to the brothers, he replied, 'I have not
yet become a monk, but I have seen monks.' This is followed
by a long story about how Macarius left for the desert—a
story that 'profits the soul' (*psychōphelēs*) and concludes with the
words, 'This is why I said "I have not yet become a monk, but
I have seen monks."' "There was always a way to have them
speak without offending their humility. 'They said about abba
Macarius that if a brother came to him [with awe] as if to a
great, holy man, he did not speak to him. But if one of the
brothers would say to him as if to set him at naught, "Abba,
when you were a camel driver and you stole nitrate and sold
it, did the guards not beat you?" If anyone spoke to him that
way, he joyfully gave an answer to whatever they asked
him.'[12] Others protected their humility by stating their in-
competence in theological and mystical matters, but admitted
that they were well up in the psychology of human passions.
Was this not admitting that they had experienced them?[13]

On numerous occasions, however, they preferred running
away to jeopardizing their soul by taking care of another's.
And how could they have accepted the role when the masters
themselves unanimously protested against the view that they
had reached such perfection that they could undertake the

guidance of others? In this matter, the only way to feel secure in conscience is to accept this dangerous office only when one can no longer refuse. A perfect formula for this state of mind is found, for example, in the *Life* of Joseph the Hymnographer: 'As soon as he had arrived in Thessalonica, he entrusted himself to the care of a certain man who excelled in mortification and piety. Because of his eminent virtue, he had undertaken the care of the brothers in the venerable monastery of the great God-the-Saviour; he had accepted this charge *ou diōxas, alla pneumatikōs diōchtheis*, not by pursuing it, but by being pursued himself, spiritually.'[14] The same word play is found a little further down, when the question arises about Joseph receiving the priesthood.[15] Such security is found only in obedience. At the basis of any exercise of authority there must be submission, or rather the superior's submission to the will of God must always be the very soul of his superiorship, as the conformity of his commands to the will of God is the only legitimate basis for the authority given to him. The list of qualities demanded of the spiritual father is enough to confound any courage that is not foolish recklessness. One of the most famous masters in this matter, Symeon the New Theologian, knew this well. First, here is the portrait he draws of the spiritual father along the lines of his own ideas: He is

someone who examines himself diligently, and discovers that he is free of all desire for glory, without any trace of pleasure or of cupidity pertaining to the body, free of avarice and resentment, perfectly meek, unaware of anger; someone who is kindled by love and desire, even to tears, at the mere mention of the name of Christ, and who is, moreover, in mourning instead of his brothers and weighs the sins of others as his own, while he reckons himself whole-heartedly as the greater sinner; and next, if he sees in himself the abundant grace of the Spirit shining instead of the sun, perfecting the inner heart; if he clearly perceives that the miracle of the Burning Bush is being repeated inside him, so that, united to the inaccessible divine fire, he burns without being consumed, because his soul is free of all passion; furthermore, if he humbles himself and judges himself by no means fit, but unworthy, knowing the weakness of human nature, but still trusting the grace from above, and the aptitude it confers; and if he undertakes this task eagerly because he is moved by grace, rejecting every human reasoning[16]; next, if he risks his life for no other purpose than fulfilling God's commandment and loving his brothers; and if, over and above what has been said, he has a mind that is free from all worldly thinking, and if he is wholly covered by the beautiful tunic of humility, so that he does not act in a middling manner toward his helpers, but is the same with everyone in goodness, in openness, and innocence of heart.[17]

Synonymous expressions such as 'next', 'furthermore', and others are used several times on this page. There remains one last example, the supreme warranty:

And even then, he would not dare accept this duty of office without the counsel and the desire of his spiritual father. But let him humble himself, and let him do this because [his father] commands it, and with his prayers; and let him accept this charge only because of the salvation of his brothers. If he knows that his father partakes of the same Spirit and has been judged worthy to receive the same knowledge and wisdom so that he says nothing that is contrary to the will of God, but says what is pleasing to God and profitable to the soul, according to this same charism and degree. For want of this, he will be found to obey man and not God, and will be deprived of the glory and the charism that has been given to him. If he finds a good helper and spiritual advisor, his enterprise will be auspicious and more secure, and he himself will feel more humble. . . .[18]

As he usually does, Symeon of Saint Mamas here lays down as a principle what he has lived himself. He had a marvellous spiritual father, Saint Symeon the Studite, and he, in turn, remained the best supporter of Arsenius, his spiritual son who had become hegumen. There are lines of successors each leaning on his predecessor, a kind of spiritual succession. But where such a succession does not exist—for monastic history has always known beginnings or new beginnings without a personal or institutional link with what precedes—where no authority intervenes to reassure the person who has been asked to function as spiritual father, one can understand that many refuse to attempt to get out of it by using one of the stratagems we have mentioned.

2. PRAYING FOR ONE'S SPIRITUAL CHILDREN

If he nonetheless accepts, what duties does he assume? First, and this goes without saying, the obligation to practice the required virtues so that his influence will be of spiritual profit to his disciple. By visiting frequently, the latter must acquire the virtuous habits he does not possess, through conscious imitation, and also mimetism, even through some sort of *endosmosis*. The virtues, while resulting from human effort, are a gift of God. Prayer is therefore needed to acquire them. And the perfection of the christian life does not consist only in the practice of morality; the charisms which can only come from God are also needed.

Virtues are performed through assiduity and attention; they are acquired through our battles and toils, while the spiritual charismata are gifts accorded by Christ to those who struggle. For example, fasting and chastity are virtues, because they make pleasure wither and hold the fires of the body in check. They are the work of our free will and decision. But to practice these virtues without difficulty and to arrive at purity and perfect impassibility is the highest gift of God. On the contrary, to rule over irascibility and nascent anger is a great struggle, no moderate toil. But to arrive at the point where one experiences no commotion from them and one possesses serenity of heart and perfect mildness is the work of God alone.[1]

One should therefore pray harder to obtain such gifts.

In a word, irrespective of the angle from which the religious life is viewed, it imposes, first of all, the obligation to pray for the one we claim to guide through it. Out of the essential need of his role, the spiritual father must be the one who prays for his spiritual children. The sayings of Saint Antony already attest to the disciples' habit of counting on the intercession of their fathers in God.[2] Above all, it is Saint Barsanuphius who allows us to be present, so to speak, at this practice; he and Saint John illustrate how this habit had acquired the status of a principle, a law. 'Father, pray for me', this is the formula that often introduced the disciple's request.[3] Saint John Climacus holds this intercession of the spiritual father for his children in such high esteem that he recommends that the latter attribute all graces received to the merits of the former. This efficacy of prayer explains to a large extent the marvellous results of this spiritual fatherhood.

Moreover, this prayer for spiritual children is part of the general obligation to pray for others, according to the oldest christian tradition. What is unique to it is that, according to the same tradition, it is advisable to say special prayers for those to whom divine Providence has united us more especially, if only by having us meet them. Saint Polycarp, before suffering martyrdom, prayed for two hours 'remembering all who had ever come his way (during his long life of eighty-six years), both small and great, high and low, and the whole Catholic church throughout the world.'[4] What would the specialists of unceasing prayer, the Desert Fathers and their heirs, not do for the children God had given? They had care of souls, and to have care of souls means devoting oneself to this spiritual welfare as to one's own salvation; it means giving them a privileged place in the unending supplication addressed to God by one's entire life transformed into prayer. 'The advisor is nothing but a man who plays the role of Christ. Having become the mediator between God and men, he performs before God the sacred work: the salvation of those who obey him.'[5] Let us remember that Christ 'is living forever to intercede for all'.[6] Thus, through their very function, the fathers must pray for their spiritual children. They should pray twice as hard when the latter ask them for prayer, as is their obligation as disciples.

A brother asked John the Prophet, 'Father, pray for me, for the love of Christ. And tell me if it is good to frequently ask the Fathers to pray for us, even when they have assured us that they do.' John's answer: 'Brother, I have often written to you on the subject of prayer; it is a command of God. We have the duty to pray for one another, especially when we have been asked by others; we are debtors twice. We can therefore not fail to do our duty. As for asking prayer from the Fathers, it is useful. It is written, "Pray for one another".[7] Also, "It is not the healthy who need the doctor, but the sick".[8] One should therefore not neglect this practice, but be reminded of the importunity of the widow with the unjust judge.[9] It is indeed true that our heavenly Father knows what we need, even before we ask him. Why did he not say, "Do not ask"? On the contrary, he said, "Ask and you will receive," and so forth. It is therefore good to ask so that we may receive, according to his promise. When you ask for prayer, say as follows, "Abba, I am not doing well. I beg you, pray for me as you know I need the mercy of God." And God will have mercy on you, as he wishes. For love towards man (*philanthropia*) belongs to him, and to him the glory for ages and ages. Amen.'[10]

A father's prayers follow the disciple everywhere, and the certainty he has of this gives him great peace. With it, he will escape from danger, whereas he would perish without it.

A solitary old man had someone who waited upon him, and lived in the village. When he had not come for several days and the old man lacked the things needed to do his work and to restore himself, he felt sorrow because of it. Then he said to his disciple, 'Go to the village.' The disciple answered, 'I will do what you wish, father.' But the brother was afraid of going near the village because of a scandal, though he promised he would go in order to obey the father. The old man said to him, 'I have confidence in the God of our fathers: he will protect you from all temptation.' Having prayed, he sent him off. When the brother arrived at the village, he asked where the one who waited upon the old man lived. Having found the house and knocked at the door, he found no one there except one of the attendant's daughters. When she had opened the door and the brother had asked her why the one who took care of the old man had not come, she encouraged him to enter the house at once, and proceeded to lead him in. When he did not want to enter, she grew stronger and dragged him in. When he saw that he was being driven into sin, and that his thoughts urged him, he sighed and exclaimed to God, 'through the prayer of the one who sent me, save me in this hour.' When he said this, he unexpectedly found himself at the river bank next to the hermitage; and he returned to his father without dishonor.'[11]

In an apophthegm which perhaps lies at the origin of this story, abba Ammonas advises, 'At whatever hour a temptation presents itself, say, "God of the virtues, through the prayers of my father, remove me (from this danger)."'[12] At any rate, the story became famous. It was quoted and glossed by Saint Dorotheos,[13] in admiring terms not expressive of doubt:

Behold the power of virtue. Contemplate the power of the word (*rhēma*), namely how much help is brought when one has recommended oneself to the prayers of one's (spiritual father), by saying, 'Deliver me, O God, through the prayers of my father.' Consider the humility and the devotion of both. They were in want, and the old man wished to send the brother to the one who bought supplies; but he does not say, 'Go.' He says to him, 'Do you want to go?' Likewise, the brother does not say, 'I'm going.' He says, 'I will do as you wish.' He was afraid both of a possible scandal and of disobeying his father. Later, when the want had become extreme, the old man says to him, 'Certainly, you will go.' And he does not say, 'I have confidence in God that he will protect you.' But he says, 'I am confident that the prayers of my father will protect you.' Likewise, the brother, at the moment of temptation, does not say, 'Deliver me, God,' but 'because of the prayer of my father, O God, deliver me.' The one and the other put their confidence in the prayers of the father. . . .'

God's help does not preclude the possibility of sinning. One should not, on the pretext of having been sent by authority and accompanied by fatherly prayer, expose oneself to more danger than is reasonable.

If you know, or have heard that the visit you are asked to make is fraught with danger, ask your abba, 'What have you decided I should do?' Then do what he tells you. If you have not said anything because of forgetfulness, but have gone away at his orders, and while you are on the way you recall that you forgot to talk to him about it, it is necessary to return. Pray to God and say, 'Lord, forgive me my negligence, and because of the demand of your saint, lead me according to your will, in your goodness and mercy. Save me and protect me from all evil. . . .'[14]

Unquestionably, as the result of negligence, some come dangerously close to the precipice, even fall into it. But their father's prayer does not abandon them. 'The disciple of a great abba was so beset by temptation that he returned to the world to become engaged. In his sadness, the old man prayed to God in these words, "Lord Jesus Christ, do not let your servant be tainted." When the brother was about to consummate the marriage, he died, escaping dishonor.[15] Another man, named Abraham, a disciple of abba Sisoes, was tempted by the demon; and the old man saw that he had succumbed. He stood up straight, stretched his hands toward heaven and prayed to God, "God our Saviour, who take no pleasure in the death of the sinner, but wills that the sinner turn from his way and live, watch over your servant Abraham and deliver him from the devil's temptation." The disciple was healed at once.'[16] This prayer has been embellished by someone who was undoubtedly bothered by the earlier formulation, which is as follows: 'Standing up at once, abba Sisoes stretched his hands to heaven and said, "God, whether you want it or not, I will not let you go before you heal him." And the disciple was healed at once.'[17] Certainly this decisive summation is the earliest. It is found again as such in the *Vitae Patrum*[18] and in the *Paradise* of Ananjesus.[19] Blessed the person who has a spiritual father of such daring, such charity. They must have been rare at all times, and the mitigation to which they subjected the brave appeal of Sisoes proves that the heroic times of prayer for another had ceased at least since Paul Evergetinos.

Meanwhile, if such intercession were always to show its efficacy with the same promptness, that would be too easy and not sufficiently salutary. Is there a more excellent divine favor than being forced to persevere in prayer?[20] Anyone, above all the spiritual father, who believes that he must collaborate in the saving of a soul, will sometimes have to pray for a long time before seeing any result to his supplications. 'After having struggled for fourteen years not to succumb, one day someone revealed his temptations to the entire community gathered in the church. An order was then given, and all did penance and prayed for him for a whole week, and peace

returned.'[21] This unusual fact proves a customary law: someone who knows another's trials must help him. Normally,
only the spiritual father knows them, and he above all must
pray and suffer together with the other. Saint Barsanuphius
allows us to notice that he does not fail in this. 'I have often
written to you that we must pray for one another, by the
commandment of God; especially when we are asked to do
this, we become indebted to it. We can therefore not fail to do
our best.'[22]

It also happens that a disciple's ill will makes all intercession
vain. The words of Saint Antony are still valid: 'No prayer by
another frees anyone from praying for himself.'[23] Here is
someone beset by temptations.

> He went to a certain highly respected old man, and asked
> him, saying, 'Most blessed father, put your solicitude
> into praying for me, for the spirit of lust is attacking me
> mightily.' When the old man heard his, he prayed inten-
> tly, day and night, asking the mercy of God for him.
> However, the same brother returned and asked the old
> man to pray for him still more earnestly. Likewise, the
> blessed elder, in all solicitude, began to pray for him
> more earnestly. The old man saw the brother return to
> him frequently, asking for prayers. Greatly saddened, he
> wondered why the Lord had not heard his prayer. That
> same night, however, the Lord revealed to him the reason
> of the monk's negligence and sloth. He saw the monk
> sitting down, and the spirit of lust playing before him in
> various shapes of women, and he took pleasure in these.
> He saw the angel of the Lord standing near, deeply impa-
> tient with the same brother because he neither arose nor
> threw himself to the ground in prayer to God; but more
> and more he took pleasure in his thoughts. . . .

The old man understood that his prayers had not been heard
through the fault and the negligence of that brother.

And the old man said to him, 'It is your own fault, brother, because you take delight in evil thoughts!'

Then the old man indicated how such thoughts should be resisted. 'Hearing this, the brother repented in his heart. He earned the mercy of the Lord, and the spirit of impurity departed from him.'[24]

From earliest times, the custom of asking for a prayer—or a blessing—from the spiritual father before any undertaking was established. There is a rather long story which was evidently written to recommend such prayer rather than to bear witness to it. An old man living in a cave in the Thebaid had a disciple; he gave an admonition every evening, prayed, and then sent the disciple away to retire. This disciple, whose father had fallen asleep during the customary evening exhortation, resisted the temptation seven times to wake him up, 'so that the prayer could be said'. The thought of quietly retiring for the night without this prayer did not even occur to him. In ecstasy, the old man saw a throne and seven crowns promised by God to this faithful disciple.[25]

The obligation of praying for one's spiritual children led nonetheless to soul-searching questions. Here we grasp the delicacy of soul of these tough ascetics. What should one ask God for one's spiritual children? To be delivered from temptation, or the strength to oppose them victoriously? 'Because we are lazy, you and I, we ask for one thing instead of another. Here is my opinion on this subject. The perfect fathers ask that God would do to each what is profitable to him. If advantageous, God leaves the weight of the passions to make him practice patience. If it is advantageous to be delivered from the passion, God will cause him to be freed from it. We attribute this to the foresight of God.'[26] The ancient Fathers acted in different ways, and their examples with regard to this point need an exegesis: Barsanuphius knew the plea Sisoes addressed to God. Others, the greater number (and Barsanuphius knew this), considered mostly the usefulness of the temptation, and for their disciples they demanded the grace of confidence and courage.

'If you will, my son, I will pray the Lord to remove this assault from you.' But the other replied, saying, 'Though I suffer distress, I feel that a good fruit is perfected in me. Because of this assault, I fast more and spend more time in prayers and vigils. I pray, however, that you obtain for me the mercy of God, that he may give me the strength to bear up and struggle according to the rules.' Then the holy old man said to him, 'Now I recognize, son, that you surely understand how a spiritual struggle borne patiently is profitable to your soul's eternal salvation . . .'[27]

Who is right—Sisoes or others? Barsanuphius knew that the Fathers were never wrong, because they never contradicted one another:

Sisoes prayed for his disciple, because he was inspired to pray this way. The other old man, or rather the others, prayed according to a certain inspiration. As for maintaining that what happens to people happens for their profit, this is a clear obligation, since the Apostle says, 'In all things give thanks.' Moreover, all things are possible to the person who has faith: to bear the weight of passion with confidence, to be patient, to endure, to accept everything like Job. God does not tempt man beyond his strength. Only, if the saints would not be there a man may on occasion become a traitor because of his cowardice.[28]

Another matter of conscience: does humility not forbid the intercessor to believe that his prayers for another have been heard? 'When a man sends an advocate to plead his cause with the king, the petitioner does not cease praying himself that what may be heard is not the advocate but the entreaty he has directed to the king. You do likewise: pray that [your petition] may be heard [in my prayer for you]. According to your request, I pray for everything: for your bodily health and the salvation of your soul. If my prayer is heard (for God replies to everyone), I attribute this to your prayers. I am not a lawyer who has learned how to plead. I am not a just man: I do not have the power of the word. But I view myself as a slave charged with an errand. Therefore, may the Lord hear the prayers. Pray for the wretch I am.'[29] Thanks to such rivalry in tenderness, the humility of both remains intact; and charity can be displayed, and one does not have to be afraid that it may be distorted either by too great harshness or by an excess of softness.

In a fine article in the review *Aegyptus*, Maria Teresa Cavassini gives us a concrete visual picture of the practice of prayers demanded and given between spiritual children and their father. The father is a monk named Paphnutius. We are in Egypt, probably in the fourth century. There is a set of seven letters on papyrus,[30] the content of which corresponds entirely to what the *Sayings of the Fathers* have taught us.

The correspondents of Paphnutius the monk are almost exclusively preoccupied with eternal salvation, and ask the monk for prayers to obtain the graces they need. Ammonios asks to be freed from the temptations of the devil and from human traps. Pianios asks for mercy for his sins, from which he want to be delivered (through the prayers of Paphnutius). Heraclides seeks the help of Christ, the only one to assist him in the great sufferings in which he finds himself. Valerie, who is very ill, asks for health of the body, and her faith in the power of prayer is so great that she is sure grace will be obtained: 'I have believed and do believe that if you pray for me I will find recovery.' All appeal to the monk's prayers because they 'are accepted through your holy charity; on the other hand, the correspondents also offer their personal prayer for the 'beloved father,' so that the Lord may keep him:

'. . . may divine Providence watch over you for a long time, while you always remember us'.[31]

We are lucky to have the formulations of prayers spiritual fathers offered for their children. Let us cite two of them. The first is by Saint Pachomius:

Lord God, you commanded us to love our neighbors as ourselves. May you know the secrets of my heart, I beg you. Do not despise me when I cry to you for their salvation. Out of pity for them, fill them with awe so that, knowing your divine power, they may serve you in truth, strong in all things because of the hope in your holy promises. For my soul is too afflicted for them, and all my senses are greatly troubled.[32]

The dissenting monks for whom the saint prayed in this manner ended by clearing the field of the darnel they were, and the field of the Lord produced fruit better than ever.

The second prayer seems to have less historical value. It is taken from the *Vita Barlaam et Joasaph*, two characters who, in so far as being Christians, never even existed. Nonetheless, anyone who would read this 'hagiographic romance,' while keeping the common eastern ascetic and monastic doctrine before the eyes, will not fail to notice that the author has been able to present a true catechism of spirituality in an imaginary or borrowed framework. The prayer of Barlaam for Joasaph represents the average type of prayer every spiritual father had to say for his children according to God. The unknown author[33] gives us two formulations:

At the moment he left Joasaph, who had become a Christian,

'Barlaam, curtailing his lamentations, prepared himself for prayer, his hands raised to heaven: "God and Father of our Lord Jesus Christ, who have steeped in light the things that were in darkness, and who created from noth-

ing what can be seen and is unseen, who made your
creatures turn back to you, and did not allow us to depart
on account of our senselessness, we give thanks to you,
and to your power and wisdom, our Lord Jesus Christ,
through whom you created the ages, and who raised us
up when we had fallen, forgave us when we had transgressed, and led us back when we were lost in error; who
redeemed us when we were captives, and who, through
the precious blood of your Son and our Lord, called us
back to life when we were dead. Accordingly, I call upon
you, and upon your only Son and your Holy Spirit. Be
mindful of this intelligent sheep which is led to the altar
by me, an unworthy man; and sanctify his soul through
your power and grace. Visit the vine which has been
planted by your Holy Spirit, and make it fruitful in fruits
of justice. Make it strong, confirming your covenant in
him. Tear it away from the deceit of the devil. Teach him
to do your will through the wisdom of the Holy Spirit.
Do not take your help away from him. Together with
me, your unworthy servant, let him inherit your unending blessings, because you are praised and glorified for
ages and ages. Amen.'"[34]

At the point of leaving this world, Barlaam continued to
pray for Joasaph:

Lord, my God, who are present everywhere and fill all
things, I give you thanks because you have been mindful
of my lowliness.[35] You have allowed me to finish the
course of my pilgrimage in the orthodox unity and on the
path of your commandments. And now, O very good
Master and most inclined to mercy, receive me into your
eternal tabernacles; do not remember how often I have
sinned against you, knowingly or unknowingly. Preserve
likewise your faithful servant here present, of whom you
wanted me to be in charge, me, your useless servant.
Remove from him all the vanity and vexation of the evil

one. Make him superior to the most intricate snares which the devil sets to trip up 'all those who desire to be saved [*pantōn tōn thelontōn sothēnai*: one of the ancient definitions of a monk]. Destroy, almighty God, all the power of the beguiler before the face of your servant. Give him the strength to tread underfoot the head of the enemy of our soul, that brought destruction. Send upon him from above the grace of your Holy Spirit, and add strength to him for the invisible conflicts [*aoratous parataxeis*, invisible warfare, is 'spiritual combat' in Origen's language], that he may receive from you the victory crown, and may your name, O Father, and that of your Son and of the Holy Spirit, be glorified in him. For yours is the glory and the praise for ages. Amen.[36]

The text continues: 'Having prayed in this manner, and after embracing Joasaph with fatherly affection and a holy kiss,[37] [Barlaam] left for the blessed voyage' of eternity. However, his role of intercessor was not yet finished. Hardly had 'this distinguished son buried his spiritual father' than he, in turn, immediately prayed: 'Lord my God, hear my voice . . .; save me through the prayer and the intervention of Barlaam, your servant . . .'[38] Such is the rule of spiritual fatherhood: *it continues after death*. Abba Daniel reports that the great Arsenius told him one day, 'Be a comfort to your father (*anapauson ton patera sou*), so that after he has gone to the Lord, he may pray that things go well for you.'[39]

3. CARRYING PART OF THE BURDEN

Praying for one's spiritual children already means carrying their burden, since of all ascetic works prayer is the one that ultimately demands the greatest effort, and because such prayer for the disciple obtains either relief from pain or greater strength to bear it. Another excellent and frequently meritorious ways of carrying another's burden is to listen with patience when he tells of his trials and temptations, to reply with kindness to questions that are repeated over and over again, and to receive the same visits and to hear the same confidences yet again without getting tired.[2] One more way of observing Saint Paul's precept is to take on oneself the penance another has earned by his fault or the prayers requisite for him to obtain pardon. This is a work of charity the ascetics undertook even outside the father-spiritual child relationship, but it is clear that this relationship turned such devotion into a more pressing, more habitual obligation. Saint Christodoulus quotes this decisive maxim as coming from Saint Gregory the Theologian: 'The norm of all spiritual direction (*pneumatikēs prostasias*) is to always neglect one's own interest for the profit of others.'[3] The heaviest load to carry on the road to christian perfection is the struggle against the enemy of salvation: the demons and the accomplices they find in our bad habits which have become a second nature. Anyone who accepts being a spiritual father commits himself to sustain in spirit those who struggle, by all the means of the most intelligent and devoted charity at one's disposal. 'You, spiritual father, guide of this holy flock, be equitable towards the brothers, full of solicitude, anxious to keep a fatherly disposition towards them. Indeed, I adjure you, take care of all, be pre-occupied with all, support and sustain, exhort, encourage, teach, console, give health to the sick, help to the weak, strength to those who are afraid, bring back the ones who make mistakes, forgive seventy times seventy according to the word of the Lord. Having imitated the Lord, it is better that we have to account for our condescension in letting pass a detail of the obligations instead of being condemned as unmerciful and without fatherly affection for having demanded extreme justice.'[4]

When the spiritual father is not an hegumen, his action will have to take very discreet forms. He will not have at his disposal certain external means of procuring the good of the souls entrusted to him; but although, on the human plane, certain interventions are not allowed, he knows he has the power of charity, before God. There is an invisible way of carrying one another's burden, based on the communion of saints. The 'vicarious satisfaction' of which theology speaks with regard to the Redemption also exists in spiritual fatherhood. Pretending to pay someone else's debts when one is a sinner oneself, would appear to be, or could be, presumptuous. But it can also be simple, very pure, charity. 'See what a proud man I am,' Barsanuphius wrote to someone who felt crushed by the weight of his sins.

> I am the toy of the demons, and because I imagine having charity according to God, I am forced to say to you, 'from now on I carry half of your burden'. From now on God will come to your help once more. I have spoken as one who is out of his mind, for I know that I am weak and without strength, deprived of any good work. Nonetheless, my insolence does not allow me to despair. I have a Master whose heart is sensitive, compassionate, the friend of man. He stretches his hand out to the sinner til his last breath. Be attached to him, and he will arrange all things better than we could even ask or imagine. To him be glory for ages and ages. Forgive me, brother, and pray for me.[5]

We would think that the recipient of this letter should have been delighted, filled with gratitude. Alas! He was one of those acrimonious people nothing can ever satisfy.

> Upon seeing these words from the spiritual father, 'I carry half of your burden,' the brother, saddened because Barsanuphius had not announced full remission to him, returned to the charge by begging him to grant it fully for the love of Christ. This is the answer given by Barsanuphius: 'Brother, your charity surprises me! You understand nothing about charity according to God! First of all, God knows that I view myself as dust and ashes, nothing at all, absolutely. Meanwhile, if I happen to tell someone about a thing that is beyond my ability or be-

neath my power, it is because I speak and am moved by the charity of Christ, knowing full well that I called myself nothingness, a useless servant. Since you did not understand what I told you—I made you a participant [in my works or merits]. I told you that I carried half of your sins. I did not say, I carry one third, and let you carry more that I do, a heavier burden. Moreover, I said what I said to banish self-love,. Nor did I say two thirds, thereby indicating that I am stronger than you are; such a manner of speaking would have been vainglorious. Carrying more belongs only to the perfect who have become brothers of Christ, who gave his life for us, and like those who love us to do the same by virtue of a perfect charity. What is more, had I not spoken as I did, I would have done something that is alien to the spiritual work. I will not be so vain as to take everything to my account, nor am I jealous of you, since I have made you a participant of this happy conversion. If we are brothers, let us divide our Father's fortune in half, and then there will be no injustice. And if you want to throw everything on me, I agree with this also, by virtue of obedience. Forgive me: an excessive charity makes me ramble. Meanwhile rejoice in Jesus Christ, to whom be glory for ages and ages. Amen.'[6]

We shall meet this awkward correspondent of Barsanuphius again.

The spiritual father cannot take upon himself the burden of the past so completely that the disciple would be entirely absolved from all repentance. The very redemption of Christ who has taken away the sins of the world leaves each person the obligation of adapting himself to it by practising the theological virtues, and by means of all the asceticism they require to exist and develop. But it is a burden, ultimately the heaviest one for a soul concerned with salvation, and one which the director assumes without reservation, by the mere fact that he consents to this role. Abba Isaiah the Solitary stated this very clearly 'to the brothers who wish to stay with him': 'Take care not to neglect the observance of my regulations; for otherwise, forgive me, I will not allow you to stay with me. If you observe them, secretly and openly, I will give God an account for you. If you do not observe them, I will ask you to account for your negligence as well as for my exhortation. The Lord will protect from evil the life of the person who observes my regulations secretly and openly, and he will guard against the temptation that could arise secretly or openly.'[7] Isaiah does not quote the Letter to the Hebrews, though he knew he could: 'Obey your leaders [your hegumens] and do as they tell you, because they must give an account of the way they look after your souls. . . .'[8] Nor did Saint Barsanuphius cite the Letter when he restated the same idea to abba Paul, who needed reassurance. The saint had already written him: 'Brother, I will gladly lay down my life for you.' But a scriptural passage, even one from the Gospel, even the Lord's own words, might sound like a cliché. Abba Paul calls for a more personal word: 'If you know that I am overly disconcerted, Father, give me your word that you, master, will answer to God for me, and that I have nothing to fear. That will put an end to my sadness and my trouble. For I am greatly tormented. . . .' The answer: 'Had you understood what I wrote you, you would have seen that [what you ask of me] is exactly what I said to you. For to say 'I give my life for you' means in other words that I will vouch for your charity [before God].' This is followed by some advice. 'Be at peace, therefore, think of your sins and of how you will meet God. I vouch that I will answer for you on the day God will judge man's hidden deeds. Therefore, do not doubt any longer, for if you do, things will become much worse. It is the enemy that makes the sweet turn bitter; may the Lord make all his undertakings against us useless from the outset. Henceforth, do not be concerned with other things. The Lord has lifted disquiet from you; and the wicked demon, seeing you freed through the prayers of the saints, has tried to leave you a little smoke from this temptation. Pray for me, brother, so that he would not tell me too,

"You who teach others, why not teach yourself?"[10] Do not stumble over these points any more; you would cause pain to the one who loves you. May the Lord protect you under his wings.'[11]

Surely this is the most important thing: to take on oneself responsibility for the other's eternal salvation. To measure the worth of a similar work of charity among the Fathers, we should recall how seriously they themselves took this matter to heart. The spiritual father is not just a physician who charges nothing (the *anargyroi*, those without silver!), combined with a pharmacist who distributes remedies for free according to the occasional needs of his clients; he is also someone who is ill with those who are ill, one who frees his children from the most oppressive dangers and worries by taking these upon himself. The inexperienced newcomer no longer runs the risk of losing his way by mistaking his own will for that of God. The anxious question 'Am I on the road to salvation?' is no longer asked from the moment there is a father to answer it for him and offer his life for him. It remains for the disciple to be humbly and boldly submissive to him, to live in holy unconcern, while the father adds to the great work of his own salvation the formidable risk of discovering the will of God for this child of God given him by the heavenly Father, and of proclaiming this will to him with prudent solicitude, so that the child can love it, accept it, and fulfill it as a son. The Art of Arts, as was said. In the order of grace it is above all the most excellent form of charity, as in the order of visible realities the highest proof of love is to give one's life for those one loves. If the true spiritual fathers are prone to mention as their slogan the words of Saint John, 'to lay down our life for the brothers,' this is not an accommodating hyperbole. It is a great, magnificent, heroic truth, and like all things of beauty subject evidently to counterfeiting, but this can only be perpetrated by people deadened by a lack of intelligence or an excess of self-importance.

There is one last burden which the spiritual father can and must take upon himself if he is an hegumen. Among the ignorant, some might think that this service is easy to render! In monastic language, in a climate of christian perfection, it is nonetheless the opposite of a jest. 'When we laid matter [that is, our fortune] on the abbot's back, without leaving a thing in our hands, God knows and bears witness that we had no reason to think that the abbot would be grateful to us; it is we who should be grateful to him, because he has been weighed down by our burdens, and has freed us from cares.' Let us quote the rest, even though it is no longer related to material goods.

> The apostle Peter has said, 'Submit to all human authority for the Lord's sake,'[13] and James states that, 'For whoever keeps the whole law but fails at one point, has become guilty of all.'[14] It is for this reason that one should not follow one's own will: one should blame oneself in everything, and thus find the mercy of God. But if the demon fools him [the monk, no doubt] to the extent that he has a high opinion of himself by thinking he has done something good, he loses everything he has done. Therefore, while doing what you do, have humble feelings, while saying, 'Forgive me, Lord; I have burdened the abbot by throwing my entire burden upon him'. May the Lord Jesus Christ save us. Amen.[15]

Material goods and man's own will are certainly linked; are the former not the most usual means of satisfying the latter, to the destruction of all peace and recollection? 'Should I,' a postulant asks, 'distribute my goods through the intermediary of the abbot? And how to distribute them, and to whom?' The answer:

> May the Lord bless you, my child. You want to be carefree, and you do not want it, harassed as you are by your own will. Simply state what you want to reserve for the cenobium, and what you consign to the needy, and worry no more. This is obedience: no longer freely to

dispose of oneself. What is more precious than the soul? The Lord has said that it is more precious than the world. If, therefore, you have surrendered it to God and to your spiritual father, why do you still hesitate to consign the rest as well? See how vainglory and lack of faith wage war upon you secretly. If you act this way, it is because you have not even entrusted your soul to them for good. It you want to attend to God, give up all preoccupation, and I will carry your cares, with the one you will designate. Only this: you try to become *amerimnos* (unconcerned, free from care) before God. And forgive me, in the name of charity.[16]

4. LOVING ONE'S SPIRITUAL CHILDREN

This is a spiritual father: a man who takes his children's peace and progress in virtue so to heart that he does not hesitate to take upon himself, as far as he can, their past with their sins and the penance they require, their present with its worries of the moment, and their future with the need to discern for them the will of God. What remains is for the disciple to do this will of God. But even in this, a father will help effectively with his prayers, and he will lead him by the example of his life.

All this occurs in an atmosphere of benevolence, made up of human goodness and divine charity. There is infrequent reference to the spiritual father's love for his children, for the simple reason that it is never questioned. It is something understood and it would be ludicrous to express it frequently, as it is ridiculous to utter a tautology. Fatherhood is the type and the source of every other affection. What is peculiar to it (and particularly felicitous) is that even in its human form it admits less than other affections of that weakness which self-love demands of others, and which the others dare not deny because of a lack of real good will. Paternal love is a strong love and, to the very measure of this strength, a true love. While other types of love center around a type of manifestation which is always the same or does not vary greatly, and is consequently diminished by familiarity, if not boredom or disgust, fatherhood has at its disposal such a range of feelings that it is able to draw from it what is needed to 'bewitch another's ills' in an infinite variety of human situations. Saint Theodore the Studite knew what he was saying when he declared, 'Nothing is so much to be desired as a father according to God.'[1] If he is worthy of this name, everything is lovable in him because, as a spiritual person, he desires to act only for the good of his children, like God himself. 'All those who are children of God are also necessarily heirs of his benevolence and forbearance, of his patience, of his philanthropy and charity. For if they are children of God, they are also gods, they are also lords. And if God is light, they are also illuminators. Thus, if God is inconvenienced by the demands addressed to him, if he is annoyed by them, so are they. If, on the contrary, he is saddened when someone asks nothing of him, and is joyful when he is asked, so are they. You must love your neighbor as yourself, the Old Testament says[2]; and the New which reveals perfection, commands us to risk our life for one another, as the Perfect Son of the Perfect One has given his life for us. The saints therefore rejoice when they are asked, perfect as they are, like their Father is perfect. Therefore, ask them; they will give you without growing weary. Unlike me, they are not indolent or cowardly. Pray that I may become one of them. . . .' This is how Saint Barsanuphius expressed himself, replying to someone who had apologized for bothering him too often.[3]

Moreover, just as natural fatherhood, once the children have grown up, is transformed more and more into a friendship in which the remnants of filial respect and fatherly affection rightly combine to make this friendship *sui generis* the most exquisite of all friendships, the image of the friendship-charity that unites us to God, so spiritual fatherhood gradually evolves into something so delicate and at the same time so pure—in a word, spiritual—that it is hard to find a name for it in the human affective vocabulary. One must think of the Holy Trinity from which it proceeds and to which it leads:

> Andrew, servant to God most High, co-servant of me the stunted, peace to you and to our other co-servants, from God the Father and our Lord Jesus Christ. I want to let you know that even before your request, I committed you to the holy, adorable, consubstantial and life-giving Trinity without beginning, by an act of *presentation* which is a protection against all evil. Meanwhile, I do not want you to ignore the following: that there is another more formidable presentation, one which is more frightening and unavoidable, more desirable and lovable, more honorable, and more glorious. Which one? Listen. When our adversary, the enemy of the good, will be covered with shame on hearing the blessed, life-giving voice of our Saviour utter these words full of joy, gladness, and exultation, 'Come, you, whom my Father has blessed, take for your heritage the kingdom prepared for you since the foundation of the world'. Then the great presentation will take place, when the kingdom will be handed to the Father. This one counts, and there is no other beside it. Hear how it will be accomplished: each of the saints will bring with him the children he will have saved for God, and with a loud voice, with great freedom and ease, to the amazement of the holy angels and of all the heavenly powers, he will say, 'Here I am with the children whom God has given me.' Then he will hand them over to God and himself with them; and God will be all in all. Pray that we may get there. . . .[5]

Souls that through a united effort tend towards this unity in God sometimes reach it already here on earth. Here below, nothing equals the union of two hearts equally filled with God, when they know one another perfectly for having prayed, toiled, hoped, trembled and struggled together—and for not having kept secrets from one another for years (the disciple revealed everything to the father, and the father formed the disciple in his image). A paradoxical intimacy is then established, equally composed of detachment and attachment, because detachment itself, by freeing the soul from every trace of self-love, gives attachment a strength, a serenity, and a certainty that belong only to the divine order of charity: Pachomius and Theodore of Tabennisi, Barsanuphius and John the Prophet, Plato and Theodore the Studite, Symeon the Studite and Symeon the New Theologian, and others, not omitting Barlaam and Joasaph, who were expressly invented by someone who knew byzantine spirituality very well to represent the ideal of a father and son according to the spirit. They agreed to part because they knew that they were not leaving one other; their separation in space leaves this union, which is spiritual, intact. 'Why did you leave me? But you did not leave me. How did you depart from me? But you are in me.'[6] When two persons are united in such a way, distance still causes suffering, but it is a transfigured suffering, and one no longer knows whether in itself this is not joy. At any rate, it leaves intact both the unceasing joy of an invisible presence, and the fortuitous joy of a presence regained. When Joasaph finally came to the entrance of the cave where Barlaam lived,

> He knocked and said, 'Your blessings, Father.' Upon hearing his voice, Barlaam came out of the cave and recognized through the spirit the one who could hardly be recognized (so greatly had he changed). But Joasaph recognized his spiritual father at once, as endowed with the same facial features. The old man, turned toward the East, and said a prayer of thanksgiving. After the 'Amen,' the two hastened to embrace at once, quenching the desire of long duration, without being sated. When they had embraced each other abundantly and reflected, they sat down. . . .[7]

Spiritualizing a human being does not mean searing the heart, but freeing it from all false love in order to let it manifest all the gradations of human feelings in the service of divine charity.

NOTES

1. SHOULD ONE ACCEPT SUCH FUNCTIONS?

1. Walther Voelker, *Das Vollkommenheitsideal des Origenes* (Tübingen, 1931) 169-75.
2. See Karl Heussi, *Der Ursprung des Mönchtums* (Tübingen, 1936) 167.
3. *Alph.*, Sisoes n. 16; PG 65: 397A [CS 59:215-16]; *Vitae Patrum* V, 15, n. 46.
4. *Vitae patrum*, n. 43.
5. *Ibid.*, n. 81; PL 73: 967B.
6. *Ibid.*, n. 15.
7. Irénée Hausherr and G. Horn, ed. and trans., *Vie de Syméon le Nouveau Théologien par Nicétas Stethatos*, *Orientalia Christiana* 12 (Rome, 1928) n. 30, p. 40.
8. Acts 1:1.
9. Rom 2:21.
10. Leontius of Neapolis, *Vita S. Symeonis Sali Confessoris*, Prol. n. 1; PG 93: 1669AB.
11. *Alph.*, Macarius n. 2; PG 65: 260-61 [CS 59:106]; n. 31, col. 273C [113].
12. *Ibid.*, n. 31.
13. See *Alph.*, Poemen n. 8; PG 65: 321C-24A [140].
14. John the Deacon, *Vita S. Josephi Hymnographi* n. 7; PG 105: 945B.
15. *Ibid.*, n. 13, col. 952A.
16. See R. Hofmann, *Die heroische Tugend*, p. 161ff. *Sine humano ratiocinio* came to be one of the signs of heroic virtue, according to the theologians that inspired Cardinal Lambertini.
17. Symeon the New Theologian, *Logos* 88, ed. Denis de Zagora (Venice, 1790) 507; *Oratio XXIV*; PG 120: 435AC.
18. *Ibid.*, p. 207; PG 120: 435D.

2. PRAYING FOR ONE'S SPIRITUAL CHILDREN

1. Symeon the New Theologian, *Logos* 88, ed. Denis de Zagora (Venice, 1790) vol. 1, p. 508, cl. 2=PG 120: 436C.
2. *Alph.*, Antony n. 16 [CS 59:3].
3. For example, *Letter* 459, p. 227; *Letters* 503, 504, 505, p. 248, etc., ed. Nicodemus the Hagiorite (Venice, 1816).
4. *Martyrium Polycarpi* VIII. 1; trans. Kirsopp Lake, *The Apostolic Fathers*, vol. 2 (Cambridge: Harvard University Press, 1959) 323.
5. *Pseudo-Basilian Monastic Constitutions*, ch. 22, n. 4; PG 31: 1409A.
6. Heb 7:25.
7. Jas 5:16.
8. Mt 9:12.
9. Lk 18:1-8.
10. Barsanuphius and John, *Letter* 541, p. 263.

11. *Vitae patrum* III, n. 144; PL 73: 788C-89A; for a somewhat longer version, see *ibid.*, V, XIV, n. 16, col. 951A-C.

12. *Alph.*, Amoun n. 3; PG 65: 120B [32].

13. *Doctrina* I, n. 16; PG 88: 1637C [See also, 'On Renunciation,' in *Dorotheos of Gaza. Discourses and Sayings*, trans. Eric P. Wheeler, Cistercian Studies 33 (Kalamazoo, 1977) 90.—ed.]

14. Barsanuphius and John, *Letter* 383, p. 195ff.

15. Evergetinos, *Synagogē* I, ch. 39, p. 136.

16. *Ibid.*, p. 135.

17. *Alph.*, Sisoes n. 12; PG 65: 396A [214].

18. VI, II, 14, PL 73: 1003C.

19. Paul Bedjan, *Acta Martyrum et Sanctorum* VII (1897) 601.

20. See 'Nilus', *De Oratione*, ch. 34; PG 79: 1173D.

21. *Ibid.*, col. 877, n. 4.

22. *Letter* 541, p. 263.

23. *Alph.*, Antony n. 8 [4].

24. *Vitae patrum* V, 19; PL 73: 878AB; for a longer version, see *ibid.*, III, 13; col. 748B-46B.

25. Paul Evergetinos I, ch. 39, p. 136ᵇ=*Vitae Patrum* V, VII, 43, PL 73: 903B-4B.

26. Barsanuphius, *Letter* 482, p. 194.

27. *Vitae patrum* III, n. 8, PL 73: 742D-3A.

28. *Letter* 482, p. 194.

29. *Letter* 70, p. 38.

30. P. Lond. (1923-1929).

31. Maria Teresa Cavassini, 'Lettere Cristiane nei papiri greci d'Egitto,' in *Aeg* (Anno XXXIV, 1954) 280ff.

32. *Vita S. Pachomii Abbatis Tabennensis*, caput XXXII, PL 73: 252AB. The *Vita Prima*, n. 38, ed. François Halkin (Brussels, 1932) p. 23, gives a shorter formula.

33. See Halkin's authoritative statement in a review of Franz Dölger's book, in *AnBoll* 71 (1953) 475-80.

34. *Vita Barlaam et Joasaph*, ch. 21; PG 96: 1053C-56A.

35. See Lk 1:48.

36. *Vita Barlaam et Joasaph*, ch. 39; PG 96: 1232AB.

37. See Rom 16:16, etc.

38. *Vita Barlaam et Joasph*, ch. 40; PG 96: 1233B.

39. *Alph.*, Arsenius n. 35; PG 65: 101C [14].

3. CARRYING PART OF THE BURDEN

1. *Alph.*, Agathon n. 9; cfr n. 8 and n. 29; PG 65: 111B [18-19].

2. See above, pp. 59-61.

3. *Hypotypose de S. Christodule* n. 28, ed. Miklosisch-Mueller, *Acta et Diplomata* VI, p. 69.

4. Prologue of the *Typikon* of the Evergetis, by Timothy, ch. 17, ed. Dmitrievskij, *Opisanie . . .* I, p. 537ff; the same 'Catéchèse au preposé' is found in the *Typikon* of the Theotokos *tōn Hēliou Bōmōn*, ch. 41, *loc. cit.*, p. 755; in the *Diataxis* of Nilus for the monastery of Our Lady of Machairas in Cyprus, ch. 55, Miklosisch-Mueller, *Acta . . .*, V, p. 426.

5. Barsanuphius and John, *Letter* 167, p. 88.

6. *Ibid.*, *Letter* 168.

7. Abba Hēsaion, *Logos* 1, n. 2, ed. Augustinos Iordanites (Jerusalem, 1911) 3.
8. 13, 17.
9. *Letter* 57, p. 29.
10. Rom 2:21.
11. *Letter* 59, p. 30.
12. 1 Jn 3:16.
13. 1 Pet 2:13.
14. Jas 2:10.
15. Barsanuphius and John, *Letter* 242, p. 133.
16. *Ibid.*, *Letter* 252, p. 137.

4. LOVING ONE'S SPIRITUAL CHILDREN

1. *Epistolarum Liber* I, 2, *Platōni pneumatikō patri*, PG 99: 909B.
2. See Lev 19:18.
3. Barsanuphius, *Letter* 481, p. 237.
4. Heb 2:13; Is 8:18.
5. Barsanuphius, *Letter* 221, p. 111ff.
6. Theodore the Studite, *Epistolarum Liber*, 3; PG 99: 920A.
7. *Vita Barlaam et Joasaph*, cap. 37; PG 96: 1218Cff

V

THE NEED FOR OPENNESS OF HEART

1. THE PROPER FOCUS OF OPENNESS

FOR NO OTHER CHAPTER of this study do we have
so many documents. Constantly, untiringly these
works teach the need for spiritual direction, or more
specifically for 'openness of heart' (*ouverture d'âme*) which is
not only, not even primarily, 'openness of conscience' (*ouverture de conscience*). What is essential is to show the spiritual
advisor not one's sins but one's thoughts (*logismoi*). In more
recent times we have seen novices being asked to confess their
former life to the hegumen so that he might know them. During the more ancient times about which the *Vitae Patrum* testi-
fy, the remembrance of the years passed in the world, perhaps
in sin, is never brought up except to exhort to compunction
(*penthos*)—without the slightest allusion to a detailed confession one would make either for one's peace of mind, or even
less to make oneself known. What the spiritual father needs to
know and the spiritual child ought to reveal to him are one's
actual dispositions which can be inferred from the 'movements
of the heart' (*mouvement des esprits*), without any need to stir up

the past, a too detailed remembrance of which might do more harm than good. 'When past sins are remembered in detail (*kat'eidos*, literally, in appearance) they harm a man of good hope. For if they again arise in the soul accompanied by grief, they repel hope; and if they are visualized without grief, they again introduce the old defilement within,' wrote one of the most famous spiritual masters.[1] It is worthwhile to cite the paragraph that follows, the greek text of which is supplied by the latin editor Galland with a *Caute legas* (read with caution notice):

> When the mind [*nous*, we would say, 'the soul'], through self-denial, embraces hope alone, then, under the pretext of confessing, the enemy represents old sins as in a picture, in order to awaken passions consigned to oblivion by the grace of God, and to harm a man secretly. For then, even if he is shining and filled with aversion for the passions, he will become perplexed, detained by the vices that were perpetrated. If he is confused and loves the passions, he will familiarize himself with these suggestions, so that such a remembrance will indeed by an anticipation (of sin) instead of a confession. If you want to bring a blameless confession to God, do not recollect your faults in detail, . . . (you would defile the mind), but resist their enticement magnanimously.[2]

Despite the impressive authorities by means of which Galland justifies his *Caute legas*—Jean Marie Branchelli, Bellarmine, Labbé, and Combefis[3]—this recommendation of Saint Mark the Ascetic is not suspect; it touches neither upon theology nor upon the sacrament of penance. It is entirely psychological, made up of experience and discernment for the use of people tending most energetically toward the goal to be reached, perfection through union with God. Mark the Ascetic's observation expresses a law which has often been observed by all true masters of the spiritual life. The author of *The Cloud of Unknowing* says the same thing when he writes at the end of his book: 'It is not what you are or what you have been that God sees with his all-merciful eyes, but what you want to be.'[4]

What is important for the director to know and even more for the disciple to reveal are 'movements of the heart' (of the mind), suggestions, inner promptings. When such an impulse or inner prompting develops into an outward deed, into consent of the will, it would be too late to show all this to the director. One must then go to a confessor, and resolve not to wait next time. The psychology of the ascetics, even before Augustine, differentiated between moments of temptation. There is the *prosbolē* (suggestion in thought), which is free from blame (*anaitios*), as Mark the Ascetic demonstrated against the Messalians, at this point predecessors of the Jansenists.[5] Next follows the *syndiasmos* (coupling), an inner dialogue with the suggestion (temptation), then *palē* or struggle against it, which may end with victory or with consent (*synkatathesis*), actual sin. When repeated, such acts produce a *pathos* (passion) properly speaking, and in the end, a terrible *aichmalōsia*, a 'captivity of the soul,' which is no longer able to shake the yoke of the Evil One.[6]

The proper object of *exagoreusis tōn logismōn* (revelation of thoughts) is the first stage of this process, the *prosbolē*. One must crush the serpent's head as soon as it appears. To massacre the children of Babylon from their tenderest age; to uproot the plant before it grows strong roots—these are classical metaphors in the matter. All this is done through an entire strategy: *nepsis* (vigilance), watchfulness, the guarding of the heart (*custodia cordis*) and of the mind, prayer, especially the invocation of the name of Jesus, and so forth.

An essential part of this war is specifically recourse to the spiritual father. An anonymous 'old man' will speak in the name of all:

When evil thoughts harass you, do not hide them, but tell them at once to your spiritual father. The more one hides one's thoughts, the more they multiply and the stronger they become. As a serpent flees instantly as soon as it has left its hole, so an evil thought dissipates as soon as it begins to be disclosed. Like a worm in wood, so a (hidden) evil thought devastates the heart. The person who discloses his thoughts is soon healed. Whoever hides them makes himself sick through pride.[7]

These classic comparisons indicate that the Fathers were not unaware of the bad effects of repression.

Meanwhile, this is not the only reason that makes revelation of thoughts indispensable. There are two others which are more important because they are no longer merely psychological but properly ascetic and spiritual: the need for discernment (*diakrisis*) and the necessity of denying one's own will (*voluntas propria*).

2. REASONS FOR THIS DISCLOSURE

Diakrisis in the spiritual father is required so urgently because it is *ex hypothesi* lacking in younger, and indeed many older, people. Hence the terrible danger of illusion, exaggeration, of theoretical and especially practical errors. One is on the road to ruin, 'if one is not restrained by the bit of prudence and discernment.'[1] On this crucial point it is once again Saint Antony who was to formulate the fundamental axioms. He says: 'There have been some who broke their bodies by asceticism, but ended far from God because they lacked discernment.'[2] Also, 'I have known monks who after performing great labors have fallen into madness, because they counted on their own works; in their delusion they ignored the command that says, "Ask your father, let him teach you."'[3] Finally, the most meticulous of those who preach disclosure of thoughts will never say anything stronger than Saint Antony's last sentence of the *Apophthegms*: 'If it can be done, a monk must fearlessly tell the elder how many steps he has taken or how many drops of water he drinks in his cell, to discover whether he thereby makes a mistake.'[4] Indeed, Saint Antony 'had seen all the enemy's snares spread over the earth. Sighing over this, he says, "Who can escape them?" Then he heard a voice saying, "Humility."[5] Moreover, temptations are necessary: no one will be saved without them.'[6] The demons have power only over the presumptuous who do not use the appropriate means of resisting them. Through prayer and openness of heart with one's spiritual father, hell itself will contribute to the sanctification of the elect, despite itself.

On the contrary, everything is to be feared when one trusts one's own lights. 'Abba Poemen said, "In no one does the enemy take such pleasure as in the person who does not want to reveal his thoughts."'[7] We could make a fine collection by gathering the more or less frightening stories designed to convince the ascetics. Saint Antony has already told one[8] of a young thaumaturge who came to a sorry end. Everyone knows the one about poor Hero, told by Palladius in his *Lausiac History* and by Cassian in a longer version.[9]

And then again, another one, named Ptolemy, had lived a life which is difficult or impossible to describe [at the beginning he had lived beyond Scetis at a place called *Klimax*, that is, the Steps, where no one could live because the brothers' well was eighteen miles away]. He had brought many Cilician vessels, and during the months of December and January he collected the dew (there is much dew in those regions) with a sponge, and he remained there for fifteen years. Having alienated himself from the teachings and the company of holy men and from the profit and the frequent partaking of the mysteries [the sacraments], he left the straight road to such a degree that he said things were not important in the least.[10] Hedged in by such satanic thoughts, they say that poor Ptolemy lost his mind; he was rumored to roam as far as Egypt, surrendering to gluttony and drunkenness, and speaking to no one. This misfortune happened to Ptolemy as a result of his presumptuousness, according to what is written, 'Those who have no direction, fall like leaves.'[11]

We cannot transcribe here the rather long but instructive story of James of Jerusalem, a disciple of Saint Sabas, who committed greater and greater stupidities every time he allowed himself to be carried away by his generosity.[12]

Furthermore, Cassian (for once!) summarizes this teaching of the Fathers very nicely:

> In order to more easily lead [young monks] to this result [true humility], they warn them against a dangerous confusion, and teach them not to conceal evil, ruinous thoughts in their heart but to disclose them to their elder as soon as they arise, and not to entrust anything to their own discernment while forming a judgment—but to believe to be good or evil what the senior has declared so after investigation. Thus it happens that the cunning enemy cannot besiege an inexperienced, unaware monk: he cannot by any craft ensnare someone he sees protected not by his own discernment but by that of his elder, someone who cannot be persuaded to conceal the suggestions he throws into his heart like fiery darts. The most subtle demon cannot hurl down or destroy a young monk, unless he has enticed him to conceal his thoughts either through pride or through shame. They claim that the universal and clear proof that a thought comes from the devil is that we are ashamed of disclosing it to the elder.[13]

The quotations from Cassian, and others, were inserted into the *Vitae Patrum*[14] and the *Synagogē* of Paul Evergetinos,[15] which proves the importance attached to them. Philoxenes of Mabbug, who did not know Cassian, his contemporary, agreed with him when, to frighten a monk who was too keen on contemplation, he mentioned in his hearing the case of Assuana, a well known hymnographer who committed suicide, the result of not sufficiently discerning spirits, and of someone named Adelphus who for the same reason became the leader of Messalianism, the great heresy in eastern spirituality.[16]

Saint Pachomius even went so far as to say that 'many men . . . killed themselves. One, in a state of ecstasy (*hōs ekstatikos*), threw himself off a cliff. Another disemboweled himself with a sword. . . . Others followed different methods. It is very bad indeed not to confess one's passion [the temptation of blasphemy] to a knowledgeable man before it becomes a chronic condition.'[17] Without the spiritual advisor's counsel, everything is suspect, especially among the young. More than suspect, to be condemned out of hand, because it can only lead to disaster, on the pretext of greater perfection. 'A certain brother, renouncing the world and having accepted the monk's habit, became a hermit at once [evidently without consulting anyone], saying, "I want to be a solitary". But when the neighboring men heard about it, they came and threw him out and made him go around to all the cells of the brothers and do penance before each one, saying, "Forgive me, I am not a solitary, but someone who recently became a monk."'[18] To this anonymous tale can be juxtaposed very nicely the detailed story which the great hagiographer Cyril of Scythopolis told about himself.

When the time had come to fulfill the prophecy of Saint Sabas, who had predicted that Cyril would be his disciple,[19] the young man left his father's house, attended the dedication of the new church of the Theotokos at Jerusalem, and went to the lavra of Saint Sabas to meet the venerable John the Hesychast, ninety years of age,

in order to entrust all his interests to him and to receive from him counsel pleasing to God. I heard him say to me, 'If you want to be saved, take up residence in the monastery of the great Euthymius'. But I, young and vain as I was, scorned his order and went down the Jordan with the intention of establishing myself in one of the monasteries in that region. Not only did I not succeed in this, but for six months I was also seriously ill in the lavra of Calamon [close to the Dead Sea]. As I had fallen into great sadness and anxiety because of my isolation as a stranger (*xeniteia*) and my weakness, and because I did not live under the yoke of a community, this enlightened old man appeared to me in a dream and told me, 'You have been punished enough for disobeying the order I gave you. Get up right now and go to Jericho where you will meet a monk named Gerontius in the guest quarters of the monastery of Abba Euthymius. Enter the monastery with him, and you will be saved.' As soon as I woke up I arose and, comforted at once, I received Holy Communion, took nourishment and went up to Jericho; and the fathers were amazed at this sudden great change. In this manner I settled in the monastery of Saint Euthymius in the month of July [543] and from then on I often went to see him to confide to him everything that was of concern to me.[20]

Toward the end of the tenth century—the time when Symeon the New Theologian was ejected from the Studios because of his attachment to his spiritual father—Patriarch Antony (974-978 or 980), himself a Studite, tells us that *exagoreusis* fell into disuse among the monks. We still have an exhortation he gave to lead them back to it.[21] *Exagoreusis* is the foundation of all asceticism. Antony proves this from Holy Scripture (but there, the references are mostly to the confession of sin), then from the classical comparison with bodily ailments: 'What happens with the infirmities of the body also happens with the ailments of the soul: the physician applies his care and cure to the place he has seen with his eyes and diagnosed well. But the person who surrenders to his own tastes and acts according to his own ideas, without revealing his soul's disease to his spiritual father through *exagoreusis*, draws upon himself the frightening verdict (Isaiah 5:21), "Woe to those who think themselves wise and believe themselves cunning." Physicians themselves need other physicians when they are ill, for their infirmity ruins their art. . . .' The author of the *Scala Paradisi* expressed himself more or less in these same terms: acknowledged bruises do not get worse but will be healed.[22] Nothing gives so much power to demons and to the enemy's suggestions as entertaining them in your heart. The soul that is attentive to *exagoreusis* is held back from sin as by a brake.

What is more luminous than a soul devoted to this exercise? Those who have experienced it know this: what hope, what freedom from care, what liberty they acquire! And also, what absence of fear, even before death, what a mitigation of the struggles, what a quieting down of thoughts; finally, what purity of soul! What good is it to talk so much? You, man, enter into yourself. Examine the disposition of your soul when it severely judges and stigmatizes its own thoughts; how it is disposed when it wants to leave them unacknowledged, and one does not want to be instructed by another. You will be competent to rectify everything. By always postponing and by retreating, without any profit, you prove from the facts that the enemy has revealed his mystery to you: you are afraid of offending him and of losing his friendship by disclosing this condition to spiritual persons.[23]

The rest of the text blames the Studites for having abandoned this fundamental practice, 'as if we had risen above human nature and the human condition.' The old Studite who had become a patriarch knew how to use irony on his colleagues who had remained monks: 'But I am perhaps the only one to be subjected to evil thoughts, and my words derive from the fact that I judge others according to my own passions, while you are without evil passion or thought or prompting! Ah! Lord, Lord of all, if that were only possible! . . . But it is not; it is not' (p.10). The result was laxity because charity disappeared and all types of self-love, haughtiness, and harshness developed.

A century and a half later, in the *Typikon* he wrote for the monastery of the Holy Saviour at Messina, its first archimandrite Saint Luke enumerated the causes of laxity he prided himself in having eliminated: the use of meat, vulgar conduct in visits that were all too free, idiorrhythm ('self-sufficiency'), latrophagy (eating in secret), *peculium* (private savings), and so forth. 'In their place were introduced *exagoreusis*, good order, obedience, and humiliations. . . .'[24]

Together with the need for discernment (*diakrisis*), what also compels the revelation of thoughts is that basic precept of striving for perfection: the *abneget semetipsum* ('let one deny oneself'). In the common language of the eastern ascetics (and of Saint Benedict), the self to be denied is one's own will (*voluntas propria*). *Ekkopē tou oikeou thelēmatos*, the cutting out of one's own will, is one of the sovereign mottos of monasticism. Now is not the time to explain its theory. We need only say that, according to the Fathers, this is done through obedience. Here again, there is good reason to limit ourselves chiefly to ancient times, to situations when the spiritual father was not an hegumen and when, as a consequence, he did not give orders for the good of an organized community, but only to assure the peace and promote the progress of one disciple.

Here, Saint Antony gives us only a very general principle: 'Obedience together with continence (*meta egkrateias*) tames the wild beasts.'[25] But his maxims quoted earlier with reference to discernment also hold true for obedience. After him, with the help of experience, it was understood better and better that there is no virtue without self-denial, no conformity to the will of God without the sacrifice of one's own will, and no charity without the uprooting of a perverse self-will (*philauteia*). There also would be discussions on the relative pre-eminence of eremiticism and of cenobitism, and one of the arguments in favor of the latter would be the more perfect practice of obedience. Nothing could be more unreasonable than to choose a spiritual father according to the drift of one's natural inclinations.

A brother said to a famous old man, 'Abba, I would like to find a senior according to my own will, and to stay with him.' The old man said, 'You do well to search,

Master!' . . . The other did not understand what the old man had said. And after it appeared that the old man had approved of this, the old man said to him, 'And so, if you find an old man according to your own will, you plan to stay with him?' 'Yes,' the other replied, 'this is exactly what I want, if I could find one according to my will.' Then the old man said to him, '[All this] is not so you can follow the old man's will, but so he will follow yours, so that you can lead an easy life.' The brother understood what he said. He arose, threw himself to the ground in repentance, and said, 'Forgive me . . .'.[26]

A true zeal for perfection, on the contrary, leads one to prefer a spiritual father who is demanding, energetic, and not to be manipulated.

The best father will be the one who succeeds best in securing the sacrifice of this *voluntas propria*, for it is built like a wall between God and the soul.[27] This is so serious that 'if you would see a young man ascending into heaven by his own will, catch him by the foot and throw him to the ground, because it is not profitable to him.'[28] The most famous of the spiritual fathers distinguished themselves by care in preaching this renunciation, above all Saint Barsanuphius.[29] 'Our Lord has said, "If anyone will come after me, let him deny himself, and take up his cross, and follow me." Now, denying oneself means severing one's own will in everything and to confine oneself to the *apsephiston* [indifference to all earthly profit, as not worth reckoning].'[30] In short, all *ascesis* therefore boils down to this sacrifice of self, of our *own* will. We consent to do this only with great difficulty; to see clearly into ourselves is even more difficult. We do not know which spirit moves us inwardly. One's own will, personal interest, in a word *philauteia* (self-love), thanks especially to certain sanctimonious airs, succeeds in masquerading as the love of God, of which it is the irreconcilable opponent. It is especially for this reason that one needs a clear-sighted spiritual guide, charitable enough that he is not afraid of speaking clearly.

A brother questioned an old man, saying, 'In my cell I do everything that is recommended, but I find no consolation from God.' The old man replied, 'This happens to you [four unintelligible words] because you want your will to be done.' The brother says, 'What do you order me to do, Father?' The old man replies, 'Go, join a God-fearing man, humble yourself before him by surrendering your will to him, and then you will find consolation from God.'[31]

Here is a variant of the same story. Abba Poemen says that somebody once asked abba Paisios: 'What should I do for my soul? It has become insensitive (*hoti anaisthetei*: a frightening disposition!) and does not fear God.' He answered, 'Go, join a man who fears God; his company will teach you the fear of God as well.'[32]

Certainly, to obtain this result, consultation at long intervals, as solitaries did on occasion, is not enough.[33] According to the hallowed expression, one must *kathēstai en hypotagē patros pneumatikou*, remain, persevere, be fixed in submission to a spiritual father. This is what numerous apophthegms that compare the various *politeiai* or types of asceticism[34] state or imply. Anachoretism is not yet condemned, as it is by Saint Basil, in the name of the human social character. It is not the common life that is recommended for various reasons, but a relatively eremetical life only for the advantages of submission. It is probably this eremitism tempered by the mutual presence of a master and a disciple that abba Ammonas was thinking of when he maintained that solitude is more effective in breaking self will. *One* leader and *one* disciple; understandably, this can be terrible yet marvellous! John Climacus knew the 'remarkable athlete who for eighteen years never heard with his fleshly ears the voice of his superior say, "May you be saved"; but every day with his inward sense he heard the Lord say, not "may you be saved" [an optative, and uncertain], but "you are saved" [an affirmation, and certain].'[35]

True spiritual fathers are at the same time severe and very good. Such was the Saint Ammonas we have just mentioned. 'Beloved in the Lord,' he writes, 'you whom I love whole-heartedly and whose profit I seek like my own good because you have been given to me as children according to God. . . .'[36] But precisely this charity compelled him to do everything to obtain from his children the sacrifice which is the pre-condition of every good, the renunciation of their own will. 'I hear that temptation is besetting you, and I am afraid it comes to you because of your fault. Indeed, I have learned that you want to abandon your place, and this has grieved me. . . . For I know very well that if you leave your place, it will profit you nothing, because it is not the will of God.' The rest subtly teaches how to discern what in us comes from the Enemy, or from ourselves, or what comes from God. 'Of all these things, God accepts only what is his.'[37] Specifically, God does not approve of a pretended apostolate undertaken on one's own initiative. One is an apostle only through the will of God who sends. God only sends persons who 'have overcome their own will'. And this victory over one's own will is impossible outside of solitude:[38] the entire context and the very existence of a correspondence prove that Ammonas understood 'solitude' to mean at the school of a spiritual master. 'In this, and in all other things, listen to your masters, so that you might make progress.'[39]

Likewise, Saint Barsanuphius combined an uncommon vigor with a goodness that was even tenderness. Here is a series of letters addressed to the same spiritual son. On the part of the disciple, it starts, as always, in a solemn fashion: 'I turn to your holiness, Father. . . .' The reply: 'Your holiness writes to my holiness to pray for your *theophilia* (love of God). In turn, I, the unintelligent father, demand the same thing from you, the intelligent son. . . .'[40] From being playful, the tone rapidly becomes affectionate: 'Brother, I greet you in the Lord, and I pray that he may strengthen your charity. . . .'[41] 'My brother, my dearly beloved in the Lord, the assurance of my spiritual affection for you gives me, in Christ. . . .'[42] And then, in quick succession: 'Brother *akēdiasta* [succumbing to sloth] and murmurer.'[43] 'Limp brother. . . .'[44] And this brother was ill! With those who were well, Barsanuphius got even ruder, but under the waterfall of his rebukes one senses clearly the inclination of a heart entirely filled with good will. How many people complain about lacking devotion (in those days they said 'compunction'), but believe nonetheless that they are full of good will! Only the will of God is good; all self-will is bad, it desiccates.

> Brother, you are kidding yourself by saying, 'I want,' because you do not really want. . . . What prevents the arrival of compunction in you is your will. For if a person does not cut off his own will, his heart cannot be affected. It is a lack of faith [in God and, what amounts to the same thing, in the spiritual father] that does not allow you to cut off your own will; and lack of faith proceeds from our desire for human glory. . . . This is why the most tenacious demons make sport of you and make difficult things which are easy. . . . To save a man is hard toil, brother. Cut off these three things: your own will, self-justification, the desire to please, and compunction will in all truth come to you, and God will protect you from all evil. I abjure you, brother, take care: rejoice when you are beaten, rebuked, insulted, chastised. . . . *There* is a path of salvation. It if suits you, walk on it; and the Lord will stretch out his hand. If you do not want to do this, it is up to you to watch out. For everyone has freedom for what he wants. If you deliver it over to another, you will be free of care: he will bear your worries. Choose what you want.[45]

The only *raison d'être* of spiritual fatherhood is to lead from the stage of slavery to the freedom of the children of God, according to a very ancient division of the three ways: slaves, faithful servants, and sons.[46] This blessed transformation takes place only when the human will is utterly replaced by the will of God. The person who does not consent to such abnegation deceives himself into believing that he has been or is searching for a spiritual father. What he seeks is complicity. Neither Saint Barsanuphius nor any other 'diacritic' would be a party to such deception, such a waste of time.

To finish, let us read a portion of a letter in which Saint Barsanuphius explains himself in plain language:

> Brothers, the affection [charity] of the Fathers for their children is one thing, the charity of brothers for their brothers another. The perfection of the spiritual fathers' charity for their children is such that it contains nothing that is carnal or could cause damage; the Fathers have the assurance of their state of soul which is entirely spiritual. In whatever they say or do, they have no other concern than to attend to the good of the young in all things. Animated by this charity, they do not keep silent about their faults; on the contrary, they reprove and correct their children. Indeed, it is to them that the word of Saint Paul is addressed 'reprove, rebuke, exhort'.[47] This is what your abba often does, and you do not understand when he reproves, rebukes, and exhorts you. The fact that, because of charity, he does not let faults pass, shows that his affection for you is spiritual. Everyone loves his neighbor according to his own degree of perfection. . . .[48]

These were the reasons of a personal nature that demand the revelation of thoughts. There is still another, for the common benefit. It is by practicing it that one is trained to receive it, in turn, from others. It is through this that abba Poemen became what his name signifies, an eminent shepherd of souls; and this anecdote serves as a preface to the long list—the longest of the entire *Alphabetical Collection*—of his Sayings and deeds:

> While he was still young, Abba Poemen went one day to an old man to ask him about three thoughts. Having

reached the old man, he forgot one of the three and went back to his cell. But as he was stretching out his hand to turn the key, he remembered the thought which he had forgotten and leaving the key, he returned to the old man. The old man said to him, 'You come quickly, brother.' He told him, 'At the moment when I was putting out my hand to grasp the key, I remembered the thought which I was trying to find; so I did not open the door, but have retraced my steps.' Now the length of the way was very great and the old man said to him, 'Poemen, Shepherd of the flock,[49] your name will be known throughout Egypt.'[50]

Poemen himself had learned this lesson from the ancients: 'Abba Poemen relates that abba Paphnutius said, "During the entire life of the old men, I used to see them twice every month—the distance was twelve miles—and I disclosed to them every one of my thoughts. . . ."'[51] What is true for the exercise of authority also holds for spiritual direction: one can only do it well after undergoing it properly. All the great directors began by being perfect disciples: Saint Pachomius of Saint Palamon, Saint Theodore of Saint Pachomius, Saint Dorotheos of Saint Barsanuphius, Saint Theodore the Studite of Saint Platon, and so forth.

Listening to one or another of them speaking about the need to open one's heart to the spiritual father is well worth while.

3. TESTIMONIES OF SOME GREAT SPIRITUAL FATHERS

Saint Basil, the great legislator of cenobitism, expressed his teaching on the subject in one of the shortest of his *Detailed Rules*: 'Everyone of the subordinates—at least if he wants to make progress worthy of mention and desires to lead in a firm and stable manner a life that conforms to the commands of Christ—must not keep any of the movements of his soul hidden inside, nor must he utter any ill considered word, but must reveal the secrets of the heart to his brothers who have been appointed to heal the sick with compassion and sympathy.'[1]

Saint Gregory of Nyssa did not have the same taste as his brother from Caesarea: the mystic and the philosopher stood in contrast to the organizer and moralist. In the matter before us, he became, for the benefit of virgins, the theoretician of the practice the elders had taught to monks. The entire last chapter of his *On Virginity* is devoted to this subject:[2] 'That it is necessary for the person who wants to understand this exacting type of life to be taught by someone who has achieved it successfully.' There are books, of course, but instructions given in person and deeds are clearer and more effective. Someone who wants to study a foreign language cannot not do it alone: he needs to be instructed by people who know it. It is the same in all other human enterprises. It is often dangerous to trust one's own judgment, for example, in medicine. Direction, then, is 'the philosophy', the medical science, teaching us the therapies for every passion that affects the soul. One should therefore not indulge in conjectures and intuitions, but become the disciple of an experienced master. 'Generally, in all kinds of things, youth is an unreliable counselor; it does not happen very often that one finds a serious matter managed well by someone who has not consulted gray hairs. The more a goal to be pursued is nobler than others, the more indispensable it is to provide for our security.' In virginity, then, the question is not, as elsewhere, about a loss of money or reputation or advancement, but of the salvation of the soul. Beginners must therefore above all seek a good guide and instructor in the way of *ascesis*. 'Woe to the man who is by himself with no one to help him up when he falls down.'[3] The traps awaiting the imprudent are more numerous than one could tell: vainglory, excessive fasting leading to death, 'as if God takes pleasure in these types of sacrifices'; the fantasies of visionaries 'who take their hallucinations and deceptive dreams more seriously than the teachings of the Gospel, and who call their fantasies revelation'; or, on the contrary, a relaxation that is satisfied with the name and the appearance of asceticism in a life like that of those who do not profess it. Subsequently, Gregory of Nyssa declared that in his day models were not lacking, and he obligingly drew an idealized portrait of the director he advised one to choose.

Saint Dorotheos, schooled by the two famous spiritual directors Saint Barsanuphius and Saint John the Prophet, could hardly fail to insist 'that one should not walk by one's own judgment'. The chapter is too long to be quoted here; but it would figure nicely, in the right place, in an anthology on spiritual direction, so solid and traditional is his teaching, so pleasing and persuasive his style. Unfortunately, the printed greek text is so defective that it is still better, while we wait for a critical edition, to read the intentionally literal translation by Balthasar Cordier,[5] 'a translation remarkable for its precision, its simplicity, and conciseness'.[6] As usual, Dorotheos calls on Holy Scripture and the Fathers; and sometimes, with charming ingenuity, he tells a story of which he was either the witness or the hero.

> It is said in Proverbs, 'Those who have no direction fall like leaves; safety lies in many advisors.'[7] Not 'in many advisors', as if one had to consult the first person to come along, but one must tell everything to the person one trusts, and ask advice on everything. Without this, the devil has an easy turn deceiving by means of virtue itself. His trump card is one's own will. This is why abba Poemen said, that 'one's own will is a brass wall between man and God'.[8]

An admirable line. 'If human will is added to what is right [a merit, a virtue], one's conduct will not be honorable', Poemen continued.[9] Dorotheos exclaims: 'Oh! The logic in the sayings of the Fathers!' When someone believes he is virtuous but does not humbly open the heart to someone wiser, he is lost. 'The devil detests hearing someone asking questions for the salvation of his soul.' This is easy to understand:

He [the devil] knows his trick will be discovered by the mere fact of the interrogation. . . .; he hates and fears nothing so much as being discovered, because he will no longer have the man available to set his traps. If the soul is made secure by revealing everything, she will hear someone competent say, 'do this; do not do that; this is good, that is not good; this is just, that is your own will,' and also, 'it is not the right time to do this.' Another time she hears, 'now is the right moment'—the devil then no longer knows how he can harm or overthrow her, since she is governed and guarded on all sides. In her is verified that 'salvation lies in many advisors'. This is what the Evil One does not want; he hates it. What he wants is to do evil. And he finds abundant joy in those who lack someone to guide them. They tumble like leaves.[10]

To support this last assertion, Dorotheos recalls a long story taken from the Sayings of Macarius.[11] Then he draws the conclusion from it: 'I, however, say this again, I do not know of one fall caused by a reason other than this (confidence in self). You see someone who has fallen? Know that he had appointed himself as director. Nothing is more troublesome, nothing more deadly than to govern oneself.'[12] Also, Dorotheos congratulates himself for not ever hiding anything from

his senior, abba John. I never did anything without his knowledge. Sometimes my thought said to me, 'Will the old man not tell you this? Why bother him?' But I said to my thought, 'A curse on you, on your discernment, your judgment, your good sense, your intelligence, because what you know, you know from the devil.' I went directly to ask the old man; sometimes he happened to give me the answer I had previously considered. Then my thoughts said to me, 'Now what? Don't you see it is as I told you? And you have disturbed the old man unseasonably.' And I said to my thoughts, 'But now it is good; now it proceeds from the Holy Spirit. What is your own is worthless; it is from the devil because of your passionate condition. . . .' And believe me, brothers, I was in such great repose, such great freedom from care, that I very frequently was displeased with it, as I believe I told you at another time.[13] Indeed, I had heard, 'We all have to experience many hardships before we enter the Kingdom of God,'[14] and I saw that I did not even have a single tribulation! I was afraid and embarrassed because I did not know the reason for such peace, until the day the old man pointed it out to me and said, 'Do not be distressed. Whoever devotes himself to obeying the Fathers has this peace, this freedom from care.[15]

Dorotheos concluded: 'Take care, brothers, to ask about things, and not to rule yourselves. Learn what freedom from care this habit brings, what joy, what tranquillity.' Then, with all the earmarks of an improvisation, follows this recital of a personal experience: I too have known sadness. I thought I would die of it. But God delivered me in a marvellous manner, and

since then, through the mercy of God, I have not been subject to fear and sadness. The Lord has protected me to this day, through the prayers of these saintly old men. I have told you these things so that you might know what peace, what freedom from care—and this with total security—there is in not directing yourselves and in channeling all your interests to God and to those who can guide us according to God. Likewise, my brothers, learn to ask questions, learn not to guide yourselves: that is beauty, that is humility, that is peace, that is joy. What use is there in pursuing unprofitable things? It is not possible to be saved in any way other than this.[16]

Saint Theodore the Studite. 'There are numerous exercises of virtue; but of all of them not one is as necessary as that of

exagoreusis (revelation of thoughts) and perfect obedience.'[17]
'You know how numerous the demon's traps and ruses are,
brought into play against us in various ways. No one can
escape them except through *exagoreusis* and trust in the hegumen.'[18] Faced with the same spectacle of diabolical traps set
everywhere, Saint Antony had asked himself the same question: who will avoid them? And a voice had answered him,
'humility'.[19] Saint Theodore knew the Apophthegms by heart:
he certainly believed that *exagoreusis* was the best sign of humility. 'I exhort you to let the secrets of the heart be known,
according to the word of Scripture. For it is impossible for a
plant not to perish when it is being slowly eaten by the worm
inside, or for a soul that is hiding a serpent (something un-
disclosed) not to decay or, filled with worms, not to end in
total corruption. I abjure each of you to reject the gnawer
concealed in you. . . .'[21] Also, toward the end of his life, he
stated,

> My brothers and fathers, I would like to keep silent and I
> am forced to speak. To keep silent so as not to sadden
> you; to speak because of the commandment, 'Speak,' it is
> said, 'and do not be silent. I am with you.'[22] This was
> said, it is true, by the Lord to the apostle, but this word
> also applies to those who have care of souls. . . . Tell me,
> where do they come from, these arrogant words among
> you and the unreasonable acts that follow? Is this not
> because you conceal and do not disclose your evil
> thoughts? An evil thought is the beginning, the root of
> the errors we make; if one discloses it, it disappears with
> God's help. If it remains hidden, it gradually evolves into
> a work of darkness. And from that comes death, splits
> between brothers, and so forth.[23]

Saint Theodore never grew weary of returning to this subject:
he wants 'everyone to know that for salvation (including perfection) there is nothing comparable to *exagoreusis*, or as fast'.[24]
In Theodore the Studite we hear the entire ancient tradition.

4. EXCEPTIONS TO THE RULE?

There are men and women who have sanctified themselves without spiritual direction by a human being. Such cases, not numerous and always personal, deserve mention and scrutiny to see whether they may be explained by a principle that would justify them *a priori* or whether they derive from circumstances. In other words, whether they correspond to a thesis or merely represent an hypothesis.

The thesis could be represented by the institution of hesychasm. Were the hesychasts, expressly admitted by Justinian legislation, dispensed from *exagoreusis*? Sometimes it appears that on this point there was no difference between cenobites and eremites. The *Life of Saint Paul the Younger* of Mount Latros states this explicitly:

> Then he wisely and intelligently divides those who opt for the isolated life and those who would rather embrace life in common. Except on certain points, both followed the same observances: not keeping anything hidden from the father, neither an action nor a thought whether good or bad; not doing what one could not tell him and telling him everything one would not tell [others]; doing this day and night unfailingly; not possessing anything without his knowledge, not even a needle; not allowing oneself a leave without advising him and obtaining his approval. This is what is observed without change to this day. The difference consists in this: those who live in community have a dormitory and a refectory of which the superior is in charge, as well as a vestiarian, while among the hesychasts each person has to worry about procuring for himself what is necessary. Everything else, as we have said, is rigorously the same for both.[1]

Nonetheless, we would be wrong if we understood this text in the sense that the hesychasts had to have recourse to *exagoreusis* as frequently as the other monks. The very institution of this form of eremitism is founded upon the conviction that the *acts* of *exagoreusis* could become more spaced out after a certain number of years had been spent in the cenobium. And this is for two reasons: because of the disciple's progress, and because of the perfect knowledge his father in God would have of him. One interview a week would be enough.[2] But 'a spiritual father was indispensable to the monk to a higher or lesser degree, at all the steps of the ascetic ladder, as in all the forms of monastic life,' Smirnov correctly states.

Nonetheless, there are dissenting opinions. I cite the ones I know. The *remoboth* or *sarabaites* mentioned by Smirnov are heretics in the eyes of orthodox monasticism, or at least errant, in every sense of the word. According to Cassian, the first of their errors consists in their not having any desire for cenobitic discipline, not submitting themselves to the arbitration of the father, not letting themselves be instructed in the ancient traditions to govern their own will, and not admitting the rule of discretion.[3] In a word, their error is to refuse any submission. Saint Benedict characterizes them succinctly: they are 'without a shepherd' (*sine pastore*), and the reason for this, or the aim, is that 'Their law is what they like to do, whatever strikes their fancy. Anything they believe in and choose they call holy; anything they dislike they consider forbidden.'[4] They demonstrate by absurdity how indispensable spiritual direction is.

Moreover, there are, or at least have been, hermits who do not belong to the category defined either by Cassian or by Saint Benedict, because they did not begin with regular instruction in the cenobia, to then move to the solitary life after having reached perfection in the active way.[5] Certain hagiographic stories confirm the existence of total anchorites who seemed to have had as their first principle the 'flight from men' in the absolute sense. Manifestly, every eremitic life is preceded by a 'life in common,' in the sense that no one could be born or grow up in total solitude. Cassian perhaps supposes that Saint Paul of Thebes, before the age of fifteen, received sufficient instruction and spiritual direction for a long one hundred year stay in the desert. But during this century of isolation what happened to the famous 'revelation of thoughts?' The same holds true for all the heroes of this pan-egyric literature of excessive *anachōrēsis*.[6] Whatever the historicity of such marvellous cases, the Byzantines who read them believed them, and this created difficulties with the classical doctrine that spiritual direction was necessary for everyone. Here are, for instance, the 'two little strangers' of whom Saint Macarius himself tells the heroic, but unusual adventure. Two young men, one already bearded, the other fuzzy cheeked, came to see Macarius at Scetis and said they wanted to stay in the area. The hermit believed they would not be able to persevere in the desert, and thought he would discourage them merely by telling them to build their cell. Then, he taught them how to weave baskets to provide their living. 'Following this, I went away. And they had patiently done what I had told them. But they did not come to me for three years. I was perplexed and said to myself, "What are they doing that they have not come to ask me about their thoughts? Those who live far come to me, while those who live near have not come, nor have they gone to others."' We understand how worried the great Macarius was! Two youths, with no novitiate at all, jump into eremitism all at once, without ever observing the fundamental precept of asking their father questions; were they not, like so many others, bound to end up falling into *ekstasis phrenōn* (mental derangement) with all its consequences?[7] No longer able to refrain himself, Macarius went to make an inspection tour of which we still have the detailed and admiring report. Its conclusion: 'On leaving them, I said to them, "Pray for me". They bowed down, in silence. I understood that the oldest of the two had reached perfection; the enemy was still waging war on the younger. But after a few days the older one died, and three days later the younger one. From then on, when some of the fathers went to Macarius, he led them to their cell, saying, "Come and see the martyry of the little strangers"'.[8]

This story, in that map of monasticism which the Apophthegms of the Fathers provide, must have perplexed more than one reader. We still find traces of this in the prudent exegesis which an 'old man' of a more recent period makes concerning this anecdote. 'Why did the Romans who went to abba Macarius, during the three years they lived in the neighborhood, never go to him or to any other old man to ask about the subject of their thoughts? The answer: it is because the older one was excessively wise, perfect, and humble. Had he gone to Macarius or to one of the other old men, his perfection would have been revealed, and he would have been praised in all of Scetis by the fathers who would have admired this, saying 'How has a young man arrived at perfection in three years?' But then, this young man knew he was perfect and could have had an opinion of himself which not one of the most famous fathers would have allowed himself, and could he, by virtue of such pride, be excused from a practice which all the fathers considered essential?' The exegete senses the incongruity of his own explanation. So he adds, 'Nonetheless, it is not right for us to compare ourselves to these two brothers and to neglect the teaching of the elders. Of the two brothers the older was perfect, and the younger was humble and learned from him.'[9] The casuist ensnares himself. At any rate, he subsequently lacks the spirit: a little further down he replies to a question about the young man who ascended to heaven on his own will and whom one should catch by the leg to bring him back to earth.[10] Here he is more at ease because he knows he is in the tradition: 'Certain beginners in the ascetic life are so naive and so reckless that they dare undertake things which are well beyond their capacity.'[11]

It would be better to renounce an explanation that forcefully interpolates extraordinary phenomena into a framework of normal ascetic rules. Ignatius and Xanthopoules showed their wisdom when they wrote in a chapter on submission: 'And if some of the famous Fathers were able, even without the exercise of submission, to arrive at a deifying stillness (*tēs theopoies hēsychias*) and at perfection according to God, this happened through a revelation of God and rarely.

Now, it is written: what is rare cannot be a church law,[12] just as one swallow does not make the summer. But you, who believe that true submission is some type of introduction to the excellent *hēsychia*, drop these things which happened only once because of divine ordering, and proceed according to the commands of the venerable Fathers.'[13]

Let us mention one of these rare occurrences where it appears that God through 'dispensation' makes himself directly the guide of a soul. Saint Parasceva the Younger lived as a hermit 'without having any other support in the desert except only Jesus Christ. She conversed with him, breathed him, had him as a yoke (?), as guide, saviour, benefactor, redeemer, and husband. . . .'[14] Having returned to the capital, she addressed the Theotokos: '. . . I have no other hope, no other protection [than you]; you are my expectation, my protection, my guide, my superior, my guardian, and the invisible rampart of my whole life. While I lived in the desert it was you, Lady, who were my companion. Now I am in the world; what other help can I have if not you, queen most immaculate? May you be my companion on the way, my governess, guide, refuge, and fortress for me, the weak one.'[15] But this biography of a tenth century person was written by Matteos of Myres at the beginning of the seventeenth century! Moreover, the author had enough sense of tradition to let his saintly anchoress first pass through a monastery.[16] Thus she almost rejoins the classic doctrine; at least, she does not remove herself from it as much as the 'two little Romans'. Indeed, there are voices, more or less authoritative—and late!—that dare state that the perfect do not need spiritual direction at all. 'The person who has achieved spiritual submission, (that is), the one who has submitted the flesh to the spirit, does not need human submission. For such a person, when a loyal subject, is submitted to the word and the law of God. But those in whom there still is a struggle between body and soul need to submit themselves; they should have a well-trained leader and pilot at the helm, one who arms them as best he can. Without this, we would be destroyed by invisible enemies, and submerged by the passions through lack of experience.'[17]

But are there perfect of this type? And is anyone allowed to count himself among them?

NOTES

1. THE PROPER FOCUS OF SUCH ATTENTION

1. Marcus Eremita, *De his qui putant se ex operibus justificari* n. 139; PG 95: 952B.
2. *Ibid.*, n. 140.
3. See PG 65: 896A.
4. *The Cloud of Unknowing*, trans. William Johnston (New York, 1973) 146. Cfr *Alph.*, Antony n. 6.
5. Marcus Eremita, *De lege spirituali* 142; PG 65: 924A.
6. On this psychic analysis, see Marcus Eremita, *loc. cit.*, and *De baptismo*; PG 65: 1013-21; Joannes Damascenus, *De virtute et vitio (De octo spiritibus nequitiae)*; PG 95: 93; Joannes Climacus, who already appeals to the Fathers, *Scala Paradisi, Gradus* 15; PG 88: 896CD; S. Nilus, *Liber de monastica exercitatione*; PG 79: 768BD; *Epistolarum Liber* II, 12, col. 205C; II, 79, col. 236C; Philotheus the Sinaite, etc.
7. Paul Evergetinos, *Synagogē* I, cap. 20, p. 62, col. 1.

2. REASONS FOR THIS DISCLOSURE

1. S. Ignatius, *Letter on Obedience* 12.
2. *Alph.*, Antony n. 8; PG 65: 77B [CS 59:3].
3. *Ibid.*, 37; col. 88B [9]; see Deut 32:7.
4. *Ibid.*, 38; col. 88B [9].
5. *Ibid.*, 7, col. 77B [2].
6. *Ibid.*, 5, col. 77A [2].
7. *Vitae Patrum* III, n. 177; PL 73: 798C.
8. *Ibid.*, 14.
9. Cassian, *Coll.* II, ch. 5; cfr Palladius, *Historia Lausiaca* 26.
10. For the meaning, one should take into account the paraphrase in PG 34: 1092C.
11. *Historia Lausiaca* 33; PG 34: 1092ff.
12. See *Vie de S. Sabas*, ch. 39, ed. Schwartz, p. 129ff.
13. *De coenobiorum institutis*, 4, 9; PL 49: 161-62.
14. *Liber* V, *cap.* 15, 3 and 4.
15. I, chs. 20 and 21.
16. See Irénée Hausherr, 'Contemplation et sainteté,' In *RAM* 14 (1933) 193.
17. *Vita* I, n. 96, Halkin, p. 64 [CS 45:363].
18. *Vitae Patrum* V, X, 110; PL 73: 932B.
19. *Vie de S. Sabas*, 75, ed. Schwartz, p. 180, 22.
20. *Vie de Saint Jean L'Hésychaste* 20, ed. Schwartz, p. 216ff.

21. A. Papadopoulos-Kerameus, *Antonios Stouditēs kai tina symmikta* (Jerusalem 1905) 5-12.
22. John Climacus, *Scala Paradisi, Gradus* IV; PG 88: 681B.
23. *Antonios Stouditēs*, pp. 7-9.
24. *Typikon Messanense* n. III, ed. Mai, *Patrum Nova Bibliotheca* X. 2, p. 213; Mai's greek text is badly punctuated, and the latin translation is wrong toward the end: there should be a period after *katērgnēthēsan*, and instead of 'Omnino ad norma redacta quidem sunt commercia,' one should write,'abolita sunt. Confessionem autem . . .'
25. *Alph.*, Antony n. 36; PG 65: 931CD[CS 59:8].
26. *Vitae Patrum* V, 10, 111; PL 73: 932BC.
27. *Alph.*, Poemen n. 54; PG 65: 333D-6A [174].
28. *Vitae Patrum* V, 10, 111; PL 73: 932BC.
29. See Irénée Hausherr, *Penthos. La doctrine de la componction dans l'Orient chrétien*, OrChrA 132 (Rome, 1944). [English translation by Anselm Hufstader, *Penthos. The Doctrine of Compunction in the Christian East* (Kalamazoo: Cistercian Publication, 1982).—ed.]
30. Barsanuphius, *Letter* 225, p. 140.
31. Evergetinos I, ch. 19, p. 57.
32. *Alph.*, Poemen n. 65; PG 65: 337B [176].
33. See Evergetinos, *Syllogē*, Bk 1, ch. 19, p. 57; *Alph.*, Poemen n. 65; PG 65: 337B.
34. See *Alph.*, Issac n. 2; PG 65: 181A [110]; Pambo n. 3, col. 369AB [196]; Rufus n. 2, 389CD [210-211], etc. It is true that Rufus who sings the praises of obedience over here, elsewhere utters a dithyramb in praise of the solitary life: see Irénée Hausherr, 'Le Métérikon de l'Abbé Isaïe,' in *OCP* 12 (Rome, 1946) 298-300. Contrary to what is said there on p. 300, the text in question is printed with the greek works of S. Ephrem, Edit. Rom. III, p. 234ff.
35. *Scala Paradisi, Gradus* IV; PG 88: 717C.
36. Ammonas, *Letter* 5, n. 2, ed. François Nau, POr 11, p. 447[English translation by Derwas J. Chitty, *The Letters of Ammonas* (Oxford:Fairacres Press, 1979) 7—ed].
37. *Ibid.*, p. 448.
38. *Letter* 1, pp. 432-34 [1].
39. *Letter* 4, p. 443 [6].
40. *Letter* 507, p. 249.
41. *Letter* 509, p. 251.
42. *Letter* 510, p. 251.
43. *Letter* 511, p. 251.
44. *Letter* 514, p. 252.
45. *Letter* 236, p. 127.
46. See Clement of Alexandria, *Strom.*, I, 26; ed. Otto Staehlin, II, p. 107, 25ff.
47. 2 Tim 4:2.
48. *Letter* 239, p. 174.
49. Variant: 'of angels' (*aggelōn* instead of *agelōn*).
50. *Alph.*, Poemen n. 1; PG 65: 317A [164].
51. *Alph*, Paphnutius n. 3; PG 65: 379A [202-203].

3. TESTIMONIES OF SOME GREAT SPIRITUAL FATHERS

1. *Regulae fusius tractatae, interrogatio* 26; PG 31: 985Cff; cfr 46, col. 1036AB.

2. Ed. Werner Jaeger (1952) 333-43; *De virginatate*, cap. 24; PG 46: 410ff.

3. Eccl 4:10.

4. '*Peri tou mē opheilein tina stachein tē idią synesei*,' *Doctrina* V; PG 88: 1676A. [See 'On the Need for Consultation,' in *Dorotheos of Gaza. Discourses and Sayings*, trans. Eric P. Wheeler, Cistercian Studies 33 (Kalamazoo, 1977) 122ff.—ed.]

5. Antwerp, 1647; Prague, 1726.

6. P. Brun, *Orientalia Christiana* 26 (Rome, 1932) 96.

7. Prov 11:14 (LXX).

8. *Alph.*, Poemen n. 54; PG 65: 333D=*Vitae Patrum* V, X, 60; PL 73: 922C [CS 59:174].

9. *Doctrina* V; PG 88: 1677B; Dorotheos cites from memory.

10. *Ibid.*, 1677D.

11. *Alph.*, Macarius n. 3; PG 65: 261AB.

12. Col. 1680D.

13. See *Doctrina* I, n. 70, col. 1640.

14. Acts 14:12.

15. Col. 1681BC.

16. Col. 1684BC.

17. S. Theodorus Studita, *Oratio* XI. *Laudatio S. Platonis Hegumeni*; PG 99: 812D.

18. *Grande Catéchèse*, ed. Papadopoulos-Kerameus, p. 533.

19. *Alph.*, Antony n. 7; see above, section 2, note 5.

20. See 1 Cor 14:26.

21. *Grande Catéchèse*, p. 623.

22. Acts 18:9ff.

23. *Petite Catéchèse*, ed. Auvray, p. 464ff.

24. Papadopoulos-Kerameus, *Catéchèse* 25, p. 176.

4. EXCEPTIONS TO THE RULE?

1. *Vita S. Pauli Junioris* n. 17, ed. Hippolyte Delehaye, *AnBoll* 11 (1892) 52.

2. See Smirnov, p. 23.

3. Cassian, *Collatio* XVIII, 4.

4. S. Benedicti, *Regula*, *cap.* 1.

5. Cassian, *loc. cit.*, *Regula S. Benedicti*, I.

6. See François Nau, 'Le chapitre peri anachōretōn hagiōn et les sources de la Vie de saint Paul de Thèbes,' in *ROC* 10 (1905) 387-417.

7. See *Alph.*, Antony n. 37; PG 65: 88B [CS 59:8-9].

8. *Alph.*, Macarius n. 33; PG 65: 273D [134-36]=*Vitae Patrum* III, 195 ; PL 73: 802A-3B; V, III, 2, col. 1004C-6A.

9. See E. A. Wallis-Budge, *The Paradise of the Fathers* II (1907) n. 262, p. 292.

10. See above, p. 165.

11. *Paradise.*, n. 631, p. 302.

12. See *Syntagma tōn hierōn kanonōn* (Athens, 1859) 400.

13. Ignatius and Callistus of Xanthopoulos, *Methodos kai kanōn*, *cap.* 15; PG 147: 660BC.

14. *Vie de Sainte Parascève la Jeune* n. 4, ed. Papadopoulos-Kerameus, *Analecta hierosol. stachyol.* I (1891) 440, 31ff.

15. *Ibid.*, n. 7, p. 443, 27ff.

16. *Ibid.*, n. 4, p. 440, 12ff.

17. Theognostos, 'Sur la pratique et la théorie . . .' ch. 11, *Philocalie* (Venice, 1782) 500ff.

VI

THE DUTIES OF THE DISCIPLE

IF IT IS A DUTY of spiritual persons (the gnostics, the perfect) to devote themselves to the salvation and perfection of souls, at least of those who come to them spontaneously, there are nonetheless valid objections against the actual acceptance of this ministry and fatherhood—the strongest being that no one is ever obliged to believe that he is either a gnostic or perfect! One can even ask oneself how it is ever possible to view oneself as such. On the part of the disciple, no excuse is valid: his very imperfection demands that he have recourse to the insights, the help and the prayers of another. Consequently, in practice, the initiative will always have to come from the one who *seeks* a director, as long as no type of contract intervenes, an agreement as to mutual roles.

1. HAVING A SPIRITUAL FATHER

Our first duty, then, is to have a spiritual father. Since one is needed and not easily found, one must search for him. Saints are rare at all times, at least according to what the aspirants to sainthood say.[1] The 'present generation' always seems degenerate. Saint Barsanuphius wrote that in his day (the first half of he sixth century, the time of Saint Benedict) the earth counted three men perfect before God, who surpassed human stature and had received the power to bind and loose; consequently, three men who were truly worthy of becoming spiritual fathers. 'They are John in Rome, Elijah in Corinth, and another in the eparchy of Jerusalem', where Saint Barsanuphius himself was.[2] Hesychius of Sinai, writing after Saint John Climacus, states in the opening chapter of his first *Century* that 'today purity of heart is indeed rare (*spanizei*) among monks because of its excellence and beauty or, to speak more appropriately, because of our heedlessness and indifference.'[3] This 'today' has never ceased. And this is why it has never been easy for the aspiring ascetic to accomplish his first duty which was to choose for himself a spiritual father among the great number of priests and monks he could meet in every region of the christian East. To know by which signs he could recognize them was of the utmost importance.

All the more since certain (false?) witnesses tell us that there were some who did not shrink from cheating in order to give themselves a beguiling appearance. Having an 'ascetic complexion' pointed to rigorous fasting: it was a yellow hue on an emaciated face. Very serious authorities agreed on this point: Philo the Jew had already noted that 'the ascetics are pale because of the toil that consumes them and by reason of the fear that they may perhaps not obtain the results that accord with their prayers.'[4] Saint Basil the father of monks, had a pale color, and Saint Gregory of Nazianzen, who tells us this, saw in it one of the outward signs of holiness.[5] Saint Nilus, or rather Evagrius, a deserter from the basilian community, perhaps picked up this idea and remembrance over there; at any rate he gives a warning about vainglory 'to those whose face is brilliantly yellow as the result of ascesis,' for having 'made the flower of the flesh fade.'[7] 'The beautiful flower (or healthy tint) of bodies inhabited by a noble soul is *ōchrotēs*, paleness,' Saint Gregory the Theologian adds.[8] At all times, hagiography has pointed out this phenomenon in praise of its heroes.[9] In an exhortation to his 'fathers and brothers,' Saint Theodore the Studite said, 'As we have just finished the first week of Lent, we see each other as being thinner and yellower than before.'[10]

This statement should warn us against a sign of holiness that is acquired in one week. One does not even need that much time! The science of make-up was one of these that was early brought to greatest perfection. Certain monks, if we can believe their adversaries, did not refrain from using it to give themselves a *technēton ōchron*, an artificial pale hue, without the price of even one mortification[11]; and if we append this text to the passage cited earlier, in which Theodore Balsamon— while stating that the monks have practically monopolized the ministry of confession—used the word hypocrisy twice, we may conclude that the aim of such artifice was to earn the reputation of spiritual men, adept at directing souls. That did not make the choice of a guide in the way of the spirit any easier. If one were to be taken in by it, one could even fall into the hands of heretics, for they too, the Bogomils, for example, knew how to make themselves 'look pale as a result of hypocritical fasts'.[12] Indeed, Saint Gregory Nazianzen noticed that while his friend Saint Basil had an ascetic air 'not intentionally, but in all simplicity, like a fortuitous accident',[13] the 'numerous Basils for the eye' make themselves look ridiculous by imitating him, out of ostentation. Would the Lord's recommendation to groom ourselves to hide our fasting not inspire trust instead in the fathers with a 'radiant, happy face,' like those in the *Historia Monachorum*, abba Or,[14] abba Theon,[15] abba Apollo[16] who extolled joy even to the point of assigning gloomy airs, even *penthos* (sorrow), to the Hellenes and the Jews,[17] and so on? It is true that one can at the same time be austere and radiant, as was Saint Antony. But where are the Saint Antonys found?

An ascetic look does not therefore suffice. Wisdom recommends that one does not take this into account until one has another proof of holiness. All the qualities required of the director may be summed up in two words: holiness and *diakrisis*. By what less deceptive signs can one recognize them? when one possesses these qualities oneself, one can, like Saint Athanasius of Lavra, for example, propose someone for the role of hegumen *hōs ate pneumatikon kai tō onti phronimon*, 'because he is spiritual and really prudent.'[18] But beginners? And yet it is at the beginning of the ascetic life that the problem imposes itself most urgently. 'One should reveal one's thoughts to the diacritics among the fathers; one should not give one's trust to the first man one meets,' states the title of a chapter of the *Synagogē* by Paul Evergetinos[19]; these words are taken from the Greek translation of Cassian.[20] Fortunately, Cassian adds—still in the Greek version—a sign that is more easily managed, *kai para pollōn memartyrēmenous*, 'and recommended by numerous witnesses.' This presupposes that one submits to another, that one follows an already established trend. But since everything needs a beginning, who would dare become the first disciple of an ascetic who does not yet have an established reputation? Cassian also warns against the prestige of years: having white hairs is not enough. 'Many who have revealed their thoughts while only considering age and outward appearance have fallen into despair because of the inexperience of those who listened.' A long and frightening story follows as proof; here is the conclusion, inspired by Cassian, but written by Evergetinos:

From what proceeds we learn that there is no other sure path of salvation, except each reveal his own thoughts to the diacritics among the Father, to be guided by them to virtue, while avoiding self-direction through one's own will according to one's own criteria. If by chance someone were to meet an old man or even several, simple and inexperienced, there is no reason to refuse to reveal one's secret thoughts also to the most proven of the Fathers. On account of the inexperience of some, this would be showing a lack of trust towards all and a subsequent fleeing from all. As one does with physicians of the body, one should first experience the ability of the person one meets, and only then should one reveal one's psychic traumas (*ta psychika traumata*) to him; one should no longer object to his methods of healing, but accept them with gratitude even if at the moment they make us suffer.[21]

Very well! But what if the experimentation to which I subject the physician is to be done on me, and I am the victim? Or do I have to give him the opportunity to take his chances with an *anima vili* (common soul)? Certainly, the problem becomes more and more complex. In the same Evergetinos chapter there are, in addition, six long columns of subtle explanations taken from the answers by Saint Barsanuphius, but the one thing that is related to the specific problem that is of interest to us is this: 'Teach me, Father, whom should one ask about the subject of thoughts? Should I report the answer received to another spiritual man?' Answer: 'You should ask questions from the one in whom you trust, and whom you believe is capable of bearing your thoughts: you should believe in him as in God. To ask another about the same thought would be to lack confidence and tempt [God]. For if you believe that God is speaking in his saint, what need is there to tempt God by posing the same question to someone else?'[22] The sign, then, is that I feel confident? I understand that my spiritual father, once he has been duly selected, is entitled to my unconditional trust, but how can I be sure? My inexperience as a neophyte compels me to choose a spiritual father, but makes me unable to make this choice myself. The letter we have just quoted does perhaps remove us from embarrassment through its very existence: in the church of God there always will be some spiritual persons *para pollōn memartyrēmenoi* (recommended by numerous witnesses) like the three marked out by Saint Barsanuphius.[23] One can always ask their authoritative opinion about potential spiritual fathers, at least whether they know any, naturally or supernaturally.

Saint Barsanuphius gave such a testimony to Saint Dorotheos. Things like this happen even today. It is not the voice of a crowd, but that of a man of God, which is worth far more.

Yet, here is one of the most famous Byzantine mystics whose succinct opinion nullified any proceedings of this sort. Symeon the New Theologian has dealt with our problem *ex professo* in an immensely long letter to one of his spiritual children.[24] But the answer looks like a *petitio principii*: be spiritual yourself, and you will recognize spiritual men unfailingly by visiting them often and from their mere appearance. Without this personal seeing, the testimony of all of humanity is unacceptable. 'And who, one may ask, will recognize such men, if there even are such people today? The one who is enlightened by the Holy Spirit from on high. If one claims not to know them, what reason would he have to accept the testimony of another? . . . Under no circumstance will he be able not to know the spiritual man he meets, unless he be blind. For how could one not tell with one's eyes a sheep from the wolf, and the thief from the shepherd? . . . I maintain that the one who sees and hears spiritually sees, if not substantially then at least in concept, the soul of the one he frequently sees and with whom he often visits for conversation: and he determines of what quality and worth he is. If therefore one has been granted participation in the Holy Spirit, that is recognized by sight alone . . .'[25]

S. Smirnov deals with our question[26] rather briefly; the document he produces affirms the freedom of choice rather than the principle that should guide it. The title of the paragraph formulates the thesis: 'The choice of *staretz* was held as an indefeasible and essential right of the neophyte himself.' The arguments to support the thesis are taken from abba Isaiah, Mark the Ascetic, and the *Lausiac History*.[27] These quotations add nothing to what we have said: that one should consider not age but experience—we have already heard this—and that one should not be schooled by someone who is vain—that is self-evident. Abba Apollo of the *Lausiac History* owed the attraction he had among surrounding hermits to his reputation as a spiritual man. They flocked to him, 'bringing him their souls as a gift, as if to their true father.' When abba Isaiah warns against the pretense of arrogating the office of master, this is only indirectly related to the subject, and we have spoken of this elsewhere.

By contrast, Saint Basil's *Letter* XXIII is very much to the point, and even more is the one that follows, from the ascetic discourse. One must give the new monk the spiritual *aleiptēn* (trainer) for whom he may ask.[28] Now that you have made the first step by leaving the world,

> do not throw yourself away like a worthless vessel. On the contrary, with exceeding care and intelligence, find someone who walks before you unerringly on the path of your profession, one who is able to lead those who are on their way to God, who is adorned with virtues, who through his own works witnesses to the love of God, who has knowledge of the divine Scriptures; someone who is not drawn hither and yon by distractions, who does not love money, does not meddle, is peaceful, a friend of God and of the humble, someone who is not angry or resentful, without vanity or pride, insensitive to flattery, not subject to inconstancy, and someone who puts nothing above God. If you find such a person, surrender yourself to him, spewing out your own will and casting it far from you. . . . This is the second struggle against the opponent of our salvation. The lessons of good masters are good; those of evil masters are altogether evil. If our adversary cannot persuade us to remain in the agitation and the ruin of the world, he tries to get us not to devote ourselves to a regular life, or to surrender not to a person who condemns all our faults to correct them, but to one of those who crave glory and who, on the pretense of condescending to their companions, exhibit their own vices so that imperceptibly we become subjected once more to a thousand vices and become fettered by his own chains, which are those of sin. If you surrender to a man

of great virtue, you will inherit the inward possessions he owns, and be worthy of being called blessed before God and man. If, out of concern for the body you seek a master who is able to condescend to your passions, or, to say it better, to tumble down with you, in vain will you have endured the struggle to renounce the world, since you will have surrendered to a dissolute life by taking a blind guide who will push you into the pit. And if one blind man leads another, both will fall into a pit.[29] It is enough for the disciple that he should grow to be like his teacher;[30] this is a divine word, and it does not fail.[31]

These observations of Saint Basil are still the clearest ones on the question. Nevertheless, they are more negative than positive; the great Doctor is especially afraid that one may choose a guide according to the desires of 'one's own will'. In this he agrees with all the Fathers. Furthermore, in basilian monasteries, it had been provided for that such misleading masters not be found; a novice could make a choice but only among 'elders' recognized by competent authorities as being able to direct.

We must stop here, without asking for more precision on this delicate subject than what the Fathers give us. In monasteries that do not allow spiritual fathers other than the hegumen, it is clear that for cenobite candidates the choice of a director is limited to the choice of the community he will enter and whose statutes and customary laws he will have to accept. If the case arises he can also pass to the authority of another hegumen, according to an established procedure. Judging from the legal texts such a transfer seems very difficult; in reality it has been much more frequent than would appear. This is a legal question: it is not appropriate for us to deal with it.

2. FAITH AND SUBMISSION

Nonetheless, it has to be said that this freedom seems to fit only into some type of *epikeia* (benevolent application of the rule) or of ordering (*oikonomia*).

This is what Symeon the Studite, the spiritual father of Symeon the New Theologian stated explicitly:

> If you have come to trust a brother in the cenobium and you reveal your thoughts to him, never cease going to him, brother, to tell him the thoughts that come to you daily and at every hour. It would be advisable that all go to confession to the hegumen, but since some do not disclose their thoughts to him, on account of their great weakness and the distrust they have of him, I speak in this manner through condescension. At least one should not leave the one for another by lending an ear to the suggestions of the enemy who makes you afraid of becoming a burden in order to prevent you from seeing this brother often, the confidant of your thoughts, and to persuade you either to give up confessing or to go to someone else; for if we continue to go to the first, we will acquire greater trust in him; we will derive great profit from his own life; no one will reprimand our way of life and all will praise us for keeping the faith so well. On the other hand, if we neglect to reveal our thoughts frequently, we fall into the trap of despair. Even if we go to another spiritual father—which is not allowed if this man is from our own monastery—all our brothers will accuse us of losing confidence in the first, and we will incur God's severe condemnation; and the spiritual guide to whom we go will suspect that the same thing will happen to him. We will get into a habit of changing from one to another, and will never ceasing seeking to know stylites, recluses, and hesychasts to confess to them, only to lose faith in all of them, to stagnate without progress and, what is worse, to bring malediction down on ourselves. Because of this, take care to be faithful until death, unswervingly, to the spiritual man to whom you confess from the beginning. Never be scandalized because of him, even if you see him committing fornication. Thus you will never suffer damage. But if, as we have said, you

scorn him and go to another, you will become the cause
of many scandals, and you will also accuse all the others:
you will open the paths of perdition to yourself. But
Lord, Lord, deliver us from all lack of faith, from all
indiscreet searching, and protect us by your divine
grace.[1]

It was appropriate to transcribe this passage at the opening of
what remains to be said about the duties of the disciple to the
father. We only have to come back to the concepts expressed
in it and support them with some testimonials.

That one must remain faithful to his spiritual (guide) once
he has been chosen is easy to understand, if spiritual fatherhood is not an empty word. Now is the time to read a few
letters of Saint Barsanuphius that follow the one already mentioned (see above, p. 189). One has confidence or not; to run
from one director to another is to tempt God. Indeed, the
questioner goes on, 'but what if a thought continues to harass
one after asking the father about it?' The answer of John the
Prophet: 'This is because someone, after listening, has remained passive, and has not completely and carefully done
what was ordered. He should remember his error and do
exactly what he has heard. If it is God who speaks in his
saints, he does not lie.'[2] Here are objections that come straight
from experience and from human reality:

Should one ask the same person about the same thing a
second time? I know cases, Father, when I heard someone tell me, 'Don't do this.' And when I asked the same
one about the same thing, he told me, 'Do it.' What does
that mean?'

The answer by John the Prophet is worth its weight in gold:

Brother, the judgments of God are like the mighty deep[3];
God puts in mouth of the fathers words that correspond to what the disciple has in his heart, either to test

him or because his heart has changed and he wishes to
hear something else, or because others, involved in the
same thing, have changed and God speaks differently
(than he did the first time) in his saint, because of them.
Thus he spoke to king Hezekiah, through Isaiah. After
the prophet had told him, 'Put your affairs in order, you
are going to die,' the king's heart changed. He became
sad, and because of this he then told him through Isaiah,
'See how God has added fifteen years to your life'.[4] Now,
had he spoken through another, the thing would have
caused a scandal, because (as one may have thought) the
saints speak differently, from one another. Likewise also,
he spoke through Jonas to the heart of the people of Nineveh, saying, 'In three days I will destroy the city'.[5] And
when their heart had changed by coming to repentance,
God showed his great magnanimity and spared the city
because it had changed for the good. For this reason one
should never replace the saint from whom one asks questions. One should go to him again, for fear that it becomes necessary for God to change the answer, the occasion being provided by (the disciple) himself, and that a
scandal might result from this.[6]

Smirnov is not exaggerating when he writes: 'The disciple
must have a faith in his *staretz* that is built upon the recogni-
tion of his unconditional authority. Every doubt about his
authority, the slightest criticism of this personality or his actions is a great sin.'[7] One should not be scandalized, Symeon
the Studite tells us, even if one were to see him fornicating.
Saint John Climacus already wrote:

Go therefore, and do not permit that in all humankind
there be found a man more given to hitting and more
cutting than your trainer in the Lord. Persevere; and day
after day drink the mockery and ridicule as if they were
milk and honey. The disciple says, 'Yes, Father, but if
that father does not do his duty because of indolence?'

The old man replied, 'Even if you see him fornicating, do not depart from him, but say to yourself, "Friend, why have you come?"[8] Then you finally will see your haughtiness struck down and the flame of lust go out.[9]

This is obviously a hyperbole; to take it literally would be to forget the conditions required for becoming a spiritual father, and not to take into account the recommendations of Saint Basil. Yet bearing the faults one may detect in one's guide should be carried a long way, as long as they strengthen the disciple's patience. There is a story 'told by holy men' and reported by 'one of the old men' that teaches how the disciple can do the teacher's work and save the soul of his spiritual father. 'There was a certain old man who was a drunkard. He made one mat every day and sold it in the neighboring village. Whatever he received for it was used to buy drink. Later, however, a brother came to stay with him. He too made one mat which the old man took and sold, and spent the price of both mats on wine. But to the brother he only brought a little bread in the evening.' One understands that the poor disciple was tempted to leave. But an angel dissuaded him and announced that 'Tomorrow we will come to you,' meaning that the angels would take him to paradise. Thus it happened. 'And the old man shed tears, saying, "Alas! my son, for many years I have lived negligently, but in a short time you have saved your soul through patience." From that day on, the old man was sober.'[10]

Such stories could only occur under the particular conditions of a hermit living in the company of a disciple. Did they ever happen? The one we just quoted bears all the earmarks of one of these numerous 'stories profitable to the soul,' whose one aim was strongly to inculcate a moral lesson; all the characters in it are anonymous, from the so-called first witness to the last story teller. Indeed, the spiritual father's temptation had to come less from his flaws than from his demands or from the fact that the disciple felt misunderstood, as we would say—a handy euphemism that conceals a refusal to deny one's own will. The eternal desire to 'find a spiritual father according to my own ideas'. Fidelity (faith, *pistis* as the Easterners say) is possible only through *total* submission.

The doctrine of the eastern ascetics on this *obedience* is characterized by *absolutism*—which does not mean despotism, though in certain cases this deviation must have occurred. The distance between tyrannical authoritarianism and unconditional obedience is great. The latter must come entirely from the disciple; it is obtained more readily if the master shows discretion in exercising authority, and he knows full well that true respect is commanded through the example of one's own life. 'A brother asked abba Poemen, "Brothers live with me. Do you recommend that I give them orders?" The old man said to him, "No. You do the work first, and if they want to live [=work out their salvation], they will learn from you." The brother said, "Father, they want me to command them!" The old man replied, "No. Be a model for them, but not a legislator."'[11] Saint Basil evidently also counted more on the slow suggestiveness of good examples than on the sudden interventions of authority.[12] That did not, however, prevent him from having definite ideas about the need for universal obedience.[13] These two things go together very well: the one is like the general climate, the other intervenes at the right time either when the spiritual father—the leader of the community—judges it to be useful to the common good, or especially when the disciple comes to him to reveal his thoughts. It is the latter case we consider here because that is the proper role of the spiritual father and the authority of the hegumen derives from it. Saint Nilus wrote: 'When such teachers [as have just been described] are found, they require disciples who have so renounced themselves and their own will as to be no different from dead bodies or from the substance used by an artist. Just as the soul functions in the body at will and the body offers no resistance, and just as the artist shows his art in the material and the material does not resist him, so does the teacher apply his knowledge of virtue upon obedient disciples who do not contradict him in anything.'[14]

Saint Barsanuphius wrote: 'Every deed performed without the superior's command or permission is a theft, a sacrilege that leads to death, not to profit, even if it seems good to you.'[15]

This is the general principle. It will be expressed in many other ways. It is noteworthy that the traits mentioned by Saint Ignatius in his *Letter on Obedience* all derive from the *Lives of the Fathers*, that is, the East, except the anecdote about Saint Maurus which is indeed western but of eastern inspiration. In these venerable monastic documents, Ignatius must have read other comparisons besides that of 'a corpse' or 'inert manner.' He could have been authorized by them to say that one should consider oneself a donkey and one should obey like a camel. 'An old man said, "Be like a camel; carry your sins and allow yourself to be led, trussed, by one who knows the way to God"'[16]; be like a dog who 'goes outside when he is chased away, and enters when he is called.'[17]

This comparison to various kinds of 'pack animals' is classic in the literature of the *Apophthegms*: a donkey or a camel, or in general an *alogon*, an unreasoning irrational beast, or *ktēnos*, cattle, another's property.[18] 'A donkey is by nature as sensible, as patient, as quiet as the horse is noble, high-mettled, and impetuous.'[19] The donkey has provided the Greeks with numerous proverbs[20] always based upon the *anaisthēsia* (want of feeling) or its endurance. Since the donkey has its stubbornness and the camel its whims, other symbols came to be used to represent total submission: wax in the hands of the kneader, iron under the hammer of the smith.[21] But all this imagery is offered to the disciple! If the master misuses it to his advantage, serious inconvenience may result from it. The *Life* of Saint Germanus the Hagiorite relates a fact that is more unique than rare but which clearly shows to what excess a severity not tempered by discretion could lead: 'John, the first spiritual father [of Germanus], a record holder in walking (Athens-Thessalonika in one day—Athens-Constantinople in three days) as hard on himself as on others . . . became a victim [a martyr, Philotheus, the biographer, was to say] of his severity; for in Thessalonika, one of his "servants", treated harshly no doubt during the novitiate, hacked him to bits with an axe, along with his disciple Germanus; the latter was about to leave him when his unexpected death spared him [John] the chagrin of seeing himself abandoned by the disciple he loved.'[22]

Saint Basil does not resort to the rustic images of the Desert Fathers, but he expresses the same radicalism in a language that is entirely evangelical when he writes: 'One must be submissive until death through a prompt and punctual obedience to the superior's order, even when it seems to exceed one's strength, mindful of the example of the divine Saviour who "was obedient even to accepting death, death on a cross."'[23] The immediate reason given for this prescription is the common good; but it also derives from spiritual direction since it closely follows *Question* XXVI which deals with revelation of thoughts.

Obedience knew no physical limits. Some even went so far as to say that it should have no moral limits. 'The old man said, "If someone has faith in another and yields to him in submission, he does not have to heed the commandments of God, but entrust his entire will to the spiritual father; for if he obeys him in everything, he will not commit a fault before God."'[24] And if this anonymity raises legitimate doubts, here is a letter duly signed by Saint Barsanuphius himself.

Question: must one submit oneself to the hegumen in good things, indifferent things, and in those in which there appears to be a transgression of the commandment of God? . . . Answer: Brother, the person who wants to be a monk must have absolutely no personal will in anything. This is what Christ has taught, saying, 'I have come down from heaven, not to do my own will.' For the one who wants to do this but takes exception to that, either flaunts himself as being more discerning than the one who gives the order, or he is a toy of the demons. You must be obedient in everything, even if the order appears sinful to you. For the abba who orders you will carry the responsibility himself since he will be called to account for you.[25]

Such an opinion did, however, not have many defenders. Along the same lines Smirnov quotes a word of Saint John Climacus (according to the Russian translation): 'The one who will have delivered the disciple's soul to death will answer for everything.'[26] But would the disciple's soul be less dead for all that?[27] The two other quotations given by Smirnov (from the *Paterik* and *Saint Dorotheos*) offer nothing that matches the teaching of Saint Barsanuphius on this specific point. When all is said and done only the authority of the Great Recluse is left, but one has to admit that it carries weight.

On another point the same saint shows more frugality. 'How should one behave when questioning the Fathers? Should one inevitably carry out the answers they give?' John the Prophet replies in the name of Barsanuphius: 'Not all of them, but the ones that are given as an order. Simple advice according to God is one thing; an order, another. Advice is a directive, with no obligation, showing man the straight path of life. An order imposes an uncontestable yoke.'[28] The four inquiries that follow subsume the difficulty. How does one know whether it is advice or an order? John's reply makes us witness a real scene so well that is should be given in full:

If you go to find the spiritual father to question him about a certain thing, not to receive an order from him but to hear an answer that would be according to God, and he tells you what is to be done, you must obey at once, even then. If, having done this, you feel anxiety because of it, do not be distressed: this happens for your profit. If, on the other hand, you do not want to do it, it will not appear to you as if you transgressed a commandment, because you likewise did not accept (the answer) as an order; but it will seem to you that you scorned your profit, and for this you must condemn yourself. Indeed, one must hold that everything that comes from the mouth of the saints is for the benefit of those who hear it. The same thing is true when, without your asking anything, (the spiritual father) tells you something on his own initiative, the result of a suggestion from God. If you go to question him about something specific, intent on receiving an order, you must make a bow and ask him to give you an order. When it has been given, make another bow, to ask the blessing of the one who has given it to you, telling him, 'Your blessing, father, upon this order, and your prayers so that I may obey it.' Brother, know this: the one who imposes an order does not merely impose it, but he helps you with his supplication and prayers so that you may obey it. However, if out of distraction, you did not bow to receive the blessing, do not think that the order is null and void. It holds, even so; only, you received it contrary to the accepted fashion. If you are able to endure the weariness, do not hesitate to go back to correct things by making a bow and receiving the benediction. If you cannot do this, tell yourself that you have accepted the order as received.[29]

The letter that follows specifies even more: it is the spiritual father's intention that makes his reply an order or a counsel, not the intention the disciple had in questioning him. An order also is everything that is said by virtue of the church canons or by the Fathers in the name of their authority: but to know what one should hold on to, it is better to ask the Fathers themselves. 'But if I succumb, and transgress the commandment, what do I do? The Lord told Peter, 'you will forgive your brother seventy times seventy.' If therefore He has commanded man to forgive to such degree how much more will the One who is rich in mercy and surpasses all in compassion do it. . . .' Nonetheless, one should take care not to fall into indolence and negligence because of this. 'That would be serious. Do not despise the order even in apparently small things. . . . Through such carelessness one is led to more serious falls.'[30] Finally, what should one think of the temptation 'not to question the Saints' any longer, on the pretext of avoiding the sin one would incur in not obeying them, once their decision is known?

> Such a suggestion is most awful. Do not tolerate it! If one sins knowingly, one cannot fail to blame oneself for it. If, on the contrary, one sins because one failed to become informed, one will never condemn oneself and such ills will become incurable. That is precisely why the devil makes such a suggestion. . . . When the very idea comes to you of not being able to observe the [father's] decision on account of your weakness, question him in this manner. 'Father, I want to do such and such a thing: tell me which is worth more. I know that even when you tell me, I am unable to do it nor can I observe what you have said. I therefore want to inform myself only to be able to condemn myself for neglecting my spiritual profit.' On your part, this will be a sign of humility. May the Lord keep your heart, through the prayers of the Saints. Amen.[31]

Once we have a critical edition and a faithful translation of Barsanuphius, this will be worth more than any book in understanding the practice of spiritual direction among the eastern christian monks. Meanwhile, the distinction we have just seen, between an 'order' from and 'counsel' by the spiritual father is of little practical importance, just as it is not often found in spiritual writers, including Saint Basil,[32] for whom 'the one who disobeys excludes himself from salvation through a single sin, a single omission of a good deed.' This conclusion of D. Amand, which he himself calls 'a frightening teaching,' has been called into question. One would first have to see how the Byzantines interpreted it; Saint Theodore the Studite, the most scrupulous 'Basilian' there ever was, did not understand it differently, and the hagiographer indicates how heroically the Saints tried to conform to it. The Apophthegms of the Fathers have collected *one* anecdote concerning Saint Basil; it is not by chance that it deals specifically with obedience. Having come to the cenobium one day, the saint, 'after the suitable exhortation, said to the hegumen, "Do you have a brother here who is obedient?" The other says to him, "Master, all are your servants and hope to obtain salvation."' But Basil did not want to be diverted from his concern. 'He said to him once again, "Truthfully, do you have someone who is really obedient?"' [33] The rest indicates how even humility cannot prevail over obedience. The great Bishop of Caesarea orders the humble brother to let his hands be washed by him! This represents the height of submission since nothing is more contrary to the sense of hierarchy. [34]

The Fathers could even order *strebla*, astounding things! They were sometimes in the habit of doing this to novices, [35] to train them for unconditional obedience. The line mentioned above is mentioned by Saint Dorotheos, [36] but with a variation: 'Do you have someone here you expect to be saved (*tina tōn sōzomenōn*)?' Not understanding, the abba replied, 'Because of your prayers, Master, all (of us) want to be saved.' Basil repeats the question; then the other understood, 'for he too was a spiritual man.' One is on the path to salvation, one takes the matter of salvation and perfection seriously, only after one has decided to be obedient *everywhere* and *always*. I wonder whether Abba Isaiah, while writing 'The one who obeys is the Great one,'[37] was not alluding already to this episode with Saint Basil the Great. Meanwhile, I do not believe that the expression *blind faith* is ever found in the *Lives of the Fathers*. The Fathers did not consider blind the person who let himself be led by a guide of charismatic clearsightedness. The qualifier which may have given rise to the epithet 'blind' is that of *adiakritos hypakoē*, 'obedience without discernment,' here and now, as to a specific action. But discernment preceded when the spiritual father made the choice, and it is guaranteed forever by the certainty that God speaks through him. Even humanly speaking, it is wise to trust someone who is more prudent than you are. Proclus mentions a reflection by old Zeno stating that ready obedience (*eupeitheia*) is worth more than *phronēsis* (understanding) and *agchinoia* (cleverness of mind).[38] The *adiakritos hypotagē* must not be separated from its reason for being, which is precisely the need for discernment. It is because of the conviction that one does not have it that one presents one's problems to someone who possesses it; it is only logical to submit to his decisions. John Climacus has a still more striking sentence: *hypakoē estin apothesis diakrisiseōs en ploutō diakriseōs*, 'Obedience is putting aside discernment through an overabundance of discernment'—a definition that recalls one given by Evagrius concerning prayers, which is *apothesis noēmatōn*, 'laying thoughts aside.'[39] Saint John is fond of these 'oxymora' which in a few words gather antinomies which are an indication of intellectual and spiritual richness. To him, the paradox concerning obedience constitutes its greatest praise.   Saint Basil, unlike Saint Barsanuphius later, expressly protected the rights of the conscience and retained the right to say, eventually, 'obedience to God comes before obedience to men'[40]; but neither did he want the superior ever to order things that are preposterous or unreasoned. But if 'in superiors he does not tolerate arbitrary orders that lack all good sense as are customary among Egyptian ascetics to prove the obedience of the disciples,'[41] one should qualify this just observation of Dom Amand by adding that for Basil an order on the part of the superior does not become arbitrary and preposterous merely for the reason that its execution appears too difficult or even impossible to the subordinate.[42] 'The one to whom a task (beyond one's capacity) is given must not oppose it, because the limits of obedience reach all the way to death.'[43] The difference between Saint Basil and the Desert Fathers lies not so much in the doctrine of obedience as in the regulation of authority. It behooves the superior to regulate his orders according to reason, to adapt them to the strength and especially to the needs of each. This last consideration largely restores the possibility and usefulness of *strebla* which other prescriptions seemed to exclude. It is not always unreasonable to have preposterous things done by people who are too attached to *their* reasons, *their* reasoning. Thus among people who explicitly appeal to Saint Basil we find certain ways of behaving which would seem forbidden by the quotations from Saint Basil, if one would view these outside the eastern monastic climate. The essential interest in salvation and perfection demands the death of this perceptible attachment to self which is called one's own will or self-love (*philauteia*). All means are good to obtain this supreme result, except the ones that violate a divine commandment, that is, exactly those that would feed self-love.

In the discourse Symeon the New Theologian gave to the monks of Saint Mamas in surrendering his function as hegumen-spiritual father to Arsenius, his successor, there is a paragraph that summarizes Saint Basil's ideas. After exhorting his 'children, brothers, and fathers' to disclose all their thoughts and faults to the new superior, he continues:

> Do not conceive any dissatisfaction with his words or actions. If they should be contrary to the opinions of the Fathers, bow your head for the time being. Then, if some of you are distinguished through seniority or through life and competences, let them undertake especially to point out the inconveniences to him, according to the line of conduct described by Saint Basil. On days of irritation and bitterness, accept this with patience, for the love of God, without either contradicting or resisting it. The one who contradicts or is opposed to it is opposed to the authority of God, as Saint Paul says—in all things in which there is no transgression of the commandments of God or of the canons or of the *Apostolic Constitutions*—in all this you owe him obedience and docility as to the Lord, by necessity. On the contrary, in everything that would endanger the Gospel of Christ and the laws of his Church you do not owe obedience to him or to his orders and directives, not even to an angel who would descend expressly from heaven . . .[44]

The man who spoke this way showed an insatiable respect and veneration for his own spiritual father. During his monastic youth, he had become subservient once and for all to the old man (Symeon the Studite), whose slave he considered himself to be, ready to obey him joyfully and with haste, had he ordered Symeon to throw himself into a burning oven or into the depths of the sea. While performing the most menial tasls and greatly exhausting himself, he did not neglect his fasts and his vigils; he knew how useful they were and devoted himself to them without holding back. But the old man, to break his will, frequently ordered him to do the opposite of all this, and he forced him to eat and sleep. This was a great trial for Symeon but he endured these various exercises, for in his wisdom, the divine old man now made him taste humiliations and weariness, now gave him honor and rest. On both accounts he made him earn merit, by being opposed to his own will.[45]

Let us recall that Symeon was not an hegumen but merely a spiritual father. In turn, Symeon the New Theologian imposed 'various exercises' on his disciples, which were not always serious or reasonable. Thus one day, Arsenius, his future successor, had to consent 'to let himself be dragged throughout the entire monastery, to be a spectacle of ridicule' by other monks, while carrying around his neck the bodies of dead crows he had killed with a pole.[46] At another time, contrary to a sacrosanct monastic law, he had to eat poultry in public, or at least chew it and spit it out before 'sending it to his stomach', while listening to what was said in front of some distinguished guests: 'What a guzzler you are; once you start to eat the entire pigeon-house would not be enough to satisfy you.'—all this as punishment for a mere inner thought which his hegumen had conjectured. A bishop who had resigned and had entered Saint Mamas was not treated with more consideration.[47]

Practically the only limit to the spiritual father's authority is respect for yet a higher authority, the commandment of God. The classic examples of obedience mentioned by all the greek and latin authors even down to our own times come from the

East. Everyone knows the *exemplum* of the letter that was begun but not finished—but how many know its origin? It happened at Scetis, between abba Silvanus and Mark, his disciple, a calligrapher by profession.

He was loved by the old man because of his obedience. But there were eleven other disciples who were distressed that he was loved more than the others. Then the elders heard this, and they were grieved. One day they came to Silvanus and accused him. Taking them with him, he left, and knocked at the door of each cell, saying, 'Brother so and so, come; I need you.' Not one of them came forth immediately. But when he came to Mark's cell, he knocked, and said, 'Mark.' Hearing the old man's voice, he jumped up at once, and the old man sent him off to business. Then he said to the elders, 'Fathers, where are the other brothers?' Then he entered Mark's cell, examined his quire, and saw that he had begun to put his hand to the letter omega; but hearing the old man he had not turned his pen to finish it. The elders then said,'Indeed, abba, the one you love we also love, and God loves him.'[48]

Obedience goes hand in glove with renunciation of the world; the two virtues control each other and are measured one by the other. No one is readier to state this than Saint Theodore the Studite, who plays upon the two words *hypotagē* (obedience) and *apotagē* (renunciation).[49] It also seems that obedience will be perfect in proportion to *exagoreusis*. At any rate, 'there is nothing like the contest of *exagoreusis* and of perfect obedience; by these, the soul is enlightened and one's own will is mortified. Through them is obtained the perfect union (*eisoikēsis*) of the one who is born spiritually, with the one who engenders him.'[50] Without them, no virtue is worth anything; the other practices even become harmful. 'Where there is *exagoreusis*, there is firm trust; where there is trust, there is a cutting off of the will; and where the will is cut off

there is the perfection of obedience.'[51] This idea, the uselessness of every virtue outside of obedience, soon became an
indisputable maxim of cenobitism. We come across it at all
times, at least until the establishment of idiorrhythmy; and
even the this did not deny it on principle. Idiorrhythmy was
born, not from a revolt against obedience, but from the dividing of authority between fathers other than the hegumen.[52]
This is undoubtedly the reason why many a *Typikon* does not
want to hear about such a division of labor between the hegumen and some of these elders who remain his subordinates.
On this point, Saint Basil did not succeed in imposing his
views everywhere, not even among those who laid claim to him.

We give up the idea of transcribing or of translating the
encomia to obedience we come across in all eastern monastic
literatures. To end, let us quote yet another sentence of Saint
Theodore the Studite. While presenting himself at the monastery, Saint Plato said to Theoctistus, the novice master
(*paidiotribēs*): 'Father, I freely give everything to you: my
mind, my will, my body. Do with your servant what you
want; he will obey you in everything.'[53]

3. IN CHARITATE

The last word on spiritual fatherhood and sonship is not obedience. This is possible, and valid, only if it is accorded to
Christ himself, according to the word of Saint Paul.[1] The
superior must exercise his function as someone who is marked
by Christ: to be a doer first, then a teacher. The subordinate
must obey and submit himself as someone who renders obedience to Christ himself.[2] Saint Theodore the Studite followed an old tradition when he asked his own monks to love
their hegumen as the Apostles loved Christ. It goes without
saying that the hegumen, on his part, must love his monks as
Christ loved his Apostles.[3] 'I have only you and you have only
. . . Why call me father, if your heart is far from me?'[4]

Here we should reread the passage already quoted from the
Apostolic Constitutions: 'If the word of God, while referring to

parents according to the flesh, declares, "Honor your father and your mother, that your days may be long for you," how much more, with respect to spiritual parents, will the Word not exhort you to honor them like benefactors and intercessors with God—those who by the water have regenerated you, who have filled you with the Holy Spirit, who have reared you with the Word as with milk, bred you with doctrines, strengthened you by admonitions, deemed you worthy to partake of the precious body and blood of salvation, who made you partakers and joint heirs of God.'[5] Over the centuries, this text was to become law. We will always find it repeated, remembered, presupposed; more than one's parents according to the flesh, one must love one's fathers according to the spirit. Origen dealt with the 'order of charity' (*ordo caritatis*) in commenting on the line from The Song of Songs, *ordinate me in charitatem*, 'set charity in order in me.' Of course, one must love God above all, and love him without measure. Well before Saint Bernard, Origen gave the formulation: *Deum diligere nullus modus, nulla mensura est, nisi haec sola, ut ei totum exhibeas quantum habes*, 'In loving God, there is no limit, no measure; except this alone, that you give him everything you have.'[6] After God, one has to love like God himself those who lead us to God.

If, for example, someone toils in the word of God, instructs and enlightens our soul, shows us the way to salvation, and teaches us to live in an orderly way, he would surely be a good neighbor, but does it not seem that he should be loved much more than another neighbor who does none of these things? Even the other must be loved, of course, in so far as we are members of one body and partake of the same essence, but this one who— aside from the right he has to our love, like everyone else who is our neighbor—gives us a still more important reason for loving him in that he shows us the way to God and contributes to the salvation of our soul through the light he brings, ought to be loved much more.[7]

If someone removes me from sin or prevents me from committing sin, thereby saving me from the abyss of eternal death, 'Do you not think that, if possible, I should love him, after God, with the same fulness of love with which we love God himself?'[8] To the motive of gratitude should be added the consideration of merit, if the spiritual father is a saint; and we know he *must* be in order to fulfill his mission worthily. Thus we see spiritual children attached to their father as to their own eternal salvation. In this world their love for him can go as far as veneration, and may transfigure itself into a cult, in the liturgical sense of the word, as soon as their father has died. Saint Theodore the Studite undoubtedly had a particular aptness for behaving this way toward Saint Plato, who at the same time was his father in God and his maternal uncle. The letter, a few lines of which we will read, has been preserved, because it was kept in honor of the one saint as well as the other:

> You are my light, the ever-burning lamp dispersing the dark thoughts of my soul, the rod sustaining the faintness of my heart, the dissolution of my sadness, the promoter of my eagerness, my good news, my joy, my fear, my glory. Without you, the sun itself appears dark. Not one of the things on earth would be pleasant to me, if you were not present. What is more desirable than a true father in God? A son who loves his father knows this, if he is faithful. But is there a need for many words? I will tell you what happened: time and again, though I did not intend to come to your holy cell, it happened, imperceptibly, that I came to you as if someone had dragged me. When you asked the reason for my visit, I did not know how to answer, so greatly did my salvation depend upon you.[9]

One should read all the other letters addressed to the same (monk). And in the panegyric apparently delivered shortly after Plato's death,[10] Theodore, far from asking intercessory prayers for him, stated without hesitation: 'Now he is in heaven, deserving, I dare say, not merely the order of ascetics, but added to the choir of confessors (*choreiais homologētōn*— originally this last word meant 'martyr') since he endured their struggles. He surely also shares their destiny', and so forth.[11] In a word, Theodore canonized his spiritual father.

We will discover the same fervor of filial devotion in Symeon the New Theologian. But here, there will be drama, the drama of an entire life and an entire spirituality. The hegumen of Saint Mamas had been a novice at Studios. After only a few months he was expelled by Peter, the superior of the famous monastery, who was 'neglecting his duty and jealous' of the trust the novice had in his spiritual father, a simple monk, not a priest.[12] Having entered Saint Mamas, whose hegumen, Antony, was apparently more generous, he always remained faithful to Symeon the Studite, his 'good shepherd', and Symeon continued to direct him by paying frequent visits.[13] This went on for about ten years (977-986) until the spiritual father's death. Beginning at the first anniversary of this blessed death, in 987, and every year after that, 'the disciple, conforming to the Apostolic tradition, celebrated with great pomp the memory of this father like that of all the other saints. . . .'[14] Resentments arose. Symeon had to justify this cult to Stephen of Nicomedia, the syncellus of the Patriarch, to the Patriarch himself and to the entire synod. This has left us with a formal defense of his conduct in a detailed document dealing with the duties of disciples toward their spiritual fathers. The arguments are taken from Scripture: 'Anyone who welcomes you welcomes me; and those who welcome me welcome the one who sent me.'[15] Also, 'Anyone who welcomes a prophet because he is a prophet will have a prophet's reward.'[16] Then from the *Apostolic Constitutions*, evidently viewed as authentic laws enunciated by 'eye witnesses of the Word': 'You will honor him who speaks the word of God to you, and be mindful of him day and night. You will reverence him as the author of your salvation, for where the doctrine concerning God is, there God is present.'[17] And we already know,[18] the classical text.[19] Then follows

Saint John Chrysostom with his *Panegyric on Philogonius*[20]: 'If our natural parents are entitled to such great attentiveness on our part, how much more so our spiritual fathers.' We may omit the rest which refers mostly to the canonization performed by Symeon. But he stubbornly believed he had done this according to his right and duty, a sign of the unlimited religious attachment he had felt for his father in God while he was still alive.

Moreover, Symeon could have mentioned other patristic arguments. In the Apophthegms of the Fathers, Isidore, priest of Nitria, teaches: 'The disciples must love (*philein*) their spiritual masters as fathers, and they should respect them as leaders, in such a way that their love does not slacken their fear and their fear does not obscure love.'[21] Smirnov, who quotes this text,[22] comments: 'Here love was not the main feature of the relationship [between the disciple and his director]: it did not banish all fear.' This observation lends itself to false interpretation. Fear of the spiritual father is like the fear of God: it limits love as long as each is imperfect—a more or less servile fear and a love that is not yet truly filial. When fear itself becomes filial—we would then call it respect—it represents the most exquisite, the most spiritual element of love. Saint John Chrysostom (at least if the Migne text is correct), states explicitly that trust in and love for the spiritual father are addressed to God who, in turn, 'in unknown ways, will suggest to him that he become attached to you and kindly disposed toward you, just as you are well disposed toward him.'[23] Let us note once more that the initiative always comes from the disciple; if he wants a spiritual father who is wholeheartedly interested in his soul, he must begin by putting his trust in him and submitting himself to him wholeheartedly.

These teachings have been repeated at all times, with little variation in the expression. Here, in the fourteenth century, is Gregory Palamas:

> Moreover, if we love and honor our parents according to the flesh, how much more will you honor and love those

who have become parents to you according to the spirit, who led you from being to well being (*apo tou einai eis to eu einai*—the vocabulary of Maximus the Confessor!), who communicated to you the light of the knowledge [of God], and taught the manifestation of truth, who regenerated you through the bath of regeneration, who implanted the hope of the resurrection in you, and of immortality, and of the unending kingdom and heritage, who changed you from being unworthy to being worthy of eternal blessings, from earthly to heavenly, from ephemeral to eternal, a son and disciple no longer of a man but of the God-Man Jesus Christ, who gave you the Spirit of sonship and said, 'You must call no one on earth your father, since you have only one Father, and he is in heaven.'[24] You owe all honor and love to your spiritual fathers, because the honor given them ascends to Christ and to the Holy Spirit from whom you received the sonship, and to the heavenly Father, 'from whom every family, whether spiritual or natural, takes its name.' You will apply yourself to having a spiritual father all your life, and to showing him every sin and thought, to receiving healing and forgiveness from him . . . And you will obey them and will not contradict them, so that you do not bring destruction upon your soul. For the one who contradicts those who have engendered him according to the flesh, in things that are not prohibited by divine law, is killed according to the Law: how could the one who contradicts his fathers according to the Spirit not drive out the Spirit of God, and destroy his soul? Therefore, always, to the end, consult and listen to your spiritual fathers, that your soul may be saved . . . ?[25].

The fourth commandment of God seems to have great force with reference to spiritual fathers.

The *Century* of Kallistos and Ignatius of Xanthopoulos, which is a handbook of hesychast spirituality, likewise explains at great length the disciple's duties toward his spiritual father.[26] These two authors are widely read and they attempt to systematize what they had learned from the Fathers. Here, in fact, they especially follow John Climacus.

> The person who is truly obedient must, of necessity, possess the following virtues: a pure and unfeigned faith [trust] in his director, even to the point of seeing Christ himself in him and of obeying him as he would obey Christ, according to the word of Jesus, 'Who hears you hears me and who despises you despises me.' Everything that does not result from faith is a sin, John Climacus says.[27] The second virtue is truth [sincerity]: to be truthful in word and deed, and through a precise revelation of thoughts. The third virtue: cutting off one's own will. To the person who obeys, doing one's own will is damaging, it is said.[28] But one should cut it off willingly, and not as compelled by one's father. The fourth: absolutely not to contradict or contest. Contradiction and contestation are not concerns of religious people. Saint Paul writes: 'If anyone might still want to argue: it is not the custom with us, nor in the church of God.'[29] Contradiction and arguing are caused by a mentality accustomed to a lack of faith and proud ideas, as has been said, 'A proud monk strongly contradicts.'[30] The fifth virtue to be observed is to make a sincere and detailed confession to the superior, according to the promise we made when we were tonsured, and in some way before the awesome tribunal of Christ, before God and the holy angels. In addition to our other obligations, we must view the disclosure of the secrets of our heart as the beginning and the end (of everything).[31]

The Xanthopoulos' presuppose the love for the spiritual father more than they say. Was it necessary to state what was accepted by everyone? Emperor Manuel Palaeologus himself reminded the monks that they must 'view their superior as a father; even better, far more than a father, inasmuch as spiritual realities are more excellent than carnal things.'[32]

We have seen that it was not always easy to live up to all these duties when we spoke of the severity needed in every education, especially the ascetic. But then we viewed the problem from the superior's point of view. Seen from the disciple's perspective, the problem is not the same. The master must *show* that his love for the disciple is sincere; the disciple must *acquire* a spirituality he does not yet possess. This is why the son must feel the father's rigorousness more than the father needs to impose it on him. The aim of everything is the novice's progress; no profit from this should return to the spiritual father, at least not intentionally. Has it, in fact, always been that way? To suppose this would be naive, to want to prove it, even more so. The 'exceedingly negligent and intemperate old man' whose excesses John Climacus reports.[33] will give us an example of what it may cost a young monk to fulfill his obligations towards the master, if by the permission of Providence the latter forgets to do his. The story seemed so extraordinary to the scholiast that he thought it would be good to write a gloss on the word 'intemperate' (*akolastos*): the term is used not only when speaking of impurity, but of intemperance, even if it is inward, as in the case of anger.[34] Climacus puts the story in the mouth of a Sabaite monk named John:

In the monastery in which I lived, in Asia, there was an old man who was exceedingly negligent and intemperate. I make this known for the cause of truth, not to judge. This man, I do not know how, had acquired a disciple, still a young man, named Acacios, of a simple mind, but not imprudent. He had to suffer so many insults from this old man that the story may seem unbelievable to many. He violently attacked him not only with insults and humiliations, but every day he badly punished him with stripes and blows. The young man's patience was not without reason. Every day I saw him mistreated like some slave that could be bought. Oftentimes when I would meet him, I said, 'Brother Acacios, how are you today?' Thereupon he showed me now a black eye, sometimes an injured neck, or a head bruised by blows. Knowing how patient he was, I said to him, 'Well done; endure, and you will derive profit.' After staying with this savage man for nine years, the disciple went to the Lord. Five days after his burial in the cemetery of the Fathers, Acacios' master went to see a famous old man in the region and said, 'Father, brother Acacios is dead.' Upon hearing this, the other replied, 'Believe me, old man, I do not think so. Come and see.' The old man quickly rose and together they hastened to the cemetery of the noble and blessed athlete. Standing at the grave, he exclaims to the one who indeed was alive in his sleeping, 'Brother Acacios, are you dead?' And the wise, obedient subject, giving proof of his obedience even after death, replied, 'Father, how could it be that a man of obedience would die?' Frightened, Acacios' former superior fell to the ground in tears and asked the hegumen for a cell close to the tomb. There he lived sensibly for the rest of his life, always saying to the Fathers, 'I have murdered a man.'

A scholion absolves us from drawing the moral of this story: 'He is rightly called a superior in name, not in fact. A true superior is eager to awaken his disciple to imitate his example; he will be recognized by his works. The one was a slave to anger; the other a master of anger. How then is he shown to be the superior of one who far surpassed him in virtue?'[35]

This Acacios would certainly have deserved his name (which means, 'without malice'), had he succeeded in loving his master who was neither spiritual nor a father. Would it not have been better to look for another? Yet, there was a way to make the solution to this spiritual problem easier: namely, to convince oneself that the Fathers 'do not do this for real' (*en alētheią*), but merely to test. This is what the same John Climacus puts into the mouth of a certain Abbacyrus, whom he often saw thrown out of the refectory to go to bed unfed (*adeipnos*). 'Believe me, Father, my fathers do this to see if I can be a monk, and not for real (*en alētheią*). I know their intention, and I endure it all without difficulty.' But we ask whether under such circumstances, 'ill' treatment still remains effective. John Climacus asked this himself, and his answer seems rather negative, or at least deprecatory. 'We do not earn the title 'patient' when we bravely endure the father's mockery (*myktērismos*),[36] but when we are despised and beaten by everyone. We endure the father out of respect and out of duty. Bravely drink the *myktērismos* on the part of everyone, like a life-giving water.'[37] It is like a remedy for concupiscence, while praises and signs of esteem develop the sinful humors.[38] The bitterness of absinth is better than the treacherous sweetness of honey. 'One should therefore without disquiet trust those who are in charge of us in the Lord.'

One could fill a volume with pages of this sort taken from all the byzantine spiritual writers. Paul Evergetinos alone gathered enough material for seven chapters on this subject.[39] His sources are Saint Gregory, the *Life* of Saint Pachomius, the *Life* of Saint Antony the Younger from the time of the Iconoclasts, the *Gerontikon*, Saint Ephrem, the *Life* of Saint Theodius the Cenobiarch, the *Life* of Saint Theodore, the *Life* of Saint Euthymus, the *Voyages of Saint Peter* (the Pseudo-Clementines), abba Isaiah, Saint Barsanuphius, Antiochus Pandectes, Mark the Ascetic, Saint Maximus, the *Life* of Saint Arsenius, the *Life* of Gregory Thaumaturgus—as we see, all undisputed authorities.

This abundance of witnesses proves once again what we have said: spiritual direction is so indispensable that nothing excused the ascetic from the obligation of finding a spiritual director and remaining faithful to him, of obeying him, respecting and loving him, regardless.[40]

NOTES

1. HAVING A SPIRITUAL FATHER

1. See Irenée Hausherr, *Penthos. La doctrine de la componction dans l'Orient chrétien*, OrChrA 132 (Rome, 1944) 53-54 [translation by Anselm Hufstader, *Penthos. The Doctrine of Compunction in the Christian East* (Kalamazoo: 1982).— ed.]
2. *Letter* 565, p. 274, ed. Nicodemus the Hagiorite (Venice, 1816).
3. Hesychius Presbyter, *De temperantia et virtute. Centuria* I, 1; PG 93: 1481A.
4. Philo, *Legum allegoriae* I, XXVI, 84.
5. Gregorius Theologus, *Oratio* XLIII, *In laudem Sancti Basilii* n. 77, PG 36: 600A.
6. *Tractatus ad Eulogium* XX; PG 79: 1117D.
7. *Ibid.*, XIX.
8. *Oratio* XIV, *De pauperum amore* (Paris, 1609), p. 217A.
9. See, for example, *Vie de Léonce de Jérusalem*, Neon Ecologion (1863) 263, col. 1; *Vie de Grégoire le Sinaïte*, ed. Pomialovsky, pp. 8, 12; *Vie de Sainte Theoctiste de Lesbos*, ed. Theophilou Ioannou, p. 5, etc.
10. *Petite Catéchèse*, ed. Auvray, p. 203ff.
11. Eustathius Thessalonicensis, *Peri hypokriseos* n. 27; PG 37: 396D.
12. See A. Cronia, *Saggi di letteratura bulgara antica*, p. 75.
13. *Loc. cit.*
14. Preuschen, p. 24, 17 (CS 34:63).
15. *Ibid.*, p. 30, 15 (68).
16. *Ibid.*, p. 48, 8 (71).
17. *Ibid.*, p. 47, 13ff (78).
18. *Diatyposis of Saint Athanasius.* in Ph. Meyer, *Die Haupturkunden fuer die Geschichte der Athoskloester* (Leipzig, 1894) 124, 27ff.
19. Bk I, ch. 21, p. 67ª.
20. *Ibid.* (1861 edition) p. 67, col. 1; cfr Cassian, *Collatio* II, 13.
21. Evergetinos, *loc. cit.*, p. 68, n. 1.
22. *Loc. cit.*, p. 68, col. 1 *infra* ff=Barsanuphius, ed. Nicodemus the Hagiorite, *Letter* 358, p. 182.
23. See above, p. 186.
24. Vaticanus Graecus 1436, fol. 266-84, and frequently elsewhere.
25. *Ibid.*, fol. 269.
26. Smirov, p. 25ff.
27. As found in Migne; PG 34: 1138.
28. *Epistola* XXIII; PG 32: 296B.
29. Mt 15:14.
30. Mt 10:25.
31. *Sermo de renuntiatione saeculi* n. 2-3; PG 31: 632A-3A.

2. FAITH AND SUBMISSION

1. *Un grand mystique byzantin. La Vie de S. Syméon le Nouveau Théologien par Nicétas Stéthatos*, ed. Irénée Hausherr and G. Horn, *Orientalia Christiana* 12 (Rome, 1928) xlixff.
2. *Letter* 359, n. 182.

3. Ps 35:7.
4. Is 38:1-5.
5. Jon 3:4.
6. *Letter* 360, p. 183.
7. Smirnov, p. 49.
8. Mt 26:50.
9. Joannes Climacus, *Scala Paradisi, Gradus* IV; PG 88: 724B.
10. *Vitae Patrum* V, 16, 18, PL 73: 972D-73B.
11. *Alph.,* Poemen n. 174; PG 65: 364D.
12. See *Regulae fusius tractatae, interrogatio* 7; PG 31: 928-33C.
13. See Amand, *L'ascèse monastique de Saint Basile* (Maredsous, 1948) 326-35.
14. S. Nilus, *Logos asceticos, Tractatus de monastica exercitatione,* ch. 41; PG 79: 769D-72A.
15. *Sermo de renuntiatione saeculi* n. 4; PG 31: 633B.
16. Evergetinos I, ch. 19, p. 57, col. 1.
17. *Vitae Patrum* V, 15, 64, PL 73: 964D.
18. See Theodore the Studite, *Grande Catéchèse* 63, ed. Papadopoulos-Kerameus, p. 443; A. Mai, *Patrum Nova Bibliotheca,* vol. 8 (Rome, 1871) 134.
19. Buffon, cited by Littre, art. '*ane.*'
20. See Suidas, s.v. *onos,* ed. Adler, III, p. 540-43.
21. See, for example, Theodore the Studite, *loc. cit.* See above, n. 18.
22. *AnBoll* 70 (1932) 46.
23. *Regulae fusius tractatae, interrogatio* 28; PG 31: 989BC.
24. *Vitae Patrum* V, 14, 12, PL 73: 950B.
25. *Letter* 285, p. 154.
26. In the 1862 Moscow edition, p. 34.
27. A note by the Russian editor states that 'the one who has mortified the passionate will in himself is a father.' This is based on John Climacus, *Scala Paradisi, Gradus* IV, *Scholion* 5 (PG 88: 729CD): 'He speaks of the superior. He has accepted in himself the subject's will which he has put to death, so to speak. He will give an account to God for his subject.' All these interpretations presuppose a text that differs from Migne's, which reads: 'The one who has piously put to death his own soul (*kai mononouchi ethanatōsen auton*) will answer for all.' Therefore, it is the disciple himself, unless the reference is to Christ who remained obedient unto death and will be the defender (*apologēsetai*) of those who, like Him, put no limit on their obedience.
28. *Letter* 365, p. 185.
29. *Letter* 366, p. 186.
30. *Letter* 368, p. 186.
31. *Letter* 369, p. 187.
32. See Marcel Viller, *La spiritualité des premiers siècles chrétiens* (Paris, 1930) 70; Dom David Amand, *L'ascèse monastique de Saint Basile* (Maredsous, 1948) 264-68, especially 283.
33. *Alph., De magno Basilio;* PG 65: 137BC.
34. See *Alph.,* John Colobos, n. 7.
35. See *Alph., Joseph of Panephysis,* n. 5 (CS 89:103).
36. *Doctrina* I, n. 17; PG 88: 1640A-C.
37. *Logos* III, n. 3, ed. Augoustinos Iordanites (Jerusalem, 1911) p. 11, 7.
38. *Proclus ad Hesiod., Op. et D.,* 291; see von Arnim, *Stoicorum veterum fragmenta* I, p. 46, n. 225.

39. Nilus, *De oratione*, chs. 69, 70; cfr John Climacus, *Scala Paradisi*, *Gradus* XXVIII; PG 88: 112A.
40. *Regulae brevius tractatae*, *interrogatio* 114; PG 31: 1160A.
41. Amand, p. 332.
42. *Reg. brev. tract.*, *interr.* 28; PG 31: 989B.
43. *Ibid.*, *interr.* 152; PG 31: 1181D.
44. *Un grand mystique*, n. 66, p. 90.
45. *Ibid.*, 12, p. 20.
46. *Ibid.*, n. 49, p. 64.
47. *Ibid.*, n. 56, pp. 76f.
48. *Alph.*, Mark, *disciple of Abba Silvanus* 1; PG 65:273D-96A (CS 59:145-46).
49. *Laudatio S. Platonis hegumeni* 9; PG 99:812C.
50. *Ibid.*, c. 10; 812D
51. *Ibid.*, 32; 836B.
52. Cf. *An Boll* 70 (1952) 40, n. 2.
53. *Eloge*, n. 9; 812A.

3. IN CHARITATE

1. Eph 6:5.
2. Theodore Studites, *Epistola* 43; PG 99: 1245C.
3. See *Grande Catéchèse*, ed. Papadopoulos-Kerameus, p. 456.
4. *Ibid.*, p. 540.
5. See above, p. 18.
6. *Origenis in Canticum Cantic.*; PG 13: 156A.
7. PG 13: 156A.
8. See Hélène Pétré, 'Ordinata Caritas. Un enseignement d'Origène sur la charité,' in *RSR* 42 (1954) 40-57.
9. *Epistolarum Liber* I, 2; PG 99: 909BC.
10. See PG 99: 848Cff.
11. *Ibid.*, 44,. col. 848Bff.
12. *Vie de Syméon*, ed. Irénée Hausherr and G. Horn, *Orientalia Christiana* 12 (Rome, 1928) n. 11 and 12.
13. Nn. 23 and 24.
14. Nn. 72 and 81.
15. Mt 10:40.
16. *Ibid.* 41.
17. *Constit. Apostol.*, VII, 9, ed. Funk, p. 398.
18. See above, p. 208.
19. L. II, ch. 33, Funk, p. 115.
20. *De beato Philogonio* VI; PG 48: 747-49.
21. *Alph.*, Isidore the priest n. 5 (CS 59:107).
22. Smirnov, p. 53.
23. *Scala Paradisi*, *Gradus* IV; PG 88: 705; trans. Lazarus Moore, *The Ladder of Divine Ascent* (Boston, 1978) 39.
24. Mt 23:9.
25. Gregory Palamas, *Decalogus christianae legis*; PG 150: 1096Cff.
26. *Opuscula ascetica*; PG 147: 653-64.
27. Indeed, John Climacus says this, PG 88: 681A, but it is Rom 14:23, understood in an accommodating sense.

28. See Climacus; PG 88: 1112C.
29. 1 Cor 11:16.
30. Climacus; PG 88: 965D.
31. *Century*, col. 656A-C.
32. *Chrysobull* of 1406, ed. Ph. Meyer, *Haupturkunden* (Leipzig, 1894) 206, 17-19.
33. *Gradus* IV; PG 88: 720B-21A.
34. *Scholion* 86, col. 757D.
35. *Schol.*, 88, col. 760A.
36. In ascetic language, this term looks like a *terminus technicus*, as it occurs very frequently.
37. *Gradus* IV; col. 713AB.
38. Col. 717AB.
39. Bk I, chs. 33-39, pp. 115-37.
[40.] [On friendship, see Dom André Louf, 'L'accompagnement spirituel aujourd'hui,' in *Vie Consacrée* n. 1 (1981) 32-43. English translation by Luke Harris, "Two Idols of Spiritual Companionship," in *Hallel: A Review of Monastic Spirituality* (Autumn, 1985) 104-15, and Brian P. McGuire, *Friendship and Community. The Monastic Experience, 350-1250*, Cistercian Studies, 95 (Kalamazoo, 1988)—tr.]

VII

THE REVELATION OF
THOUGHTS IN PRACTICE

NOTHING IS MORE EVIDENT than the obliga-
tion not to hide anything from the spiritual director.
Still, we would like to know how this was done in
practice. Those who read St Barsanuphius can watch day
after day the spectacle of questions and answers between the
disciple and the master. The one thing they have to remember
is that ordinarily such conversations took place live (*viva voce*).
The case of the Great Recluse is an exception for which we
can appropriately thank Providence.

First, before someone goes to *tell* what passes through his
head or the heart or though his imagination or through one's
disposition (of mind), one must become aware of it oneself.
Some psychologists maintain that for reasons of health it is
better not to become too self-aware: the best human organs are
those we are inattentive to. But this principle cannot be applied to the moral life; here, the first law will always be the
Socratic *gnōthi seauton* (Know Thyself). This is why examination of conscience is absolutely indispensable. Philosophers of
all schools—from Plato to Epictetus, from Marcus Aurelius to
Plotinus and beyond—have unanimously recommended and

practiced it, and had it practiced. The reason for this is simple: to renounce examination of conscience is to renounce 'philosophy' itself which is the pursuit of wisdom; and which claims that wisdom means *life* according to reason, and not merely nor mainly 'intellectualism'. Among Christians is to be added the '*Probet autem seipsum homo*' ('let a person examine himself')[1] out of respect for the holiness of God. The ascetics have always understood this well. A few reminders: Origen[2] offers a remarkable questionaire, under two rubrics: *quid sit ipsa [anima] et qualiter moveatur, id est quid in substantia et quid in affectibus habeat* (the soul must know what she is in herself, and how she is actuated; that is to say, what she is like essentially and what she is like according to her dispositions). In other words, one should try to discover what stage one is at, where our desires tend, and what our dislike is aimed at. A catalogue of virtues and vices will render great service. 'Anger, for example: does one suppress it with some and give vent to it with others? . . . Or sadness: does one overcome it for certain things but not for others, or in everything? It is the same for fear and the other vices that are opposed to the virtues,' and so on. Furthermore, this is not the only time Origen wrote on this subject.[3] When Evagrius Ponticus, following Origen, established his sequence of 'the eight evil thoughts' and applied his acumen on the particularities of each, and especially when in his *Antirrheticus* he makes an impressive list of the various suggestions, he leads his reader to an increasingly acute introspection. The treatise *De malignis cogitationibus (On Evil Thoughts)* could be entitled *Manuductio ad examen cogitationum (A Guide for the Examination of Thoughts)*. There is no need to bring up once more the Desert Fathers, whose voice we hear through Evagrius and Cassian.[4]

Saint Dorotheos too returned to the same subject more than once; in addition to the two examinations (morning and evening), he recommends that one examine oneself 'every six hours'.[5]

We will not mention other names, that would be too easy. But an observation is called for: it is not the examination of conscience as such that constitutes the best preparation for *exagoreusis* (revelation of thoughts), save as a sacramental confession. In so far as the latter is an unveiling of thoughts (*logismoi*), what should above all precede it is what byzantine ascetic idiom calls *nepsis* (watchfulness). One should always stand guard at the door of one's heart or mind, and ask every suggestion that presents itself, 'Are you one of ours, or from the opposing camp?'[6] And precisely because one knows, by hypothesis and from experience, that one is often unable to tell the wolf from the sheep—the devil transforming himself into an angel of light—one will never run out of questions to ask the spiritual director, thanks to this unceasing attentiveness. Perhaps it would be better to forget these? Indeed, if the spiritual father invites us to; but until then, it is better to submit all of them to him and to remember the answers until the next consultation. A well-known anecdote reported by John Climacus illustrates the point very well. In a certain monastery, he notes how 'the person in charge of the refectory had a habit which intrigued me greatly. He carried a small book, hanging from his belt, in which he used to jot down the thoughts that came down to him during the day, and he showed all these to the superior. He was not the only one to do this. I discovered that more of the others did the same thing, on orders of the cenobiarch.'[7] This custom must not have been regular or even widespread, since John Climacus did not know it before visiting this monastery, and he himself does not recommend it. If he reports it nonetheless, it is because he approves of vigilance over one's thoughts and their divulgence. Furthermore, with a monk, above all a solitary, such thoughts engrave themselves spontaneously in a memory that had to remember few other things. In so far as someone was intent on referring to some of them and attributed great importance to them, they had to be revealed. It could happen, however, that one would be forgotten, as we have seen with abba Poemen; as soon as it emerged once more in his memory, it became subject to disclosure.

In view of all this, we might think that the spiritual father would not have a minute's rest, especially in a community, and when he was its hegumen. Indeed, famous abbots of the past admitted that receiving confidences and responding to the consultations of their subordinates was a heavy task,[8] even a drudgery; but there must have been set times for this. The refectorian of whom John Climacus speaks and his notebook prove this. And then, except for scrupulous and restless spirits, life itself, age, experience and the practice of daily account making had gradually to reduce the maddening exuberance of thoughts to just a few, always the same, which the disciple could rapidly mention and the master could analyze. What is true for 'openness of heart' is also true for the 'particular examination of conscience.' The ancients knew the latter but did not often speak of it because a general examination faithfully made would itself become a particular examination[9] as long as one's temperament or environment did not change. Thus we see Saint Dosithee running to his spiritual father at every whim. Dorotheos took his problems seriously but not tragically, and never said that Dosithee was wrong in relating them. By contrast, Saint Barsanuphius, the 'Great Ancient', was in charge of the most advanced monks in the same monastery of Seridos, future candidates for the hesychast life. Here we see, taken from life, the phenomenon of the concentration of thoughts. In the collection of *Letters* edited by Nicodemus the Hagiorite[10] the words *tou autou . . . pros auton* recur frequently: '*From the same* Barsanuphius (or John) *to the same* consultant'; and what is usually presented is the same problem, taking on different aspects or nuances at successive times. Thus we hear, for example, of a certain abba Euthymius who returned for advice several times[11]; then of a sick man named Andrew, whom we have already met,[12] and so forth. Andrew, happy to live close to the Holy Recluse, had spoken, appropriately enough, of his illness. Barsanuphius consoled him by assuring him that 'God demands nothing else except thanksgiving, patience, and prayer for the forgiveness of sins,' and by adding some words, complicated as are all declarations in which a little shame is added to the delicacy of feelings: 'See how proud I am! The demons make sport of me, and I imagine having true godly charity! I cannot refrain from telling you, "From this moment on, I take upon myself half your burden. Once again, God will come to our help".'[13] All this was very comforting, but Andrew suffered from rheumatism and consequently from melancholy. 'He was saddened because the saint had told him, "I take upon myself half your burden," instead of promising him total remission. . . .' Barsanuphius explained to him why he could not speak otherwise. The sick man did not know how to behave with his companion who was equally ill. Having no physical strength, Andrew was led to ask himself whether salvation could even be achieved.[14] He even feared that his rheumatism came from the demons; furthermore, he could not fast, and in his dream he saw wild beasts. In short, on all sides he was beset by the temptation of sadness. Barsanuphius never tired of commanding him: Fear not! Your illness comes from God, for your salvation. Was Job not a good friend of God? One day, after receiving a letter from the Grand Old Man, the sick man was healed. Joy and enthusiasm—soon followed by new anxious questions concerning the 'canon' to follow for health recovered! The wise Barsanuphius moderated exaltation and fervor as he tried to raise the other's despondency.[15] Health did not last; there are stomach problems: 'After midnight, my mouth is dry, and so are my eyelids and my hands and feet. When I wake up my body begins to shake, starting with the stomach. I am falling apart; I become like mud. I wanted to recite a psalm, but I could not with my lips; if I try to pray from memory, sleep overtakes me. I no longer know what to do; I see how hampered I am in the work of salvation. . . .'[16] And this goes on, without Barsanuphius getting tired of hearing it or of restating the same thing: that Andrew is an impressionable fellow whose exaggerated reactions never allow him to find or observe the golden mean.

To another who had many questions (*Letters* 60 to 89 are addressed to him) and who perhaps ended up by discovering himself how he exaggerated, Barsanuphius wrote: 'One should not ask questions about all the thoughts that are [in your mind]; they are fleeting, but [ask] only about the ones that persist and wage war on man. Take a man who is insulted by a whole crowd of people; he scorns injuries and becomes utterly indifferent. But if some one person attacks him and wages war on him, then he lodges a complaint in the presence of the magistrate. Thus it is with this matter [of thoughts].'[17] As if by chance, this was the last letter to that correspondent.

Spiritual direction does not exempt the disciple from making use of common sense, or prayer, or his own good will. Many diabolic suggestions or others will disappear by themselves; the ones that linger or return persistently are to be the subject of a report to the spiritual father.

> Brother, do not rush into the discernment of thoughts that come to you. You are not qualified for this. If you continue, they will agitate you at will like someone who knows nothing of their deceptions. If they bother you, say to them, 'I do not know what species you are. God who knows will not let you confound me.' Turn over your powerlessness to God, by saying, 'Lord, I am in your hands. Come to my help, and deliver me from their hands.' But mention the thought that lingers in you and wages war upon you to your abba, and he will heal you, through God.[18]

This is what normally happened: once the after-effects of the influences undergone in the world had been eliminated, the ascetic simply became himself with the temperament he had since birth and his early years. The relative but very real solitude and the monotony of the monastic environment gradually erased habits of thinking and acting that did not result from basic human nature itself. And this clearing away made one's essential character traits stand out more clearly. All spiritual life simplifies (which does not mean 'impoverishes'), especially if it is pursued steadfastly in a favorable surrounding. This is why as one progressed, recourse to the spiritual father could be less frequent. The incontrovertible evidence for this is the great fact of hesychasm. To be a hesychast one had to start with years in the common life, under the supervision of the hegumen. Once this trial had been undergone to the superior's satisfaction, one could occupy an isolated cell, to return to the community only once a week to attend the liturgy and see one's director. To them applied the advice of John of Lycopolis (?): 'Discern your thoughts devoutly, according to God; if you cannot, ask the person who is able to discern them.'[19] Some even went so far as to state: 'The person who has achieved spiritual submission and has subjected the body to the spirit does not need to be subservient to man. He is subject to the Word of God and to the Law, like one whose obedience has been well-proven.'[20] 'An old man said, "The one who wants to live in the desert needs to be a doctor, not one who needs to be taught—otherwise he will suffer because of it."'[21] The eternal question is whether there are such perfect men who will assuredly remain so.

All the others, especially in cenobitic monasteries, remained subject to the obligation of accounting for their thoughts. Materially, however, this law was not the same everywhere. Here is another question that awaits some patient researcher who would go through the *Typika*, the *Diatypōseis* (Rules of monastic orders), the *Hypotypōseis* (Outlines, Characteristics), and other documents of this genre. A few indications: in the cenobium of Saint Euthymius, *exagoreusis* must take place daily, at night.[22] The same ordinance, or custom, is found in the *Life* of Saint Leontius of Jerusalem,[23] and in the *Typikon* of Pacourianos.[24] Antony the Studite (974-980) mentions the same rule, which had evidently passed into disuse. His short homily to the monks of Studios[25] is but an echo, a distant one of almost two hundred years, of the exhortations and complaints of the great Saint Theodore. 'Daily confession,' he writes in one short sentence, 'brings daily enlightenment.'[26] The *Constitutiones Studitanae* prescribed that the hegumen 'leave the choir every morning at Orthros, at the beginning of the Fourth Ode. He should sit down for confession (*eis ten exaggelian*), receive the brothers who come to seek him and give salutary spiritual care to each one.'[27]

The *Typikon* of Our Lady the Beneficent imposes two sessions on the hegumen. 'The superior must sit down twice a day in an isolated spot. All other affairs being ended, including the care of administration and of organization, he must bring the greatest care to listening to those who wish to confess, and prescribe a suitable cure for each. We decree that the first session be after the morning psalmody has started; at that moment, he will attend to those who always remain in the monastery and are not occupied with some ministration. After Compline he will look after those who deal with services outside and inside.'[28] A much later document, the *Typikē Diataxis*, decreed by Nilus, hieromonk and hegumen, for the monastery of the Most Holy Mother of God, which he founded in 1210, describes the same practice in greater detail, in chapter eleven:

We must also speak about the salutary *exagoreusis*. At every vigil (*argypnia*) and on the occasion he will choose himself, the superior must leave to go to the diakonikon. All other affairs being ended, including worries of administration and management, he must bring the greatest care to listen to those who wish to confess, and suggest a suitable remedy to each. Let him be authorized (for he may not have enough time since the brotherhood has increased) to charge those whom he wishes among the priests or even among the most devout brothers wearing the great habit to receive confidential thoughts from the majority of monks who are less educated. By this I understand the thoughts of every day and of every hour which quite obviously one must allow and condone, because they are easy to control and do not cause persistent trouble. As for those that require a more attentive medical examination, those who receive their avowal must report them to the superior, who will apply a suitable cure.[29]

The rest of the text is an impassioned exhortation to practice *exagoreusis*.

One would like to have been present at one of these interviews between the spiritual father and his child in God. For want of recordings and television we are reduced to guess work. But we can still reconstruct things, at least in great outline. In detail, there must have been an infinite variety of *duration* and *manner*. As for duration, all indications lead us to believe that *exagoreusis* was generally short. This is evident for crowded monasteries; but how Saint Theodore the Studite managed to grant each of his consultants even a few minutes will always remain a mystery to us when we hear it said that at the best times his flock numbered a thousand monks.[30] Also, we should remember that Theodore had under his jurisdiction not only the monastery of John the Baptist at Studios, in Constantinople, but also the daughter houses at Saccoudion, of the Cathars, of Hagios Christophoros, and so forth. It is obvious that Theodore could not have heard daily confessions in each of these distant dependencies. For example, to Sophronius, the superior at Saccoudion,[31] he declares: 'I have given you power equal to the one I, the weak one, have received from God in this governance.' That Saint John the Baptist had an exceptional number of monks remains likely, though the number cannot be specified. Saint Theodore certainly tried to remain within the customary limits.[32] 'On average, this number was not higher than thirty or forty.'[33] The *Typika* rather frequently defined the minimum or maximum number of monks to be admitted. 'Never more than forty,' the founder of Saint Michel of Mt Auxentius decreed[34]; sixteen for the choir, twenty-four for work. 'Not less than eighty,' the founder of the Pantokrator monastery in Constantinople ordered.[35] For Our Lady Kosmosōtēria (Saviour of the World) at Aenos (1152), the *Typikon* wanted fifty religious for the choir, twenty-four for poor-relief[36]; but further down,[37] it gives the superior the power, or rather the advice, to still increase this number 'in so far as he believes that the monastery revenues would allow this.' A similar clause is found elsewhere, for example, for the monastery of the Most Blessed Theotokos *tōn Heliou Bōmōn* which was to have 'twenty monks in the main monastery honored by the name of the Most Glorious Lady and Theotokos, and twenty in the *metochion* (dependency) it owns in the capital'. 'If, as we hope, the Lord decides that still others hasten to the monastery because of the virtue of its inhabitants and for the preservation of the cenobitic state; and if, in addition, the Lord provides what is needed for subsistence—due either to the wise administration of the possessions of the monastery by superiors or to the offerings we expect the friends of Christ to make, so that there will be enough to support even more—no one will be opposed to an increase in the number of monks as high as the superior wants it and he has available cells.'[38]

For Our Lady of Pity at Stroumitza,[39] Manuel, the founder, 'decrees that there be ten monks; but if through the most pure intercession of the Mother of God the (possessions) of the monastery increase, the number of monks will also be increased.' This corresponds exactly to what Saint Basil says in the *First Ascetical Sermon*,[40] and this number has a mystical meaning: 'The spiritual law does not want those who eat the mystical Pascha to be less than ten; hence it is necessary that the ten-fold number of those who practice the spiritual life together be increased rather than decreased.' There are other mystical numbers given to justify and sanctify a fixed number of monks. The number seven, for example, inspired Michel Attaliates to write this amazing commentary:

I set and determine the number seven as the number of monks in this monastery (though for the time being, because of the lack of resources I have established only five), given the fact that this number is virgin and honorable and preferable. It is according to this number that the cosmic periods and the length of the week and the course of the stars were coordinated by the all-powerful ordinance of God; among the ancients as well as the moderns this number is dear to mystics because it is virgin (as I have already explained) for the main reason that, within the decade, it neither engenders nor is engendered, from which follows, I am convinced, that the good news was brought to the Holy Virgin and Mother of God by Gabriel who, unlike the others, keeps the septenary number in his name.[41] I therefore decree that seven be the number of monks when, through the grace of God, resources will increase with the procurator, the hegumen, and the porter.[42]

After such considerations, the number seven would seem to be forever immutable! The *Typikon* continues: 'If, with the help of our infinitely good God and of his undefiled Mother full of grace, the resources of the orphan school and of the monastery increase (as I am confident in our Lord Jesus Christ that some of these will arrive), then the number of seven monks will also be increased in proportion to the increased revenues. . . .'[43] If we add up all these calculations and all this mystagogy, the result is that the virgin number of seven monks probably never existed at the monastery of the Most Merciful Saviour, first because of a lack, and then an overabundance, of resources.

In monasteries of nuns the difficulty had to be greater still, if the hegumen had to receive 'the revelation of thoughts'. We are not well informed about the number of religious in each community; in general, it appears not to have been high. For the monastery of the Most Holy Mother of God Full of Grace, at Constantinople, founded or restored by Irene Ducas, the *Typikon* wanted twenty-four sisters; resources permitting, they could go to forty, but no higher. Also, such increase would be allowed only if the sisters 'keep without infraction the canon and the rule of cenobitic order as we have established it; and the great number does not prevent observances from being followed faithfully. If the growth of the community would be the cause of some irregularity, we decree that this number be abandoned altogether; indeed, we are most anxious for cenobitic orderliness, not the high number of religious.'[44]

A wise prescription, which unfortunately was not followed by another Irene who will be mentioned later.

Taking these data into account, one is led to conclude that the preoccupation with being heard by the hegumen played a less important role than did economic considerations, setting the number of subjects to be accepted. 'We do not want to fix a number, but you shall have as many as you can feed. . . .'[45] It is also difficult to establish the average, except to let it fluctuate between seven (in fact, even less) and eighty (occasionally, probably more). At any rate, the number of *exagoreuseis* to hear was so large that the hegumen, between his other duties and occupations had severely to limit the time given to each of his subjects. It is evidently to obviate this inconvenience—sometimes it might be better to say this nullifying impediment (*impedimentum dirimens*)—that many *Typika* willingly or unwillingly appointed other spiritual men to help the hegumen receive intimate confidences; and even when not one legal text existed, the authority of St Basil was there to permit, if not impose, such a plurality of spiritual fathers.

On this subject we are better informed about the Desert Fathers, because many of the apophthegms are specifically the account of one visit, one query and a response. Most frequently, even when we admit that the redaction of the saying condensed historic fact, we note that everything happened in a few words. The law of silence, the fear of useless words (words about which Saint Basil was to say such fearsome things!), the austerity of the profession, unquestionably also the desire to be clear, to facilitate remembrance of the answer and to make it more effective, the very seriousness of the questions that were raised, and the solemnity of a ministry which both sides knew to be very great and of a properly mystical, if not always sacramental, order—all this contributed to impose a seriousness that excluded everything unnecessary, all chatter, even more all jesting. The *nihil est melius quam tacere* (nothing is better than to be silent)[46] reaffirmed its value, as soon as the problem which had compelled someone to speak had been solved. But there was a higher reason for imposing brevity by making all prolixity superfluous: the strong belief in the spiritual and inspired character of the *Verba Seniorum*. One did not dispute with them: one had to remember their oracles and meditate upon them. At the most, when they were obscure, one could ask for further clarification. Yet even this was always given in a sententious, laconic style. Moreover, many of the questions were asked by neophytes who needed generalized maxims, or by people anxious to have in one short phrase a panacea for all their ills. The most frequent question, 'Tell me how I can gain salvation?' was also the most general and admits of answers that were less precise. 'Abba Pambo asked abba Antony, "What should I do?" The old man replied, "Put no trust in your own righteousness; do not regret a thing of the past; control your tongue and your stomach".'[47] Sometimes, however, a consultant's particular situation allowed the other to be more specific, while remaining marvelously concise: 'A brother who stayed with other brothers asked abba Bessarion, "What should I do?" The old man said, "Be silent, and do not compare yourself to others".'[48] Even when a consultant insisted with a boldness that is rather rare, on obtaining greater clarity, the dialogue hardly got longer because of it: every new question provoked a concise answer, and soon the conversation stopped, because even the most dim-witted disciple understood that he had to meditate on what he had heard instead of pressing for more.[49] The discourse became a little longer, however, when the abba wrapped his answer in a parable or a fable.[50] Such indirect methods usually betrayed the embarrassment of a person who was unsure of himself or who wanted to spare another's weakness. Only rarely did the master agree to discuss things; if an obstinate disciple did not let himself be convinced, it was better to ask God to change the disciple's heart or to think of a stratagem to make him understand his error indirectly. Abba Sisoes combined these two methods when he invited to prayer an angry young brother intent on avenging an insult. 'He says, "Let us pray, brother." Standing up, he said, "God, we no longer need you to care for us; we bring about vengeance ourselves." Hearing this, the brother fell at the old man's feet and said, "I will no longer contend with my brother. Forgive me, abba".'[51]

Like oral consultations, letters of direction almost always answered specific questions, and with the same conciseness. The edition of Saint Barsanuphius and Saint John by Nicodemus the Hagiorite contains 836 letters (questions and answers), which take up 386 pages in 4⁰. Many contain only a line or two, even one word, while others runs to a maximum of two pages. Those of Barsanuphius are generally a little longer than John's. What is most admirable in them, along with discernment, is the great variety of feelings (for men who had become impassible!); beginning with humor[52] and moving through good-heartedness, graciousness, tenderness, to vehemence, even violence—all this in the service of souls, always. The spiritual father must give his life for them, most often drop by drop, insofar as his other indispensable obligations allowed, if there are any that surpass the duty of charity. 'Children are not expected to save up for their parents, but parents for their children,' according to the words of Saint Paul[53] to the Corinthians whom be begot in Christ through the Gospel.'[54] Also, though the official texts do not speak of this, we must believe that the spiritual fathers, even as hegumens, were available for emergency cases, aside from the times set for the cenobites' daily revelation of thoughts *(exagoreusis)* or the hesychasts' weekly disclosure. Saint Theodore the Studite who, while Saint Plato was still alive, went to see him very frequently even without having a specific reason, found nothing to criticize if someone came to him outside the regular meeting every morning. In other respects, it was in the interest of the monks to leave their director at least time for prayer and the quietude needed to renew his provisions of charity in the relationship with God—in other words, to renew the degree of tranquillity *(hèsychia)* that was indispensable to abiding in the spirituality which he had to bring his disciples.

One good way of making the task of the spiritual director

easier was not to mix with the *exagoreusis* elements that would make of it something entirely different from a 'confession'.

> If by chance some disagreement or dispute arises, confess not by accusing one another, while each presents himself as being innocent; that would be to seek trials rather than a confession. Do not talk about your material needs either; you have all the time to do that. But now is the time for *exagoreusis* and for the medical treatment of your psychic diseases. If you have to mention a dispute, make haste to pin all the blame and the responsibility for the fault, whatever it might be, on yourself. In the case of other diseases, explain them clearly in order to reap a two-fold profit: to reach perfect health of soul and to be attired by glorifying humility, the possession of which makes us truly similar to God who says, 'learn of me; for I am meek and lowly in heart.'[55]

The best way to gain time is to do everything in its time. The best way to profit from the time of *exagoreusis* is to do, more than ever, that which the ascetic should be ready to do all the time: blame himself. What is often the most difficult in the task of the spiritual father would then become easier: the need to convince of their wrong persons who stubbornly believe that only their environment prevents them from being saints or from appearing as holy as they convince themselves they are deep inside. A passage which spiritual men like to quote is most applicable here: 'Answer not a fool according to his folly: lest you also be like him. Answer a fool according to your wisdom; lest he be wise in his own conceit.'[56] Of all obsessions, the most tenacious with such senseless folk is that of their own immunity from error. The spiritual father would not wish to cause them harm by encouraging their illusion; like a wise surgeon, he would therefore have the courage to cause some pain. Some will recover their health by accepting surgery; others will come to dislike the practitioner. Nonetheless, he will have done his duty—and will have stopped wasting his time.

Nonetheless, even if everyone, fathers and children, follow the rules of *exagoreusis* and spiritual direction as best they can, the latter, to be effective, will demand something else beside a mere 'confession' followed by an *epitimia* (penance). If the director at the same time exercises other functions that are too absorbing, he will have neither the time nor the freedom of mind needed to listen with interest, to reflect and pray comfortably, and lastly to respond wisely. Though it is easy to write, 'all other affairs being ended,'[57] the *ochlēsis* (annoyance), the awkward interference of administrative and economic concerns, threaten to create an obstacle to spiritual fatherhood and diminish the efficacy of direction. While reading the *Typika*, one has the feeling that in cenobia where all power was concentrated in the hand of the hegumen, the ancient revelation of thoughts came to resemble a confession of sins more and more. The vocabulary of *exagoreusis* still persisted, but its meaning became restricted, its scope narrowed. Instead of a soul-to-soul relationship made up of fatherly interest and filial trust, what remained was a series of regulations and interviews of a canonical nature. A few more steps in that direction, and spiritual fatherhood became congealed in administrative reports—regulated. Where the initiative had originally come from the disciple and was directed to a trusted spiritual guide, little by little codification and control through authority asserted themselves. A superior easily forgets that he is bound to elicit from his very being what subordinates are obliged to; he is not to impose it through his power over them. Trust cannot be coerced; at the very least, trust on command will go no further than strict obedience to an order, if such trust can even reach this *minimum* in an enduring fashion. The filial 'openness of heart' (*ouverture d'âme*) which was aimed at future healing in particular, transformed itself into a painful accusation which viewed almost nothing but the past. The 'spiritual father' became nothing more than a giver of absolution, a tariff maker of *epitimias* (penances). This is why S.J. Smirnov's book, despite its title, *The Spiritual Father in the Ancient Christian Church* (Sergiev Posad 1906), deals with hardly anything but confession, except in the opening chapter. And this chapter ends with pages of disillusionment (70-75).

By way of conclusion, let us now view the institution of spiritual direction (*starčestvo*) from a new point of view: *how it functioned in life*. During each flowering of monasticism (which usually coincided only with the beginning of its growth in every new christian region and consequently occurred within the walls of monasteries founded or directed by great ascetics) the institution of *starčestvo* came close to the ideal. But, as we know, the customs of monachism degenerated rapidly everywhere and the relationships of a high moral order between an old man and a disciple which lay at the basis of the institution became all but inaccessible to the majority, the common monks. Yet the *starčestvo* did not disappear altogether. Its outer forms became so hardened that its existence was prolonged for a very long time, so that it continued to exist here and there, even in present-day monasteries. Over the years, however, an entirely different and undesirable content manifested itself under the forms of *starčestvo*. . . .[58]

According to Smirnov, what caused the institution[59] to disappear was ambition and the lust for power (*l'esprit de domination. Libido dominandi*). The responsibility for such decline lies primarily with the superiors. 'Power spoils (i.e. corrupts) a person: it develops pride, a big *ego*, vaingloriousness, arrogance, and a lack of respect for the one subjected to such power. Attractive in itself, power became an object of ambition on the part of unworthy people. All this can be observed in the ancient *starčestvo*. . . .' Such an observation imposes itself on anyone studying the documents (books mostly written by dignitaries) as it imposed itself on me, independently of Smirnov. Indeed, his statement is supported by many texts. We have cited others in profusion (See above, Chapter VI: The Duties of the Disciple, p. 185); they will excuse us from adding more.

Unless hegumens, abbots, superiors, archimandrites, and others put their greatest care in becoming truly spiritual men—try as they might to exhort the monks to practice *exagoreusis* (they have done it so often)—their very exhortations more and more alienated the hearts and minds of those they had to win. If they were not truly charitable, their recipes and exhortations did not cause hearts and minds to open to virtue and the attraction of charity. Clearly, the subordinates too carried their share of responsibility for the slackening of the bond between them and those who were or should have been their fathers.[60] The murmurers (*murmurantes*) in particular— and their misdeeds have been stigmatized so frequently— never realize how much evil they cause by injecting the poison of their bitterness into the souls of their brothers and sisters.

Spiritual fatherhood is too fragile a reality to put up for too long with mediocrity and human folly. It dies much faster from this than the assassins would wish. But it is beautiful and divine enough to deserve every effort, every sacrifice, on the part of both the spiritual fathers (mothers) and the children.

NOTES

1. 1 Cor 11:28.
2. *Comment. in Cant.* II, ed. Wilhelm Baehrens, VIII, p. 143ff. *Origen, The Song of Songs. Commentary and Homilies*, trans. R. P. Lawson, ACW 26 (Westminster, Maryland, 1957) 130.
3. See Walther Voelker, *Das Vollkommenheitsideal des Origenes* (Tübingen, 1931) 25-62.
4. *Collatio* I, 20: '. . . *oportet nos iugiter obseruare et universas cogitationes quae emergunt in corde nostro sagaci discretione discutare.*' Ed. Michael Petschenig.
5. *Doctrina* 11.
6. Jos 5:13; see Evagrius, *Antirrheticos*, 'pride' n. 17; *Letter* 11; Barsanuphius, *Letter* 89, p. 47, ed. Nicodemus the Hagiorite.
7. John Climacus, *Scala Paradisi, Gradus* IV; PG 88: 701D.
8. See above, S. Theodore the Studite, p. 61.
9. According to the simple meaning of the term, without supplementary practices.
10. *Biblos Barsanuphiou kai Ioannou* (Venice, 1816).
11. *Letters* 150-166, pp. 74-87.
12. *Letters* 167-214; see above, pp. 142ff.
13. *Letter* 167, p. 88.
14. *Letters* 171 and 172.

15. *Letters* 177-181.
16. *Letter* 182.
17. *Letter* 89, p. 46.
18. *Letter* 142, p. 71.
19. See Jean Muyldermans, 'Un texte grec inédit attribué à Jean de Lycopolis,' in *RSR* 41 (1953) 526.
20. Theognostos, 'Sur l'action et la contemplation,' ch. 11, *Philocalie*[1], p. 500, col. 2.
21. *Vitae Patrum* VII, 19, 6, PL 73: 1044D.
22. *Vita Sancti Euthymii*, n. XV, ed. Jean-Baptiste Cotelier, *Ecclesiae*, vol. II, p. 213ff.
23. *Neon Eclogion* (1863) 260, col. 2.
24. Ch. 13, ed. L. Petit, *ViVr* 11 (1904) 30ff.
25. Papadopoulos-Kerameus, *Antōnios Stoudités kai tina symmikta* (Jerusalem, 1905).
26. *Ibid.*, p. 9.
27. *Constitutiones Studitanae*, ch. 22; PG 99: 1712B; see Julien Leroy, 'La vie quotidienne du moine studite,' in *Ir* 27 (1954) 33.
28. *Typikon* of Our Lady of Evergetis, ch. 7, ed. Dmitrievsky, *Opisanie*, I, p. 261ff.
29. Franz Miklosisch-J. Mueller, *Acta et Diplomata Graeca*, V, p. 403ff.
30. See *Bios kai Politeia, Vita et Conversatio Sancti Patris . . . Theodori Praeposisiti Studitarum*; PG 99: 148C.
31. *Grande Catéchèse*, 55; ed. Papadopoulos-Kerameus, p. 393ff.
32. See Julien Leroy, p. 27, n. 3. Cfr n. 27.
33. Raymond Janin, 'Eglises et monastères de Constantinople byzantine,' in *REB* 9 (1952) 152.
34. Dmitrievsky, *Opisanie*, I, p. 780.
35. *Ibid.*, p. 671.
36. *Typikon* n. 3, *Izvestia de l'Institut archéol. russe de Constantinople* 13 (1908) 21.
37. N. 88, p. 62ff.
38. Ch. 5, Dmitrievsky, p. 725.
39. *Typikon* n. 5, *Izvestia de l'Inst. archeol. russe de Const.* 6 (1900) 72.
40. *Sermo asceticus*, n. 3; PG 31: 873CD.
41. Because this name has seven letters? Or because its numerical value in Greek is a multiplier of 7: 154 = 7x22?
42. The greek text is not any clearer than this translation.
43. *Typikon* of Michel Attaliates, ch. 6, Miklosisch-Mueller, *Acta et Diplomata* V, p. 71.
44. *Typikon Sanctae Mariae Gratiae Plenae*, ch. 5, Mikl.-Mueller, V, p. 337.
45. *Typikon* of the Evergetis, ch. 23; Dmitrievsky, I, p. 641.
46. *Vitae Patrum* VII, 30, 1, PL 73: 1050D.
47. *Alph.*, Antony n. 6; PG 65: 77A (CS 59:2).
48. *Alph.*, Bessarion n. 10; PG 65: 141C (42).
49. See *Alph.*, Peter the Pionite n. 2; PG 65: 376C-7A (200-201).
50. See, for example, *Vitae Patrum* V, 15, 88, PL 73: 968A-9A.
51. *Alph.*, Sisoes n. 1; PG 65: 391C (212).
52. Truthfully, humor is indeed rare. One example: Question, 'If I make a blessing with the left hand, not being able to use the right, is this not out of order?' Answer, 'Until further notice, when *I* want to make the sign of the cross on my right hand, I do it with my left' (*Letter* 534, p. 277).
53. 2 Cor 12:14.

54. 1 Cor 4:15; see Evagrius, *Letter* 61, ed. Wilhelm Frankenberg, p. 610, *in medio*.

55. *Typikon* of the Evergetis, ch. 7, *loc. cit.*, p. 622ff (see n. 45).

56. Prov 26:4-5; cfr Evagrius, *Antirrheticos*, Preface, ed. W. Frankenberg, p. 473.

57. See above, n. 28, *Typikon* of the Evergetis, ch. 7.

58. Smirnov, 70ff.

59. In Russian, *institout*.

60. See Smirnov, p. 74.

VIII

THE EFFICACY OF DIRECTION

SPIRITUAL FATHERHOOD is remarkably effective if each side, 'father and son,' conforms to all the demands we have described. Let us first learn about the affirmation of this spiritual fruitfulness. We will then ask the Easterners about the reasons for it.

As we have done previously, let us put the example of a remarkable success at the opening of this chapter. Once more it will be Symeon the New Theologian. He simply attributed all the graces he has received—and they make him one of the greatest byzantine mystics—to his father in God. 'Our blessed and saintly Father Symeon [the Studite] had so suffered as to surpass many of the saintly Fathers of earlier times. He so endured tribulations and trials that he became an equal to many of the most illustrious martyrs. This is why he has been glorified by God. He became impassible and a saint, having received the Paraclete, so to speak, wholly within him; and then, like a father bequeathing a heritage to his son, he, in turn, filled me, his unworthy servant, with the Holy Spirit, and this effortlessly and freely.'[1] This fact is all the more remarkable since the disciple admits having known years of sloth during which

> I do not know how to explain this, love and confidence in that saintly old man remained in my heart, unknown to myself. It is because of this and through his prayers that after years had gone by, God, the lover of humankind, was merciful to me; through him, He drew me away from my great blindness and freed me from the depths of evil. Although unworthy, I was not entirely unattached to him for I confessed to him all that was happening to me, and when I was in town I frequently went to his cell, though in my heedless ways I neglected to follow his precepts. [2]

This is unquestionably the most shining example one could show to indicate the remarkable effects of spiritual direction according to the ancient tradition. The New Theologian never wearied of thanking God for the grace through which all the others were channeled to him, that of having had a true father according to God. In the midst of the most lyrical flights of his *Hymns of the Divine Loves*, he pauses to remember him. [3]

Let us have as close a look at these results as the documents will allow us. First, we should remember what we have read about the need for direction. It is direction *alone* that protects the ascetic from the errors and dangers to which he is exposed as a result of his inexperience in the ways of the spirit. That in itself would suffice to give us a most noble idea of it. But there is more, aside from this negative aspect. First, the exclusion of danger becomes a positive blessing in itself, through the security it provides. Saint Dorotheos has described this feeling for us with his usual affability and with the cogency a personal anecdote conveys. Let us simply add what this same author tells us about the importance of peace of soul. It is the proper blessing of the sons of God, according to the evangelical beatitude (*makarismos*), 'Happy are the peacemakers: they shall be called sons of God.'[4] 'What is more blessed than the soul which has arrived at this degree?'⁵ Such peace thus comes from God our Father. It is not surprising that it is found in filial confidence in the spiritual father, since he is invested with this fatherhood.

> You do not have the experience of unmurmuring obedience (*hypakoēs adiakritou*), nor do you know its peace. I remember one day asking abba John, the disciple of abba Barsanuphius: 'Scripture tells us that we must enter the kingdom of heaven through much tribulation; and I see that I do not have the slightest tribulation. What do I do? Will I not lose my soul?' For I had neither tribulation nor cares. If I ever happened to have a thought (that could have caused me trouble), I took my writing tablet and wrote it down for the old man (for I questioned him in writing); and before I had finished writing, I felt the profit and the relief this caused me, so great was my freedom from care and my peace. But since I did not know the power of this virtue (of submission to the spiritual father), and I heard that one had to enter the kingdom of heaven through much tribulation, I was worried when I saw that I did not have a single tribulation. To my question, the old man wrote back, stating: 'Do not be worried. It is not your business. Anyone who falls down in obedience to the Fathers possesses such freedom from care (*amerimnian*) and such peace (*anapausin*).⁶

Saint John Climacus calls this condition 'freedom from anxiety, from care' (*amerimnia*): 'the work of *hēsychia* is [precisely] this unconcern for all things, reasonable and unreasonable.'⁷ This is why submission to the spiritual father constitutes the indispensable preparation for the hesychast life, the glory and blessedness of which Saint John Climacus cannot praise enough; it is a quietness of divine origin, given by the Holy Spirit. But if one has obtained it, one must say to oneself that this happened because of the spiritual father's prayers. 'One day I asked one of the most competent Fathers in what way the virtue of obedience was connected to humility. He said to me, "The obedient man who has discernment, even if he were to raise the dead and receive the gift of tears or the gift of reconciling enemies, will always believe that it is the prayer of his spiritual father that accomplished this".[9] This is this general principle Symeon the New Theologian observed with respect to Symeon the Studite. The spiritual fathers, on their part, believed in the power of their intercession in favor of their spiritual children, as they knew they were obliged to pray for them.[10]

A spiritual father can transfer the Spirit to his disciples, as Elijah once did to Elisha. At least, this is often stated explicitly, and it is implicit in the principle of John Climacus: to attribute all graces to the prayers of the Fathers. The two saints Maximus and Dometius, 'sons of Valentinus, King of the Greeks,' stayed with the 'old man Agabos' in Syria for seven years. And when the latter 'went to sleep peacefully, a double portion of his spirit was upon them, as in the past a double portion of the spirit of Elijah was upon Elisha.'[11] Saint Maximus and Saint Dometius, two 'Romans' are the eponyms of the convent of Varamus that still exists in Nitria.[12] The devil himself bears witness that Saint Macarius took on a resemblance to Saint Antony in the same manner Elisha resembled Elijah.

> Admittedly Antony too has been a master (*magister*) to you, since it is he who gave you the habit; and you have struck me with your humility, in that in all humility you accepted advice from this Antony, and you put him (in the rank of) a god by the charity of your humility. And when I try to affect you through the passions, you at once say in the depth of your heart and with victorious faith, 'He is my physician and my healer on the mountain and the river'.[13]

A century later, Emperor Leo I (457-474) had a particular esteem for the monk Daniel who, at the very gate of the capital, renewed the admirable life of Symeon [the Stylite]. As Elijah formerly bequeathed his prophetic spirit to Elisha together with his mantle, it appears that the Antiochian Stylite, together with his monastic cowl, transferred upon the Stylite of Constantinople the heritage of his ascetic virtues, the same gift of miracles, and the same assiduous admiration of the crowds.[14]

To these texts could be added others which, either by mentioning Elijah and Elisha or by not mentioning them, confirm the same transferral of graces from the spiritual father to the disciple. This is all the more understandable since the eastern monks unanimously link the very institution of their way of life to the great prophet; Athanasius already attests to this in the *Life* of Saint Antony.[15]

If we now seek the reasons for this efficacy, let it be permitted to indicate one that catches the eye, even though the documents do not insist on it. This 'openness of heart' (*ouverture d'âme*) practiced daily and maintained assiduously prevents the formation of these complexes which modern psychoanalysts struggle so hard to unravel. We need only express in modern terms the great truth which has been stated so often—that wounds which have been declared do not become worse—to indicate the human benefit of direction understood in the manner we have described. The true joy and lightness of soul which Saint Dorotheos describes for us and which is the prerogative of all those who routinely devote themselves to *exagoreusis*, according to Saint Barsanuphius, perhaps deserve to kindle in us a little bit of nostalgia, if not about days when superiors were above all spiritual fathers, even if they had others to help them in their function, then at least about a time *when there were* spiritual fathers, superiors or not. The eastern monk, faithful to the tradition of total lucidity towards a psychiatrist accredited by God himself, could not but arrive at this childlike serenity which the hagiographer frequently attributed to him, together with the seriousness of an old man.

And would this not be one of the causes that explains that longevity so frequent among them, at least in heroic times when, according to Antony's precept, one had to give to the father an account of all the steps one had taken and all the drops of water one had drunk?[16]

By our liking, they may have seen too much supernatural intervention in this phenomenon of peacefulness. But even that is not as certain as we may be led to believe. They did not altogether ignore experimental psychology. It is certainly to this that Saint Dorotheos refers when he confides to his audience, that merely by taking down a thought to mention it to my spiritual father, 'even before I finished writing, I experienced profit and relief from it—so great was my security and my peace.'[17] Long before Saint Dorotheos, the *Vitae Patrum* did not uniformly teach that the usefulness of direction depended on cure-alls prescribed by the director.

> A brother said to an old man, 'See, abba, I frequently ask the Fathers to give me an earnest reminder for the salvation of my soul, and I do not remember a thing of what they tell me.' Now the old man had two empty vessels, and he said to the brother, 'Go, bring one of the vessels and pour water in it: rinse it, pour it out, and put it back in its place, all shiny.' The brother did this several times, and the old man said to him, 'Bring both vessels at once.' And when he had brought them, he said, 'Of the two, which one is cleaner?' The brother answered, 'The one I put water in and cleaned.' Then the old man said to him, 'son, thus it is with the soul that frequently hears the word of God; though the soul remembers nothing of what she asked, she is nonetheless cleansed more than the soul that did not inquire.'[18]

I could undoubtedly have gone on more about this purely physical causality. But this problem is like the famous 'demonism' of the Fathers: they knew very well and said on occasion that one sometimes does not need a demon at all to tempt us. What does it matter? A demon or the troubled subconscious; the result is the same, a temptation. And this is what must be overcome. Likewise, to explain the fortunate results of *exagoreusis*, what difference does it make whether there is a direct intervention by God or an interplay of the psychic laws caused by God? From this point of view, a thorough examination of the *Apophthegmata Patrum* (*Sayings of the Fathers*) would perhaps reveal that the Fathers had a still more extensive knowledge of these laws. And thus the benefit of discernment, in the sense of the right mean adapted to everyone's condition seemed not to have had anything miraculous in the least, though the discernment that allowed spiritual men to find this right mean did not come about without a charism. Medicinal science can be miraculous, even when the remedies prescribed by it do not function outside natural laws. One example among many. 'An old man was asked by a brother, "How do I find God? Is it by fasting, or through toil, or in vigils, or by acts of mercy?"' This is a problem often debated, and one that often imposes itself on everyone coming into this world. More than once the Desert Fathers have been accused of attaching too much importance to ascetic practices. Here, then is the answer: you will find God 'in all the things you have listed—and in discernment. I tell you that there are many who have tormented their flesh, and because they did this without discernment, they came away devoid of profit. Our mouth smells of fasting; we know all the Scriptures by heart; we have devoured [the psalms] that came from the heart of David; but we do not know what God required of us, humility.'[19] The humility that would make us go to a diacritical father would prevent us from exhausting ourselves for nothing. Spiritual direction assures health of the soul and the body. 'Discernment is the begetter and the guardian and the director of all the virtues.'[20] It is the 'royal road' on which one walks cheerfully because the guide deserves our full trust.

One of the most distressing and harmful psychic diseases is scrupulosity; psychiatrists and confessors know something about it. Now, it is a fact that in the ancient literature of spirituality, theoretical as well as practical and historical, there is little of it, perhaps none at all.[21] On the other hand, in it we often come across examples of the ease with which very holy people could on occasion rise above rules and regulations which seem apparently to have been sacrosanct. The occasion for this was usually a neighbor's need, and what gave them this ease was their *discernment*. Someone who had never tasted bread in fifty years now did not hesitate a second to eat meat in order to save a lost soul[22]; even when it is merely a matter of showing charity, for example, toward a guest, because 'One must be hospitable and share joyfully,' the title of a little book states,[23] and in it we read apophthegms of the Fathers as well as excerpts from Cassian. He gives us the general principle, heard from the lips of an egyptian Father. 'When you receive brothers why do you not observe the fast, as is done in Palestine?' The answer: 'The opportunity to fast is always with me, while I do not always have you. Fasting, however useful and necessary, is an offering of our free will. God's law requires the fullness of charity of us. Receiving Christ in you, I must feed him. After leading you out, I shall be able to compensate in myself by a stricter fast for the hospitality offered for this sake. The sons of the Bridegroom cannot fast as long as the Bridegroom is with them; but when he has gone away, then they will fast appropriately.'[24] All this is the work of discernment, and therefore of direction, as the anecdote cited above indicates. And what beautiful moral—and physical— health this presupposes and maintains! Let us read the few lines that follow in the *Vitae Patrum*:

> The same one also said, 'We came to another old man, and he made us eat. When we were sated, he insisted that we take a little more. When I said to him, "I can't," he replied, "I have already set the table six times for brothers who came by. I always ate with them, and I am still hungry. But you, eating here for the first time, say that you cannot eat more?"[25]

What is true of fasting also applied to other monastic observances, for example, silence. To speak out of love of God for the good of the neighbor is not to break silence. The discernment of abba Poemen overthrows the fragile constructions of formalism with a flip of the finger, a flash of wit: 'So and so seems to observe silence but he talks all the time because his heart judges others. So and so speaks from morning till evening and he observes silence, for he says nothing that is not profitable.'[26] One more maxim of wisdom which only a 'Shepherd' (*Poemen*) could state with such assurance: His disciples knew that for the good of their soul there never was a prohibited time, not even 'sacrosanct Lent,' which certain famous people like Gregory Nazianzen believed should be spent without uttering one word.

> A certain brother came to abba Poemen during the second week of Lent and told him his thoughts. Having obtained peace because of the answer, the brother said to him, 'A little thing almost prevented me from coming to you.' The old man said, 'Why?' He replied, 'I was afraid that no one would open the door because of Lent.' Abba Poemen replied to him, 'We have not learned how to close a wooden door; we prefer to keep the door of our tongue locked.'[27]

In this entire chapter, and in the many anecdotes that could be added to it, there is a human atmosphere which is all the more liberating as one element is excluded from it, self love with all its small-mindedness. 'A certain brother came to a certain solitary and when he left, he said, "Abba, forgive me, because I obstructed your rule." He replied, "My rule is to receive you with hospitality, and to dismiss you with peace."'[28] Another who, likewise out of charity, had not followed his habits, was asked, 'Abba, are you saddened because of this?' He answered, 'My sadness would be to have followed my own will.'[29]

In short, the great benefit of direction-discernment is the *inner freedom* it brings; no 'captivity' (*aichmalōsia*) or physical bondage can oppose it for long. In inner freedom, the very feeling of guilt, of the sinful state, looses everything it could have that is oppressive, maddening, morbid, or pathological. There is nothing christian about 'The morbid universe of sin'—and to get away from it there is no need for a 'Morality without sin'. The one requirement is to take seriously the Lamb of God who has taken away the sins of the world. The person who claimed that among byzantine monks there was an almost hysterical sense of sin,[30] only saw one aspect of the situation. Nothing was more alien to the 'Fathers' than crushing sinners. Anyone who submitted to their guidance knew how easily forgiveness was obtained, on the one condition that one asked for it.[31]

The rare 'old men' who disheartened their clients were condemned severely. Another little book of the *Vitae Patrum, De eo quod non oporteat judicare quemquam (That it is not Proper to Judge Anyone)* is partly related to this, even totally as far as the spirit is concerned.[32] Certain well known stories originated from there, such as the one about the saint who, in a meeting that had been called to judge the case of someone who had been accused, presented himself with an enormous bag of sand on his back and in his hand a little basket containing a few grains of sand. 'This bag filled with sand represents my sins; and since they are numerous I have put them on my back, so as not to be grieved by them. The few grains of sand are the sins of my brother; they are in front of my eyes, and by means of these I practice judging my brother. . . .'[33] This Pior is no-one to scorn! Thus the gathered Fathers said, 'Indeed, this is the way of salvation.' Bessarion deserves even more attention. His lesson sounds like bugle call for the Last Judgment. 'A brother who had sinned was driven out of the church by the priest. Whereupon Bessarion rose and went out with him, declaring, "I, too, am a sinner".'[34] Above all monastic authorities stands Saint Antony. It is he, the ideal type of purity and discernment, who received and kept with him on the mountain a brother who had been expelled from the community of an abba Elias. Then he sent him back to the cenobion, but the brother returned. 'They did not want to receive me,' he said. Whereupon the great Antony sent them this message: 'A ship suffered shipwreck on the sea; it lost all its cargo, and hardly made it to shore. And you want to throw into the sea that which was brought safely to land.'[35] Likewise, abba Poemen upbraided an anchorite who was merciless toward a brother who had sinned.[36] Understanding of and compassion for the sinner sometimes went so far that a modern editor such as H. Rosweyde felt it necessary to observe that 'the judgment of Macarius is to be admired, not imitated' (*Mirandum Macarii judicium, non imitandum*).[37] It is this note which is astonishing. Macarius thought he was imitating the patience of God; and the Fathers knew that it is inexhaustible.

> An old man was asked by a soldier, 'Does God accept repentance?' The reply 'Tell me, my dear, if your cloak is torn, do you throw it away?' Answering him, the soldier said, 'No, I mend it and use it again.' The old man said to him, 'If you spare your own vesture, would God not be kind to his own image?'[38]

At this rate, being a sinner and admitting it to men of God who have such convictions would be almost enviable. 'Mourning for lost salvation,' *penthos*, becomes joy-bringing repentance (*charopoion penthos*) when one lives in this environment and breathes this spirit. The spiritual direction of the Fathers freed one from all anxieties and made the heart rejoice in truth and charity.

On one point, it is true, they were demanding. But is was specifically in order to excise the great cause of all neurasthenia: one's own will (*voluntas propria*), *philauteia* (love of self), the false, morbid sense of self. On this point they made no compromise, because they knew and believed that from this derived all moral evil, in the double meaning of the term: all sin and all suffering that is not merely physical. We have sufficiently cited their opinions about this, especially that of abba Isaiah and of abba Barsanuphius. These are neither abstract hypotheses nor mere deductions made on the basis of certain philosophic or scriptural principles; experience and psychological reflections told the Fathers that their teaching was true. But the practice of direction slightly changed the application of the principle. They also knew that self-love did not die from this one blow (*ekkopē*); they brought to its manifestation, 'one's own wills', in the plural. Out of consideration for the weak, they often proceeded with amazing precautions and adaptations. A young man maintains that he is not able to endure anything painful, whether it be working with his hands or giving alms. Abba Joseph of Panephysis advised him. 'At least, keep your conscience free from all evil with regard to your neighbor, and you are saved.'[39] Another told abba Poemen that his occupation was to cultivate a field and give the proceeds away in alms-giving. Abba Poemen (the Shepherd) told him, 'You do a good work'. Abba Anub, Poemen's brother, protested, saying, 'Do you not fear God for speaking this way to that brother?' Poemen remained silent. After two days, however, he had that monk-farmer sent for and told him, in Anub's presence. 'What did you ask me the other day? My mind was elsewhere.' The brother repeated what he had said.

Abba Poemen said to him, 'I thought you were saying this about your brother who is a layman. However, if you do this, it is not the work of a monk.' Hearing this, the other was saddened. He said, 'I do not know how to do anything except cultivate my field.' When he had left, abba Anub began to make excuses with abba Poemen, saying, 'Forgive me.' Abba Poemen said to him, 'I knew from the beginning that this was no work for a monk, but I spoke to him according to my soul's disposition. I encouraged his soul to make progress in charity. Now he has departed sorrowfully; and yet he will continue that work.'[40]

Together with the precept of renouncing one's own will, we sometimes find a merciless severity, sometimes an unexpected condescension. To understand the reason for this difference, one would have to understand each consultant's 'state of soul'. But what we know very well is that discernment was the highest law. There was severity when a commandment of God was at stake; but patience and forbearance when it was only a matter of an ascetic rule. Pambo did not have Poemen's kindness when a deluded brother one day asked him, 'Why do evil spirits prevent me from doing good to my neighbor?' The old man said, 'Do not talk that way, otherwise you make God into a liar. Say rather, "I do not want to practice charity at all." God has refuted [your evil pretense] when he said, I have given you the power to tread under foot scorpions and serpents, and all the power of the enemy[41]; why then do you not tread under foot the evil spirits?'[42] Both ways of doing derive from the same source—benevolence. They tend toward the same goal—freedom of soul. They are measured by the same rule—discernment. Uprooting one's own will amounts to changing self-love into love, to detoxifying the soul of her pathogenic disposition (*diathesis*) called, so appropriately, self-will (*philauteia*), in order to make a person into the perfect image of God through the 'blessed passion of holy charity' (*tou makariou pathos tēs hagias agapēs*).[43] A person thereby becomes happy; and it is to such *divine* happiness that spiritual fatherhood wanted to lead people, by means of its various demands for total openness (of heart and mind), absolute trust, unending renunciation (of self), in the most perfect discernment possible.

Whether all this transcended natural causality could be legitimately discussed. While being aware of the distinction between the natural and the supernatural, the Fathers hardly ever spoke of it as part of the practical question of salvation and perfection. To them, everything was the work of God, especially spiritual progress by way of direction. One became a father in God only by being spiritual first; and by means of all the ascetic purifications, one became spiritual by receiving the charisms needed for direction: *diakrisis* (discernment) and prophecy (or the gift of the word). On the disciple's part everything was based on faith and tended toward the perfection of love. The Spirit of God is the only sanctifier. If he uses a human mediator, the latter only speaks and acts in the name of the Spirit. This conviction, held by both sides, master and disciple, gave the practice of direction a guarantee and an effectiveness quite superior to natural causality. Far from destroying the latter, they appropriated, magnified, and multiplied it.

Whatever the value of the hypothesis linking the spiritual men of the fourth and succeeding centuries to the 'prophets' of apostolic times, it is certain that the living tradition demands the same authority for the spiritual fathers as the *Didache* and the *Epistle of Barnabas* had for the prophets of their time. One should listen not to a man, but to the Spirit 'who dwells and speaks in him'.[44] 'You will not test or judge a prophet who is speaking in the spirit. Every sin will be forgiven, but this sin will never be forgiven.'[45] Dom Ildefons Herwegen had reason to write: 'However far removed monasticism is from the Apostolic age, nonetheless there cannot be the slightest doubt that it is consciously linked to the early church at all times. The ascetic life desired to be nothing other than the *apostolic* life at a time the world had invaded the church.'[46] He then quotes Cassian, *Conference* VII.31.4 (PL 49:712), where 'spiritual men' (*viri spirituales*) seem closely linked to the apostles. However, one does not read in Cassian that 'the spiritual men should be designated as successors of the apostles.' They are accredited by 'the signs of Apostolic powers' (*signa apostolicarum virtutum*).[47] Their decisions are sometimes compared to 'divine oracles'.[48] Yet one should not neglect the *velut* that softens this expression: *hac beatissimi Joseph institutione atque doctrina velut divino oraculo confirmati (in Aegypto residere maluimus)*; 'By this instruction and teaching of the blessed Joseph we were confirmed by, as it were, a divine oracle (and preferred to stay in Egypt).' But when all is said and done, it is not in Cassian that the clearest statements about this are to be found. With him, as in the Apophthegms, the supernatural value of the *rhema* (word, saying)[49] uttered by the Fathers is more frequently presupposed than stated explicitly. The argument one could draw from this would be more convincing; but for it one must read the *Sayings* from beginning to end.[50]

Certain occasional pronouncements still deserve mention. To the one quoted by Dom Herwegen,[51] let us add one from the *Alphabetical Collection*, Sisoes 17: 'Abba Ammon of Raithou asked abba Sisoes, "When I read Scripture, I am thinking of preparing a careful discourse, which could serve as an answer to a question." The old man said, "This is not necessary. Try rather, by purity of spirit, to acquire serenity and gift of speech"'. Still others could be collected. It is perhaps better to rely on some later spiritual men who only swore by the Fathers. Such are Saint Barsanuphius and John the Prophet, his *alter ego*, and his disciple, Saint Dorotheos. There is little chance that they would wrongly interpret doctrines with which they nourished themselves daily. Now, nothing is more evident than the faith Barsanuphius had in the spiritual character of the answers the Fathers had given to the questions of their spiritual children, even when the latter were bishops like the one who one day sent a list of candidates for the diaconate to the Great Recluse. To the prelate's surprise, the ascetic replied: 'In order not to speak from my own knowledge, I recited a prayer, and then I said what God had authenticated to me. It is not because of my ability that this letter was uttered by me. When it was needed, God opened even the mouth of [Barlaam's] ass.'[52] Moreover, it is possible that the answers of the Fathers helped the demons trouble someone momentarily, but

> do not let yourself be diverted from asking. The Fathers impose nothing that is either heavy or harmful, since they are disciples of the One who said, 'My yoke is easy and my burden is light.' Later, we will verify the usefulness of our questions by the result; and we will join our voice

to that of the psalmist who wrote, 'You have changed my sadness into joy.'[53]

'The Fathers say nothing without God's help, though it can happen that they are occasionally mistaken because the dispositions of the heart may have changed in the meantime. People without either faith or intelligence may then denounce them as liars. But it matters little to them; since they follow the example of the Master, they care nothing about human vainglory.'[54] When dealing with an upright mind, Barsanuphius explained his convictions with all the simplicity one could desire:

> Consider. You are a professor of worldly wisdom, and you have students. When you dictate a letter to one of them, will your student write what you want or will you leave him to write what he wants? Obviously, he will write what you will say, not what he would like. Likewise also the saints: it is not they who speak from their own knowledge. It is God who speaks in them as he intends it: sometimes in a veiled fashion, sometimes clearly. And to convince you that this is so, the Lord himself told his disciple, 'It is not you who speak, but the spirit of my Father who speaks in you.' Consequently, he speaks as he wants it, and not as they want.[55]

The professor was convinced by these reasons. But he asked another question: 'How is it that, according to what we read, the saintly Fathers of former times received from God everything they demanded?' The answer: 'No, they did not receive everything they asked for. They wrote only about what they received.' The proof: the story of the epileptic demoniac.[56] A new question: 'Why do saints not receive everything they ask for?' The old man wrote:

> God does everything for human profit . . . God treats you, and also the saints, with consideration. He is con-

siderate to you, by preventing you from becoming proud by patently receiving everything you ask for. And he treats the saints with consideration by preventing them from becoming proud about the revelations they clearly make in their discourses. They are not greater than the Apostle Paul who writes, 'In view of the extraordinary nature of these revelations, to stop me from getting too proud I was given a thorn in the flesh, an angel of Satan to beat me.'[57] Go, watch yourself, and let us pray that God gives you a strong heart and an untiring faith. Do not be scandalized by the saints. The spirit of God who speaks in them makes no mistakes. For in them is accomplished the word of Scripture, 'Your spirit is good; lead me into the land of uprightness.'[58] Having heard this, the professor felt reassured in the Lord. He went away joyfully, thanking God, and glorifying the saints.[59]

The last reason that explains the wondrous efficacy of obedience to the spiritual father is that in it meet all the 'activities of the commandments,' and these are so great that they made Evagrius cry out in amazement.[60] Saint Barsanuphius, who did not like Evagrius, agreed with him on this point: 'The one who asks the Fathers, fulfills the Law and the prophets.'[61] This is more or less what Saint Gregory was to say: 'To be sure, the single virtue is obedience which implants the other virtues in the mind, and protects the ones that have been implanted' (*Sola namque virtus est obedientia quae virtutes caeteras menti inserit, insertasque custodit*).[62] We would falsify the spirit of the Fathers if we were to understand this line in the sense of administrative, formal obedience, severed from its context or its vital surroundings; and this environment is the mutual relationship of spiritual fatherhood and sonship. Only there does the spiritual fecundity of the spiritual life grow, develop, and expand in all directions. Abba Poemen said, 'Do not entrust your conscience to someone in whom you do not have complete trust.'[63] This is a basic principle, and if we ask the reason for it, we would not be wrong in thinking that the efficacy of direction depends on the disciple's trust even more than on the master's 'spirituality'. Not for nothing must the initiative come from the disciple; likewise, not for nothing does the disciple's trust have the same name as the theological virtue of faith (*pistis, fides*). In fact, it is faith in one of its most essential functions: believing that through spiritual persons God guides, directs, and sanctifies 'those who want to be saved'. This conviction ran so deep that some (but not in the first generation) went so far as to say that God would send an angel to the person who was unable to find a man of trust to whom he could open his heart. "If something bothers me and I do not feel sufficiently at ease with anyone in whom I could confide, what do I do?" The answer:

> I believe that God will send his grace to help you, if you ask him earnestly. In Scetis there was a wrestler [an ascetic] who conceived certain thoughts, but was unable to disclose them because he did not have the requisite full confidence (*plērophoria*) in anyone. So he was ready to leave. And behold! The grace of God appeared to him in the form of a virgin who consoled him, saying, 'Do not go elsewhere. Stay here with me. Know that, from everything you have heard, no harm has occurred.' He let himself be persuaded, stayed and immediately his heart was healed.[64]

If we were to set up, in descending order, a hierarchy of causes that make the spiritual father-son relationship so effective, we would put the disciple's faith (trust) on top, since this is what makes someone take the first step in the ways of direction. It is also the first in worth, because everything depends on it, just as all evil comes from a lack of faith. As Symeon the Studite wrote: 'Lord, Lord, deliver us from all lack of faith, from all indiscreet searching, and keep us in your divine grace.' Obviously, this faith presupposes the spiritual character of a future director. But it would be inoperative if the disciple's faith did not goad it into action. Of all the master's actions, the most essential and the most effective is prayer for his children to God. What proves this are two facts, two customs so deeply rooted that they acquired the force of law: before revealing one's thoughts one must ask for the father's prayers; and once the victory has been obtained and grace received, it is to the same prayers that one must attribute all merit.[65] We have seen the second of these laws clearly explained by Saint John Climacus. We also see it put into practice each time the disciple, whether questioned or not, tells his spiritual father, 'Thanks to your prayer, everything goes well.'[66] It is possible that this sentence, born of a profound conviction, ended up by becoming more or less a polite formula among ascetics. The request for prayers is specifically declared obligatory by Saint Barsanuphius, but we also see the practice long before him. The following answer by Saint Antony even seems to suggest that certain brothers already counted rather too much on the prayers of the father. 'A brother said to abba Antony, "Pray for me." The old man said to him: "Neither I nor God will have mercy on you unless you have made a zealous effort and have asked God".'[67] There were different ways of asking for a spiritual man's prayers. Two brothers went together to see abba Zeno (Zeno the Prophet, the father of Peter the Iberian (?): 'The first one, to make his confession, bowed down before the old man and asked him, with many tears, to pray for him. . . . The other, having told the old man his "thought," added softly and negligently, "Pray for me," but he did not ask insistently.' It is not surprising that, upon meeting one another a little later, the first one could say, 'God has healed me through the old man's prayers' (note this formulation: it is perfect in every respect!); and that the other had to admit: 'In spite of my openness I have not felt any result from the cure.'[68] Are we to understand that even prayers become effective only through the medium of the 'client's' faith? At any rate, such prayers are necessary. The most frightening malediction is: 'Woe to you . . . because the Fathers no longer pray for you.'[69]

In the third place, the effectiveness of spiritual direction

depends on the charism the father possesses of being the instrument of the Holy Spirit. We know that the disciple must
be deeply convinced of this: his faith consists in believing this.
There is no need to insist more on it here. But what must be
said again is that this pneumatic character does not work automatically; it is not thaumaturgy dependent on the will of the
person who has the gift. If there is thaumaturgy, it has results
only if it is provoked by the one who solicits, as is generally
true of any other miraculous power. All the same, it is not at
all certain that even the most enthusiastic praisers of spiritual
fatherhood counted its wondrous blessings among the number
of miracles. For this, the ancient Fathers believed too strongly
in the ordinary providence of God; and they knew that it was
not miracles in the strict sense that deserve our greatest admiration, for the simple reason that they are not, as such, the
doings of christian spiritual men. 'They are numerous, those
who have performed astonishing miracles—chasing demons,
purifying lepers, and giving health back to the sick—but who
nonetheless did not reach the wisdom of the other world, since
it is much higher than anything that is admirable in this
world'. (For example, the Corinthians, according to I Cor 3).
'Performing miracles in front of unbelievers does not prevent
one from being jealous or angry; but to understand the wisdom of christian hope is only possible if one's understanding is
pure. . . . Now, that [understanding the life that follows the
resurrection] is, in its grandiose worth, more profound than
the gift of miracles, just as the soul is more inward than the
body.'[70] The same author also resolutely consigned the gift of
miracles to the 'psychic degree,' the one intermediate between
the somatic and the pneumatic: 'Just as the soul is located
between corporality and spirituality, in that in this world it is
neither like a body nor like the perfect spirituality of the angels, so is the gift of miracles kept between error and truth, in
order to remove from error and to lead to the truth. For this
reason, the life of the other world, being superior to error, is
superior also to miracles, since over there no one needs to be
removed from error.'[71]

I do not maintain that all the eastern ascetics shared these ideas. As elsewhere, there were in the East too many people who were fond of miracles, too ready to shout 'a miracle', too inclined to view a miracle as a proof of holiness. We find traces of this mentality as early as the *Vitae Patrum*. However, one should not mistake a mere mention of thaumaturgy for an indication of exaggerated thaumaturgism. Saint Antony performed miracles,[72] but that did not prevent him from lamenting a thaumaturge,[73] from being ironic at the expense of monks who were too keen for visions and extraordinary divine interventions.[74] That is, he did not confuse discernment, the pre-eminent gift of the spiritual father,[75] with the supernatural.[76] And to quote one more witness through whom the Fathers of the first generation speak: John Cassian assures us that his heroes attached less importance to the miracles they had performed or which God had performed through them than to inner holiness: 'My purpose is to speak not about God's miracles, but about the way to reform our manner of living, and the attainment of the perfect life' (*non de mirabilis Dei, sed de correctione morum nostrorum et consummatione vitae perfectae*).[77] The entire *Conference* XV, the Second Conference of abba Nestoros on 'Divine Gifts,' has no other intention than to inculcate this truth. It is possible that our ascetics had been put on their guard by various 'aretalogies' (spiritual gift systems) which were being hawked by sects of all types to proselytize.[78] Saint Theodore the Studite still echoed this tradition when he told his religious that only charity marks the true disciple of Christ, to the exclusion of miracles which 'heretics too, in our day as before, can perform'.[79] In the second half of the eleventh century, Nikon of the Holy Mountain, in chapter 43 of his *Pandectes* (lit., the receiver of all), only intended to be a summary of patristic doctrines, warns against the prestige of 'signs, prophecies, visions', and other marvellous events. What is important, is 'a just faith, and to fulfill the will of the Lord'.[80]

If it is not correct to see in this belief in the charism of direction a particular case of belief in miracles, even for the three reasons of efficacy we have just enumerated—the disciple's faith, the spiritual father's prayer, and the spiritual character of the answers given and received—all the more strongly do we have to exclude all 'illuminism' in stating the benefits attributed to the disclosure of the soul *qua talis*, leaving aside the question of the advice received, either because it was not given or because it had been forgotten.[81] What is true and remains true even in our age of psychologists, is that this naturally beneficent activity of frequent and complete *exagoreusis* was multiplied by the disciple's religious faith and by a religious sense of his responsibility in the master. Even more: the conviction on both sides—that during the practice of direction asked and given, a true spiritual generation occurred through participation in the very fatherhood of God—could not fail to give this practice a special value, and to transpose the relationship of master and disciple to a level of higher effectiveness. A mere professor or casuist could not be a true father. The eastern ascetics knew what they were saying when they put spiritual fatherhood above natural fatherhood.

NOTES

1. *Vaticanus Graecus* 1436, folio 77, cited in Irénée Hausherr and G. Horn, ed. and trans., *Un grand mystique byzantin: La Vie de Syméon le Nouveau Théologien par Nicétas Stéthatos*, *Orientalia Christiana* 12 (Rome, 1928) xlii.
2. *Vie*, lxff; cfr Basile Krivochéine, in *Christian East* nn. 7 and 8 (Winter 1953-1954) 220ff. [*Idem.*, *In the Light of Christ. Saint Symeon the New Theologian* (949-1022). *Life-Spirituality-Doctrine*, trans. Anthony P. Gythiel (New York: Saint Vladimir's Seminary Press, 1986) 18-19.—tr.]
3. *Divin. Amor.* XV; see Karl Holl, *Enthusiasmus und Bußgewalt beim griechischen Mönchtum* (Leipzig, 1898) 18.
4. Mt 5:9.
5. See Dorotheos, *Doctrina* I, 4, PG 88: 1664BC.
6. *Doctrina* I, 17; PG 88: 1640CD.
7. Climacus, *Scala Paradisi*, *Gradus* XXVII, PG 88: 1109B.
8. *Ibid.*, *Grad.* XXV.VII, and frequently elsewhere.
9. *Grad.* IV, PG 88: 705D-8A.
10. See above, pp. 129ff.
11. E. Amélineau, *Hist. monast.* (Paris, 1894) 269ff. Amélineau translated as follows: '*comme autrefois l'esprit d'Elie se dédoubla sur Elisée.*' This passage is quoted by Smirnov, p. 63, n. 3, with an amusing variant, '*son esprit se déboucha sur eux*,' 'his spirit uncorked itself upon them.'

12. Cfr *Alph*. Macarius n. 33; Evelyn White, *The Monasteries of Wadi* *Natroun* (New York, 1932) 38-104; P. Peeters, in *AnBoll* 57 (1939) 104.
13. 'Vertus de Saint Macaire,' in Amélineau, *loc. cit.*, p. 121.
14. L'abbé Marin, *Les moines de Constantinople* (Paris, 1897) 266ff.
15. *Vita Antonii* n. 7, PG 26: 835B; the *Life* of Saint Pachomius cites this passage, *Vita* I, n. 2, ed. Halkin, p. 2 (CS 45:298); Saint Basil, Saint Gregory Nazianzen, Saint Jerome, Saint John Chrysostom, Saint John Cassian, and others repeat the same idea.
16. *Alph.*, Antony n. 38, PG 65: 87B (CS 59:9).
17. *Doctrina* I, n. 17, 'De renunciatione,' PG 88: 1640C (CS 33:91).
18. *Vitae Patrum* III, 178, PL 73: 798Cd. In Bk V. X. n. 92, col. 929AB there is a redaction that is a little forced, and therefore by a later hand.
19. *Vitae Patrum* V, X, 91; PL 73: 9280ff.
20. *Ibid.*, IV, 42, Pl 73: 84A=Cassian, *Collatio* II, 2.
21. See N. Jung in *DThC*, s.v. '*scrupule*.'
22. *Vita Sanctae Mariae Meretricis Neptis Abrahae Eremitae*, PL 73: 656B (Translated by Benedicta Ward, *The Harlots of the Desert*, CS 106 [Kalamazoo, 1987] 97).
23. *Vitae Patrum* V, *liber* XII, PL 73: 943B.
24. Cassian, *Instit.* V. cap 24=*Vitae Patrum*, V.XIII.2, PL 73: 943Dff.
25. *Ibid.*, col. 944B.
26. *Alph.*, Poemen n. 27, PG 73: 329A (CS 59:171).
27. *Vitae Patrum*, n. 5, col. 944C=*Alph.*, Poemen n. 58 (174-75).
28. *Vitae Patrum* V, XIII, 7, PL 73: 945A.
29. *Ibid.*, n. 8, PL 73: 945.
30. Steven Runciman, *Byzantine Civilization* (New York, 1970) 106, 169.
31. See Irénée Hausherr, *Penthos*, *OrChrA* 132 (Rome, 1944) 26ff. [English translation by Anselm Hufstader, *Penthos. The Doctrine of Compunction in the Christian East* (Kalamazoo: Cistercian Publications, 1982).—tr.]
32. *Liber* V, 9, PL 73: 909C-12B.
33. *Ibid.*, 911B=*Alph.*, Pior n. 3 (CS 59:199-200).
34. *Alph.*, Bessarion n. 7=*Vitae Patrum* V, 9, 2.
35. *Alph.*, Antony n. 21, PG 65: 81 (6)D=*Vitae P.*, V, 9.1; col. n. 1.
36. *Alph.*, Poemen n. 6, PG 65: 320BD=*Vitae P.*, V, 9, 7, 910CD.
37. PL 73: 1019, n. 1.
38. *Vitae Patrum* VI, 30; PL 73: 1019D.
39. *Alph.*, Joseph in Panepho n. 4, PG 65: 229B (101-102)=*Vitae Patrum* V, 10, 31, PL 73: 918A.
40. *Vitae Patrum*, *loc. cit.*, n. 46, col. 920-21B.
41. Lk 10:12.
42. *Vitae Patrum* V.9.66; PL 73: 924A.
43. Maximus the Confessor, *Capitum de Charitate Centuria* III, 67, PG 90: 1037A.
44. *Epist. Barnab.*, 16, 10, and elsewhere.
45. *Didache* XI, 7.
46. Ildefons Herwegen, *Vaterspruch und Mönchsregel* (Münster i. W., 1937) 12.
47. *Collatio* XVII.23; PL 49: 1076B.
48. *Coll.*, XVII.31; PL 49: 1087A.
49. On this concept, see Eero Repo, *Der Begriff 'Rhēma' im Biblisch-Griechischen.*—I. '*Rhēma*' *in der Septuaginta* (Helsinki, 1951); and the review by Antoine Guillaumont in *REG* (1954) 318ff.
50. See Karl Heussi, *Der Ursprung des Mönchtums* (Tübingen, 1936) 164ff.

51. *Alph.*, Zachary n. 3; *Vitae Patrum* VII.26; PL 73: 1124D= *Historia Lausiaca*; Reitzenstein, *Historia Monachorum und Historia Lausiaca*, p. 190.
52. *Letter* 913, p. 373.
53. *Letter* 699, p. 334. (*Letter* n. 700 is missing from the edition of Nicodemus the Hagiorite.)
54. *Letter* 829, p. 383ff.
55. *Letter* 885, p. 360 (through typographical error, 460).
56. Mt 17:14-21.
57. 2 Cor 12:7.
58. Ps 142:10.
59. Barsanuphius, *loc. cit.*, p. 361.
60. Evagrius, *Cent.* II, 9.
61. *Letter* 701, p. 335.
62. *Moralia in Job*, XXXV.14.28, PL 76: 765B.
63. Evergetinos, Bk 1, ch. 2, p. 71=*Alph.* Poemen n. 80; PG 65: 341C, but here the text is almost certainly wrong.
64. Evergetinos, p. 72.
65. For example, Barsanuphius, *Letter* 541, p. 263.
66. *Vie de Saint Dosithée*, ed. P. Brun, *Orientalia Christiana* 26 (Rome, 1932) 82.
67. *Alph.*, Antony n. 16; PG 65: 80D (CS 59:4).
68. Evergetinos, Bk 1, ch. 21, p. 65.
69. See John Moschus, *Pratum spirituale*, ch. 55, PG 87: 2909B.
70. *Johannes von Lykopolis. Ein Dialog über die Seele und die Affekte des Menschen*, ed. Sven Dedering (Leipzig, Uppsala, 1936) 10-12; French translation by Irénée Hausherr, *Jean le Solitaire (Pseudo-Jean de Lycopolis). Dialogue sur l'âme et les passions des hommes*, OrChrA 120 (Rome, 1939) 35ff.
71. *Ibid.*, p. 12, trans. p. 36.
72. *Vita Antonii*, for example, ch. 24, PG 26: 865A.
73. *Alph.*, Antony n. 14 (CS 59:4).
74. *Ibid.*, n. 12 (3).
75. Cfr *ibid.*, n. 8 (3).
76. *Vita Antonii* 12, PG 26: 861AB; *Alph.*, Antony n. 14, PG 65: 80BC.
77. *De Coenobiorum Institutis, Prefatio*; PL 49: 59A.
78. See Reitzenstein, *Hellenistische Wundererzählungen* (Leipzig, 1906).
79. Theodore the Studite, *Petite Catéchèse*, ed. Auvray, p. 413.
80. See Charles De Clercq, *Les textes juridiques dans les Pandectes de Nicon de la Montagne Noire*. Codif. can. orient., Fonti II (Venice, 1942) 53.
81. See above, p. 247.

IX

SPECIAL CATEGORIES

LMOST ALL THE DOCUMENTS used in the
preceding pages belong to monastic literature. It
could not be otherwise. Spiritual direction was not
taught and practiced to perfection except among monks. Only
for them do we have adequate information about it. Moreover,
in the East, as in all christian lands, the direction of other
categories of faithful was always modeled on the one practised
in the monasteries, for various reasons we do not have to
explain *ex professo*. Only those who in some way aspired to
perfection sought a director of conscience; and the monastic
state has been, and will be, at all times the classic type of this
tendency. Only those who had the necessary gift and experience could give profitable direction; and these gifts and experience were found only among those who had progressed
in the ways of perfection. These, monks or not, were called
ascetics by the Easterners; in fact, they were almost always
monks or former monks who had become bishops. Two
classes of believers persuade us to make special observations
about their spiritual direction: the nuns (*moniales*) and lay
persons.

1. THE DIRECTION OF NUNS

That an adjustment had to be made is evident; and it is important to know for what reasons. Certainly, not so much because of 'womens' frailty', which is how moderns think. Among non-christian philosophers the ones who agreed with Musonius that 'women too must philosophize' (*hoti kai gunaixin philosopheteon*)[1] were rare. By contrast, christian theologians, with the exception of some later ones, missed a few chances to confirm the equality and sometimes the superiority of the 'weaker sex' with respect to virtue. Yet, in the *Stoicorum Veterum Fragmenta* edited by J. von Arnim,[2] only two texts are found in favor of this equality, and both are by Clement of Alexandria.[3] On this point, as on others, Clement did his best to indicate how the philosophers agreed with his theology. A good Christian in this respect, he taught explicitly that

> the virtue (*arete*) of men and women is the same. The God of the one and the other is One; the Pedagogue of the one and the other is One. One the church, one the moderation, one the sense of shame; common is is the food . . ., breathing, vision, hearing, knowledge, hope, obedience, charity: all this is similar. And those whose life is in common, have common grace, a common salvation; common also is charity and education.'[4]

According to the Lord, difference of sex has reference only to the present world.[5] The eternal reward

> is offered not to male and female but to the human person, when this unique being will no longer be torn apart by concupiscence. Common, therefore, to men and women is the name 'man' (*koinon oun kai to onoma adrasi kai gunaixin ho anthropos. Viris itaque et mulieribus commune nomen homo est*).[6]

We must insist on this because, in more recent times, under the pretext of psychology and physiology, a retrograde movement has occurred, away from evangelical ideas. After Galen and Hippocrates, the ancients certainly knew the essentials of these two sciences. And the Fathers realized that what was against them was not learned anthropology but the male prejudice of the common people that had been upheld more or less tacitly by the philosophers. That did not prevent the most learned among them from stating, with Origen, that the true difference between human beings was not a matter of sex, but of soul.

Divine Scripture never recognized the division of men and women according to sex. Before God, there is no difference of sex; but one is called man or woman according to the difference of soul. Before God, how many of the female sex are not counted among the brave men? And how many men are not counted among the soft and weak women? Do you not think that the one who says, I cannot comply with Scripture. I cannot sell what I own and give money to the poor;[7] I cannot turn the other cheek to someone who slaps me on one cheek;[8] I cannot bless someone who curses me;[9] I cannot answer with a prayer (when I am maligned)[10]—has to be classified as a woman? Someone says I cannot fulfill other similar commandments, does it not seem to you that he is to be counted among women who can do nothing manly?[11]

Procopius of Gaza was inspired by this teaching when he wrote, 'Everyone of us is immediately called a female when he is cast down from the state of intelligence and is ensnared by passions and vices toward which nature is prone. . . . If, on the contrary, he avoids the vices and would strive for the high ground of virtue, he is valued as a male.'[12] Saint Gregory of Nyssa speaks likewise, but with a different aim: to take away from woman any excuse she might draw from sacred texts badly understood; for example,

'God made man in his image.' 'The man (*ton anthrōpon*),' the woman says. 'What does that have to do with me?' He did not say *tēn anthrōpon*, a man of female gender. By using the masculine article, he has specified the masculine sex. But to prevent stupidity from saying that the word 'man' only applies to the male, Scripture has added, 'male and female he created them'.[13] Equally with the man, woman possesses *to kat'eikona gegenēsthai*, to have been made according to the image of God. Both natures are held in equal honor; the virtues (*hai aretai*) are the same; the condemnation the same. Let her not say, I am weak! Weakness is in the flesh, but strength is in the soul (*en psychē to dunaton estin*). Let the image of God then be held in equal honor, let virtue be equally honored, and the demonstration of good works. There is no excuse for anyone who tries to set up the weakness of the body. And this is not all. Tender and compassionate (the female sex) is strong in steadfastness, strong in vigils. When could a manly nature (*anthrōpou physin*) match its strength with a feminine nature leading a vigorous life? When can a man imitate the endurance women have in fasting, the loving labor they show in prayer, the inclination they have for tears, their readiness to do the good . . .? Do not turn your attention to the 'outer man': all that is plaster. The soul resides inside, behind the veil of a weak body. A soul nevertheless; the souls are honored equally, the one difference is in the veils.[14]

Some people do not believe that this oration is by Saint Gregory of Nyssa. Nonetheless, the passage quoted nicely recalls the praises given to Macrina, Gregory's sister. However, this is not important. The Greeks read and approved such thoughts not only because they believed they were by Gregory of Nyssa, but also because they saw them as being conformed to those of many other great Doctors, not to mention the Gospel. While speaking of his mother, Saint Gregory Nazianzen—called The Theologian (through autonomasia)—states that she was 'in body a woman, but, in character, superior to her husband'.[15] In connection with his sister, The Theologian exclaimed:

'O feminine nature who has surpassed the masculine in the common struggle for salvation, thereby proving that between the two there is a difference of body but not of soul.'[16] In the Preface to the *Ascetica* (*Ascetic Treatises*), after recalling and glossing the military terms used by Saint Paul to describe the christian life, Saint Basil—to prevent excuses by the weaker sex—warned explicitly that 'This discourse is aimed not only at men. The female sex is also part of the military service of Jesus Christ because of the strength and fortitude of their soul (*tē psychikē andreią*, the psychic manliness). They are not excluded because of weakness of the body, and several (that is, many) were not inferior to men. There were some who distinguished themselves more valiantly. Among them are these who make up the choirs of virgins. Among them are those who shine through the struggles of faith and the victories of martyrdom. Moreover, not only men followed Christ while he moved among us; and the service (*hē leitourgia*) of the Saviour was performed by both.[17]

In support of this text, G. Hermant, the old (1673) translator of the *Previa Institutio Ascetica*, cites two documents. The first is by Gregory of Nazianzus.[18]

'Saint Gregory of Nazianzus, in the *Instructions* he gives to virgins, whose defense he undertakes against the people of the world who imagine that the practice of abstinence is an impossible condition because of the frailty of their sex, opposes his own experience to this false claim. "I have known men and women who have sentiments that are entirely in heaven, and keep a perfect purity of body; if there is a difference between the sexes, it is visible only in that men have a stronger, more vigorous body. As for the rest, the cultivation of virtue is the same; they march together on the road leading to life eternal, and in this no one has anything more than the other except the difference of his merit and his toil. . . ." '[19]

The other document cited by G. Hermant is by Saint Nilus of Sinai:

> In levying an army from abroad, only young men are selected; old men are rejected, children are left behind, slaves are scorned, women are utterly avoided because of the frailty of their sex. But in the battle led according to God and in levying the army of piety, old men are called, young men run forward, children hasten along; moreover, slaves make haste with great self-confidence, women are not rejected; but they hasten against the devil courageously and boldly. They fight it out, the enemy being overthrown. They put up a trophy and every day they are crowned against their enemy.[20]

On rare occasions, even the Desert Fathers had a chance to express their judgment about the aptitude of women for the ascetic life. Bessarion and his disciple discovered in a cave a solitary who was busy plaiting a rope. He refused to answer their greetings, and did not even raise his eyes. A few days later they came to the cave again, and found the solitary dead. While they got ready to bury him, they noticed that he was a woman. They drew a lesson from this: 'See how women overthrow Satan; but we behave indecorously in cities.'[21] Obviously they felt humbled. Even more humiliated was the monk of whom the *Lausiac History* speaks, and who went to Saint Macarius to tell of his grief. He was in the habit of saying three hundred prayers a day; he carried three hundred pebbles, and he counted his prayers by throwing away a pebble.

> Abba Macarius, I am greatly cast down . . . In that village lives a certain virgin who is in her thirtieth year of the ascetic life. Many tell me that she does not eat any day but Saturday and Sunday, and every day she says seven hundred prayers. When I heard about this I condemned myself that I, born a man with all this manly strength, could not say more than three hundred prayers.[22]

Anecdotes of this type are a reaction against the male superiority complex. Perhaps some were invented for that reason. The 'Lives' of Saint Marina, Theodora, Hilaria, and other women who endured the hard discipline of a male monastery incognita do not have to be authentic to tell us their intent: to make us admire the courage of their heroines. Their views were disseminated in all the tongues of christendom.[23] The *Historia Religiosa* of Theodoret offers more solid guarantees of historicity. The Bishop of Cyrrhus had seen with his own eyes incredible feats of austerity accomplished by syrian hermits and stylites; but after having 'the life of the most excellent of the men' parade before our eyes, he judged it worth the trouble 'also to commemorate women whose struggles were not easier but rather harder.' The men are Symeon the Stylite, 'the great wonder of the inhabited world',[24] a Zebinas or a Polychronius 'who surpassed all men of his time by assiduity in praying',[25] or a Petrus the Galatian, who had begun 'the combats of philosophy' at the age of seven and persevered in them until the age of ninety-nine,[26] and so on. The saintly women 'are all the more worthy of the highest praise: as they were given a weaker nature, they showed the same determination as the men, thereby freeing their sex from its ancestral shame'.[27] The ultimate explanation of this superhuman phenomenon is obviously not physical strength,[28] for no strength, even masculine, would be sufficient for this; it is 'divine and holy charity,' the love of God and Christ. Of this love, women are certainly as capable as men; they even may possess the special charism of falling in love with the divine Bridegroom, Christ.[29]

They also have the example and the help of the Blessed among all women, 'the Queen of the choirs of virgins,'[30] the 'joy of holy women'.[31] 'In all truth, the mother of all those who live according to the gospel,'[32]—according to Saint Nilus, the mother above all of those who lead the ascetic, monastic, and apostolic life. The Virgin is *holkas tōn thelontōn sōthēnai*, 'the raft of those who want to be saved' (in the language of the Fathers, these are also the ascetics).[33] Mary is 'the fortification of virgins, of all those who flee to her; the column of virginity, the gate of salvation.'[34] She is 'the beautiful nursing mother of virgins, the one who dresses holy souls for their Bridegroom.'[35] She knows weaving and embroidery well, these pre-eminent arts of women, 'to make vestments of incorruption with the wool of the Lamb born to her, and to clothe the faithful in them.'[36] In short, although most of the titles given to the Virgin by eastern piety[37] praise her privileges in relation to God or her role in relation to all christians, it can nonetheless not be denied that all women, especially virgins, have benefited from the blessing given to this woman wherever the action of the evangelical leaven has penetrated. 'The Virgin, the advocate of Eve' (*Evae Virgo Maria . . . advocata*).[38]

Christian women should become conscious of their dignity; the most distinguished representatives of Christianity never ceased repeating that their dignity equals that of man. Saint Basil, together with his brother Gregory, apparently noticed that prejudice did not give way easily, even in the minds of the women who should have the greatest interest in eliminating it. Would they somehow get something out of it? Let us have one of them tell them. Before climbing the funeral pyre, the martyr Julitta

> exhorts the women standing nearby not to grow weak in the toil of piety, and not to adduce the weakness of their nature. We were made, she says, from the same dough as men. We were created in the image of God in the same manner they were. Woman, on a par with man, was made capable of virtue by the Creator. What are we then if not, by birth, the very same as men? To fashion woman, God has taken not only flesh, but also bone from bones[39]; and because of this we owe the Master constancy, fortitude, and patience exactly as men do. Having said this, she jumped into the fire.[40]

One only wonders why the great bishop opened his homily with the usual tag about 'the great athletic contest which Julitta, the most blessed of women, endured manfully in a woman's body . . . if it is fitting to call someone, who makes the weakness of woman's nature disappear through greatness of soul, a woman.'[41]

Harsher words about women or words addressed to them would be uttered by ascetic writers, reminding them of the modesty that suits them well,[42] and above all giving fair warning to imprudent men unaware of their own male psychology. But no longer would anyone dare view women as being spiritually inferior. This was to be apparent in spiritual direction. First, because women came to be viewed as being capable of giving direction under the same conditions as men; secondly, because the direction given to them would not differ essentially from that given to monks, though a great appeal would be made to their love of the Heavenly Bridegroom and the example of the most Blessed Virgin Mary.

That nuns could serve as guides to others derived from the simple fact that they could become spiritual and thus be qualified to receive the title *Amma* (Mother), corresponding to that of *Abba* (Father). Palladius asserts this explicitly, or has it stated by the saintly abba Piteroum in two chapters that are worth rereading here,[43] not only because this story was inserted into the *Vitae Patrum* under the name of Basil himself, but especially because its vivid details were intended to destroy stubborn, ancient, and harmful prejudices in the minds of the women and their guides.

St Basil, the bishop, relates that in a monastery for women there was a virgin who pretended she was crazy and vexed by a demon. She succeeded so well in this that the others would never eat with her. She had chosen a life of performing menial service, never leaving the kitchen. As the common saying goes, she was the mop of the whole house . . . She had wrapped her head in rags, and in this used to serve everyone. The other virgins had their hair cropped and wore cowls. Not even once did any of the four hundred virgins ever see her eat; during her entire lifetime she never sat at the table. From no one did she accept even a piece of bread, but she only wiped off the crumbs from the tables; she was satisfied with this food alone, while cleaning pots. She never did anyone any wrong. No one ever heard her murmur; she never talked to anyone, either a little or much. She was beaten by everyone, lived with the loathing of all, and endured all their curses. One day an angel of the Lord appeared to Pyoterius [or Piteroum], dwelling in the desert at a place called Porphyrites. He speaks to him in these words, 'Why,' he says, 'do you think you are something great, like a saint, because you are staying in this place? Do you want to see a woman who is holier than you are? Go to the woman's monastery at Tabennisi, and there you will find someone who has a band on her head [the old Latin version has *coronam*, in Greek *diadēma*, a crown]. Recognize that she is better than you are. While she, alone, struggles day and night with very many people, her heart is never away from God, while you stay in this one place and never go anywhere, letting your heart and mind roam in all the cities of the world.' He went to the above mentioned monastery at once, and asked the prefect of the brothers to lead him to the women's monastery. As he was a man not only famous for his lifestyle but indeed also advanced in years, they let him enter in complete trust. Having entered, he wanted to see all the sisters, but among them he did not see the only one for whom he had come. He finally said, 'Bring them all to me; it seems to me that one is missing.' They said to him, 'in the kitchen we have one who is an imbecile [in Palladius, *salem*, in Greek *salē*, the name for a halfwit].' This is how they call the one who is vexed by demons. He says, 'Bring this one to me, too, that I may see her.' Hearing this, they begin to call her. But she did not want to hear, sensing something, I believe, or perhaps knowing it through divine revelation. They say to her, 'Saint Pyoterius wants to see you.' Indeed, he was a man of great fame. When she was shown to him, and when he saw the rag on her head, he fell down at her feet, saying, 'Bless me'. She, too, fell down at his feet, saying, 'Bless me, master'. All the sisters were astonished and they said, 'Abba, do not suffer such an insult. The one you see is an idiot.' But Saint Pyoterius said to all of them, 'It is you who are idiots, for she is an amma to you and to me.' This is how they call spiritual women. 'And I pray,' he says, 'that I may be found worthy of her on the Day of Judgment.' Hearing this, they all fell at his feet, each one confessing her own sins. One said that she had poured dirty water on her from a bowl she was cleaning; another remembered having beaten her often; still another lamented that she had filled her nose with mustard. All conveyed that they had inflicted outrages of all sorts on her. The saint prayed for all of them, and left. After a few days, not being able to bear such glory and unwilling to have the other nuns heap praise on her, believing that she was burdened by the excuses of the ones and the others, she secretly left the monastery. Where she would have gone, and to what place she went, and how she may have died, no one could ever find out.[44]

Ammas—this is what spiritual women were called or, according to a variant, 'spiritual mothers.'[45] *Amma* recalls the semitic *Em(ma)* related to the Coptic *mau*, as *abba* is a transcription of the Hebrew. And in the same way as *abba*, in itself, refers only to the ability one had to become a spiritual father, and not to the actual exercise of this fatherhood, so the title *amma* does not correspond in the least to superior or abbess, as is indicated by the example we gave. Even more than men, many holy women during their entire life were able to hide the high spirituality that eventually would have allowed them to help others on the road leading to God. On rare occasions did Providence reveal the excellence of their virtue and charisms to someone holy. Saint Zosimas, for example, was such a holy man: he gave Saint Mary of Egypt, a converted *meretrix* (harlot), the name 'spiritual mother,' and asked for her blessing, because he had had proof of her eminent holiness.[46] He even called her *mater mea*, my mother,[47] undoubtedly because he knew he was indebted to her for a great grace. Saint Theodore the Studite expressed himself no differently when writing to women, nuns or not, whom he considered saints. For example, to the patrician Irene who had suffered for the cause of truth: 'Christ has triumphed in you and through you, distinguished woman, friend of martyrs, finally, my mother. For in my mind I call you by this name. Like a companion in the struggle, closer to me than those who are close to me in the flesh, this is how the Spirit joins together the ones who are born of him.'[48]

However, only, or especially, those women, who habitually exercised motherly functions were mothers spiritually—the hegumenas or superiors of communities, the ones addressed by the Latins 'with the disgraceful title abbatissa.'[49] They were the 'mothers of their monasteries', as Pachomius was the father of his. Her religious were truly her daughters especially if she had received them into the house, like the woman of whom the *Vita Theodosii*[50] speaks. She 'had left the world and presently serves God together with the children born of her according to Christ'. She must 'govern the flock of God entrusted to her in a saintly way, as spiritual mother (*hagiōs hōs mētēr pneumatikē*), giving an example through herself of what is ordered, not demanding anything that is beyond one's strength, giving her charity equally to all, not giving preference to someone because of a family relationship.'[51] As with the monks, this governance had to be above all inward, and not in the least either purely administrative or despotic. Neither spiritual fatherhood nor spiritual motherhood must destroy the sense of essential brotherhood expressed by the nouns brothers and sisters. The community was called *adelphotēs*, a brotherhood,[52] and it is as such that the mother had to guide it in the ways of the Spirit.

The sisters who have you as their head must explain their affections to you, and that to which each one is more inclined. You must receive such 'openness of heart.'[53] You must exhort the one, encourage the other, warn a third; in one word, prescribe the appropriate remedy for each. Let tedium not defeat you in this. God supports us. We only have to begin; he teaches the knowledge (*gnōsin*).[54]

Theodore gave the hegumen Euphrosyne the same rights and obligations as to himself, with regard to the revelation of thoughts by subordinates. This was the general custom if not the law; as much as monks, nuns needed spiritual direction, and for this they had to go to their mother. Only for sacramental confession would there be special arrangements. The *Lives* of the holy women hegumens presuppose such practice everywhere. The question as to whether the superior could allow others to assist her in this office was not raised because women's monasteries generally had a restricted number of religious, fixed by the foundation charter, and which could not be surpassed: twenty four, thirty, forty at most, as the Empress Irene says.[55]

The *Life* of another Irene, hegumen of the monastery of Chrysobolanton in Constantinople, in the ninth century, gives us precise information about the manner in which the direction of sisters was practiced, for the author of the *Life* states explicitly that the saint had been nourished by the *Vitae Patrum* to the point that she spoke only of these.[56] She could not have allowed herself something that did not perfectly conform to the tradition. First, before being elected hegumen, she 'was not unaware that the remembrance of past misfortunes was a snare of the Clever One, as the eye of her understanding had been purified. At once she disclosed all such thoughts to her guide and conductor, and through *exagoreusis* (revelation of thoughts) she found that she had been freed from such a trap, and could continue to devote herself to the exercises she had begun.'[57] Having become hegumen, with the blessing of the patriarch Saint Methodius, she occupied the cell reserved for superiors, and behind a closed door prayed to the One who sees in secret, imploring God to help her in governing the sisters. Bathing the ground with her tears, she asked that powerful help be given her from above. 'It is you,' she said, 'who are the good Shepherd. You told your disciples, there is one Master, Christ. You are the gate of the sheepfold, you lead to eternal salvation. You are Lord and Master. If you are our guide, come to the aid of your servant and your little flock here present; always protect us against the plunder of the wily, invisible wolf. You know our weakness and know that we cannot succeed in anything at all without the help that comes from you'.[58]

Then the new superior gave a sermon to herself which fittingly expressed the biographer's view of the duties of a spiritual mother.

Poor, weak Irene, do you understand the burden which Christ has put on your shoulders? Souls for whom God became man and shed his blood have been entrusted to you. You have heard it: the entire universe is not worth one soul. If, on Judgment Day, everyone must give a reckoning for each vain word, you certainly are not unaware, are you, of how greatly the one in charge will have to suffer for a lost soul, if she did not do all she could to save her? You must see to it that you pray more, show more endurance in fasting, bear the infirmities of your sisters, endure all things with generosity and kindness. Do not let your own unconscious failings become the cause (of a fall) for one of your sisters. Without attentiveness, the word of Christ that says, 'If the blind lead the blind, they shall both fall into the ditch,' would be fulfilled for you.[59]

The exhortation she then gave to her daughters is less related to our subject, as it deals with the monastic life in general. However, one statement is worth retaining; Irene knew that she would be ineffective as a teacher, inasmuch as her religious, she said, are all taught by God himself (*Theodidaktoi*). Nonetheless, as she had been placed at this post by the inscrutable judgment of Providence, 'I beg you not to view me as a school teacher but as a counselor, a sister bound by conscience to fulfill these functions. "Woe to me," the Apostle says, "if I do not give you profitable advice." Endure the words of my unworthiness; they are spoken to you out of charity.'[60] The sermon then continues at length without any reference to the 'revelation of thoughts' (*exagoreusis*). But this is not because the wise hegumen was not preoccupied with it. She may have sensed astutely that trust could not be gained on command, at least not on the part of sensitive souls. In the same century, the same Byzantium, Saint Theodore the Studite was more blunt with his monks when he said, 'God knows you; but I must know you, too.'[61] Irene preferred to take this very important matter up first with God himself. Here she gave proof of a rare boldness which clearly illustrates how important the object of her request seemed to her: what led her to it was undoubtedly a sense of duty but above all her 'maternal gut-feeling' (*entrailles maternelles*). Moreover, we read between the lines that the idea of such a 'paradoxical and frightening' request had not come to her from the beginning, but doubtlessly after she had experienced the difficulty of 'openness of heart'. Thus she said to herself—and this indicates her faith in God—'If the Lord would give me the grace through the gift of discernment (*diakritikos*) to know what my sisters are doing in secret, I could correct the ones who sidestep the issue, and encourage those making progress to run more energetically along the path of virtue.' 'She clearly realized the greatness of this charism.' But she did not want to be diverted from asking for it insistently with tears and genuflections, because (and let us note the reason) she was not unaware that 'this charism is the second highest among those that are distributed by the Spirit for the edification of the church, in proportion to the degree of faith. As the Apostle says, "God has set some in the church, first, as Apostles, secondly, as prophets".'[62] Irene obtained what she asked for. An angel was sent to her who said, 'According to your request, the Lord has sent me at your service for the benefit of those who must receive the heritage of salvation.[63] I will always be with you, and I will show you clearly everything that is done in secret all day long.'[64] Such a privilege was no longer ordinary, even though there is no lack of 'discerning ones' (*dioratikoi*) in the history of eastern spirituality. What is remarkable in this is that, despite this gift of 'second sight' (*prophētia*), Irene did not consider herself excused from giving all her time and care to directing her daughters.

> After Orthros, she who had spent the entire night up-right in prayer, gave some relaxation to her body, and took some rest (as was her custom). Then she entered the sacristy and called everyone of her sisters to her, by name. She let her sit beside her; and then, very naturally, she led the conversation to hidden, secret things. She aroused the conscience by adroitly touching upon the movements of the soul and the sisters' inner thoughts. Thus she provoked a confession of faults and repentance, and had a complete correction promised to her.[65]

Among the sisters, this gave her a reputation for supernatural clairvoyance; and even people from outside came running to her to test her second sight and to profit from her lessons.

Apart from what is miraculous or legendary in this account, this example lets us see the practice of *exagoreusis* (revelation of thoughts) in monasteries of women. Everything happened as with the monks; here we see how the nuns daily practiced 'opening their hearts' (*ouverture de conscience*) to the 'spiritual mother.' We could have arrived at this conclusion solely from the fact that, like this saintly Irene, the nuns had no spiritual books aside from Scripture and the *Lives of the Fathers*. Furthermore, in the *Apophthegmata Patrum (Sayings of the Fathers)* they found, at their alphabetical place, the sayings of *ammas*

Saint Theodora, Sarah, Syncletica ranked alongside those by *abbas* Antony, Arsenius, or Poemen. At the time there were no 'books for women', as a certain abba Isaiah discovered around the year 1200. Fully conscious of removing himself from the tradition, he undertook to do 'what no one had done for centuries'—putting together a book composed exclusively of apophthegms by holy women, for the use of a nun of noble birth, Theodora, the daughter of the emperor Isaac II Angelus. We still have the result of this work, inedited in Greek,[66] but printed three times in the russian translation of Theophane the Recluse.[67] Now, far from introducing new doctrines or even adapting certain teachings to the feminine temperament, Isaiah gave his lover of God, under the title *Mētērikon* quite simply a *Patērikon* with all identifying marks removed. He attributed the Fathers' sayings to the Mothers, without bothering in the least to soften them or vary them for the use of the 'weaker sex'. Far from lessening any of the ascetic demands, Isaiah merely wanted to prevent his daughter from saying that 'only to men is it possible to practice strict virtues, thanks to the strength of their nature.'[68] Specifically, nothing had been changed for the practice of *exagoreusis*; for example, what a brother said to abba Sisoes, Isaiah had said by Saint Melania to the blessed Matrona, and so forth.

This fact sufficiently illustrates something the ancient Easterners were convinced of: they did not believe that a great distinction needed to be made between ascetics of either gender, though they certainly taught the need for adaptation. But for them, adaptation was a matter of discernment (*diakrisis*) as to other types of temperament or of circumstances. The ascetics of the ancient christian East were of the opinion that such an adaptation to woman's nature, with all the individual shadings it allowed, would generally be better assured by a woman rather than a man, provided she was entirely 'spiritual' and deserved the title *amma* in the sense given to it by Palladius. In such a case she would carry the name Mother as rightfully as Saint Antony carried the name Father. The biographies of holy women had as their title *Bios kai politeia tēs hosias Mētros hēmōn tēs deina,* The Life and Conduct of Our Holy Mother (so and so).[69] Nil Diasorenus, a much later writer, it is true— Metropolitan of Rhodes in the fourteenth century—even attributed to them a certain motherhood with reference to Christ: 'Christ does not hesitate to call them his mothers.'[70] According to the same author, their spiritual fertility elevated them well above physical motherhood. Nonetheless, this *Matrona* had no spiritual children other than her own virtues. Had the occasion presented itself, however, she could have generated such virtues in other souls whose mother she really would have been from then on. Indeed, when sisters called their hegumen by this name—for example, while Saint Athanasia lay dying, the gathered community said, 'Our holy mother'[71]—they certainly understood, or ought to have understood her this way: 'Our blessed mother, guide and teacher,' 'Dominica, mother and in all respects a teacher filled with love for God and for her children.'[72] 'Indeed, she was Spirit-bearing (*pneumatophoros*), and had an understanding that was divinely enlightened and altogether translucid.' In one *Life*[73] traces are found of a spiritual mother who was not an hegumen. But the kind services of this subordinate did not rule out recourse to the superior. 'Each time (the young Eupraxia) had been tempted in her sleep [i.e. had a bad dream], she told this to a sister called Julia who was extremely virtuous and greatly loved her, helped her in all her work, and always gave her good advice according to God.' Thus, she quietly sent her to the 'superior' to have the generous resolutions the novice was eager to make evaluated by her. The *Life* adds that the hegumen surpassed all others in heroism. Let us notice the nice title the biographer gave her: '*Ho kalos iatros hē hēgoumenē,*' 'the good physician, the saintly hegumen, full of affection for her children.'[74] It was this affection that led her to make this reproach to the virtuous Eupraxia: 'Why, O child, do you hide your activities from me?' The activities in question referred to certain heroic acts toward a possessed woman. And yet this hegumen (whose name the biographer forgot to tell us!) was also directly enlightened by God.[75] She was *theophōtistos.*[76]

The superior's supernatural insight did not excuse the sisters from telling her everything. Indeed, grace was tied in with *exagoreusis*.

The one thing the 'spiritual mother' could not do was to give absolution. Hence the need for a spiritual father to administer the sacrament of penance. Although this does not pertain to our subject, we should nonetheless mention that in connection with this confessor's functions there were, as might be expected, two tendencies. One wanted to limit these functions as much as possible; the other to increase them until the hegumen's role was thereby diminished more or less. Here is another subject for research, one that would be far from easy. One would have to be careful not to confuse the 'spiritual father' with any 'old man' invested with any authority whatever in a monastery for women. Within this context, Smirnov is wrong in the short paragraph he has devoted to the subject. Nothing proves that the fatherhood of Petrus, Eponychus, and of other 'holy, sedate monks'[77] suppressed the motherhood of Pachomius' sister or of those who succeeded her, by making it superfluous. If they carried the title of 'father' of sisters,[78] even before their nomination by Pachomius, his sister was 'the mother of virgins'. 'Subsequently, many heard about her (Mary, the sister of Pachomius); they came to stay with her, and courageously practiced ascesis with the woman who was their mother and their excellent *senior* until the day of her death.'[79] The Bohairic *Life* continues: 'When our father Saint Pachomius noticed that the number of women had increased somewhat, he assigned an old man named *abba* Petrus to be their father, a man whose word was seasoned with salt, in order that he might devote himself to talking to them frequently about Scripture for the salvation of their soul.' His role was therefore above all doctrinal, that of a preacher or lecturer. Moreover, Petrus was in charge of supplies, for example, of raw materials for the manual labor done by the religious. As to the rest, the monasteries of nuns followed exactly the laws and customs of the monasteries for men, and in them the 'mother' had the same privileges and obligations as the 'father' did with monks.

Also, abba Elias and abba Dorotheos who devoted themselves to a large monastery of virgins in Athripe, Upper Egypt, were not the spiritual fathers of these women. Their role, which they assumed spontaneously out of compassion, consisted in maintaining or re-establishing peace among the some three hundred *ascētriae* (women ascetics) who had been accepted there, thanks to Elias' generosity. If he listened to them patiently, [80] it was not in his capacity as confidant but as mediator; for, 'having come from different ways of life, they continually fought among themselves.'[81] 'Elias was succeeded by Dorotheos, a well tested man who had grown old in a praiseworthy active life. As he could not stay in the monastery itself in the same way (as his predecessor, who had received an evangelical charism), he shut himself up in an upper story and had a window installed overlooking the women's monastery, a window he opened and closed. He constantly sat at the window, warning the women to stop fighting among themselves. And thus he grew old in the upper room. The women could not climb up there and he could not go down, for there was no ladder.'[82]

Still another fact must be pointed out, one which shows the equality of both sexes in things spiritual. The interdiction against women teaching in the church[83]—let us not forget that the same Saint Paul wanted them to be *kalodidaskaloi*, teachers of that which is good[84]—did not in the least prevent them, according to the Fathers, from propagating good, spiritual doctrines. *The Banquet of the Ten Virgins* by Saint Methodius of Olympus and the *Life of Saint Syncletica*, a parallel life to that of Saint Antony, are enough to prove this. Furthermore—and this is even more significant—the Apophthegms of the 'Mothers' were admitted into the collection of Apophthegms of the Fathers, in alphabetical order, not at the end in an Appendix we might suspect of having been tacked on. If these women-*seniores* were less numerous, as they are in our litanies of saints, the time has come to say that numbers play no role in the matter. What counts is the presence of these women; this is a fact that has doctrinal value, based on a principle. Their small number merely has a sociological and historical significance.

Far from weakening the superior's role, Basilian discipline, through certain surprising prescriptions, indicates how much he wanted to maintain it. Question 110, 'When a sister (*adē-lphēs*) confesses to a priest, is it necessary for the superior (*presbytera*) to be present?' Answer: 'It will be more becoming and more prudent if the superior herself declares the sister's fault to the priest who can prudently and skillfully suggest a penance, and a way of correcting herself.'[85] This presupposes that the sister had first admitted her fault to the superior. The priest is no doubt necessary since we deal here with sacramental confession[86]; this did not excuse her from the *exagoreusis* to her 'superior.' The answer to the next question is characterized by an eloquent conciseness. 'When the priest orders something to be done by one of the sisters without the knowledge of the superior, does the latter have reason to complain?' Answer: *kai sphodra*, 'and greatly.'

Where the direction of souls was to become most difficult for the superior was in the institution of Shenoute, in Upper Egypt. 'The superior of the nuns was not on an equal footing with the father; she depended on him, particularly for the application of the penal code. She could proceed on her own authority only in matters of physical punishments . . . Shenoute demanded that he be informed of all matters of some importance.'[87] Neither the sisters nor the spirit of the Gospel had to congratulate themselves on this.[88] The ruthless founder does not seem to have got what he wanted, to be informed about everything. 'Many things were hidden, even from the old man, his delegate among the sisters.'[89] As always, masculine rudeness merely set off feminine astuteness. And between these two forms of the same stupidity, the peace of souls and charity found themselves in bad shape. The extremely discrete male intervention wanted by Saint Basil certainly had greater value. Meanwhile, everyone admitted the need for a spiritual father, and for only one. The *Typikon* of Irene has a special chapter entitled, 'That all the religious must be under one spiritual father.'[90] The one who needed help the most was the superior. If she carried her charges lightheartedly, it was perhaps because she underestimated her obligations, like the hegumen of whom the *Spiritual Meadow* speaks, who thought she could leave a sister seized by a demon to her sad lot. However, the hegumen had a brother who was a bishop.

> One day when the brother came to visit her at the monastery, he noticed the poor sick woman and asked his sister, 'Does it please you that this sister is tormented by the demon and acts indecorously? Do you not know that you, as hegumen, bear responsibility (*krima*) for all the sisters?' She said to him, 'And what can I do against the demon?' In return, the bishop replied, 'What have you been doing here all these years?' Having said a prayer, this bishop purified the sister from the demon.[91]

If the superior had a sense of her responsibility and her own inadequacy, she would be the first to seek a guide, a counselor, someone to give her support, without being imposed on her. Thus Saint Eusebia-Xene addressed this prayer to God: 'God, who are present everywhere and see us wandering about, do not scorn us; do not abandon us who, after leaving our houses and parents for you, have chosen to live away from home. May it please you to send a savior and a sure guide, as at one time you sent Paul to Thekla, so that, following his foorsteps, we, the unfortunate and downcast, may follow your path without stumbling.' The Lord granted her prayer by sending her a priest, named in fact Paul, whom she asked 'to be a father to her according to the Spirit; and she would depend upon his care and solicitude.[92] Had this Eusebia read the sermon *On Repentance* of John the Faster (d. 595)? At any rate, she put into practice the advice we see given there to the virgins: 'Seek Paul, as Thekla did, to hear from him the things

he will say to you.'[93] 'Accordingly, listen to the good counselors; more than parents according to the flesh, parents according to the Spirit have more solicitude and love for the
weak; "who is weak that I am not weak?" '[94] Thus Saint Paul
was taken as the model of the spiritual father, in remembrance
of his solicitude for Saint Thekla.

As for the norms that informed the nuns' spiritual direction,
we have already said that they did not vary when they passed
from the monasteries of men to communities for women.[95] It
must be added that the nuns do not seem to have wanted rules
written especially for them. Pachomius had sent his *Rule* so
that the nuns could learn it by heart, obviously not as a mere
memory exercise, but so that 'educated according to the same
rules, they may apply themselves to live according to God'.[96]
Thus communities of sisters followed exactly the laws and
customs of monasteries of men, and in them the 'mother' had
the same prerogatives and obligations as the father had among
monks. The laws of the ascetic life, written by men for men,
presupposed that virtue (*vir*-tus, manliness) and courage (*an-
dreia*, manhood), despite their names of pagan origin, which
make of them prerogatives of men, were not lacking in woman's nature. We still sing, *Fortem virili pectore laudemus omnes
feminam*, 'Let us all praise a strong woman of manly courage.'
But here language surrenders to a male pretense that is not
worth refuting, except by *deeds*. In *narratives*, there is undoubtedly not one *Life* of a woman saint—they were all written by men, until quite recent times—that does not praise its
heroine for having 'a manly soul'.[97] One *Life*, without blinking
an eye, speaks of a sex change[98]; others, more specifically,
of replacing 'womanly weakness' with a 'manly will.'[99] This
goes so far that the Empress Irene, in a long prayer addressed
to the Blessed Virgin for a monastery she had just founded,
asked the blessed among all women, the 'All Immaculate Virgin and Mother,' 'once and for all to protect from all ambushes
this flock consecrated to your Magnificence, to masculinize in
virtue what is womanly in the brotherhood (*adēlphotēs*), so always to protect this beautiful sheepfold with [her] all powerful

right hand, that the old serpent would not find in it another Eve to whom he could whisper his deadly sophistries. . . .'[100] One could have believed, or hoped, that after the Most Blessed Virgin and because of her, it would no longer have been necessary for women to masculinize themselves in order to gain the Christians' esteem and admiration. One does not reform habits of language rooted in the most remote prehistory. The most astounding symptom of this atavistic prejudice is what we read in the *Life* of 'Our Holy Mother Matrona': 'Having cut her hair close to the skin . . . and pretending to be a eunuch, Matrona had called herself Babylas, and went to the monastery of Bassianos. Admitted by the monks, she immediately prepared herself for spiritual combat . . . to such a high degree that it was universally admired how a man affected with the weakness unique to eunuchs can show such endurance in toil that he strove zealously to surpass all the monks. . . .'[101]

From all this, which could be corroborated by other evidence, it is evident that the women themselves would have felt offended had anyone sweetened the principles of the monastic life for their use. Necessary adaptation cannot consist of a lowering of the common ideal of all christian perfection. This is not a matter of quantity, dosage, phrases, verbal and conceptual shadings, but of quality and imponderables—in one word, of spirit. Consequently, no one could write better practical 'translations' of a text to be used by sisters than the spiritual mother, someone who is truly mother and truly spiritual. She will do this all the more competently as, to quicken her theoretical teaching, she keeps before her eyes, even more in her heart, the devotion to the Blessed Virgin Mary and the love of the Lord Jesus, Bridegroom of souls.

Beginning with the first treatises *De virginitate* we see an appeal being made to these two loves. In his text, Saint Gregory of Nyssa returns three times to the Virgin Mary:

What was accomplished bodily in the inviolate Mary, when the fulness of the Godhead appeared in Christ by the grace of virginity, is accomplished in every soul that remains virgin. The Lord does not come with bodily presence, since, according to Saint Paul,[102] 'we know Christ no longer according to the flesh.' He dwells in the soul spiritually, and his presence brings that of the Father, as the gospel tells us somewhere.'[103]

In chapter IX, Gregory of Nyssa makes the life of virginity go back to Miriam, the sister of Moses, but he knows that this opinion is conjectural; at any rate, the prophetess Miriam merely prefigures Mary the Theotokos.[104]

The thought of the most Blessed Virgin makes the struggles of the ascetic and virginal life lovely; the love of the heavenly Bridegroom gives the strength to do battle victoriously. The frequency with which greek authors writing for nuns return to this subject shows how much importance they attached to it. They were right, unquestionably. Even though every soul, regardless of gender, is betrothed to Christ, according to Origen's explicit teaching,[105] and since as a consequence no difference in sex is valid theologically—psychologically it is obvious that nuptial symbolism would fit better with woman's nature. After its very remote beginnings,[106] the great masters of the spiritual life, even the church itself, hardly use this vocabulary again except for the use of virgins dedicated to God (*virgines Deo sacrae*). But then they used it with a freedom that would bring a smile to many a modern imagination more prudish than chaste.[107] However, the numerous treatises *De virginitate* deal too much with generalities for us to use them here. To obtain information about the direction of sisters by a spiritual father, there is hardly anything, except the letters addressed to one or another of them in particular. Also, to use them they would have to be rather numerous and addressed to the same person. Fortunately, this is the case for the correspondence of Saint Theodore the Studite. We have, among other things, a series of letters to 'The Hegumen Euphrosyne' which superiors could read with great profit even today.[108]

Euphrosyne had succeeded her mother Irene in directing her monastery. Theodore had promised the mother he would help her daughter.[109] He could not break his promises, 'if it is possible for a sinful man somehow to be useful.' How did he proceed? Not as a dry moralist or a mere casuist. He was able to put affection at the service of charity, while teaching how faith and the love of God should rule charity. At the death of Irene, he sent a first letter, one of genuine condolence: he understands and unreservedly shares the sorrow of his correspondent. Was the deceased not also his mother through her virtue? 'In what manner has the venerable *ammas* flown away from us, this Christ-bearing woman (*hē christophoros gynē*), this treasure of chastity, this head adorned with grace, this sanctuary of piety . . . this holy temple, this olive-yard of compassion, (and so forth)?'[110] In another letter of condolence, Theodore did not fail to remind other people that the Christian must not grieve like those who have no hope. To Euphrosyne he made no recommendation of this sort. He waited until the sense of faith returned by itself; and indeed soon he was able to write to her: 'How splendid was the letter from your Reverence; in it is made known your grief for the death of your holy mother, and a reminder of hope! Not to feel pain at all, not to cry over the departure of the dead is justly reprehensible (it is a sign of insensibility). Likewise, to allow oneself to be broken by grief beyond measure belongs to those who have no hope in the resurrection.' Theodore could then exhort his spiritual daughter; she was ready to listen to him and profit from his advice. What is of interest to us here is what he told her about her role as superior.

> Direct your attention to guiding the sisters, ruling them in the Lord, with all forbearance and sympathy. Demand the fulfillment of obligations, not urging too vehemently, but as a nurse would take care of her children, even risk her life for them. On the other hand, do not relax the reins completely, which would cause dissolution and confusion, and would show lack of love for your children

(*aphiloteknia*). . . . You know that all their eyes are on you as upon God; they view you as a reconciler between them and God. If you act this way, it is clear that on their part they must not aspire to do anything but what you, their teacher (*hē didaskalos*) desire, order, and declare. Truly, they should act like true daughters toward the mother, like the members of the body toward the head, like the flowers toward the rose bush.

In a city where convents were numberless, one danger lurked for hegumens, the temptation to conformity.

Do not look hither and thither, saying, 'this monastery does this, that monastery does that.' This is harmful; we must judge ourselves by the norm of the commandments, not by that of the neighbors. From this, no one can secure straight marching, or to walk in a manner that is worthy of God.

The end of the letter indicates that Theodore was thinking not only of the hegumen but of her entire community .

Do you see, sister and spiritual mother, how the love of God has compelled me to speak candidly with you? I would not have done anything more had I talked to my mother and my own sisters; except that all of us are the body of Christ; and we invoke one Father, our good God. For this reason, we are all brothers of one another, joined in one body, partakers and co-heirs. Hence our affection for you and for your salvation, as Christ loves this, and as we have been instructed. Peace to you, Mother and Teacher. Peace to the sisters (*eirēne tais adelphais*), in Christ Jesus our Lord. Amen.[111]

Saint Theodore always supported his spiritual daughter. He reminded her of the greatness of her function and of the obligations deriving from it. 'Rule the flock of God which has been entrusted to you with holy awe, like a spiritual mother (*bōs mētēr pneumatikē*), not like a human ruler, presenting yourself as an example of what has been commanded; not demanding anything that is beyond one's strength; bestowing your love equally upon all, not giving preference to someone for reasons of filiation.'[112]

> Do you see the laws that have been imposed upon us by truth? And what does the great Peter say? 'When the chief shepherd appears, you will be given the crown of unfading glory.'[113] What praise for you to be able to exclaim before God, 'Here I am, with the children (*ta paidia, puellae*, the daughters) the Lord has given me.'[114]

The great Studite knew the difficulty of the common life well enough to be preoccupied above all with the unity between souls, and this depended chiefly on the superior. Euphrosyne was afraid she had no one who really supported her. When reading about this fear, Theodore sensed pain (for his sensitivity was very great, and he had done everything for Irene's daughter), but he was very cautious not to say, 'I am here!' This would have been very imprudent; in the first place, did he even know where he might be tomorrow? What he knew well and never forgot, not even in moments of greatest surrender to human friendship, was that we should put our trust entirely in God, of whom even the best creatures are, and only can be, intermediaries. Relying on human support, without recalling that it is a gift of God, replaceable by another, is to insult Providence, to lack faith, to get away from truth, and run the risk of a well deserved disillusionment. When clouds gather on the horizon, the threat of a storm can make the inhabitants of convents tremble more than other people; when the barbarian invasions were near, did Saint Augustine not write a long chapter in his *City of God*[115] to reassure the pious souls who were more afraid of their imperiled virtue than of the prospects of death? At the beginning of the ninth century, times were troubled enough for an hegumen of nuns to be deeply apprehensive, in as much as peddlers of alarming news rarely missed an opportunity to ply their sad trade. 'What is rumored by the people terrifies you, you say. But you have God for your champion, and you have the help of your mother's prayers. Throw all your cares upon Him, and He will take it upon himself to help you with the arrangements to be made. You say that you have no one really to protect you? But you have the One who stands in the front line, the One you you have vowed to love, the Lord. Next, you have the guardian of your life, the angel who snatches you away from all evil. Courage, therefore; and do not be downhearted! . . .'[116]

Instead of trembling, trying to foresee events that may never happen, the hegumen should be entirely devoted to her role as mother. Let her be generous, Theodore states, in providing the material things her daughters need: food, drink, clothing, and the rest.

> Only, let them be of one purpose, of one mind, of one soul, one will. Let all things be in common, let there be no private ownership, no dissension; and then all the things necessary for salvation will be fulfilled; and the beautiful, rapid course of the cenobitic life will have been traversed. Then for ages and ages they will dance with you, their distinguished, godly-minded (*theophronos*) holy mother.[117]

Above all, the spiritual life, the goal of everything, must be attended to. To do this, it is good for the superior 'to have a soul in whom she may confide everything that happens;[118] just as the sisters find refuge and protection in you. For they must lay all their affections on you as a burden,[119] and that to which each one is more inclined; and you must receive such openness of heart. You must console one and encourage another; you must strengthen a third; in a word, give the appropriate remedy to each. Let tedium not defeat you in this. God supports you: we only have to begin, and he teaches the knowledge (*kai autos didaskei gnōsin*) . . . .'[120]

Another letter by Theodore is not a reply, but a spontaneous sign of his solicitude. 'Presently, we visit your Reverence through this letter, desirous to know how you continue to lead the spiritual life holily and healthily; this is our obligation, inasmuch as you have entrusted yourself to our lowliness (after the death of your mother).'[121] The letter has no other goal than to comfort and encourage, without there being a special problem to be treated. Theodore had heard praises about Euphrosyne's convent and, far from intervening at once to beat down possible thoughts of vanity, he used the opportunity to challenge her to keep making continued progress towards higher and higher perfection.

> We hear again and again of the excellent things you do, mostly while directing the sisters, keeping them united in one soul through charity, being vigilant in what regards God: prayer, psalmodies, and reading; but also in hospitality, dividing things for the care of souls through largess. What the eye is to the body, that, I hear, your monastery is to Byzantium. Let God be praised for this; your mother rejoices about this more than can be said, for the saints are privileged to see the virtuous deeds of their disciples. Rejoice therefore, good teacher and true mother according to God. Let others have worldly glory, renown, diadems, and crowns of short duration. The cross of Christ will be enough to you; the life accepted from God, your community of virgins so dear to Christ, and, if you wish, the words of God more precious than gold and stones, the bright garment which is the following of Christ—things which are more excellent than all the goods in the world, earnest-money of the kingdom of heaven.[122]

This letter should not put us on the wrong track. Theodore was no flatterer. When he heard that the Reverend Mother Euphrosyne was getting ready to dismiss a sister about to leave, he agreed with her evident pain but did not understand why she resigned herself so easily to it. 'Wise and intelligent as you are, do you not recognize duty on your own?' Studite canon law admitted only two kinds of leave from the convent: one for the perfect religious who had been duly elected superior of another house; the other for the imperfect religious who, after long and fickle care, chose to go over to another 'fraternity' in the hope of becoming better over there, after an understanding between the two superiors. As for mere re-entry into the world after the 'sacrament' (*mystērion*) of profession, Theodore considered it inadmissible, and forever. On this point, his morality perhaps sinned a little by excessive severity; the psychological sensitivity of Euphrosyne, at grips not with principles but with reality, ultimately saw things more correctly. At any rate, the direction he gave her, and especially its tone, showed that the hegumen of Studios was able to oppose, with intransigent rectitude, not only Leo the Armenian, the emperor 'named so well after a wild beast,' but also—and this is perhaps more difficult—the ideas of a nun, his spiritual daughter.

Theodore also wrote to sisters who were not hegumens; but more rarely, it seems, even though it is impossible to make the statistics of this correspondence. The letters we have (some inedited ones remain) were written for special circumstances: persecution and dispersal of communities, bereavement, blessings received, questions asked. The 'direction' given is mostly limited to the general principles of christian perfection, except when the correspondent found herself in an exceptional situation, cloistered or exclaustrated, or when she had asked for personal instruction on some specific point. Of course, the teaching of the Studite corresponded to the spirit of his spirituality, which was above all concerned with *praxis*.

You ask to be instructed in the way you should pray. The Lord himself has taught this well in the *Our Father*, and by undertaking to ask, not for anything temporal, but for his kingdom and eternal justice. The one thing to add is what has been determined by the Fathers: first, to give thanks to God, then to confess to him sins committed; finally to ask for their forgiveness and other salutary requests. Therefore, when you prepare yourself for prayer, thank God for creating you out of nothing, for having freed you from all error by giving you the vocation of knowing himself and for actualizing it, far from pagan and heretical error; then, for everything He has arranged so that, after you enjoyed the common life in the world, you were received in the bosom of the monastic life 'equal to that of the angels' (*eisaggelos*)—all graces, the very thought of which is capable of moving the soul to compunction and to the shedding of tears. From this comes enlightenment of heart, peace of spirit, and the desire for God. When this dwells in the heart, rejection of all evil follows. When you make your thanksgiving ascend to God in this manner, speak this confession to him: Lord, you know how much I have sinned against you and how much I sin every hour. Regard this sin, this fault, committed knowingly or unknowingly, without, however, imprudently recalling those whose detailed remembrance harms the soul. From this will spring for you the grace of humility with contrition of heart and fear of divine retribution. After this, request, lament aloud, beg the Lord to forgive you your past and to strengthen you for the future with a view to pleasing him, saying: 'No longer, Lord, will I provoke your anger; besides you, who are truly worthy of love, I will no longer love things. And if I offend you again, I will fall down before your mercy, that strength may be given to me whereby I may please you.' If another good thing to be accomplished comes to your mind, ask for it earnestly. Having done this, ask the Holy Mother of God to have mercy on you; and the holy angels, especially the one who guards your life, that he may watch over you and protect you; the Forerunner, the apostles, all the saints, the ones you particularly used to invoke and the one whose memory is celebrated that day, therein, it seems to me, lies the power of prayer (*tes pros-*

euchēs tēn dynamin), although everyone prays in different words, and not like everyone else, and the one who prays does not always use the same words. But it seems to me that the essence is necessarily the same for all.[123]

With respect to the spiritual life as a whole, the other letters addressed to sisters presented the same doctrine, one that was hardly predisposed toward illusion, even the mysticism of prayers. If there is mysticism (and there certainly is), it is identified with the life of faith and charity, according to circumstances: fidelity to the laws of the christian and the monastic state in time of peace; in time of persecution, steadfastness in orthodoxy, even to martyrdom. Did perfection, for Theodore, not lie in the 'martyrdom of submission'?[124] This does not mean that Theodore was unaware of the vocabulary of mysticism, dionysian or other. For Dionysius the Pseudo-Areopagite, *theoptia* (the vision of God) was granted to the angelic orders,[125] the prophets and especially Moses[126] and some 'purified intelligence' like Carpus of Crete.[127] In a reply to a recluse, Theodore speaks of *theoptia*. To believe that she had touched on the subject in her letter would not be speculation. Here is what her spiritual father conveyed to her:

> To those who dwell in the common life (of the world) it is not possible that the eye of the understanding (*dianoias*) will be purified to such a degree that it is intent upon God without a barrier, the attachments of the flesh making them see badly as if through some rheum. But to us who must renounce everything and who received the order to carry only the cross of Christ, seeing God (*theoptian*) is easy; namely, not to think or consider anything except how to please God and to serve him with a pure heart, all carnal affections having been severed.

Then follow the usual recommendations on how to be faithful to the commandments.[128]

By proposing a spirituality of this type to nuns, Saint Theodore merely made them start down the road he himself followed. He had found the secret of his heroic love of Christ during his exiles, in prisons, through cruel torture.[129] The monks too showed magnificent examples of courage. We are less well informed about the nuns. Nonetheless, there is one letter we must cite because in it we sense the spiritual father's joy and pride.

> If there is one thing I, the lowly one, am bound to do, it is to encourage and prepare you for the struggle, you who are indeed my sisters and mothers, as Truth himself has said. For Christ, you have suffered being deprived of your spiritual mother, separation from one another, the confiscation of your monastery, and incarceration after being flogged for confessing the truth. What can I say to give an encomium worthy of your merits? That in this time in which we live—when princes and subjects have gone astray and have thrust aside the words of Christ for fear of death, monks and nuns, except for a very few, among them—an entire brotherhood, thirty persons, in a single convent have had this unanimity and have fought for Christ a victorious battle worthy of Sebasteia, with the one difference that of the thirty nuns not one gave in.[130]

Saint Theodore's spiritual direction had proved itself. Moreover, using the greatest discretion on the subject of the mysteries of the contemplative life, he remained in the lineage of the most famous masters: not only the entire school of Saint Basil and Saint Barsanuphius, but also Evagrius of Pontus himself. Though his *Centuries* and *Gnostic Chapters* repeat or ceaselessly presuppose an appeal to 'knowledge of the Holy Trinity' or 'the vision of God' (*theoptia*), he hardly mentions this in his exhortation *To A Virgin*, while finding intimate accents in describing the amiability of the 'heavenly Bridegroom'.[131] The surest way to arrive at christian contemplation is not the reading of mystical texts[132]; it is the one that was followed first by all the saints, the martyrs, and then their followers, the heroes and heroines of 'the martyrdom of conscience' or of 'submission', that is of renunciation in all its forms.

Five hundred years after Saint Theodore the Studite, the metropolitan Theoleptus of Philadelphia had to direct (outside of his diocese) a princess who had become a nun, and hegumen of the convent of Mary Full of Grace. This direction was often done by letters to the hegumen or through instructions addressed to the whole community; and the correspondence as well as the discourses still exist in a contemporary (early fourteenth century) manuscript. Already the articles of V. Laurent[133] and of S. Salaville[134] let us view Theoleptus as the representative of a classical spirituality totally centered around detachment; though the same Theoleptus also wrote a *logos* on 'secret occupations' (*krypta ergasia*), and a few brief chapters which, in the opinion of the editors of the *Philokalia*, seem to have favored hesychasm.[135] If hesychasm is found there, it is according to the ancient, not the new, method. As far as spiritual direction is concerned, what Laurent has told us about it makes us regret that the manuscripts have not yet been edited. 'Hardly out of adolescence (she had remained a widow since the age of sixteen), Irene took the direction of her monastery firmly in hand. She possessed learning, a precious advantage for a woman in governance . . .'[136] Certainly, 'but this cultivated mind who managed the affairs of her convent with a rare practicality seems to have given up her administrative habits only with great difficulty when directing souls.' Not that she lacked humility! At least, she was wise enough to do her share of 'the most menial and repulsive tasks. She did not disdain working in the kitchen. On the advice of her director, she cared for the sick sisters with her own hands.'[137] Despite signs of good will, the governance of the princess-hegumen does not seem to have yielded the desirable spiritual fruits. 'Her director had constantly to reprimand her for her too great severity. . . .' The result: 'petty quarrels, small incidents that constantly disrupted the peace of the community.' What added to the seriousness of the problems were reports by the hegumen, soon denied by letters from subordinates, which led the prelate to believe that 'order reigned in the monastery.' 'Irene had acted with the good intention not to sadden her spiritual father.'[138] If that is true, she did not understand one thing about her obligations, either toward her director or her daughters. 'The bishop condemned her severely, and told her bitterly, "Very well. I have been deceived, and it is you who have lied to me. However, you did not lie to man, but to God".' He even threatened to break things off. Evidently, he knew that everything would yield to this supreme argument. For 'Irene was a worried woman . . ., bewildered by the slightest accident . . . When the mail did not satisfy her expectations, she got upset and cried that she had been abandoned. She conveyed her agitation' to those around her. Under such conditions, the princess-hegumen, before reaching the age of forty, 'tired of being misunderstood, decided to give up her post and to retire either to some hermitage or to Philadelphia, close to her director. Nonetheless, she resigned herself and remained at the head of the monastery until the end [of *her* life?].'[139]

Would Theoleptus not have done better to accept the offer of resignation? Perhaps he was afraid of having such an unaccomodating spiritual daughter too close to him. In the case of Irene, had there not been an original irreparable malpractice? The entire teaching of the ancients which we have expounded condemned the haste with which the young widow was styled, or styled herself, hegumen. She hardly had taken the time to change her first name Irene (*Eirēnē*) to Eulogia, 'before she took the direction of her monastery firmly in hand'. Was her title of empress (*basilissa*), which she held from her deceased husband, the equivalent of *ammas* or spiritual mother? Could her instinct for domination have replaced the virtues of charity, sweetness, and justice necessary to her office? Above all, could her early bookish education (for we are told that she possessed learning) have compensated for the indispensable discernment she never had? No art or science can be learned by rushing headlong into practice without having learned the basics. In matters of the mind, even more in those of the Spirit, someone who rushes ahead will never reach the end. Irene Eulogia Choumnaia Lascarina Paleologina could have become a good hegumen, had she been given the opportunity to make an apprenticeship of it according to the rules. Her husband's name and her father's great fortune seemed to have been sufficient reasons for dispensing with this. Nicephoros Gregorias, the byzantine historian,[140] who is too partisan to let us accept his judgments uncritically, believed that he was praising the princess-hegumen when he wrote that she always presented herself as an empress (*basilissa*) and a lady (*kyria*)— we would like to know what her subordinates thought of this—that she wanted and built for her community a magnificent edifice which, thanks to her, became even more famous for virtues than for its magnificence[141]—but is modesty not also a christian virtue?—that in these splendid buildings there were soon over a hundred nuns. Had the founder, Irene Comnena, been wrong in prohibiting that the number forty be exceeded or even reached, if the high number could bring the risk of less regularity?[142] This self-styled hegumen undoubtedly felt that she was above such old-fashioned practices. She even found the time to get involved with politics or, with what then amounted to the same thing, theological controversies. On Saturday and Sunday, 'Irene held parlor during which all the events in Byzantium were echoed; . . . crowds of friends must have hastened to these weekly gatherings, for her rude director denounced on several occasions the dangers of such gatherings to a sensitive heart. . . .'[143] Furthermore, the abbess had to manage, first with her brother, the general and rhetorician John Choumnos, then by herself, the enormous family patrimony;[144] for Nicephoros Choumnos was 'scandalously rich'.[145]

We hardly dare recall the ancient teachings about the qualities and duties of spiritual father or motherhood. However, let us be allowed to call to mind Saint Synclectica, the 'faithful disciple of Saint Thekla'.[146] Born rich, of great beauty, she too had given herself to God from her teenage years by taking as her slogan, *Ego Dilecto meo et Dilectus meus mihi* (My Beloved is mine, and I am his). When she was able to get rid of all her possessions, instead of savoring the sacrifice by retaining her esteem and a taste for the vanities sacrificed, she said: 'Now I have acquired a great name and there is nothing I can give to my Benefactor . . . since everything belongs to him.'[147] 'One cannot at the same time have the green stalk and the ripe ear. Likewise, in the spiritual life, it is impossible to produce heavenly fruit while being surrounded by worldly glory. The leaves must fall, the haulm must dry, if one wants to have a harvest.'[148] To begin teaching before one has covered the entire course of the practical life is especially dangerous.[149] We are told, still by the panegyrist Gregorias that the hegumen was not averse to doing some very menial tasks such as caring for sick sisters or performing her tour of duty *even* in the kitchen (*achri ton optaneion*—literally, in the roasting place), but the manner in which this is said makes us suspect that Irene acted that way more out of condescension than conviction. Human consequence which believes it must be humble by occasionally sharing the living conditions of simple people perhaps humiliates them more than it humbles itself. Irene was perhaps despised by them because they sensed that in view of human and christian dignity, it is petty to give value to 'the greatness of an established order', especially after someone has professed *metanoia* (repentance), by substituting thoughts of Jesus Christ for worldly ideas. Irene Eulogia Choumnaia changed her first name, her clothes, but not enough of her ideas and feelings. V. Laurent states that 'with a rudeness and an ill-controlled nervousness she uniformly asked of her daughters what an excessively taut will tempered by tribulation allowed her to dispense generously: blind obedience and docility.'[150] Let us be allowed to ask *when* and *where* she practiced obedience, since she had become an hegumen right away? Certainly not her father's house: 'The pride of the Choumnos, flattered by this premonition [of an illustrious destiny] surrounded the newly born with some sort of cult. . . .'[151] When such destiny was realized even beyond parental ambitions it became idolatry. Here is what Irene's father wrote after the death of the prince, her husband: 'I and the mother from whom you were born, and your brothers will always be, and wish to be, what you yourself want or could desire (us to be), even when you command as mistress (*hōs kyria*). We will always surround you like slaves (*hōs douloi*), hastening to serve you in everything and in every way. Not one of the things you desire will remain undone, as long as it is in our power to do it.'[152] In this statement, we will certainly allow for the elements of grief on that occasion, and of rhetoric, but the father, 'an impenitent rhetorician',[153] knew which arguments had to be used to get something from his daughter. What about Irene's attitude toward her spiritual father? Disregarding the fact the she used trickery and resisted him more than once to the point of making Theoleptus of Philadelphia angry and wearied, there is a difference between docility toward a far away spiritual father to whom one says everything, and an everlasting subjection to one woman's autonomy, always present. The case of the empress-hegumen Irene Eulogia demonstrates, *per reductionem ad absurdum*, the need to maintain the ancient doctrines on how to accede to governance. Theodore the Studite has given us the lapidary formula: *apo tou archesthai kalōs aneisi tis epi to archein ennomōs*[154]: 'The one who would learn to command well must, as they say, first of all learn how to obey'[155]—otherwise he governs badly. If that is true for all exercise of authority, how much more true is it for spiritual fatherhood or motherhood? Because of a lack of firmness in adhering to such principles, Theoleptus of Philadelphia, and others like him, condemned themselves either to rudeness or to weakness, and always to failure.

After the death of Theoleptus, Irene had another director. A great deal of the correspondence she exchanged with him— thirty six letters sent and as many answers—has been preserved. Laurent announces that the collection will be studied at the first opportunity; this work promises to be most interesting. It is already clear that the charitable presupposition

Laurent made has not turned out to be true: 'Having been appraised of the inconveniences of being directed from afar, she chose one of these local innumerable monks of the capital. . . .'[157] The empress-hegumen, before as afterwards, preferred a spiritual father at a safe distance.

Saint Gregory the Theologian took the trouble to write heroic verse about the way in which a virgin consecrated to God should behave toward her spiritual father:

> Above all, serve God. Then honor the priest,
> Christ on earth (*Christon epichtonoin*), who shows you life.
> Direct yourself to him swiftly, submit to him in silence.
> Through him tend on high, rejoicing; submit your faults to him;
> So that, quivering a little, you lift off to the heights.
> Be dead to all others.[158]

2. THE SPIRITUAL DIRECTION OF LAY PERSONS

We will have few things to say on this topic, for two reasons:
1) because lay people had less recourse to direction since, as was true for monks, the initiative always had to come from the one who consulted, not from the one who directed. Their 'spiritual father' was most often the one who gave them absolution during confession.
2) because the same general principles as for religious applied to the minority that asked their confessor for something else aside from absolution and penance (*epitimia*). First all were invited to perfection, according to the very teaching of the Lord[1] which is applicable to all Christians. No orthodox thinker ever thought of dividing Christians into two categories according to the degree of charity toward God and neighbor to which they were called. The distinction between the just and the perfect, as the anonymous author of the *Book of Degrees*[2] explained it, is heretical. The distinction between believers

and gnostics in Clement of Alexandria corresponds to a human fact, not a divine law. When Saint John Chrysostom enumerated nine degrees through which one reached 'the height of philosophy,'[3] he addressed himself to christian people in general.

> The stadium of virtue is open not only to men but also to women; the Divine One who awards the prize (*ahtlothetēs*) generously awards the same prize to the one gender and the other; for the one who has decided to complete, neither sex, nor fortune, nor bodily weakness, nor difference in profession nor anything whatever is an obstacle. It does not happen here that the man is taken and the woman left, that the great lord and the rich one are deemed worthy to run and the slave and the poor are turned away as unworthy, that the adult is admitted and the child rejected, that the person who awards prizes accepts the someone who opted for celibacy and does not accept those who passed under the yoke of matrimony. No, each gender, each class and age and way of life is called to this noble contest; all kings on earth and nations, princes, all rulers of the world,[4] young men and girls, old people and children too.[5]

The means to be used are also the same and responsibilities are similar:

> You will say (that) the one who lives in the world (*biotikon*) and the one who has given himself to God once and for all are not the same. Both do not fall from the same height and this is why their words are not the same. In this you are utterly wrong, if you say that different things are demanded from monks than from those living in the world. The one difference between them is that one takes a wife and the other does not, but the account they will both have to render is the same. For someone who for no reason gets angry with his brother offends God equally

whether he be a monk or a secular; and someone who looks at a woman to desire her, whether he be in this state or that one, will be punished by the same penalty, for adultery. I would rather say that the secular who does this is less worthy of forgiveness, for there is no equality between these two things. Indeed, the misdeed is not the same when someone who has a wife, and therefore enjoys consolation, is carried away by a woman's beauty; and when someone who is totally deprived of this is fettered by this evil.[6]

And so on, for the prohibition of swearing, laughing, for all the gospel beatitudes; nowhere does the Lord mention the difference between monks and seculars.

The Holy Scriptures know nothing of such a distinction: they want everyone, even if married, to lead the monastic life. Hear what Saint Paul says (and when saying Paul I always say Christ): when writing to men who have wives and bring up children, he asks from them the same rigorous observance that befits monks. He eliminates all luxury in dress and maintenance when he writes, I direct that women wear suitable clothes and dress modestly, without braided hair and jewelry or expensive clothes.[7] Also, someone who is self-indulgent is dead even while she lives.[8] And finally, If we have food and clothing, with these shall we be content.[9] What more could one ask from monks?

Chrysostom continues in this vein for many pages which it would be as profitable to reread now as it was in the fourth century.

In agreement with this and with the entire tradition, Saint Theodore the Studite[10] summarized this doctrine in two words, 'all things are equal' (*episēs panta*). There is a perfect equality among all Christians, monks or not, with respect to the laws of the inward, spiritual life. Yet, here too, an adaptation has to be made on two points: lay people made a vow neither of poverty nor of chastity. Nonetheless, they must practice both of these virtues according to the common commandment of God obligating everyone not only to avoid actual sin but also sin in thought, which evidently presupposes inner detachment and a limitless spiritual poverty. At the beginning of the fifteenth century, Symeon of Thessalonica wrote: 'Let every priest[11] act saintly and try to live in a way befitting monks; or let him even try to become a monk at the right time.'[12] If there were differences between spiritual direction for monks and that given to Christians in the world, they lie not either in the doctrine or in the goal professed, but in the means to be used to reach it, and this is true in the West as in the East.[13] The evolution of monastic and of lay spirituality occurred along two parallel, or approximately parallel, lines, with areas of greater widening and narrowing. An interesting study, if possible, would be to measure the mutual influence of the one on the other. In the East, the monastic spirit, born of the christian spirit, has always exercised a predominant influence on the life of the people as a whole; the books they read when they aspired to evangelical perfection were always books written by monks or former monks who had become bishops, even until recently. While the expressions of a theology or spirituality of the lay state are all modern in the West, in the East they have never existed and would have caused consternation had they even been used.

We know about the practice of direction for lay people only through some letters from famous directors. Such letters are, however, rare; more than once the correspondent, apparently a man or woman of the world, sooner or later turns out to live in a monastery. The title of a very interesting study by V. Laurent, 'La direction spirituelle des grandes dames à Byzance: la correspondance inédite d'un metropolite de Chalcedoine',[14] seemed to promise information comparable to that offered by the correspondence of Saint Francis of Sales or Mgr Hulst. In fact, the sole correspondent was a nun living in a community, in rather special conditions set up for the daughters of noble houses. Neither can the other study by the same author be used here, 'Une princesse byzantine au cloître'[16] to which we referred in the preceding chapter. Perhaps one is allowed to reason *a pari* or *a fortiori*: if nuns were allowed to see their spiritual father or write to him freely, by virtue of their social standing before tonsure, all the more strongly would devout women who remained in the world have had opportunity. But such an inference does not help us greatly.

We will be a little better informed by other, more ancient collections of letters and by the *Lives of the Saints*. Saint John Chrysostom was a great director of souls. But one should not take his *Letters to Olympias* as the main document in this respect. Anne-Marie Malingrey correctly writes: 'Letters of direction. Sometimes. But usually the director's personal preoccupations fade, he forgets himself, better to guide the soul entrusted to him. This is not always the case here.'[16] One should recall the pages which the same author devotes to the 'director'.[17] Despite everything, the case of John Chrysostom, archbishop of the capital, and of Olympias, daughter and widow of famous people at court, is too exceptional for us to spend a long time on it in a general study on spiritual direction. The case depended more on friendship than on spiritual direction. And then, Olympias herself also lived in a community. L. Meyer has written an excellent chapter on Chrysostom as a director of souls. The one thing that may be criticized is that he attaches too much importance to situations and documents that are rather removed from spiritual direction, such as, for instance, advice given to husbands on how to instruct their wives,[18] or rhetorical developments—for Chrysostom always remained the sacred orator, even in his letters—or regular treatises that were sent to Theodore, Stagiras, or Olympias. Yet one must agree with the following lines: 'Chrysostom wisely specifies the role of the spiritual director. It is not up to him to impose or even propose what the soul is perhaps not able to bear, but he must not always remain passive. If he is concerned with the soul's progress he will form and cultivate it so well that the desire for a higher perfection will be generated in it almost spontaneously.' 'As can be seen, Chrysostom had all the qualities of an excellent director of conscience. But direction was too little honored in Syria.[19] Nonetheless, John understood its advantages, and he sought to introduce it in friendship and family relationships. [This is precisely why certain documents used by L. Meyer cannot be used for spiritual direction in the narrow, exclusive sense]. In it he saw the most perfect exercise of the charity obligating all Christians and leading them to the height of spiritual perfection.'[20]

A colleague of L. Meyer, P. Resch, has also gleaned some information concerning direction 'among the first Egyptian masters.[21]' But there we are in a full monastic setting, even with Saint Athanasius, for all the writings ascribed to him, the *Life of Antony*, the *Letters to Amoun, to Dracontius*, and *On Virginity*, have ascetics as heroes or as addressees. A few lines to remember: 'Antony inaugurated some sort of pursuit of direction. After his conversion and his decision to abandon all his possessions, he undertook many visits to renowned ascetics in order to learn from each how to take a new step in virtue. Among the ascetics he frequently consulted, there was one who particularly served him as a master of spirituality.' Antony was then indeed a layman, but he had decided to sanctify himself, as many others must have done; in the early days of monasticism, there was almost no distinction between a pious lay man and a monk. Also very correct is the observation made by P. Resch: '[Antony's] entire later life, according to the *Vita*, seems to have been but one uninterrupted direction offered to the crowds; they came to seek light from his experience and example, advice to help them progress in the ways of perfection.'[22] However, are these discourses addressed to the crowds, as reported by Saint Athanasius, still direction in the strict sense, or are they not rather catechesis?

Most of the *Letters* of Saint Isidore of Pelusium are addressed to monks or clerics. But quite a few were sent to people in the world. Some of his correspondents received several: count Herminos, some thirty; a certain Maron, more

than sixty, and so on. However, the latter was some type of
Epicurean who led a happy life with a certain Martinianus,
Zosima, Eusthates, Chremon, and others. Isidore tirelessly
and vehemently preached repentance to these featherbrains.
For, despite the view of Hippocrates who advised against undertaking the cure of incurables, Isidore did not despair of
bringing the guilty to better sentiments. A study could be
written on these series of letters. But Zosima, Maron and
company belonged to the clergy of Pelusium! As for count
Herminos, we guess from the monk's answer that what he
asked for was chiefly a solution to certain exegetical and theological problems. In short, it may be said that Isidore's activity
was more the result of pastoral concern than direction; he
busied himself not only with souls desiring perfection but also
with all categories of Christians, including many bad ones. He
did not wait until they came to him for consultation; he often
made the first step. About his function as pastor and physician, he nonetheless had principles that could be applied to
direction. A *Letter* to Bishop Theodosius[23] developed these at
some length, on the subject of a text already used by Origen to
expound similar ideas[24]: that moral diseases are innumerable
and each one calls for a different treatment. Without this,
instead of healing them, one makes them worse. From then
on, 'who would be able to recognize or heal them if his soul is
not enlightened by the Holy Spirit?'

The *Letters* of Saint Nilus, less numerous, proportionately
contain some addressed to lay people. They often betray a
concern with keeping them progressing in the ways of perfection; although, more frequently, they reply to questions about
Scripture or theology. The monk of Ancyra did not like useless words. To a certain Faustianus he wrote: 'Your soul is far
removed from God; how can you ask me to send you edifying
words. You joke about secular and sacred realities. What good
is it to talk to a dead ear, unable to hear?'[25] For direction to
take place, the first condition was that the disciple decide to
move. One may have good desires and tarry on the way, held
back by all sorts of vices and faults. The director's role is then

to inform, to warn, to spur on; and Saint Nilus did not seem to have had the slightest disdain for such function: he reproved out of season, and in season (*importune, opportune*).[26] He was not afraid of recalling the last events: death, judgment, and hell.[27] In fervent souls, the stern hegumen was able to inspire feelings of trust and peaceful thoughts. A sure sign with lay people was their sympathy for monks. Let us cite a letter to Sosipater, the tribunal:

> Advancing in the knowledge of God (*tē theia̧ gnōsei*), O outstanding young man, you try to do all things by following the norms of an enlightened conscience. From this derives the fact that you generously dispense your entire fortune, a gift from God, in favor of monks because you greatly love them and think of them as you breathe, day and night, as if you had neither relatives nor children; and yet you have such a large number of them! While conversing, when you say that you are the monks' beast of burden, ready to serve them in all their needs without murmuring and with assiduity, that too is a sure sign of consummate knowledge; you certainly understand that along with their levites, God and Moses also needed their animals. Since you appraise all things according to the knowledge of God, you, friend of God (*philothee*), speak and act wisely. You positively will enter the kingdom of heaven together with the monks, because you have made yourself their attendant and helper, and together with them you will inherit for endless ages the blessings which cannot be expressed by words.[28]

There is nothing surprising in this; the monks lead the apostolic life, and anyone who receives an apostle will receive the apostle's reward. Through antonomasia, the monks are 'those who want to be saved'; the wisdom of the lay people consists in coming as near them as possible, by imitation, benevolence, and charity toward them. Human psychology is the same in all of them. If monks acted knowingly in choosing their way of life, lay people will show prudence and uprightness when they live as well as they can in the way monks should life; or if in moments of temptation they behave as the great masters of monasticism have taught they should. Saint Nilus clearly took his inspiration from such ideas when writing, for example, *To the Young Count Pierios.*[29] The letter opens by stating that one should not confuse *erōs* and *agapē*, 'as this virtuous friend of God' did. On this point, more than on any other, youth lacks discernment, and does not turn to a clearsighted Saint Nilus, as Pierios did. 'From reading your letter, I discerned the robber and his craftiness, for he is cunning at evil deeds. For the *daemon* of fornication which the Greeks used to call *erōs* knows how to adapt its ruses to various temperaments. Quickly and with no trouble, it drives into the pit of debauchery those who are inclined to lust and despise the universal judgment to come. Those who are concerned with salvation and struggle against the assault of pleasure, however, it attacks through alluring ruses.' Nilus then describes in detail the stages of temptation, from innocent sympathy to the fall. Pierios should be suspicious of his need always to be with Dionysiodorus. Even more, he should use all the classical means of a most vigilant caution: avoiding encounters, and when this is not possible, controlling his eyes and assuming a stern look, avoiding pleasantries, and so forth. In a word, we must pluck out the root of the evil which is, deeply within us, a weakness for the flesh. In vain would anyone trust 'will power'! 'Over time, a tenaciously clinging root makes the most skillfully and solidly built wall decay; it makes a rock burst asunder.' Thus one must flee, run fast, pray more, bend the knee, toil, make an 'effort of piety' (*skulmos tēs eusebeias*), use all other precautions and means . . . It is the spiritual father's obligation ceaselessly to remind one of such necessities. Psalmody is especially recommended. Saint Nilus would not have written differently to any of his novices. One senses that he was deeply interested in this still pure young man, 'an excellent offspring of an excellent root', and he trembled to see him fail. He identified with him: 'Who will ask the Lord to come to my aid and take me by the hand as he did with Peter's mother-in-law, so that temptation may be removed from me, and the fever of this detested and hateful *erōs* leave me, that I may stand up in full charity and serve the Lord in continence?'

To another adolescent, Nilus recommended observing the fourth commandment:

'Honor your father and mother, that your days may be prolonged'.[30] This is the law of the Lord. Therefore, if possible, do not leave your parents for one moment, lest, far from their supervision, their solicitude, and their good care, you meet corrupting men and fall into the trap. For especially among the young many are found to be witless pleasure-seekers, workers of iniquity, repositories of all kinds of impurity, who do the greatest damage to anyone who comes near them. Therefore, flee their contagion, the quagmire, by lovingly staying with your parents, by honoring them greatly, by heeding their warnings, and by being sheltered by the rampart of their prayers. No matter what you do for them, you will never be able to give them life as they gave it to you.[31]

This somewhat tremulous concern with safeguarding innocence was justified by an experience frequently referred to by Saint Nilus: the difficulty of correcting a habit.

A practice leads to a habit, and habit takes root like a second nature. It is difficult and painful to stir or transform a nature. Nevertheless, God can do it: nature creates no obstacle to God. . . . Therefore, one should not despair. Stronger than the evil and culpable habit is God who created us, who makes and transforms everything, as the prophet says.[32] And even when you have acquired an evil habit and it has become a second nature, do not despair (*mē apognōs*); change your mind (*metagnōthi*), and you will be saved. The Lord has said, 'Though your sins are like scarlet, they shall be white as snow;

though they are red as crimson, they shall be like wool.'[33]
These colors do not easily become extinct; they stick to
things as if they almost formed a unity of substance. The
Lord has chosen these colors on purpose to say that he
would change them into their opposite, in order to give
people better hope. Great therefore is the power of repentance (*megalē toinon tēs pronoias hē dynamis*), for it makes us
white as snow or wool, even if sin has affected the soul for
a long time, and has made her undergo a frightening
transformation.[34]

This is an echo of the *monon mē apognōs* (Only, do not despair)
that ends Saint Chrysostom's treatise *To the Fallen Theodore (Ad
Theodorum Lapsum)*. Saint Nilus is said to have been a disciple
of Chrysostom. Even the stern Isidore of Pelusia spoke this
way. They all know how difficult it is to correct an inveterate
habit. This is why Nilus gave detailed precautions to the
people in the world who confided in him. One cannot say,
'This is a small thing'. A small thing can have eternal consequences. 'Indeed, a small thing, one single night, and Judas
would have entered the kingdom of God; a small span of time
prevented the person who deserted the martyrs of Sebasteia
from receiving the crown with the others. Disregarding false
pretexts [misinterpretations, *parexegeseis*], let us exert ourselves
in an action that is good and sure.'[35] One of the most dangerous disorders was visiting the theater. Saint Nilus, like
Chrysostom, and a little later Severus of Antioch and others,
condemned it mercilessly. 'Someone who goes to the theater
to besmear his eyes and ears with a shameful desire through
which he will be besieged is an adulterer, whether he wants it
or not. With this evil deed of fornication on the conscience,
how can you tell me that your soul has received no damage
from it; she lives in captivity (*aichmalōsia*). Without being
forced in the slightest, she lets herself be led into captivity by
the demon.'[36] This was a clear warning to Niceratos, the
privy-counselor. Theodore the tribune received one that was
equally direct: 'Because of your faith, the divine Apostle has

called you a dwelling place and a temple of the Holy Spirit. How dare you bring to the temple of God the muck of courtesan songs and sordid jests, much refuse, words that harm the soul?'[37] Count Constantinus had objected that going to the theater or the hippodrome was simply recreation for the soul (*psychagōgia*). No, his director replied, 'It is supreme destruction, a most terrible damage to the soul.' The rest of the letter clearly gives us a sense of the spiritual direction Saint Nilus gave to lay people.

> If you really want to soothe your soul, hasten to a catholic church or a monastery (*askēterion*). In truth, you will find there an abundance of goods and consolation, and the best therapy for your grieving heart. On leaving the church or the monastery, examine yourself to see what you have become, and what you had become when you left the theater and the hippodrome. Then compare the results and you will no longer need someone else to teach you a lesson. The comparison will be enough to show you what great profit you have drawn from the church and from the monastery, and what damage from the circus and the theaters.[38]

Lying at the root of these counsels (and of similar ones that could be cited) there is clearly a very simple line of thought: since monks have chosen the surest path to salvation, everyone should therefore come as close to it as possible. Yet it should be noted that neither Saint Nilus, nor perhaps any other monastic founder or superior, seems to have been preoccupied with provoking monastic vocations. The *Typika* spoke of recruitment only in order to determine the conditions for admission or to limit the number of applicants to be accepted. The universal esteem of the christian people for the monastic institution made 'compelling them to come in (*compelle intrare*)' superfluous. Even the Desert Fathers had to be begged before admitting a disciple. At any rate, Saint Nilus, even when he wrote to a well disposed adolescent, never ventured to suggest that he enter monastic life; it almost seems as if such a thought never occurred to him. If the young man spoke of this first, Saint Nilus undoubtedly rejoiced in it. But there are no examples of this in the correspondence. To the young men who had written to him, he merely advised against evil and taught ways of practicing virtue, depending on each young man's situation, and in conformity with his own ideas on perfection. Here, for example, is a young man who was engaged and also a little smug. 'Since you are the son of my true friend, the blessed Eucarpios, I am greatly interested in your salvation, and I am concerned with your ideas. I write what I believe will be profitable to your soul. Take off those earrings you wear and the bracelets on your arm; give them instead to the one who will be your legitimate future spouse. If she is altogether worthy and prudent, she will not accept them, I think. . . .'[30] To another, still a bachelor, Nilus described in detail the struggle he might have to face to remain worthy of his parents and grandparents. Let him continue to think of God unceasingly through fasting, praying, and almsgiving. And once his work is finished, let him devote himself to reading church books. Despite his encyclopedic ('all around') studies and his philosophic formation, let him be humble enough frequently to ask monks, even unlearned ones, so he may receive from them spiritual provisions for the road to salvation. And then, 'when you have dismissed the business men and have some time to yourself, come to see me, and I will explain to you in detail the struggle against vice. Farewell in the Lord, dearest of my sons.'[40]

To the most beloved of his spiritual children, Nilus, the great director, could only recommend exercises of the interior life similar to those performed by monks; he was to visit them, though Nilus never asked the young man to become one of them. 'It is not merely the pursuit of virtue that brings noble crowns; praise of those who practice virtue also brings a net negotiable reward. You, lover of Christ, glorify those who fear the Lord.'[41] Esteem leads to imitation. Spiritual reading, for example, is for everyone. 'It is the devil that suggests to you that you draw no profit from reading; what he aims at is, through negligence and forgetfulness of the commandments, to take away from you all diligent thought, since from this, at the right moment, follows all right action. . . . People find great profit in reading the inspired Scriptures. If therefore you want to keep the eye of the soul (*ton ophthalmon tēs psychēs*) and maintain its keenness, so as to be led to what is best . . ., do not be sluggish in reading Scripture'[42] Especially to people in the world, prayer is even more necessary to overcome temptations, to be freed from the passions that cause them, to become detached from apparent goods, to obtain forgiveness of sin and, finally, salvation. 'One must pray,' Saint Nilus wrote to the senator Theopompos, 'in order to be freed and redeemed from long aberration, and so as not to die in an impure, reprehensible condition.'[43] On the other hand, praying to be delivered from the body, on the pretext that it is the body that causes one to sin, is unreasonable. Those who do this would be better off 'to pray for freedom from their perverse inclinations, from their passionate, impure thoughts.[44]' It is through prayer that one arrives at *apatheia* (dispassion), whether one is a monk or a lay person.[45] When one has grown old in vice, an extraordinary grace is needed to be freed from it, and this can be obtained through prayer. To a certain Martinos, a lover of harlots, Saint Nilus wrote straightforwardly:

'May our sons be like plants growing strong from their earliest days.'[46] You ask me to explain the spiritual meaning (*tēn theōrian*) of words whose literal meaning (*tēn historian*) you scorn. Well, listen to it, even though it is not what you expected. It is possible that you asked us with the intention of getting another interpretation, and not this one which you did not expect in the least. The sons of impure demons are impure thoughts, and the perverse habits that catapult men addicted to sin into evil deeds. Like plants, these sons of demons tenaciously took root in your youth, for your immorality is in full bloom, though your body has aged. Your detestable covetousness is in good health; from early youth to advanced age you have adhered to frenzied lechery. In you is fulfilled the proverb: a vice in the soul never grows old. If at least you now feel shame while reading these words, lament bitterly. Come to your senses again after your long binge. Pray that God who can do everything may work this miracle in you, shaking these loathsome plants through his divine power, plucking them out of your soul by their deepest roots, so that you may stop your harlotry.[47]

To a priest, his homonym, Nilus explained the same principle, but in a different tone: 'One must prefer prayer to Christ above all other things, and invoke the help and protection of the Holy Spirit. For there is no way to be freed from the power of corruption unless divine power holds power over us.' This is followed by a prayer formula for obtaining such grace.[48] To Pharetrios, the mechanic, Nilus wrote: 'If you determine that you are enslaved to sin, lament before the Lord with your whole heart; make an effort to pass from the inward storm and the clutches of evil to the freedom of virtue.'[49] One must also pray and especially call upon 'the precious name of Jesus', to overcome all sorts of troubles, fears, apprehensions, phobias, and so forth, sown in us by demons.[50] Indeed, the omnipotent power of prayer is one of Nilus' favorite ideas.[51] He spoke of the more advanced degrees of prayer especially, perhaps even exclusively, to monks, though this was certainly not done on purpose.

Fasting too befits lay people as well as monks, and for the same reason. To the tribune Sophronius, Nilus wrote: 'The rioting of the flesh, the obscene passions must be beaten with the whip of fasting; in this manner we succeed in submitting them quietly to reason.'[52] 'The flesh that has grown fat must grow lean: a fat belly does not make a subtle mind.'[53] Finally, all the other monastic practices are sometimes recommended for worldly people concerned about their souls: 'excessive pleasure, boundless joy, the soul's insolence inspired by repeated success, let us restrain these by sorrow and silence.'⁵⁴ 'Humankind is easily puffed up by ostentation; numerous strong curbs are needed to subdue arrogance. Sprinkled here and there in Scripture, you will find many ways of curbing and muzzling the passions contrary to reason.'⁵⁵

Of course the general principle—to come as close to the monastic life as possible—had to be qualified, or be made more specific, by taking into account the limitations of that possibility; in other words through an account of the virtues, or rather virtuous deeds, required of people in the world by their situation but forbidden to monks by their profession. By observing the evangelical counsel, 'go and sell what you have and give the money to the poor; then come, follow me', the monk, imitating the example of Antony,⁵⁶ fulfills once and for all what the man in the world must perform from day to day: the obligation to give alms. This is but one of the special manifestations of a charity equally binding to all Christians. This is also true of other virtues; they assume a thousand forms not only according to the two life states, monastic and lay, but according to the infinite variety of personal circumstances. Subsequently, every conscience that is awake often feels the need to consult a prudent person about the demands of duty or greater perfection. But such consultations can hardly be handed over to posterity. Also, what is important is not the casuist's response but the consultant's good will. Pastors and preachers devote themselves to creating or maintaining the latter. But neither pastoral nor homiletic activities are spiritual direction.

Christianity is the revelation of the fatherhood of God through Jesus Christ, and not merely its revelation but its actualization through the mission of the Word and the Holy Spirit. 'But as many as received him, to them he gave the power to become the sons of God.' The text has 'to become' (*genesthai*), like the Word 'became' (*egeneto*) flesh. Since Irenaeus, greek theology has never ceased repeating that 'The reason why the Word of God became man, and the Son of God the Son of man, is so that man, united to the Word of

God and accepting adoption, might become the son of God.'[57]
Saint Gregory the Theologian would summarize this doctrine
in his classic formulation: the Word became incarnate 'so that
I might be made God insofar as he is made man (*ina genōmai
tosouton theos, hoson ekeinos anthrōpos*).[58] This is what Saint Maximus the Confessor, in explaining Saint Gregory the Theologian, called beautiful inversion or counterpart (*kalē antistrophē*),
a reciprocity that makes God man for the deification of man,
and man God for the humanization of God (*dina tēn tou theou
anthrōpēsin*).'[59]

Saint Maximus went on to say, 'The Word of God who is of
God wants to work out the mystery of His incarnation (*tēs
autou ensōmatōseōs to mystērion*) always and in all.' In all its
activities, the almighty power of God in the service of his love
has no other goal than to transmit this communion of divine
life to his creatures, making them children of the Father
through an ever more perfect resemblance, a gradual assimila-
tion which is not only moral, in the impoverished, modern
meaning of the term but real—a continual—generation, as
Origen wrote.[60] The Fatherhood of God reaches and deifies
us through 'all that is perfect and given to us from above, . . .
from the father of all light . . . who brought us into being.'[61]
'All creation, through the pains of giving birth, cooperates in
this, 'waiting in suspense (*apokaradokia*) to see the glory of the
children of God perfected and made manifest'[62.] 'Even we
ourselves, who possess the first fruits of the Spirit, groan
inwardly, waiting for the adoption (the perfect one, which
also includes) the redemption of our body.'[63]

All the workers employed by Providence for this great
work—from the Word Incarnate and the Holy Spirit to the
most Blessed Virgin Mary and holy Church, to the last of the
occasional benefactors—all those who transmit the divine life
to us and who cause us to have this life more abundantly by
making the Father known to us, by making us believe in his
love, by trusting the fulfillment of his fatherly design, by
making us love everything he loves, by making us find in this
faith, this love, the peace of God and the joy of Christ. In a

word, all those who contribute to creating Christ in us or reforming us according to the model of Christ, partake of divine Fatherhood and deserve analogically the name of father and mother according to the Spirit, because they make us better children of God.

Thus, one understands why Christ is called our Father, the Redeemer, since He reveals to us the One Father and enables us to become his children through communion with the One Son. 'Who are your parents?' Rusticus the proconsul asked Hierax, one of the companions of Saint Justin. The martyr replied, 'Our true father is Christ, and our mother is our faith in him.'[64] Did Christ not call those his Father had given him, 'my little children' (*teknia*)?[65] Nonetheless, he was not ashamed of also calling them brothers, since the One who sanctifies and those who are sanctified are one.[66] Hence one also understands why, in the *Veni Creator*, we call upon the Holy Spirit as the Father of the Poor (*Pater pauperum*), and why the Syrians viewed him as a mother[67]—the term 'spirit' being feminine in their language. Do grammatical categories matter? Spiritual Fatherhood or Motherhood—it is all the same outpouring of charity that makes us say, 'Abba, Father'. Relying on the Word Incarnate and on the Spirit–Father, Holy Mother Church is our mother, because through baptism and through all her other sacred functions, she actualizes the power which Christ has given us for becoming the children of God; just as the most Blessed Virgin May is our Mother, not mainly by virtue of the words of Christ on the cross, 'Woman, there is your son—here is your Mother' (exegetes waited rather a long time before interpreting the text in this sense), but by virtue of her universal cooperation in the birth and growth of the Father's children, 'through him and with him and in him' (*per Ipsum et cum Ipso et in Ipso*).[68]

Yet in this continual outpouring of the Fathers' charity that continues to lead us to the kingdom of his beloved Son,[69] participation in the Fatherhood, based on the holy humanity of Christ, shades more and more into brotherhood, since, in a general sense, we have only one Father, who is in heaven. As

Christ is our brother, 'the first-born of all creation,' the Blessed Virgin Mary, our mother in all truth, remains nonetheless our sister,[70] not only because she is the daughter of Adam and Eve, as we are, but because in the divine order itself, the fulness of grace makes her first of all the daughters of the same Father whose children we are. In order to attract us to him without his Majesty frightening us too much, or rather to teach us how to love his Majesty as sons passionately, he has given us in the blessed among woman an image, motherly and brotherly, of His fatherhood. This is the masterpiece of divine 'philanthropy'.

Like Mary—though far below her and depending on her, on holy Church, Christ, and the Holy Spirit—all Christians can become spiritual fathers, while remaining brothers among themselves. They can do this according to the degree of their spirituality, that is, according to the intensity of their union with Christ in the Holy Spirit, and through Christ with God. They can and must do it, each in his or her own way, because all exercise of charity is an imitation of God. 'If someone will shoulder his neighbor's burden; if he is ready to supply another's need from his own abundance; if, by sharing the blessings he has received from God with those who are in want, he himself becomes a god to those who receive his bounty—such a person is indeed an imitator of God.'[71] One becomes the father of someone according to the Spirit, depending on how one acts toward him with Godlike charity, with the sole aim of making him rich and happy in God. For this, it is not necessary to have received any official function whatsoever. What insures fruitfulness *ex opere operato* in the communion of saints is neither rank nor reputation or uproar. It is 'faith that works through love,'[72] and the most favorable climate to make such faith and love thrive is love of silence, self-effacement (monasticism believed it had read this in the Holy Gospel). 'The proconsul says, "Do you have any children?" Papylus replies, "Even many, through God." One of the crowd exclaimed, "It is according to the law of the Christians that he states he has children." The proconsul says, "Why do you lie when stating that you have children?" Papylus says, "Do you want to know that I do not lie, but speak the truth? In every province (*eparchia*) and city there are some of my children according to God".'[73] The simple-minded woman (*salē*) whose story Palladius has told us[74] certainly deserved the name spiritual mother (*ammas*), though in her own community she was known only as a hag. The opposite can no doubt also happen, thank heaven it does not happen more often! The real spiritual fathers, the real mothers according to the Spirit are the men and women who, by radical self-denial, by renouncing every personal worldly interest—comfort and honors—have given their body and soul over to the divine Artist[76] to be molded and recreated into the image and likeness of God, by the hands which are the Son and the Spirit,[76] with the certainty that for this to take place one had to pass through all sorts of tribulations, even to the point of 'being ground like wheat,' as Saint Ignatius of Antioch said, or of 'being delivered to the fire,' like Saint Polycarp.[77] 'Give your blood and receive the Spirit.'[78] Being no longer carnal, they have become spiritual and will serve as instruments of God-Charity in performing for others the superhuman work they first accepted for themselves with the aim of giving God, their Father, children resembling Him (*patrōzontes*),[79] through the indelible family mark,[80] 'a love that is rich and ungrudging'[81]—in other words, the twice-blessed divine beatitude, the 'blameless joy,'[82] of knowing that one is loved by God and of being able to love like God, unselfishly.

Rome, Pentecost 1955
Wichita, Great Lent 1988

NOTES

1. THE DIRECTION OF NUNS

1. Musonius, *Apomn.* III, c. 8, p. 249 Perlkamp, cited by J. Stobée, *Eclogae* II, 31, n. 126, ed. C. Wochsmuth-Hense, vol. 2 (Berlin, 1884) 244.

2. 4 vols. (Leipzig, 1923-1924).
3. *Strom.*, IV. 8; PG 8: 1272A-76A; ed. O. Staehlin, *GCS* 2: pp. 272 and 277.
4. *Paedagogus* I. 4; PG 8: 260C.
5. Lk 20:34.
6. *Paed.* I. 4; PG 8: 261A.
7. Mt 19:21.
8. Lk 6:29.
9. Lk 6:28.
10. 1 Cor 4:13.
11. Origen, *In Librum Jesus Nave, Homilia* IX. 9; ed. Baehrens, II, p. 356.
12. Procopius Gazaeus, *Commentarii in Exodum*, ch. II; PG 87: 518.
13. Gen. 1:27.
14. *In Verba, Faciamus hominem, Oratio* II; PG 44: 276A-C.
15. *Poemata de Seipso*, II, I, XI, *versic.* 60; PG 37: 1034A.
16. *In Laudem Sororis suae Gorgoniae, Oratio* VIII, n. 14; PG 35: 805B; see Severus of Antioch, *Homélie* XCII, POr XXV, p. 43 [487].
17. S. Basilius Magnus, *Praevia Institutio Ascetica*, n. 3; PG 31: 624Cff.
18. G. Hermant (Paris, 1673) 590.
19. S. Gregorius Nazianzenus, *Carminum Liber* I, *Sectio* II, *versic.* 645ff; PG 37: 620.
20. See S. Nilus, *Epistolarum Liber* IX. 4; PG 79: 552CD.
21. *Alph.*, Bessarion n. 4; PG 65: 142A (CS 59: 41).
22. *Historia Lausiaca, cap.* XXIV, PL 73: 1122C.
23. For Hilaria, see A. J. Wensinck, *Legends of Eastern Saints, Chiefly from Syriac Sources*, II, *The Legend of Hilaria* (Leyden, 1913).
24. *Religiosa Historia Seu Ascetica Vivendi Ratio;*, PG 82: 1464D. [English translation by R. M. Price, *A History of the Monks of Syria. The Religious History of Theodoret of Cyrrhus* (Kalamazoo: Cistercian Publications, 1986.—tr.]
25. *Relig. Historia*; PG 82: 1457B.
26. *Ibid.*, col. 1377C.
27. *Ibid.*, col. 1489B.
28. Theodoretus Cyrensis, *Oratio de divina et sancta charitate*; PG 82: 1497BC.
29. See col. 1504AB.
30. Romanos the Melodist, *Kontakion on the Dormition of the Theotokos.*
31. Joseph the Hymnographer.
32. S. Nilus, *Epistolarum Liber* I. 226, *Cyrillo Primati*; PG 79: 180D.
33. Georgius Pisidae, *Hymnus Acathistus*; PG 92: 1344C.
34. *Ibid.*, D.
35. *Ibid.*, col. 1345A.
36. S. Nilus, *loc. cit.*
37. See, for example, Sophronios Eustratiades, *Hē Theotokos en tē hymnographia* (Paris, Chennevières-sur-Marne, 1930).
38. S. Irenaeus, *Adversus Haereses* V. 19. 1; PG 7: 1175B.
39. See Gen 2:5.
40. *Homilia in Martyrem Julittam*, n. 2; PG 31: 240Dff.
41. *Ibid.*, n. 1, col. 237AB.
42. For example, S. Nilus, *Epistolarum Liber* II. 16, *Theodosiae Moniali*; PG 79: 249D.

43. *Historia Lausiaca*, 34 [There is an English translation by Robert T. Meyer, *Palladius: The Lausiac History*, *ACW* 34 (Westminster, Maryland, 1965).—tr.]
44. *Vitae Patrum* V. 18. 19; PL 984A-5B.
45. PL 73: 991A. See the article *Ama*, in *DACL*, vol. 1; col. 1306-23.
46. Sophronius, *Vita Sanctae Mariae Aegyptiacae, meretricis*, X; PL 73: 678 BC (CS 106: 42-43); see John Moschus, *Pratum Spirituale*, ch. 179, PG 87: 3049B.
47. *Ibid.*, col. 680D.
48. *Epistolarum Liber* II, 48; PG 99:1297A.
49. H. Lecleroq, col. 1307; the term *gerontissa* is used in modern Greek; for example, Agapios, *Eclogion* (1805) 287.
50. Usener, p. 41, 9-12.
51. S. Theodoros Studita, *Epistolarum Liber* II. 118; PG 99: 1389D.
52. For example, *Typikon* of Irene, *Analecta Graeca* (Paris, 1688) 144.
53. Translation uncertain; a critical edition of Theodore the Studite is badly needed.
54. Cfr Ps 93:10; Theod. Stud., *loc. cit.*, col. 1392B.
55. *Typikon*, ch. V, 1, 5, pp. 159-60. Palladius speaks of four hundred sisters, the *Vie de Sainte Eupraxie*, ed. Agapios, *Eclogion* (1805) 287, of three hundred, but such numbers cannot be checked and are not very likely.
56. Ch. 2, n. 12, *Acta SS* (July) 6: p. 607D.
57. *Ibid.*, n. 14, p. 607F.
58. *Ibid.*, n. 23, p. 610F-11A.
59. *Ibid.*, n. 24, p. 611AB.
60. *Ibid.*, n. 25, p. 611EF.
61. See above, p. 112.
62. 1 Cor 12:28.
63. Heb 1:14.
64. Ch. 3, nn. 30-31, p. 613DF.
65. Ch. 4, n. 32, pp. 613F-14A.
66. Codex of the monastery of Xenophon; see S. Lambros, *Catalogue of the Greek Manuscripts on Mount Athos* (Cambridge, 1895) vol. I: p. 64.
67. Moscow 1891, 1898, 1908.
68. The 1908 edition, p. 105.
69. For example, Saint Theoctista, Th. Ioannou, *Mnemeia Hagiographica*, p. 1; Saint Domnica, *ibid.*, p. 265, etc.
70. *Eloge de Sainte Matrone*, ed. Arsenii [Archimandrite] (Moscow, 1891) 11. See Saint Jerome, *Epistola XXII*. 38, *Ad Eustochium, Paulae filiam*; PL 22: 422: *"potes et tu esse mater Domini."*
71. *Acta SS* (August 14), p. 173D.
72. *Vie de Sainte Domnica*, in Th. Ioannou, p. 272-75.
73. Saint Eupraxia, in Agapios, *Eclogion* (Venice, 1805) 292ff.
74. P. 295.
75. P. 297.
76. P. 298.
77. *Estymmenos*, a medical term used by Galen, passed into the ascetic language, with a sense that is easier to grasp than to translate. *Stypho* means "to draw together, of an astringent taste; metaphorically, to be austere, gloomy." The past participle, passive voice, refers to a solidly established state. In the *Vita Sanctae Sabae* n. XXV, *Ecclesiae*, vol. III, p. 258, Jean-Baptiste Cotelier translates *andras estymmenous* as (*kai nēphalious*) as *viris gravibus et prudentibus*, which suppresses the metaphor; the arabic version of the

Vita Prima glosses felicitously, "gifted with strength, admirable in perspicuity," which Amélineau empties of flavor by his *fort vertueux*" (*Vie de Pakhôme*, Annales du Musée Guimet XVII, 2, p. 382). Further down, on p. 605, Bontouis (=*Eponychos*) is called "*un père saint, éminent envers tous, rempli de la bonté de Dieu.*"

78. For example, François Halkin, *S. Pachomii Vitae Graecae*, p. 84, 31.

79. L. Th. Lefort, *Les Vies Coptes de Saint Pakhôme et de ses premiers successeurs* (Louvain, 1943) 98 (CS 45: 50).

80. *diakouein* = to hear out to the end, hear through.

81. *Historia Lausiaca*, ch. 29.

82. *Ibid.*, ch. 30.

83. 1 Tim 2:12; 1 Cor 14:34.

84. Tit 2:4.

85. *Regulae Brevius Tractatae, interrogatio* CX, PG 31: 1157A.

86. See P. Laurain, *De l'intervention des laïques, des abbesses et des diacres dans l'administration de la pénitence* (Paris, 1897).

87. J. Leipoldt, *Schenute von Atripe und die Entstehung des nationalaegyptischen Christentums* (Leipzig, 1903) 139. [See *The Tale of Shenoute by Besa*, translated by David N. Bell, CS 73 (1983)—ed.]

88. See Leipoldt, p. 142ff.

89. *Ibid.*, p. 154.

90. *Irenes Augustae Typicum sive Regula*, ch. 16; PG 127: 103OD.

91. *Pratum Spirituale*, ch. 128, PG 87: 2992C.

92. *Bios kai Politeia, Vita et Conversatio Sanctae Eusebiae*, nn. 5 and 6, PG 114: 985D-8AD.

93. S. Joannes Jejunator, *Sermo de Poenitentia*, PG 88: 196D.

94. *Ibid.*, 1973D.

95. See S. Basil, *Praefatio, Praevia Institutio Ascetica*; PG 31: 620.

96. *Vita Altera* 28; ed. François Halkin, p. 197.

97. *Vita S Eusebiae;*, PG 114: 905A; *Vita Sae Mariae Junioris Bizyae*, n. 1, *Acta SS* (Nov.) IV: p. 692, and n. 3, p. 693C.

98. *Vita S Parasceve Junioris*, n. 1;, ed. Papadopoulos-Kerameus, *Anal. Hier. Stachyol.*, vol. I, p. 438; cfr 442.

99. *Vita Sae Domnicae*, n. 3; ed. Theophilou Ioannou, *Mnemeia Hag.*, p. 20 (8); cfr n. 1, p. 208.

100. *Typikon Irenes*, p. 144.

101. *Bios kai Politeia, Vita et Conversatio et Exercitatio Sanctae Matris Nostrae Matronae, Martyris Chiensis*, n. 6; PG 116: 925AB.

102. 2 Cor 5:16.

103. See Jn 14:12. Gregory of Nyssa, *De virginitate*, ed. W. Jaeger, p. 254, 24ff; cfr p. 306, 21-307, 7.

104. *Ibid.*, p. 323, 1ff.

105. *In Canticum Canticorum, Prologus*, PG 13: 62, and frequently elsewhere. For example, *Comment. in Matthaeum, tomos* XVII. 21; PG 13: 1340.

106. *Pseudo-Clementine Letters Ad Virgines*, Origen.

107. See, for example, Alice Gardner, *Theodore of Studium. His Life and Times* (London, 1905) 217: 'He dwells in a way that modern taste might find morbid, on the high vocation of nuns as "brides of Christ."' Actually, the concept of 'Sponsa Christi' is more alive than ever: see Pius XII, *Constitutio Apostolica de sacro monialium instituto promovendo Sponsa Christi* (21 November 1950).

108. Theod. Stud., *Epistolarum Liber* II, 113 (*Euphrosynē hēgoumenē*); PG 99: 1376D; 115, 118, 123, 134, 150, 177, 196.

109 *Letter* 113, PG 99: 1380B.
110. Col. 1378A.
111. *Letter* 115, passim.
112. *Letter* 118, col. 1389Dff.
113. 1 Pet 5:4.
114. Is 8:18. See above, p. 150; Theodore the Studite has read Barsanuphius assiduously, as is clear from his *Testamentum*, PG 99: 1816BC.
115. *De civitate Dei* I, ch. 16-28; ed. *Corpus Christianorum, Series Latina* XLVII (Turnhout, 1955).
116. *Letter* 134; PG 99: 1432B.
117. *Ibid.*, col. 1432CD.
118. This seems to be the meaning. Sirmond translates as *Animam habes in qua retractes quae contingunt.* The word *anathēsē*(PG 99: 1392B) and the entire context authorize our translation; moreover, see II. 115, col. 1384A.
119. *Anatithesthai.*
120. *Letter* 118, PG 99: 1392B.
121. *Letter* 177, col. 1548Dff.
122. *Letter* 117, col. 1548Dff.
123. *Letter* I, 42, Annae Moniali; PG 99: 1061C-64B.
124. See Irénée Hausherr, "Les grands courants de la spiritualité Orientale," *OCP* I, 129-32.
125. *De coelesti hierarchia* IV. 8; PG 3: 481B.
126. *Epistola* 8; PG 3: 1085A.
127. *Ibid.*, col. 1097B.
128. *Epistolarum Liber* II, 43, PG 99: 1245AB.
129. See, for example, *Épist. Lib.* II. 38, col. 1229Dff.
130. *Epist. Lib.* II. 49, col. 1273Bff.
131. See *Exhortatio ad Virginem*; ed. Gressman, TU 39 (1913) 146-51.
132. See Evagrius, *De Oratione*, ch. 117. See also, the commentary in *RAM* 15 (1934) 148ff.
133. "Une princesse byzantine au cloître," in *EO* 29 (1930) 29-60.
134. "Une lettre et un discours inédits de Theolepte de Philadelphie," in *Etudes Byzantines* 5 (1947) 101-15; Id., "Un directeur spirituel à Byzance au début du XIVe siècle: Théolepte de Philadelphie. Homelie inédite sur Noël et la vie religieuse," in *Mélanges Joseph de Ghellinck* S.J. (Gembloux, 1951) II: 877-87.
135. *Philocalia tōn hierōn neptikōn* (Venice, 1782) pp. 855, 862, 865.
136. *EO* 29 (1930) 54.
137. *Ibid.*, and n. 4.
138. P. 55.
139. P. 58.
140. Nicephorus Gregoras, *Romaike Historia, Liber* 29. *cap.* 7; PG 149: 208.
141. The translation made by two students, Joseph Reisacker and Nathan Rosenstein, "*quod magis virtutis causa fecit quam ornamenti*" (PG 149: 207B) is wrong.
142. See above, p. 231.
143. Laurent, p. 53.
144. *Ibid.*, p. 38, p. 49, note 5, and 58, n. 2.
145. V. Laurent, in *REB* 12 (1954) 33.
146. *Vita Syncleticae* VII, ed. Jean-Baptiste Cotelier, *Ecclesiae* II, p. 204.
147. *Ibid.*, XI, p. 207.
148. *Ibid.*, LXXVIII, p. 251.
149. *Ibid.*, LXXIX.

150. *Ibid.*, p. 55.
151. Laurent, p. 37.
152. Nicephoros Choumnos, *Sermo consolatorius ad filiam*; PG 140: 1444C.
153. Laurent, p. 37.
154. I do not know whether Theodore had read Aristotle. In any case, the thought he presents is already mentioned by the Stagirite as a traditional axiom. See *Politica*, Bk VII, 14; *The Works of Aristotle*, vol. X, trans. W. D. Ross (Oxford, 1921) paragr. 1333ª.
155. Theodore the Studite, *Epistolarum Liber* II, 196, *Euphrosynē hegoumenē*, PG 99: 1594C.
156. *REB* 8 (1950) 66, n. 2.
157. *EO* 29 (1930) 58.
158. Gregory Nazianzen, *Carmina* I, *Sectio* II *Poemata Moralia, Praecepta ad virgines, vers.* 346-50; PG 37: 605A.

2. THE SPIRITUAL DIRECTION OF LAY PERSONS

1. Mt 5:38.
2. Ed. Kmosko, *Patrologie Syriaque*, vol. III.
3. *In Matthaeum homilia* 18. 4; PG 57: 269.
4. Ps 148:11-12.
5. *Vita Sanctae Mariae Junioris, Acta SS* IV (Nov.) p. 692.
6. S. John Chrysostom, *Adversus oppugnatores vitae monasticae*, III. 15, PG 47: 372.
7. 1 Tim 2:9.
8. 1 Tim 5:6.
9. 1 Tim 6:8.
10. *Epistolarum Liber* II. 117, *Mariano spathario*; PG 99: 1388D.
11. The reference is to married diocesan priests.
12. *Responsa ad Gabrielem Pentapolitanum, quaestio* XXIII, PG 155: 881Dff.
13. See M. D. Chenu, "Moines, clercs, laïcs au carrefour de la vie évangelique," in *RHE* 49. 1 (1954) 59-89.
14. *REB* 8 (1950) 64-84.
15. In *EO* 29 (1930) 29-60.
16. John Chrysostom, *Lettres à Olympias*; *SCh* 13: p. 32ff.
17. *Ibid.*, 47-66.
18. L. Meyer, *Saint Jean Chrysostome: Maître de perfection chrétienne* (Paris, 1934) 336-63.
19. I wonder how L. Meyer was able to make such a pertinent observation in 1934. If in this book we have hardly mentioned the Syrians, it is not out of prejudice, but because there is little, if anything, on our subject, even with the greatest such as Isaac of Nineveh. It is because of this character trait that at the international monastery of Saint Sabas, the Syrians were ultimately excluded from becoming hegumen; they functioned as business managers, took care of the guest house and other "services" (*diaconies*). See A. Dmitrievsky, *Opisanie* I (Kiev, 1894) 224.
20. *Loc. cit.*, p. 362.
21. P. Resch, *La doctrine ascétique des premiers maîtres Egyptiens du IVᵉ siècle* (Paris, 1931) 194-203.
22. *Ibid.*, p. 196.
23. *Epistolarum Liber* IV. 145, PG 78: 1225D-29A.
24. See above, p. 2.
25. *Epistolarum Liber* I. 43, *Faustiano*; PG 79: 101D.

26. See *Epist.* I. 158, etc.
27. See, for example, *Epistolarum Liber* IV. 14, *Chionio Silentiario*, PG 79: 556D, or II. 154, *Orioni Ekdiko.*
28. *Epist. Liber* II. 157, *Sosipatro tribuno*; PG 79: 273D.
29. *Epist. Liber* II. 167, *Piero comiti juniori*; PG 79: 280B-85A.
30. Deut 5:16.
31. *Epistol. Liber* II. 310.
32. See Am. 5:8 (LXX).
33. Is 1:18.
34. *Epistol. Liber* II. 239, col. 321D.
35. *Epistol.* II. 288, col. 341D.
36. *Epistol.* II. 284, col. 341B.
37. *Epistol.* II. 286, col. 341C.
38. *Epistol.* II. 290.
39. *Epistol. Liber* III. 31, col. 385D.
40. *Epistol.* III. 43, col. 407D.
41. *Epistol. Liber* II. 277, col. 339B.
42. *Epistol. Liber* II. 198, col. 304C; cfr II. 208, col. 309C.
43. *Epistol. Liber* I. 330, col. 201C.
44. *Epistol.* I. 227.
45. Cfr *Epistol.* I. 178; II. 52, etc.
46. Ps 143:12.
47. *Epistol. Liber* III. 4, 365A.
48. *Epistol.* III. 256.
49. *Epistol.* II. 262.
50. *Epistol.* II. 214, 312D.
51. Cfr *Epistol.* III. 36; 253, etc.
52. *Epistol.* I. 168; see II. 167, col. 284A.
53. *Epistol.* III. 292, col. 527C.
54. *Epistol. Liber* I. 167; PG 79: 149B.
55. *Epistol.* I. 169; PG 79: 149C.
56. *Vita Antonii* n. 2; PG 26: 841Cff.
57. *Adversus Haereses* III. 19; PG 7: 939B. The Greek text cited by Theodoret, *Dialogus* I, *Immutabilis*, (PG 38: 85C) has *ton Logon chōrēsas* instead of '*commistus Verbo Dei.*' In *SCh* 34, p. 80, Sagnard correctly decided in favor of the Latin version, and translated, '*pour que l'homme entre en communion avec le Verbe de Dieu*' (*Ibid.*, p. 333).
58. Gregory Nazianzen, *Oratio* XXIX. *Theologica* III. 19; PG 36: 100A.
59. Maximus the Confessor, *Ambiguorum Liber*; PG 91: 1084CD.
60. See above, p. $.
61. See James 1:17ff.
62. See Rom 8:18ff.
63. Rom 8:23. See Thomas Aquinas, 2ᵃ⁻ᵃᵉ q. 83, *artic.* 11 ad 1: 'the Saints in heaven are happy and lack only the glorification of the body, for which they pray'.
64. *Martyrium S. Justini et Sociorum* IV, ed. G. Rauschen, *Florilegium Patr.* III, pl 101; other references in Henri-Irénée Marrou, *A Diognète*, p. 192, n. 8. See above, p. 23.
65. See Jos 13:83.
66. See Hebr 2:11; Jos 20:17.
67. See Aphraates, *Demonstr.* XVIII, n. 10ff.
68. See Mauricio Gordillo, *Mariologia Orientalis* (Rome, 1955) 25 ff, and ch. III, 58-87.

69. See Col 1:13.

70. See, for example, Saint Athanasius, *Epistola ad Epictetum* n. 7; PG 26: 1061B.

71. *Letter to Diognetus*, 10. 6. Trans. M. Stantforth, *Early Christian Writings*, 181.

72. Gal 5:6.

73. *Martyrium SS. Carpi, Papyli et Agathonices*, n. 24; ed. G. Rauschen, p. 93.

74. See above, pp. 275ff.

75. See S. Irenaeus, *Adv. Haer.* IV. 64; ed. Harvey II, p. 299.

76. *Ibid.*, V. 3, p. 403, See J. Leclercq, 'Le doigt de Dieu,' in *VS* (1948) 492-507.

77. See S. Irenaeus, V. 3; Harvey II, p. 403.

78. See above, p. 61.

79. Saint Maximus the Confessor, *Expositio Orationis Dominicae*; PG 90: 885A.

80. See Saint Ignatius, *Ad Ephesios* I, '*mimētai ontes Theou, anazōpyrēsantes en haimati Theou, to syggenikon ergon apērtisate*,' 'you are imitators of God; and it was God's blood that stirred you up once more to do the sort of thing you do naturally, and have now done to perfection.' Trans. Cyril C. Richardson, *Early Christian Literature*, p. 88. In spite of J.B. Lightfoot (*Apostolic Fathers* II, section I (London, 1885) 30, note 1) on account of the context and because of the entire soul of Saint Ignatius, it seems certain to me that *syggenikon ergon* refers to the activity proper to christians, as members of the family of God, 'through the blood of God.' Interpreting Ignatius of Antioch in terms of Plutarch's vocabulary, is to forcefully introduce a streak of naturalism into a christian psychology, perhaps the most radical the world has ever known. And all this because of the word *physis* (*Ad Ephesios* I. 1); but this vague term is specified at once by 'faith and charity in Jesus Christ'; now, 'God is faith and charity united' (*Ad Eph.* XIV, 1). The *Letters* of Saint Ignatius deserve to be read under a microscope; above all, they demand to be understood from within. Their spirit must be interiorized.

81. S. Irenaeus, *Adv. Haer.* III, *Prologus*.

82. See S. Ignatius of Antioch, *Ad Ephesios*, Salutation. It is noted that Franciscus Xaverius Funk did not include the word *chara* (joy) in the *Index Vocabulorum* of his *Patres Apostolici* (Tübingen, 1901).

GLOSSARY

Abbas literally, father, in the same sense as *gerōn* (*q.v.*); later, *abba* or simply monk.

Adiakritikos, undiscerning; applied especially to what later would be called 'blind obedience'.

Agonothete, organizer or president of the public games (fights). Cfr *athlotetēs*.

Aichmalōsia, captivity; the last stage of a *pathos* (passion) that has become tyrannical and almost invincible.

Akēdia (*acedia*), etymologically, lack of care, of interest; negligence. In ascetic language, it is the sixth of the deadly sins or better of the evil *logismoi* (*q.v.*). Cassian speaks of *anxietas* or of *taedium cordis*, weariness of heart. Evagrius calls it the *noonday demon*, though the term is not to be understood in the sense given to it in Paul Bourget's novel *Le démon de midi* (1914). *A.* is mental or spiritual torpor, a general uneasiness of soul, for no particular reason. If one gives in to it, it has lamentable results, mainly inconstancy; if one overcomes it, this gives rise to deep peace.

Akēdiastēs, a monk who fell victim to *akēdia*. Cfr *RB* 40.

Akribia, accuracy, precision, care.

Amerimnia, literally, freedom from care. Could have the same meaning as *akēdia*, but means precisely the opposite. *Akēdia* is the lack of taste for things spiritual; *amer.*, the freedom from temporal cares (cfr Mt 6:25), detachment, unconcern.

Amerimnos, free from care. Cfr. *Amerimnia*.

Amma, spiritual mother.

Anchorite, one who withdraws (*anachoreo*) from the world.

Anenergēsia, a word used by Dionysius the Pseudo-Areopagite in *The Celestial Hierarchies* (PG 3:396Aff), meaning inactivity, inefficaciousness. In *De charitate* II, 40 (PG 90: 997B), Maximus the Confessor calls *anenergēsia* a false inner peace, due to a momentary falling asleep of the passions.

Antirrhesis ('counter statement'), a method of spiritual warfare which consists of answering an evil suggestion with an appropriate line from Scripture (cfr. Mt 4:3-12).

Apatheia, the state of impassibility or dispassion, understood in the christian sense. [For a correct understanding of this term, see T. Špidlík, *The Spirituality of the Christian East*, trans. A. Gythiel, Cistercian Studies Series 79 (Kalamazoo, MI 1986) 270-81]

Apophthegma, an unadorned, usually short statement dealing with a concrete situation, made by one of the *Desert Fathers* (*q.v.*). The collection of such aphorisms, known as *Apophthegmata Patrum*, created a new literary genre for which the christian East showed a distinct preference. [*Apophth. Patrum, Alphabetical Series*, PG 65: 71-440. English trans. by Benedicta Ward, *The Sayings of the Desert Fathers* (Cistercian Publications-Mowbrays 1975). Selections from the *Anonymous Series*, trans. Ward, *The Wisdom of the Desert Fathers* (SLG Press 1979). Lucien Regnault, *Les sentences des Pères du désert. Apophthegmes inédits et peu connus.* 2 vols. (Solesmes 1970]

Aphōtistos, unenlightened (or unbaptized, baptism being called *phōtismos*, illumination).

Apsephiston, from *psephos*, a vote. Total detachment that manifests itself through the habit, or at least the resolve, not to give to oneself, and not to expect from another, a vote for any type of superiority. Cfr. Barsanuphius, *Letter* 269: 'Father, what is the *apsephiston?*' Answer: 'Brother, the *apsephiston* is not to consider oneself the equal of anyone, and not to say about a good work, "I have done this." ').

Arētalogy, the recital of the wonders wrought by a divinity.

Askēsis, spiritual training. [S.P. Brock, 'Early Syrian Ascetism,' in *Numen* 20 (1973), 1-19; Resche, P., *La doctrine ascétique des premiers maîtres égyptiens au IVᵉ siècle* (Paris 1931)]

Askēterium, a dwelling occupied by ascetics.

Askētria, a woman ascetic. [See S.Brock, and S. Harvey, *Holy Women of the Syrian Orient*, trans. with an Introd. (Berkeley: University of California Press, 1987)]

Athlotete, a judge at public games. Cfr. *Agonothete*.

Basilissa, the wife of a *Basileus*, emperor; or simply a woman belonging to a ruling house either through birth or allegiance.

Bogomils, adherents of a sect originating in Bulgaria, the origins of which go back to Manicheism. This heresy, stressing the idea that the world was created by Satan and is therefore evil, came to be associated with the Cathars ('pure ones') and the Albigenses.

Cenobites, those who live the common life (*koinos bios*). The first cenobium was founded by St Pachomius at Tabennisi in the Thebaid, *c.* 315-20. Shenoute (d.451) was the coptic abbot of a cenobium at Atripe, in Lybia. [Mgr. Stephanos, 'Les origines de la vie cénobitique,' in *CoC* 49 (l. 1987), 20-37]

Charisticarius, a lay person (man or woman), who has received a monastery *in commendam* (in commendation), first to administer it, soon, in fact, to draw income from it. The *commenda*—the placing of a *beneficium* in the hands of one not entitled to it canonically—was one of the main reasons of the deterioration of the monastic life. [Gautier, P., 'Réquisitoire du patriarche Jean d'Antioche contre le charisticariat,' in *REB* 33 (1975), 77-132]

Christophoros, literally, one borne by Christ or one who bears Christ (depending on the stressed syllable); a saint, one who is perfect. Cfr. *Pneumatophore*.

Desert Fathers, ascetics who withdrew to the deserts of Egypt (Nitria, the Thebaid, Scetis), Syria, and Palestine (Gaza) during the fourth and fifth centuries), even earlier, to lead a life of prayer, solitude, and self-denial. [D.J. Chitty, *The Desert a City. An Introduction of Egyptian and Palestinian Monasticism under the Christian Empire*, 2nd ed. (St. Vladimir's Seminary Press, 1978): P.A. Fevrier, 'La ville et le "désert." A propos de la vie religieuse aux 4e et 5e siecles,' in *Les mystiques du désert dans l'Islam, le judaïsme et le christianisme*, Conf. Assoc. des Amis de Sénanque (Gap 1975) 39-61; A. Guillaumont, 'La conception du désert chez les moines d'Egypte,' in *RHR* 183 (1975), 3-21] L. Regnault, 'Les Apophthegmes et l'idéal du désert,' in *Commandements du Seigneur et libération évangelique. Études monastiques proposées et discutées à Saint-Anselme, Febr 15-17 1976. (Rome: SA 70).

Diadochus, a title commonly given to the various successors, for example, in the Athenian Platonic school; a presumed heir.

Diakonikon, a place where sacred vessels and vestments are kept, supervised by deacons.

Diakrisis, discernment of good and evil, of the divine and the demonic, of what is appropriate to do. Consequently, discretion, the golden mean (*via media*).

Didaskalia, instruction, oral or written.

Didaskalos (masc. or fem.), one who teaches.

Dioratic, clearsighted, one who is gifted with the charism of *diorasis* (insight), the mystical ability to see what is invisible to common mortals.

Entalma or *entalteria grammata*, a written document from the competent authority, authorizing a priest to hear confessions.

Epikeia, a Greek term used by moralists since Aristotle's time, with varying shades of meaning: equity, moderation, a reasonable opinion. 'A benevolent application of the legal rules' (cfr *DDC*, s.v.).

Episkopos, etymologically, an overseer; then, a bishop.

Epitimia, a penance (often tarified) whether sacramental or not, imposed because of a fault committed.

Ergasia kryptē, literally, secret work; that is, a hidden austerity, or especially an entirely inward manner of praying.

Eudialytos, easy to be dissolved or overcome.

Eulabēs, reserved, respectful, pious (cfr. Lk 2:35: old Symeon is just and *eulabēs*).

Exagoreusis, a word derived from the verb *ex-agoreuo*, to speak out, to make known, 'to confess'. The 'revelation of thoughts' (in Russian, *otkrovenie pomyslov*) to an elder; later, sacramental confession.

Gerōn, literally, an old man (*senex* in the *Vitae Patrum*; in Russian, *staretz* (pl. *startsy*). A title of respect and dignity given to certain ascetics one considers to be truly spiritual. Synonym: father, *abba*. [M. Mathei and E. Contreras, 'Seniores venerare, Juniores diligere. Conflit et réconciliation des génerations dans le monachisme ancien,' in *CoC* 39 (1977), 31-3]

Gnōsis, literally, higher knowledge, divine science.

Gnōsimachoi, opponents of knowledge, heretics who resisted religious and biblical knowledge. Cfr. John of Damascus, *De haeresibus* 88 (PG 94: 757A).

Hēgumēn, a superior of monks or sisters (from the verb *hegeomai*, to lead the way).

Hēsychia, quiet, stillness, tranquility. The relatively eremitical life (*ēremikos bios*) granted to certain monks after years of the cenobitic (or common) life. Hence, a hesychast, hesychasm. [Every G., 'The Study of Eastern Orthodoxy: Hesychasm,' in *Religion* 9 (1979), 73-91].

Hieromonk, a monk priest, one in Holy Orders.

Hypotypōsis, constitution of a monastery.

Idiorrhythmy, literally, a type of life according to one's own (*idios*, personal) ways (*rhythmos*). In ancient texts, *id.* was a synonym for one's own will (*voluntas propria*); consequently, the term referred to a monastic regime granting each one freedoms that were hardly compatible with the ancient discipline.

Idiōta or *idiōtēs*, literally, a private person (not engaged in public affairs); an unlearned person, one who lacks basic skills.

Isangelic (isaggelos), equal to the angels; the term refers to the life style of the early ascetics.

Kardiognōsis, knowledge (*gnōsis*) of the heart (*kardia*); a charism.

Kath'hyperochen, with excess or superabundance.

Lathrophagy, the habit of eating secretly.

Lavra (laura), a group of cells scattered in the desert. Later, the term was used to designate certain large monasteries.

Logismos, in ascetic language, the good (or more frequently, evil) thought (from the verb *logizomai*, to reflect), at all stages of its development. Cfr. a syllogism, a putting together (*syn*) of thoughts. [For an analysis of the term, see T. Spidlík, *The Spirituality of the Christian East* (Cistercian Studies Series 79), 238ff.]

Makarisms, the Beatitudes in the Gospel.

Mandra, an enclosed space, a fold; hence figuratively, a monastery (cfr. archimandrite, the leader of a *mandra*).

Megaloscheme, a monk wearing the great (*megas*) habit (*schēma*, *habitus*). The highest of the three levels of the monastic profession in the East: l) the lowest (*rhasophore*); 2) the intermediate (*mikroscheme*); 3) the highest (*megaloscheme*). Such a distinction of degree was fought by the ancients, especially Theodore the Studite.

Mēlōtēs, literally, a sheep skin, part of the monastic garb in the East, especially in Egypt. It was worn particularly while traveling: 'Take up your sheep skin and depart' (*The Alphabetical Collection*, 5). On its various forms, see Ph. Oppenheim, OSB, *Das Mönchskleid im christlichen Altertum* (1931), 119-30.

Messalianism, the heresy of the Messalians (in Syriac, 'the praying ones') or Euchites (from the Greek word for prayer, *euchē*). This great (fourth-century) heresy is a complex phenomenon, being at once Pelagian and quietistic. *Messalianism*. exalted uninterrupted prayer above all other obligations such as working. More seriously, *M.* maintained that grace and the Holy Spirit could be experienced sensibly or consciously (*aisthētos*), and that a person united to God no longer needed ascetic practice or instruction, the root of sin having been removed. [Meyendorff, John, 'St. Basil, Messalianism and Byzantine Christianity,' in *SVTQ* 24 (4. 1980) 219-34].

Metanoia, a change of mind (heart), hence repentance (*penthos*) or penitence. There is also the great metanoia (*megalē metanoia*), made by going down on hands and knees and touching the ground with the forehead, and the little metanoia (*mikra metanoia*), a low bow.

Metochion, a property, a dependence of a monastery, with a few monks to administer it (cfr the word *cella*, as in La Celle-Saint-Cloud). 'All real estate (*immobilia*) belonging to church or monastery, found at a certain distance from this church or monastery' (J. Pargoire, *Echos d'Orient* 9 (1906), 371.

Mone, monastery.

Monachos, monk (from *monos*, alone). [Guillaumont, A., *Aux origines du monachisme chrétien. Pour une phénoménologie du monachisme*. Spiritualité orientale 30 (Begrolles, Abbaye de Bellefontaine 1979). Judge E.A., 'The Earliest Use of *monachos* for "monk," and the Origins of Monasticism,' in *JAC* 20 (1977), 72-89. Morard Françoise E., 'Monachos, Moine: Histoire du terme grec jusqu'au 4ᵉ siècle,' in *FZThPh* 20 (1973), 332-411; 'Some Further Thoughts on Monachos,' in *VC* 34 (1980), 309-401]].

Myktērismos, a sneer, a mockery (from *myktēr*, nostril); sarcasm to be endured, coming from the spiritual director or others.

Nepsis, wakefulness, attention, from the verb *nephō* (to be vigilant, mindful). The term and the reality to which it pointed played an important role in Eastern spirituality; hence, the Wakeful Fathers (*neptikoi patēres*).

New Prophecy, a term associated with a second century christian movement that viewed certain believers (e.g., Priscilla and Maximilla, followers of Montanus) as favorite messengers of the Holy Spirit. *New Pr.* was called by its opponents *kataphrygianism*; 'the heresy of the Phrygians'.

Oikonomia (economy), refers to 'divine dispensation', the Incarnation and Redemption, as contrasted to theology or the doctrine about God *in se*. In legal terminology, *oik*. means accomodation, indulgence, *epikeia*, *q.v.*

Old Man, a literal translation of *gerōn*. There is no need to look for a more modern term. All christian traditions have used the old noun: *gerōn*, *senex*, *saba*, *khello (hello)*, *staretz (q.v*, *beri*, and so forth—even the Arabic *shayk* (sheik).

Oxymoron, a witty statement (*moros*), all the more pointed (*oxys*) because it is presented as a paradox whereby two contradictory terms are used together, as in a discordant concordance (*concordia discors*), an eloquent silence, and so forth.

Paidariogeron, 'boy-old man,' a child or young person of precocious wisdom.

Paideusis, training, education. Also, *castigatio* (chastisement), since *paid*. was frequently rough. The term is often associated with God, as in Rev. 3:19.

Palē, the inner struggle, the third movement of a temptation, which can end either with victory or consent, *synkatathesis*, *q.v.*.

Paraenetic, literally, exhorting; hence *paranesis*, a classical literary genre, the art of giving exhortations.

Parexegesis, false exegesis.

Patērikon, a calendar giving a brief account of the exemplary lives and virtues of a monastery's holy men. [Leloir, L., 'Les orientations essentielles de la spiritualité des Pères du désert d'après les "Paterica" arméniens.' in *RThPh* 24 (1974), 30-47].

Pathos, from the verb *paschein* (to suffer), 'a disease of the soul,' an inner evil disposition, a passion, created in the soul as the result of repeated consent of evil thoughts (*logismoi*, *q.v.*).

Philanthropy, spontaneous love (*philein*) for man (*anthrōpos*). Early christians used the term frequently when speaking of God's 'love for mankind.'

Philauteia, self-love, a spontaneous attachment to oneself. A synonym for one's own will (*voluntas propria*), the single root of all the vices, especially in the writings of Maximus the Confessor.

Philosophia, in christian usage, frequently refers to the ascetic life, the *agōn* (struggle) for virtue and against vice. More precisely, ancient texts use the phrase *philosophia empraktos* (a lived philosophy) or *di'ergōn* (through deeds).

Plērophoria, a sense of plenitude, like *euphoria* is a feeling of well-being. Hence, assurance, certainty. In modern Greek, *pl.* means information, a report.

Pneumatikos patēr, spiritual father is a term already well authenticated in patristic texts by the fourth century. Cfr 'Pater spiritualis' in the *Verba Seniorum*, PL 73: 833-1066. *Abba: Guides to Wholeness and Holiness East and West*, ed. John R. Sommerfeldt. Symposium on Spiritual Fatherhood/Motherhood, Abbey of New Clairvaux, 12-16 June 1978. Cistercian Studies Series nr. 38 (Kalamazoo, MI 1982).

Pneumatophore, a bearer (*pherein*) of the Spirit (*pneuma*), a synonym of *pneumatikos*, 'one who is spiritual.' Refers to the person who bears the Spirit or is borne by the Spirit, depending on the tonic accent. Hence, inspired, prophetic. [Bilaniuk P.B., 'The Monk as Pneumatophor in the Writings of Basil the Great,' in *Diakonia* 15 (1980), 49-63].

Politeia, in ascetic language, a type of life or a particular ascetic practice, a rule of life.

Presbyter, literally, one who is *presbyteros*, which is the comparative of *presbys*, an old man (*senior*); frequently, a priest. The meaning of the term is sometimes ambiguous, as, for example, in St. Basil. Evagrius too plays upon the double meaning of the term.

Prosbolē, literally, an assault. Hence, the first suggestion of an evil thought (*logismos*, *q.v.*) before the free will can intervene.

Protepistatos, the first among the four directors (*epistates*) governing Athos, the Holy Mountain.

Remoboth (*remnuoth*), according to St. Jerome in *Letter* 22, 34 (PL 22: 419), 'a despised class of monks.' The same group is called *sarabaites* (*q.v.*) by Cassian and Saint Benedict.

Rhēma, a spoken word, an utterance (as differentiated from *logos*, which may be translated as 'inward word,' 'thought' or 'reason'). *Rh.* was used especially when referring to an

authorized, inspired answer. In the *Apophthegmata*, we frequently hear 'Speak a word, Father.'

Sabellianism, a doctrine associated with Sabellius (*fl.* 220
A.D.), who attempted to reconcile Monarchism (the traditional term for Monotheism) with trinitarian theology.
Sabellius viewed Christ as a mode of divine activity (*Modalism*) rather than as a separate person. The *Sabbellians* were
called *Patripassionists* by their opponents, indicating that the
Father (*Pater*) had suffered (*pathein, pati*) on the Cross.

Salos (fem. *salē*), a term unknown in classical Greek, refers to
'an imbecile, one who is half-witted.' Hence, 'a Holy Fool.'
[See J. Saward, 'The Fool for Christ's Sake in Monasticism,' in *East and West. One Yet Two: Monastic Tradition East
and West*, Orthodox-Cistercian Symposium, Oxford Univ.
26. 8-l. 9, 1973. *Cistercian Studies* 29 (Kalamazoo, MI 1976)
48-80, and *id.*, *Perfect Fools: Folly for Christ's Sake in Catholic
and Orthodox Spirituality* (Oxford-New York, 1980)]

Sarabaite, a term of egyptian origin, referring to 'the despised
type of monks' living under no rule, no leader, according to
their own sweet will (*phantasia*). Cfr the *Rule of Benedict*, chapter l, inspired by Cassian, *Conference* 18. 7; see also, *Remoboth*.

Schēma, the holy monastic habit. Cfr. *Megaloscheme*.

Silentiarius, a functionary in charge of silence (good order), or a
member of the imperial court (*silention*); a privy-counselor.
Sil. never meant hesychast (*q.v.*); John the Silentarius, is
merely a bad translation of 'John the Hesychast.'

Simple (or 'mere') *knowledge*, is knowledge in the actual, philosophic meaning of the term. This type of knowledge is to be
contrasted to 'true knowledge' (*gnōsis alēthinē*) which referes
to higher knowledge in the christian sense, and is reserved
for purified souls.

Starčestvo, the institution of the staretz, *vide infra*.

Staretz, the russian translation of *Gerōn*, (*q.v.*). [John B. Dun-
lop, *Staretz Amvrosy* (Mowbrays 1972); Macarius, Staretz of
Optino, *Russian Letters of Direction 1834-1860*, trans. Iulia de
Beausobre (St. Vladimir's Seminary Press 1975)]

Streblos, twisted, distorted, lacking good sense.

Stylites, one who lives on a pillar (*stylos*). [Elizabeth Dawes and Norman Baynes, trans. *Three Byzantine Saints. Contemporary Biographies of St Daniel the Stylite, St Theodore of Sykeon and St John the Almsgiver* (St Vladimir's Seminary Press 1977); I. Pena, P.I.Castellana, and R. Fernandez, *Les Stylites syriens*, Studium Biblicum Franciscanum, Collectio minor 16 (Milan 1975)

Syndiasmos, literally, the coupling (with an evil thought); it is the movement that follows the *prosbolē* (q.v.), which means 'suggestion,' the first stage of a temptation, before the struggle (*palē*) or the consent.

Synkatathesis, mental consent, the second movement of an evil thought, *logisomos (q.v.)*.

Synkellos (*syncellus*), literally, a cell-mate; a church dignitary, an assistant or counselor to a patriarch or archbishop.

Theologia, in the mystical sense, the contemplation of things divine, the highest degree of the spiritual life (ascent), after *praxis* and *theōria physikē* (natural contemplation, or an understanding of creation, in God).

Theophilia, love (*philia*) of God (*theos*).

Theophore, one who is united to God, inspired by God, spiritual. Cfr. *Pneumatophore*.

Theophōtistos, enlightened by God.

Theopteia, the vision of God, a mystical term. Cfr. Dionysius the Pseudo-Areopagite, *Epist.* 8 (PG 3: 1085) and elsewhere. [Mark S. Burrows, 'On the Visibility of God in the Holy Man: A Reconsideration of the Role of the Apa in the Pachomian *Vitae*,' in *VC* 41 (1987), ll-33; V. Lossky,, 'The Problem of the Vision Face to Face and Byzantine Patristic Tradition,' in *GrOThR* 17 (1972), 231-54]

Typikon (Pl. *Typika*), a collection of the liturgical and ascetic rules of a particular monastery.

Kterotic Typikon: 'What is called *K.T.* is a charter imposing an organization upon a given community, indicating the main lines and certain details of the type of life to be followed; to use Western parlance, the *K.T.* constitutes an amalgam of the Rule, the Constitution, the Regulations and the Customary' (J. Pargoire, in *EO* 9 (1906), 367).

Liturgical Typikon: 'A *L.T.* is a text that fixes the calendar for a given church, specifying the various offices for each day of the year with all the parts; to speak in terms of Latin usage, it presents something of a Missal, a Breviary, a Ceremonial and an Ordo' (*Ibid.*) [H. Delehaye, *Synaxaires byzantins, ménologues, Typica* (London: Variorum Reprints 1977)]

LIST OF NAMES

For names marked by an asterisk, see Selected Bibliography

Abacyrus, Syria, end of the sixth or seventh century.

Abraham, hermit in the Hellespont, and his niece Maria, sixth century.

Acacius, Saint, monk, early sixth century.

Adelphos, Messalian monk, fourth century.

Agabos of Baramos (?).

*Agapios Landos (A. the Cretan), monk, ascetic writer, d. before 1664.

*Agathon, Saint, abba, third generation of Scetis, *c.*400.

*Alexander of Jerusalem, Saint, bishop, d. 251.

Ammoes, abba, fourth century.

Ammonas, abba, fourth century.

Ammonius, abba, Theban, fourth century.

*Amoun, Saint, founder of the monastaries in Nitria, d. *c.* 350.

*Amphilochius of Iconium, Saint, bishop, wrote against the Messalians (*q.v.*), *c.* 341/3-394/400.

Andreas Salos (*ho salos*, 'the fool'), Saint, Ephesus, 880-946.

Andrew, correspondent of St Barsanuphius.

Anoub, abba, brother of Poemen, end of the fourth century.

Antiochus (*Pandect*) *of St Sabas*, monk, Palestine, early seventh century.

Antony the Great, Saint, Middle Egypt, the father of christian monasticism, *c.* 250-*c.* 355.

Antony of St Mamas, end of the 10th century.

Antony the Studite, patriarch of Constantinople, d. *c.* 980.(

Antony the Younger, Saint, anchorite on Mt. Olympus (Bethynia), *c*, 785-865.

Apollo, abba, d. *c.* 395.

Arethas of Caesarea, bishop, c. 850-after 932.

Arsenius the Great (*A. ho megas*), Saint, anchorite, famous Desert Father, 354-450.

Arsenius of St Mamas, hegumen, succeeded Symeon the New Theologian in 1005.

Assuana, Syrian hymnographer, fourth century.

Athanasia, Saint, abbess on the island of Aegina, ninth century.

Athanasius the Great, Saint, patriarch of Alexandria, Antony's biographer, 295-373.

Balsamon, patriarch of Antioch, writer of canon law commentaries, d. after 1195.

Barlaam and Joasaph, legendary saint's life, but also a masterful exposition of ascetic doctrine, probably by St John of Damascus.

Barnabas (*Epistle of*, though the Apostle Barnabas is not its author), opposes Old Testament to Pauline teaching, between 130 and 140.

Barsanuphius (*ho megas gerōn*, 'The Great Old Man'), Saint, recluse at the monastery of Seridos in Gaza, wrote at least 396 *Letters of Direction*, d. *c.* 540.

Basil the Great, Saint, hierarch, bishop of Caesarea in Cappadocia, d. 379.

Benedict of Nursia, Saint, the founder of Western monasticism, 480-543.

Bessarion, Saint, Egyptian anchorite, second half of the fourth century.

Christodoulos of Patmos, Saint, founded the monastery of St John on Patmos, wrote a *Hypotyposis*, which is partly auto-biographical, partly monastic regulations, c, 1020-1093.

Clement of Alexandria, the father of speculative theology, c. 150- before 215.

Clement of Rome, Saint, bishop, Pope, end of the lst century.

Cyril of Scythopolis, lavra of St Sabas, monastic biographer, c. 524- after 558.

Daniel, abba, fifth century.

Daniel of Raithou, Sinai, wrote a biography of St John Climacus, seventh century.

Daniel the Stylite, Saint, Constantinople, the second of the first great Stylites ('Pillar Saints'), 409-493.

Diadochus of Photice, bishop, ascetic writer, c. 400- d. before 186.

Didachē (*tōn dōdeka apostolōn*, 'The Teaching of the Twelve Apostles'), deals with moral duties and church rituals, last decades of the second century.

Didascalia Apostolorum, Syrian, deals with christian morality, discipline,and church constitutions, first half of the third century.

Diognetus (Letter to), deals with christian worship and daily life, second half of the second century.

Dionysius the Areopagite (Pseudo-), theologian and mystic, wrote between 480 and 530.

Domnica, Saint, fifth century.

Dorotheos of Gaza, Saint, ascetic writer, *fl.* middle of the sixth century.

Dosithee, Saint, disciple of St Dorotheos, d. *c.* 530.

Elias, abba (?).

Elias of Crete, metropolitan, wrote a commentary on the *Scala Paradisi* of St John Climacus, end of the eleventh-beginning of the twelfth century.

Ephrem the Syrian (E. Syrus), Saint, Edessa (Mesopotamia), the greatest poet of the Syrian church, 306-373.

Eponychus, monk of St Pachomius, fourth century.

Eulogius, priest, fifth century.

*Euphrosyne, Saint, hegumen of the monastery of Theodosius (near Alexandria), d. *c.* 470.

*Eupraxia (Euphrasia), Saint, anchorite in the Thebaid, *fl. c.* 380-410 (?).

*Eusebia-Xene, Saint, d. second half of the fifth century.

*Eusebius of Caesarea, bishop, the father of christian hagiography, *c.* 263-*c.* 340.

*Eusthatius of Thessalonika, metropolitan, theologian and classicist, official rhetorician of the church and the court, *c.* 1115-1196.

*Euthymius the Great, Saint, founder of monasteries in Palestine, 376-473.

*Evagrius Ponticus, monk of Scetis, ascetic writer, *c.* 345-399.

*Evergetinos (Paul), Byzantine monk, compiler of the *Evergetinon*, a famous anthology in four Books, arranged according to ascetic subjects (*hypotheseis*), 1054.

*Germanos the Hagiorite (G. of Lavra, George Maroules of Thessalonika), Saint, spiritual director, 1252-1336.

Gorgonia, Saint, sister of St Gregory of Nazianzus, *fl. c.* 370.

*Gregory Dialogos (Gregorios ho dialogos, Gregory I, the Great), Saint, Pope, wrote the *Dialogues*. He is the vital link between the patristic period and the Middle Ages, 540 (?)-604.

*Gregory of Nazianzus, Saint, hierarch, surnamed 'the Theologian,' on account of his orthodox teaching on the Trinity, 329-390.

*Gregory of Nyssa, Saint, brother of St Basil the Great, mystical theologian, *c.* 335-394.

*Gregory Pacourianos, wrote his *Typikon* (*q.v.*) in 1083.

*Gregory Palamas (G. of Neo-Caesarea), archbishop of Thessalonika, mystic theologian and defender of hesychasm (*q.v.*), 1296-1359.

*Gregory Thaumaturgus (G. the Wonderworker), Saint, bishop of Neo-Caesarea (Pontus), *c.* 213-*c.* 270.

Hesychius of Sinai (*H. the Priest*), monk, probably later than St John Climacus and Maximus the Confessor, eighth-tenth century.

Hilaria, Saint (?).

Hilarion (*Brother*), reputed author of the *Satire against the Hegumens*, twelfth century.

Hilarion of Gaza, Saint, Palestine, *c.* 291-371.

Horsiesi (*Orsisius*), the second successor of St Pachomius, d. *c.* 380.

Ignatius of Antioch, called 'Theophoros' (God-bearer), Saint, Martyr, *c.* 50-*c.* 110.

Irenaeus of Lyons, Saint, the father of Catholic theology, succeded Saint Pothin in 177-78.

Irene, Empress, 752-803.

Irene, Saint, mother of St Euphrosyne, fourth century.

Irene of Chrysobolanton, Saint, hegumen, 826-874 (?).

Irene Comnena, wrote her *Typikon* in 1118.

Irene-Eulogia-Chumnaia-Paleologina, founder of the convent *Tou philanthropou Sotēros* in 1308.

Isaac, priest of the Cells, Nitria, fourth century.

Isaac of Syria (*I. of Nineveh*), ascetic author, seventh century.

Isaiah, Byzantine monk, compiler of a *Mētērikon*, *c.* 1200.

Isaiah, monk, Monophysite author, d. 488.

Isias (Esaias) of Scetis, fourth century.

Isidore, priest of Nitria, fourth century.

Isidore of Pelusium, Saint, ascetic writer, *c*, 360/70-435.

James of Jerusalem, disciple of St Sabas.

James (Jacob) of Sarug, Syrian bishop, author of metrical homilies (*memrē*), *c* 449-521.

Jerome, Saint, hagiographer, translator, first among the ancient Western exegetes, *c.* 340-420.

John, abba, Athonite, end of the thirteenth century.

John, abba, ex-robber, ninth century.

John the Almoner (*Johannes Elimosinarius, J. the Merciful*), Saint, patriarch of Alexandria, 555-616 (?).

John of Apamea (*J. the Solitary, Pseudo-John of Lycopolis*), Syrian monk, probable author of the writings falsely attributed to John of Lycopolis, fifth century.

John Chrysostom ('J. of the Golden Mouth'), Saint, hierarch, great exegete, orator, and spiritual writer, 344 (?)-407.

*John Cassian, Saint, summarized the traditions of the desert in his writings, *c.* 360-433.

John Climacus (*J. the Scholastic*), Saint, author of *Klimax tou paradeisou* (*Scala Paradisi*), a compendium of old monastic doctrines, before 579–*c.* 649.

John Colobos (*Johannes Curtus*, 'the Short,' 'the Dwarf'), Saint, monk of Scetis, d. *c.* 409 (?).

John of Damascus, Saint, dogmatic theologian, writer of hagiographic texts, probable author of *Barlaam and Joasaph*, *c.* 675-749 (?).

John the Faster (*Johannes Jejunator*), *c.* 530 (?)-595.

John of Gaza (*J. the Prophet*), Saint, disciple of St Barsanuphius, *q.v.*, wrote 446 *Letters of Direction*, d. *c.* 540-50.

John of Lycopolis, Saint, Egyptian monk, one of the great figures of Egyptian monasticism, *c.* 304-395.

John Moschus, monk, author of the *Leimonarion* (*Pratum Spirituale*, *The Spiritual Meadow*), *c.* 540-619.

John Saba (*J. of Dalyatha*), Nestorian hermit, reputed author of *Barlaam and Joasaph*, eighth century.

John the Solitary (*J. of Apamea*), *q.v.*

John of Thebes, fourth century.

John of Thessalonika, archbishop, d. *c.* 630.

Joseph the Hymnographer, 816-886.

Joseph of Panephysis, abba, fifth century.

Joseph of Thebes, abba, fourth century.

Julitta, Saint, Martyr under Diocletian, fourth century.

Justin Martyr, philosopher, d. *c.* 165.

Leontius of Jerusalem, patriarch, c. 1176-1184/5.

Leontius of Neapolis, Cyprus, hagiographer, *c.* 590-*c.* 650.

Longinus, abba, early sixth century.

Luke, Saint, archimandrite of Messina, twelfth century.

Macarius the Great (*M. of Egypt*), Saint, father of the monks of Scetis, *c.* 300-*c.* 390.

Macrina the Younger, Saint, sister of Saint Basil the Great, superior of one of the earliest communities of women ascetics, c. 330-379.

Malachy, abba, hegumen of Lavra (Mt. Athos), then archbishop of Thessalonica, thirteenth century.

Manuel II Paleologus, emperor, founder of Stroumitza, and one of the most remarkable writers of the age, 1350-1325.

Marina, Saint, (?).

Mark, disciple of Silvanus, fifth century.

Mark the Ascetic (*M. the Hermit*), ascetic writer, d. probably at the beginning of the fifth century.

Mary, sister of St Pachomius, fourth century.

Mary of Egypt, Saint, d. 442.

Mary the Younger of Bisya, Saint, d. 9078.

Matoes, fifth century.

Matrona (also called *Babylas*), Blessed, c. 420-520.

Matrona of Chio, Saint, d. 1462.

Maurus, Saint, disciple of St Benedict, sixth century.

Maximus the Confessor, Saint, great theologian, c. 580-662.

Maximus and Dometius, Saint, of Scetis, brothers, fourth century.

Melania the Younger, Saint, 383(?)-439.

Methodius the Confessor, Saint, patriarch of Constantinople, d. 847.

Michel Attaliates, historian and jurisconsult, wrote a *Typikon* in 1077 for the monastery he founded in Rhodosto.

Mios, abba, end of the fourth or fifth century.

Moses, Saint, abba, Nubian ex-robber, end of the fourth century.

Musonius Rufus, Stoic, during the reigns of Nero and Trajan.

Nicetas Stethatos (*N. Pectoratus*, 'the courageous one'), biographer of Symeon the new Theologian, early eleventh century-after 1054.

Nicodemus the Hagiorite, compiled the *Philokalia*, a collection of patristic and hesychast writings, 1748-1809.

Nilus, hieromonk (*q.v.*).

Nilus of Ancyra (*N. of Sinai, N. the Ascetic*), spiritual writer, d. c. 430.

Nilus Diasorenus, metropolitan of Rhodes, fourteenth century.

Olympias, Saint, widow of Nebridios, received seventeen consolatory letters from St John Chrysostom, c. 361-408/9.

Or, abba, d. c. 391.

Origen (surnamed Adamantius, 'the man of steel'), perhaps the greatest scholar of christian Antiquity, c. 185-255.

Pachomius the Elder, Saint, founder of cenobitic monasticism in Tabennisi, c. 287 (292?)-346.

Paesius, brother of Poemen, end of the fourth century.

Palamon, abba, teacher of Pachomius.

Palladius, bishop of Helenopolis (Bethynia), wrote the *Lausiac History*, 363-420/30.

Pambo, Saint, anchorite in the desert of Nitria, 307 (?)-374 (?).

Paphnutius (called *Kephalas*, 'big-headed,' because of his knowledge of Scripture), disciple of St Antony, fourth century.

Parasceva the Younger, Saint, 10th century.

Paul of Latros (*P. the Younger, P. the Stylite*), Saint, monk on Mt Latros, d. after 395.

Paul the Simple, Saint, hermit in the Thebaid, c. 340.

Paul of Thebes, Saint, first hermit (older than St Antony), d. 342 (?).

Peter, apa, monk of St Pachomius, fourth century.

Peter of Galata, Saint, hermit, c. 340-d. 430.

Peter the Iberian, Monophysite author, c. 409-488.

Peter Pionita, disciple of abba Lot, fifth century.

Peter the Studite, tenth century.

Pezos, hieromonk (*q.v.*) of Caracallas, fourteenth century.

Pior, Saint, anchorite in the desert of Nitria, c. 350 (?)

Piteroum (*Pyoterius*), abba, fifth century.

Philis, Scetiote abba, fifth century.

Philotheus of Batos (P. *the Sinaite*), monk, ascetic writer, after St John Climacus, ninth-twelfth century.

Philotheus Kokkinos ('the Redhead'), polygraph, historiographer, end of the thirteenth century-1377.

Philoxenes of Mabbug, Saint, bishop of Hierapolis (or Mabbug), syrian monophysite theologian, c. 450-518 (?).

Platon of Sakkoudion, Saint, hegumen (*q.v.*) in Bethynia, 735-814.

Poemen (Poimen, 'the Shepherd'), Saint, d. c. 450.

Polycarp of Smyrna (P. means 'abundant fruit'), Saint, Martyr, *fl. c.* 177.

Polychronius, Saint, end of the fifth century.

Procopius of Gaza, christian rhetorician, head of the school of Gaza, wrote long biblical commentaries in the form of *catenae*.

Ptolemy of Scetis, illusionist monk (*Lausiac History*).

Romanus the Melodist, the most renowned of the Byzantine hymnographers, sixth century (?).

Rufinus of Aquileia, oldest Latin christian historian, c. 345-410.

Rufus, bishop of Majuma, biographer of Peter the Iberian.

Sabas the Elder, Saint, Byzantine monk, founder of the great Lavra ('Mar-Saba'), 439-532.

Sabas of Latros, 11th century.

Sabas of Vatopedi (S. *the Younger*), Saint, Athonite monk, d. 1349.

Sanamon, monk of Saint Pachomius.

Sarah of Scetis, Saint, amma, fourth-fifth century (?).

Seridos, Saint, founded a monastery near Gaza, sixth century.

Shenoute of Atripe, second abbot of the 'White Monastery,' Sohug (Upper Egypt); next to St Pachomius, the most powerful organizer of Egyptian monasticism, 334-451.

Silvanus, monk of St Pachomius, fourth century.

Silvanus, Saint, abba, fifth century (?).

Sisoes, abba, Scetiote ascetic (there are several ascetics by this name; in the *Alphabetical Series*, there *Sayings* are ascribed to one), fifth century.

Sophronius of Saccoudion, eighth-ninth century.

*Stephen the Younger, Saint, Martyr, monk on Mt Auxentius, 715-764.

*Symeon of Emesa (S. Salos, 'the fool'), Saint, d. *c.* 570.

*Symeon the New Theologian, hegumen of the monastery of St Mamas, the first and perhaps greatest Byzantine mystic 949-1022.

*Symeon the Studite (called *ho eulabēs*, 'the Pious'), spiritual father of Symeon the New Theologian, *c.* 916-986.

*Symeon the Stylite, the Ancient, Saint, the first and most famous Stylite, 389-459.

*Symeon the Stylite, the Younger, Saint, 521-592.

*Symeon of Thessalonika, theologian, liturgist, metropolitan from 1416 to 1429.

*Syncletica, Saint, Egypt, d. c. 400.

*Theoctista of Lesbos (the name means 'fashioned by God'), Saint, solitary, d. 872 (?).

*Theoctistus, Saint, hegumen, disciple of St Euthymius the Great, d. 466.

Theodora, daughter of Isaac II Angelus, *fl. c.* 1200.

Theodora, Saint, fourth-fifth century.

Theodore of Petra, fourth century.

*Theodore Studites, Saint, hegumen, one of the most important monastic reformers *c.* 759-826.

*Theodore of Tabenna, third successor of St Pachomius, 314-368.

*Theodoret of Cyrus, bishop, hagiographer, 393-466.

*Theodosius the Cenobiarch, Saint, founder of the monastery of Theodosios, 423-529.

*Theoleptus of Philadelphia, metropolitan, wrote letters to Irene-Eulogia-Chumnaia-Paleologina.

Theonas, fifth century.

*Theophan the Recluse, important Russian spiritual author, *c.* 1815-1894.

Theophylactus of Bulgaria, writer and prelate, c. 1030-1108.

*Xanthopoulos, Ignatius and *Kallistos*, noteworthy scholars (Ign. *fl.* 1360; Kall., d. 1363).

Zachariah, abba, end of the fourth century.

*Zacharias Rhetor (*Z. Scholasticus*), church historian and biographer, *c.* 465-536.

Zebinas, Saint, anchorite, fifth century.

Zeno the Prophet, Saint, fifth century.

*Zosimas, Saint, d. before 550 (?).

TABLE OF ABBREVIATIONS

I. DICTIONARIES, PERIODICALS, COLLECTED WORKS

Acta SS	*Acta Sanctorum*, Brussels-Paris 1836ff
ABR	*American Benedictine Review*, the American Benedictine Academy 1939ff
ACW	*Ancient Christian Writers*, Westminster (Md) 1946ff
Aeg	*Aegyptus. Rivista Italiana di Egittologia e di Papirologia*, Milan 1920 ff
AnBoll	*Analecta Bollandiana*, Brussels 1882ff
BAH	*Bibliothèque archéologique et historique*, Paris 1882ff
BHG	*Bibliotheca Hagiographica Graeca*, Brussels ²1909ff
BHO	*Bibliotheca Hagiographica Orientalis*, Brussels 1910ff
BMGrSt	*Byzantine and Modern Greek Studies*, Oxford 1975ff
BNJ	*Byzantinisch-Neugriechische Jahrbücher*, Athens-Berlin 1920ff

BS	*Bibliotheca Sanctorum*, Rome 1958ff
ByzAr	*Byzantinisches Archiv*, München 1956ff
Byz(B)	*Byzantion (Revue internationale des études byzantines)*, Brussels 1924ff
ByzSt	*Byzantine Studies*, Washington 1971ff
ByZ	*Byzantinische Zeitschrift*, Leipzig 1892ff
C	*Concilium*
Cath	*Catholicisme*, Paris 1948ff
CE	*The Christian East*, London 1920ff
ChH	*Church History*, New York 1932ff
CoC	*Collectanea Ordinis Cisterciensium Reformatorum. Collectanea Cisterciensia*, Forges 1965ff
CO	*Communio*, 1966ff
CS	*Cistercian Studies Series.* Spencer, Washington, Kalamazoo, 1969ff
CSCO	*Corpus Scriptorum Christianorum Orientalium*, Paris 1903ff
DACL	*Dictionnaire d'archéologie chrétienne et de liturgie*, Paris 1903-1953.
DDC	*Dictionnaire de droit canonique*, Paris 1935ff
DHGE	*Dictionnaire d'histoire et de géographie ecclésiastiques*, Paris 1912ff
DOP	*Dumbarton Oak Papers*, Cambridge Mass., 1941ff
DOT	*Dumbarton Oak Texts*, 1967ff
DR	*Downside Review*, Stratton-Bath 1880ff
DSAM	*Dictionnaire de spiritualité ascétique et mystique*, Paris 1932ff
ECR	*Eastern Churches Review*, 1966. *Sobornost*
EO	*Echos d'Orient*, Paris 1897ff
EuA	*Erbe und Auftrag*, Beuron 1919ff
FZThPh	*Jahrbuch für Philosophie und spekulative Theologie*, 1914, *Freiburger Zeitschrift für Theologie und Philosophie*, Freiburg 1954ff
GCS	*Die griechischen christlichen Schriftsteller*, Berlin-Leipzig, 1897ff

GrOThR	*The Greek Orthodox Theological Review*, Brookline Mass., 1954ff
GrBySt	*Greek, Roman and Byzantine Studies*, Durham 1958ff
HThR	*The Harvard Theological Review*, Cambridge Mass., 1908ff
HZ	*Historische Zeitschrift*, Munich 1859ff
Ir	*Irenikon*, Amay-Chevetogne 1925ff
Ky	*Zeitschrift für Osteuropaische Geschichte*, 1935. *Kyrios*, Berlin 1936ff
JSS	*The Journal of Semitic Studies*, Manchester 1956ff
JAC	*Antike and Christentum*, 1950. *Jahrbuch für Antike und Christentum*, Münster 1956ff
JThS	*The Journal of Theological Studies*, London 1889ff
NRTh	*Nouvelle Revue théologique*, Louvain-Paris 1879ff
NS	*Nea Sion*, Jerusalem 1904ff
Numen	*Numen. International Review for the History of Religions*, Leiden 1954ff
OrChr	*L'Orient chrétien*, Beirut 1972ff
OrChrA	*Orientalia Christiana Analecta*, Rome 1935ff
OCP	*Orientalia Christiana Periodica*, Rome 1935ff
OstKSt	*Ostkirchliche Studien*, Würzburg 1951ff
ParO	*Parole d'Orient*, 1970ff
PG	*Patrologia Graeca*, Paris 1857ff
PL	*Patrologia Latina*, Paris 1878ff
POC	*Le Proche-Orient chrétien*, Jerusalem 1951ff
POr	*Patrologia Orientalis*, Paris 1904ff
PS	*Patrologia Syriaca*, Rome 1894, 1958-1965
RAM	*Revue d'ascétique et de mystique*, Toulouse 1920ff
RBen	*Revue Bénédictine*, Maredsous 1884ff
RBSt	*Roman and Byzantine Studies*, 1959ff
REB	*Revue des études byzantines*, Paris 1946ff
REG	*Revue des études grecques*, Paris 1888ff
RHE	*Revue d'histoire ecclésiastique*, Louvain 1900ff
RHR	*Revue de l'histoire des religions*, Paris 1880ff

RHS	*Revue de l'histoire de la spiritualité*, Paris 1924ff
RITh	*Revue internationale de théologie*, Bern 1893ff
RivS	*Rivista di Storia*, 1964ff
RLM	*Revue liturgique et monastique*, Maredsous 1924ff
RLR	*Revue des langues romanes*, Paris 1869ff
ROC	*Revue de l'Orient chrétien*, Paris 1986ff
RQ	*Renaissance Quarterly*, the Renaissance Society of America 1947ff
RSLR	*Rivista di Storia e Letteratura Religiosa*
RSR	*Recherches de science religieuse*, Paris 1910ff
RThPh	*Revue de théologie et de philosophie*, Lausanne 1913, 1951, 1968ff
SA	*Studia Anselmiana*, Rome 1933ff
SCh	*Sources Chrétiennes*, Paris 1941ff
SE	*Sacris Erudiri*. Jaarboek voor Godsdienstwetenschappen, Steenbrugge 1949ff
Sob	*Sobornost*, London 1979ff
Soc	*Societas*. A Review of Social History
SteT	*Studi e Testi*, Rome 1900ff
StudMed	*Studi Medievali*, Turin 1904ff. *Nuovi Studi Medievali*, Bologna 1928ff
StM	*Studia Monastica*, Montserrat 1959ff
StT	*Studies and Texts*, Waltham Mass., 1963ff
SVTQ	*St Vladimir's Seminary Quarterly*, 1952ff. *St. Vladimir's Theological Quarterly*, New York 1969ff
Th	*Theologia*, Athens 1923ff
ThLZ	*Theologische Literaturzeitung*, Leipzig 1878ff
ThPh	*Theologie und Philosophie*, 1915ff
ThZS	*Theologische Zeitschrift aus der Schweiz*, Basel 1883ff
TM	*Travaux et mémoires*, Athens 1966ff
TU	*Texte und Untersuchungen zur Geschichte der altchristlichen Literatur: Archiv für die griechisch-christlichen Schriftsteller der ersten drei Jahrhunderte*, Leipzig-Berlin 1882ff
TS	*Texts and Studies*, Cambridge 1891ff
VC	*Vigiliae Christianae*, Amsterdam 1947ff

Vi	*Viator*, Berkeley 1970ff
VS	*La vie spirituelle*, Paris 1869ff
ViVr	*Byzantina Chronika. Vizantijskij Vremennik*, Leningrad 1869ff
WBSt	*Wiener Byzantinische Studien*, Vienna 1956ff
WS	*Word and Spirit*, Still River, Mass., 1979ff
ZAM	*Zeitschrift für Aszese und Mystik*, München 1926. *Geist und Leben*, 1957ff
ZDMG	*Zeitschrift der Deutschen morgenlandischen Gesellschaft*, Leipzig 1947ff
ZKTh	*Zeitschrift für katholische Theologie*, Vienna 1878ff
ZNW	*Zeitschrift für die neutestamentliche Wissenschaft und die Kunde der Aelterer Kirche*, 1900, Berlin 1934ff
ZRGG	*Zeitschrift für Religions-und Geistesgeschichte*, Marburg 1948ff

II. INDIVIDUAL WORKS

Amand, *Ascèse*	Dom Amand, *L'ascèse monastique de St. Basile*. Maredsous 1948.
Amélineau, *Hist. monast.*	E. Amélineau, *Histoire des monastères de la Basse Egypte* (= Annales du Musée Guimet 25). Paris 1894.
Altaner, *Patrol.*	B. Altaner, *Patrologie. Leben, Schriften und Lehre der Kirchenväter*. Freiburg i. Br., 1955.
Bremond, *Pères*	J. Bremond, *Les Pères du desert*. Paris 1927.
Budge, *Paradise*	Sir A.T. Wallis Budge, *The Paradise or Garden of the Holy Fathers, being Histories of the Anchorites, Recluses, Monks, Coenobites, and Ascetic Fathers of the Deserts of Egypt between A.D.*

	CCL *and* A.D. CCCC. New York 1909.
Cotelier, *Ecclesiae*	J.B. Cotelier, *Ecclesiae Graecae Monumenta*, 4 vols. Paris 1677-92.
Delehaye, *Mélanges*	H. Delehaye, *Mélanges d'hagiographie grecque et latine*. Brussels 1966.
Delehaye, *Styl.*	H. Delehaye, *Les saints stylites*, 4 vols. Brussels 1923
Duchesne, *Histoire*	L. Duchesne, *Histoire ancienne de l'église*. Paris 1908.
Festugière, *Antioche*	A.J. Festugière, *Antioche païenne et chrétienne*. Paris 1959.
Festugière, *L'ideal*	A.J. Festugière, *L'ideal religieux des grecs et l'évangile* (Coll. Etudes bibliques). Paris 1932.
Festugière, *Moines Or.*	A.J. Festugière, *Les moines d'Orient*. Paris 1962.
Festugière, *Moines Pal.*	A.J. Festugière, *Les moines de Palestine*. Paris 1963.
Heussi, *Ursprung*	K. Heussi, *Der Ursprung des Mönchtums, eine Studie zur Geschichte des Mönchtums und der frühchristilichen Begriffen gnostiker und pneumatiker*, Tübingen 1936.
Holl, *Enthusiasm*	K. Holl, *Enthusiasm und Bußgewalt beim griechischen Mönchtum*, Leipzig 1894.
Meyer, *Haupturkunden*	Ph. Meyer, *Die Haupturkunden für die Geschichte der Athoskloester*. Leipzig 1894.
Miklosisch-Mueller, *Acta*	F. Ritter von Miklosisch-J. Mueller, *Acta et Diplomata Graeca Medii Aevi Sacra et Profana*. Athens-Vienna 1860-90.

Papadopoulos
Kerameus,
Analekta

A. Papadopoulos Kerameus,
Analekta
hierosolymitikēs stachiologias. Hē
Syllogē anekdotōn kai spaniōn
hellenikōn syngraphōn peri tōn kata
ten Hēoan orthodoxōn ekklessiōn kai
malista tēs tōn Palaistinōn. St
Petersburg 1891-98.

Papadopoulos
Kerameus,
Antonios

A. Papadopoulos Kerameus, *An-*
tōnios
Studites kai tina symmikta,
Jerusalem 1905.

Papadopoulos
Kerameus,
Monumenta

A. Papadopoulos Kerameus,
Monumenta
Graeca et Latina ad Historiam
Photii Patriarchae Pertinentia, 2
vols. St Petersburg 1901.

Reitzenstein, *Hist. Mon.*

R. Reitzenstein, *Historia*
Monachorum und Historia Lausiaca.
Göttingen 1916.

Rufinus, *Historia*

Rufinus, *Historia Monachorum in*
Aegypto. PL 31.

Viller, *Spiritualité*

M. Viller, *La spiritualité des*
premiers siècles chrétiens. Paris
1930.

von Campenhausen,

Kirchliches Amt

H. von Campenhausen,
Kirchliches Amt und
geistliche Vollmacht in den ersten
drei Jahrhunderte. Tübingen 1953.

White, *Monasteries*

H.G.L. White, *The Monasteries of*
Wadi'n Natrun, 3 vols. New
York 1932.

SELECTED BIBLIOGRAPHY

AGAPIOS LANDOS

PRIMARY SOURCES. ORAL OR WRITTEN (henceforth A.) *Hamartolōn sōtēria* (*The Salvation of Sinners*). Venice, 1641.

SECONDARY SOURCES (henceforth B). Irénée Hausherr. 'Dogme et spiritualité orientale.' *RAM* 23 (1947) 26ff.; *id.*, 'Études de spiritualité orientale.' *OrChrA* 183 (1969) 168ff. Eugène Michaud. 'Les légendes du "Salut des pécheurs" du moine Agapios Landos.' *RITh* 8 (1900) 766-71. L. Petit. 'Le moine Agapios Landos.' *EO* 3 (1889-1900) 278-85. *Id.*, 'Agapios Landos et la Revue internationale de théologie.' *Ibid.*, 4 (1901) 303-5.

AGATHON

A. *Vitae Patrum*. PL 73:751ff. For specifics, see 'Index of Persons and Places,' in *The Sayings of the Desert Fathers. The Alphabetical Collection*. Trans. Benedicta Ward (Oxford-Kalamazoo, 1975); and *The Wisdom of the Desert Fathers. Apophthegmata Patrum* from the *Anonymous Series*. Trans. B. Ward. Oxford: Fairacres, 1975. See also, 'Index of Persons and Places,' in *The Lives of the Desert Fathers*. The *Historia Monachorum in Aegypto*. Trans. Norman Russell. London & Oxford: Mowbray, 1980-Kalamazoo, MI., CS 34, 1981.

B. De Buck. 'De sancto Agathone.' *Acta SS*. vol. 9 (October). Paris 1869, 896-908.

ALEXANDER OF JERUSALEM

B. Duchesne, *Histoire*, 433ff., 458ff. Jerome. *De viris illustribus* 62.

AMOUN

A. *Apophthegmata Patrum*. PG 65:85-88. Ward, *The Sayings of the Desert Fathers*, 31-2. Rufinus. *Historia Monachorum* xxx. PL 31: 455:57. Trans. Norman Russell, *Lives of the Desert Fathers*, *q.v.*

B. H. Delehaye, 'Saints de Chypre.' *AnBoll* 26 (1907) 186-7. Duchesne, *Histoire*, vol 2. 492-7.

AMPHILOCHIUS OF ICONIUM

A. K.G.Bones (Mpones), ed. *Amphilochiou Ikoniou* (*ca.* 341/5-395/400) '*Peri pseudous askēseos*.' Athens 1979. G. Ficker, ed. *Amphilochiana* I. 'Treatise Against the Messalians,' 23-77. Leipzig 1906.

B. K. Holl, *Amphilochius von Ikonium in seinem Verhältnis zu den grossen Kappadoziern*. Tübingen, 1904.

ANDREAS SALOS

B. Augustinos monachos, ed. *Bios kai politeia tou hōsiou patros hēmon Andreiou tou dia Christon Salou*. Jerusalem, 1912. *Vita* (*Bios*) by Leontius of Neapolis. PG 92: 1669-1748. *Bios* by Nicephorus. PG 111:627-888. E. Benz, 'Heilige Narrheit,' *KY* 3 (1938) 1-55. G. da Costa-Louillet, 'Saints de Constantinople aux VIIᵉ, IXᵉ et Xᵉ siècles,' *ByZ(B)* 24 (1955-1956) 179-214. J. Grosdidiers de Matons. 'Les thèmes d'édification dans la vie d'André Salos,' *TM* 4 (1970) 277-328. Hilpisch. 'Die Torheit um Christi Willen,' *ZAM* 6 (1931) 212-231. S. Murray. *A Study of the Life of Andreas, the Fool for the sake of Christ.* Leipzig, 1910. L. Ryden, *The Andreas Salos Apocalypse.* Greek text, trans. and Comment., *DOP* 28 (1974) 197-261; 'The Date of the Life of Andreas Salos,' *DOP* 32 (1978) 127-155. J.T. Wortley, 'The Life of St. Andrew the Fool,' *Studia Patristica* X (TU 107) Berlin 1970, 315-19; 'A Note on the Date of the *Vita Andreae Sali*,' *Byz(B)* 39 (1969) 204-8; 'The *Vita Sancti Andreae Sali* as a Source of Byzantine Social History,' *Soc* (1974) 1-20.

ANTIOCHUS

A. *Pandect of Sacred Scripture.* PG 89:1415-1848.

ANTONY THE GREAT

B. Athanasius. *Bios Antōniou (Vita Antonii).* PG 26: 835-976. L. Bouyer. *La Vie de St. Antoine.* Saint Wandrille, 1950 (2nd ed.). Spiritualité 22. Bégrolles-en-Mauges: Abbaye de Bellefontaine, 1978. N. Devilliers. *S. Antoine le Grand, père des moines.* Spiritualité orientale 8. Bégrolles: Abb. de Bellefontaine, 1971. Muchú O'Diarmuid. 'St. Anthony of Egypt: the Man and the Myth.' *CS* 20 (2. 1985) 88-97. W. Schneemelder. 'Das Kreuz Christi und die Daemonen. Bemerkungen zur *Vita Antonii* des Athanasius.' *Pietas*: Festschrift B. Koetting (1980) 381-392. L. von Hertling. *Antonius der Einsiedler.* Innsbruck, 1925.

ANTONY THE STUDITE

A. A.P. Kerameus, ed. *Protropē eis exagoreusin* ('Instruction on Confession,' to the monks of Studios), *Nea Sion* 2: 808-15.

B. Leo the Deacon. *Eulogion.* PG 117: 892ff.

ANTONY THE YOUNGER

B. F. Halkin, ed. *Vita, AnBoll* LXII (1944) 210-25.

A. Papadopoulos-Kerameus, ed. *Syllogē Palaistinēs kai Syriakēs Hagiologias*. Saint Petersburg, 1907, 186-216.

ARSENIUS THE GREAT

A. *Apophth. Patrum* (de abbate Arsenio, 1-44). PG 65: 87-108.

B. St. Theodore the Studite. 'Laudatio S. Arsenii Anachoretae.' PG 99: 849-82. (Nissen Th. Ed. *BNJ* I (1920) 241-62). Bremond, *Pères*, 544-6. Hugh G.L. White, *The History of the Monasteries of Nitria and of Scetis*. New York 1932, 476.

ATHANASIA

A. *Vita Graeca*. A. Ehrhard, ed. 'Überlieferung und Bestand der hagiographischen und homiletischen Literatur der griechischen Kirche.' *TU* L-LII. Leipzig 1937-52.
Vita Latina. Acta SS 3. Venice 1752, 170-5 *Acta SS*. 3 (1867) 168-75.

ANTHANASIUS OF THE LAVRA (A. THE ATHONITE)

A. *Typikon* and *Diatypōsis*. P. Meyer, ed. *Die Haupturkunden für die Geschichte der Athosklöster*. Leipzig.

B. J. Mossay, 'A propos des "Actes de Lavra." Notes sur les deux *Vies* de saint Athanase l'Athonite.' *AnBoll* 91 (1973) 121-32. J. Noret, *Vitae duae antiquae Sancti Athanasii Athonitae*. Turnhout: Brepols, 1982. L. Petit, 'Vie de saint Athanase l'Athonite.' *AnBoll* 25 (1906) 5-89.

ATHANASIUS THE GREAT

A. *Bios Antoniou (Vita Antonii)*. PG 26: 837-976.

B. G.J.M. Bartelinck, 'Die literarische Gattung der *Vita Antonii*. Struktur und Motive.' *VC* 36 (1982) 38-62; 'Observations de critique textuelle sur la plus ancienne version latine de la *Vie de S. Antoine* par S. Athanase.' *RBén* 81 (1971) 92-5. Brian Brennan, 'Athanasius' *Vita Antonii*: A Sociological Interpretation.' *VC* 39 (1985) 209-27. Martin Tetz. 'Athanasius und die *Vita Antonii*. Literarische und theologische Relationen.' *ZNW* 73 (1-2, 1980) 1-30.

BALSAMON

B. Oeconomos. *La vie religieuse dans l'empire byzantin au temps des Comnènes*. Paris 1918, 118-23.

BARLAAM AND JOASAPH

B. John Damascene. *Barlaam and Joasaph*. Critical ed. and English trans., G.R. Woodward and H. Mattingly. Louvain, 1953.

BARSANUPHIUS

B. *Barsanuphius and John. Questions and Answers*. Critical ed. and English trans., Derwas J. Chitty, *POr* 31. 3. Paris: Firmin-Didot,, 1966. F. Neyt, 'Un type d'autorité charsimatique.' *Byz(B)* 44 (1974) 343-61. L. Regnault, 'Les lettres spirituelles de Jean et de Barsanuphe.' *EO* 7 (1904) 268-76; 8 (1905) 15-25, 154-60; id., 'Théologie de la vie monastique selon Barsanuphe et Dorothée,' in *Théologie de la vie monastique*.

BASIL THE GREAT

A. *Ascetica*. W.K. Lowther Clarke, trans. *The Ascetic Works of St. Basil*. London: S.P.C.K., 1925. L. Lebe, tr. *Les règles monastiques*. Maredsous, 1969; *id.*, *Les règles morales et portrait du chrétien*. Maredsous, 1969.

B. H. Delhougne, 'Autorité et participation ches les Pères du cénobitisme. Le cénobitisme basilien.' *RAM* 46 (1970) 3-32. K. Duchatelez, 'La "koinonia" chez S. Basile le Grand.' *CO* 6 (1973) 163-80. J. Gribomont, 'Saint Basile et le monachisme enthousiaste.' *Ir* 53 (1980) 123-44. H. Ledoyen,

'Saint Basile dans la tradition monastique occidentale.' *Ir* 53 (1980) 30-45. J. Leroy, 'L'influence de Saint Basile sur la réforme studite d'après les *Catéchèses.*' *Ir* 52 (1979) 491-506. F. von Lilienfeld, 'Basilius der Grosse und die Mönchväter der Wüste.' *ZDMG.* Suppl. I. 18. Deutsche Orientalisten- tag, 1968. Wiesbaden (1969) 418-35. Metropolitan Georges (Khodr). 'Basil the Great: Bishop and Pastor.' *SVTQ* 29 (1. 1985) 5-27. M. Simon, 'Plaire à Dieu selon les règles mon- astiques de S. Basile.' *CoC* 39 (1977) 239-49. Adalbert de Vogüé. 'Les *Grandes Règles* de S. Basile. Un survol.' *CoC* 41 (3. 1979) 201-26; 'The *Greater Rule* of St. Basil. A Survey,' *WS* 1 (1979) 49-85.

BENEDICT OF NURSIA

B. L. Leloir, 'Les Pères du désert et saint Benoît. Un ap- ophtegme d'Antoine.' *NRTh* 112 (1980) 197-226. M. van Parys, 'L'accès à l'orient monastique chez S. Benoît.' *Ir* 47 (1974) 48-58. Adalbert de Vogüé, 'Benedict. Model of the Spiritual Life.' *WS* 2 (1981) 59-72. Ambrose Wathen, 'Bene- dict of Nursia: Patron of Europe 480-1980.' *CS* 15 (2. 1980) 105-25.

BESSARION

B. Brémond, *Pères*, 331-3. P. Ioannou, 'Un opuscule inédit du Card. Bessarion. Le panégyrique de saint Bessarion, anchorite égyptien.' *AnBoll* 65 (1947) 107-38.

CHRISTODOULOS OF PATMOS

A. Era L. Branuse, *Ta hagiographika keimena tou hosiou Christodoulou, hidrutou tēs en Patmo monēs. Philologikē paradōsis kai historikai martyriai.* Diss. Athens, 1966. Miklosich- Mueller. *Acta* VI (1890) 59-80.

B. L. Barbier, *S. Christodoule et la réforme monastique au XIᵉ siècle.* Paris 1863. P. Gautier, 'La date de la mort de Christo- dule de Patmos (mercredi 16 mars 1063).' *REB* 25 (1967) 235-38.

CLEMENT OF ALEXANDRIA

B. Th. Camelot, *Foi et gnose. Introduction à l'étude de la connaissance mystique chez Clément d'Alexandrie.* Paris, 1945.

CYRIL OF SCYTHOPOLIS

A. *Kyrillos von Skythopolis. Bioi (Vitae)* of Euthymius the Great, Sabas the Elder, John the Hesychast, Kyriakos the Anchorite, Theodosios the Cenobiarch, Theognios, and Abraham of Krateia. Edited by E. Schwartz. *TU* 49.2 (Leipzig, 1939)

B. Paul Devos, 'Cyrille de Scythopolis. Influences littéraires. Vêtement de l'évêque de Jérusalem. Passarion et Pierre l'Ibère.' *AnBoll* 98 (1-2, 1980) 25-38.

DANIEL THE STYLITE

B. *Vita S. Danielis Stylitae.* Edited by H. Delehaye, *Les saints stylites.* Brussels, 1923. English trans. by Elizabeth Dawes and N.H. Baynes, *Three Byzantine Saints. Contemporary Biographies of St. Daniel the Stylite, St. Theodore of Sykeon and St. John the Almsgiver.* (Crestwood, New York: St. Vladimir's Seminary Press, 1977) 7-84.

DIADOCHUS OF PHOTICE

A. *Diadoque de Photicé. Cent chapitres sur la perfection spirituelle.* Edited by E. des Places. *SCh* 5. Paris, 1943. 'On Spiritual Knowledge and Discrimination: One Hundred Texts.' *Philokalia*, vol. 1 (London, 1977) 253-96. *Diad. de Ph. Oeuvres spirituelles.* Ed. by E. des Places. SCh 5bis. Paris, 1955 (new edition, SCh 5ter, Paris, 1966).

B. Irénée Hausherr. 'Les grands courants de la spiritualité orientale.' *OCP* 1 (Rome, 1935) 114-38. E. des Places, 'Diadoque de Photicé et le messalianisme.' *Kyriakon. Festschr. J. Quasten* II (Münster: Aschendorff, 1970) 591-5.

DIONYSIUS THE AREOPAGITE

B. Pl. Spearritt, 'The Soul's Participation in God According to Pseudo-Dionysius.' *DR* nr. 293 (1970) 378-92.

DOROTHEOS OF GAZA

A. *Dorothée de Gaza. Oeuvres spirituelles.* Edited by L. Regnault. *SCh* 92 Paris, 1963. *Dorotheos of Gaza. Discourses and Sayings.* Trans. by Eric P. Wheeler. *CS* Series 33. Kalamazoo: Cistercian Publications, 1977.

B. F. Neyt, *Les lettres à Dorothée dans la correspondance de Barsanuphe et de Jean de Gaza.* Louvain, 1969. L. Regnault, 'Théologie de la vie monastique selon Barsanuphe et Dorothée.' *Théologie de la vie monastique* (Paris, 1961) 315-22.

DOSITHÉE

A. PG 88:1611. *Vie de Saint Dosithée. Orientalia Christiana* 26 (Rome, 1932) 1012-23.

B. *Vita (Bios). SCh* 92 (Paris, 1963) 122-45.

EPHREM THE SYRIAN

B. R. Murray, 'Der Dichter als Exeget: Der hl. Ephraem und die heutige Exegese.' *ZKTh* 100 (1978) 484-94.

EUPHROSYNE

B. *Bios.* PG 114: 305-21. *Bios.* Edited by A. Boucherie. *An-Boll* 2 (1883) 195-205. *Vita.* Edited by Rosweyde. PL 73: 643-52. M. Kamil, 'Euphrosyne.' *Tome commémoratif du millénaire de la bibliothèque patriarcale d'Alexandrie.* Alexandria 1953, 235-60.

EUPRAXIA

B. *Bios (Vita).* BHG I. Brussels, 1957, p. 193, n. 631.
P.F. Halkin, 'Une nouvelle version de la *Vie* de Ste Eupraxie.' *AnBoll* 79 (1961) 160ff. G. Quispel, and J. Zandee, 'A Coptic Fragment from the *Life* of Eupraxia'. *VC* 13 (1959) 193-203.

EUSEBIA-XENE

B. *Bios (Vita).* BHG I. Brussels, 1957, p. 194. n. 633. *S. Eusebia seu Xenae Vita.* Edited by T. Nissen. *AnBoll.* 56 (1938) 102-17.

EUSEBIUS OF CAESAREA

B. Karl Suso Frank, 'Eusebius of Caesarea and the Beginnings of Monasticism.' *ABR* 38 (1987) 50-64.

EUSTHATIUS OF THESSALONICA

B. V. Laurent, 'Eustathe de Thessalonique.' *DHGE* 16 (Paris, 1967) 34-41. P. Wirth, 'Zur Biographe des Eusthatios von Thessalonike.' *Byz(B)* 36 (1966) 260-82.

EUTHYMIUS THE GREAT

B. *Bios (Vita):* see Cyril of Scythopolis. S. Vailhé, 'St. Euthyme le Grand'. *ROC* 12 (1907) 298-312; 337-66; 13 (1908) 181-91, 225-46; 14 (1909) 189-202, 256-63.

EVAGRIUS PONTICUS

A. The *Praktikos. Chapters on Prayer.* Trans. by J.E. Bamberger. *CS* 4. Spencer, Mass., 1970.

B. A. Guillaumont, 'Un philosophe au desért: Evagre le Pontique.' *RHR* 91 (1972) 29-56. André Louf, 'L'acédie chez Evagre le Pontique.' *C* (1974) nr. 99, 113-17.

EVERGETINOS

A. *Synagogē tōn theophthogōn rhēmaton, kai didaskaliōn tōn theophorōn, kai hagiōn Paterōn.* Edited by Nicodemus the Hagiorite and Macarius of Corinth. Venice, 1783. *Synagogē.* Athens, 1976 (Bk III), 1977 (Bks I & IV), 1978 (Bk II). *Mikros Evergetinos (The Shorter Evergetinos).* Edited by Kallikinos monachos. Athens, 1977.

B. Irénée Hausherr. 'Paul Evergetinos a-t-il connu Symeon le nouveau théologien?' *OCP* 23 (1957) 58-79. J.M. Sauget, 'Paul Evergetinos et la Collection alphabético-anonyme des *Apophthegmata Patrum.* A propos d'un livre récent.' *OCP* 37 (1971) 22-35.

GERMANOS THE HAGIORITE

B *Bios (Vita)* by Philotheos Kokkinos. Edited by P. Joannou. *AnBoll* 70 (1952) 37-114 (with Introduction).

GREGORY DIALOGOS

A. *Dialogi de vita et miraculis patrum Italicorum.* PL 77: 149-430 (Bks 1, 3, 4); PL 66: 125-204 (Bk 2).

B. Francis Clark, *The Pseudo-Gregorian Dialogues.* Studies in the History of Christian Thought 37, 1987. Claude Dageus, 'Grégoire le Grand et le monde oriental.' *RSLR* 17 (2. 1981) 243-52. F.H. Dudden, *Gregory the Great. His Place in History and in Thought.* 2 vols. London, 1905. G. Dufner, *Die Dialoge Gregors des Grossen im Wandel der Zeiten und Sprachen.* Padua: Antenore, 1968. Joan M. Petersen, *The Dialogues of Gregory the Great in their Late Antique Cultural Background. ST* 69. Toronto: Pontifical Institute of Medieval Studies, 1984.

GREGORY OF NAZIANZUS

A. *Grégoire de Nazianze. Discours* 1-3. Edited by J. Bernardi. *SCh* 247. Paris, 1978. *Discours* 20-23. Edited by J. Mossay and G. Lafontaine. *SCh* 270. Paris, 1980. *Discours* 27-31

(Disc. Théologiques). Edited by P. Galley and M. Jourjon. *SCh* 250 Paris, 1978. *De vita sua*. Edited by Ch. Jungck. Wissenschaftliche Kommentare zu griech. und latein. Schriftstellern. Heidelberg 1974. *Poemata historica*. PG 35-38.

B. Altaner, 344-51. N.Z. Davis, 'Gregory Nazianzen in the Service of Humanist Social Reform.' *RQ* 20 (1967) 455-64. M.S. Guignet, *Grégoire de Nazianze et la rhétorique*. Paris, 1911. M. Kertsch, 'Gregor von Nazianz' Stellung zu *Theoria* und *Praxis* aus der Sicht seiner Reden.' *Byz(B)* 44 (1974) 282-89. J. Plagnieux, *Saint Grégoire de Nazianze, théologien*. Paris, 1911. Rosemary Radford Ruether. *Gregory of Nazianzus. Rhetor and philosopher*. Oxford: Clarendon, 1969. Špidlík, Thomas. *Grégoire de Nazianze. Introduction à l'étude de sa doctrine spirituelle*. OrChrA 189 (Rome, 1971); 'La theoria et la praxis chez Grégoire de Nazianze.' *Studia Patristica* 14. 3 (*TU* 117, Berlin 1976) 358-64.

GREGORY OF NYSSA

A. *Grégoire de Nysse. Traite de la virginité* by M. Aubineau. *SCh* 119. Paris, 1966.

B. E. Baert, 'Le thème de la vision de Dieu chez S. Justin, Clément d'Alexandrie et S. Grégoire de Nysse.' *FZThPh* 12 (1965) 439-97. Mariette Canévet, 'Grégoire de Nysse (Saint).' *DSAM* 6 (Paris, 1967) 971-1011. Jean Daniélou, *Platonisme et théologie mystique. Essai sur la doctrine spirituelle de saint Grégoire de Nysse*. 2nd ed. Paris, 1954. J. Gribomont, 'Le panégyrique de la virginité, ouvre de jeunesse de Grégoire de Nysse.' *RAM* 43 (1967) 249-66. J.E. Pfister, 'A Biographical Note: the Brothers and Sisters of St. Gregory of Nyssa.' *VC* 18 (1964) 108-13.

GREGORY PACOURIANOS

A. *Tipik Grigorija pakuriana. Vvedenie, pereved i kommentarij [The Typikon of Gregory Pacourianos*. Trans. Introd. and

Comment.] by V.A. Arutjunova-Fidnajan. Ereven: Verlag der Akademie der Wissenschaften der Armenischen SSR, 1978. *Le typikon de Grégoire Pakourianos (décembre 1083).* Edited by P. Lemerle. Vol. III of *Cinq études sur le XIe siècle byzantin.* Paris: CNRS (1977) 113-91.

Louis Petit, 'Typikon de Grégoire Pacourainos pour le monastère de Petritzos (Bačkovo) en Bulgarie.' *ViVr* ll (Suppl. 1) 1904.

B. S.G. Kauchčišvili, 'Tipikon Grigorija Bakuriani (Typicon Gregorii Pacuriani).' Konferencija po voprosam archeografii i izučenija dervnichd rukopisej Tbilisi 3-5 nojabra. Tbilisi (1969) 21-2.

GREGORY PALAMAS

B. *Vita* (panegyric) by Philotheos Kokkinos. PG 151: 551-656 (*BHG* 718). K.G. Bones, 'Gregorios Palamas, der letztze der grossen byzantinischen Theologen.' *Th* 50 (1979) 7-21. Basile Krivochéine, 'The Ascetic and Theological Teaching of Gregory Palamas.' *ECQ* 3 (1938) 26-33; 71-84; 138-50; 193-214. Jean Meyendorff, 'Palamas (Grégoire).' *DSAM* 12 (1984) 82-106. G.C. Papademetriou, *Introduction to St. Gregory Palamas.* New York: Philosophical Library, 1973.

GREGORY THAUMATURGUS

B. *Bios (Vita).* PG 47: 833-957. *BHG* . n. 715.
Vita (Syriac). Edited by V. Ryssel. *ThZS* 11 (1894) 228-54.
V. Ryssel, *Gregorius Thaumaturgus. Sein Leben und seine Schriften.* Leipzig, 1880. W. Telfer, 'The Latin Life of St. Gregory Thaumaturgus.' *JThS* 31 (1930) 142-55, 354-62; *id.*, 'the Cultus of St. Gregory Thaumaturgus.' *HThR* 29 (1936) 225-344.

HESYCHIUS OF SINAI

A. *Les 24 chapitres De temperantia et virtute d'Hésychius le Sinaïte.* Edited by Marysse Waegeman. *SE* 22 (1974/75)

195-285. 'On Watchfulness and Holiness.'. Trans. by G.E.H. Palmer and E. Kadloubovsky. *The Philokalia*. vol I. London 1979 162-98.

B. Irénée Hausherr. 'La méthode d'oraison hésychaste.' *Or-ChrA* 9.2 (1927) 138-40; *Noms du Christ et voies d'oraison*. *Or-ChrA* 157 (1960) 253-59. English trans. by Ch. Cummings. *The Name of Jesus*. CS 44. Kalamazoo, 1978. Jean Kirchmeyer, 'Hésychius le Sinaïte et ses Centuries,' in *Le millénaire du Mont Athos 963-1963*, vol. I (Chevetogne, 1963) 319-29. Viller, 93-4. M. Waegeman, 'La structure primitive du traité "De temperantia et virtute" d'Hésychius le Sinaïte. Deux Centuries ou un acrostiche alphabétique.' *Byz (B)* 44 (1974) 467-78.

HILARION (BROTHER)

A. 'La Satire contre les Higoumènes.' Trans. by E. Jeanselme and L. Oeconomus. *Byz(B)* 1 (1924) 317-39.

B. Peter Charanis, 'The Monk as an Element of Byzantine Society.' *DOP* 25 (1971) 61-84.

HILARION OF GAZA

B. *Vita Hilarionis*, by Saint Jerome. PL 23: 29-64.
E. Coleiro, 'St. Jerome's Lives of the Hermits.' *VC* ll (1957) 161-78. Winter, P. *Der literarische Character der 'Vita Hilarionis.'* Zittau, 1904.

HORSIESI (ORSISIUS)

A. *Doctrina de institutione monachorum*. Trans. by Saint Jerome. PL 103:453-76. *Liber de S. Orsiesius*, by Jerome. Edited by A. Boon. *Pachomiana Latina*. Louvain, 1932. Translated 'The Book of Orsiesius', *Pachomian Koinonia*, vol. 2. CS 46. Kalamazoo, 1981.

B. H. Bacht, 'Vom Umgang mit der Bibel im ältern Mönchtum.' *ThPh* 41 (1966) 557ff. H. Doerries, 'Die Bibel im Mönchtum.' *ThLZ* 72 (1947) 215-22.

IRENAEUS OF LYON

B. Johannes Quasten, *Patrology*, vol. I (Utrecht, 1950) 287-313.

IRENE EMPRESS

B. S. Runciman, 'The Empress Irene.' *Conspectus of History* I. Muncie, Indiana: Ball State University, 1974, 1-11.

IRENE OF CHRYSOBOLANTON

B. *Acta SS* (28 July). vol 6 (lst ed.) 398E, 600-34. *BHG* II, p. 41. n. 952. Doukakis, C. *Megas Synaxaristes* 7 (Athens, 1893) 434-57.

IRENE-EULOGIA-CHUMNAIA-PALEOLOGINA

A. A Summary of the *Letters* written by Theoleptus of Philadelphia. S. Salavile, in *Mélanges J. de Ghellinck*. vol. 2 (Gembloux, 1950) 877-87. Angela Constantinides Hero, *A Woman's Quest for Spiritual Guidance. The Correspondence of Princess Irene Eulogia Choumnaina Palaiologina* (Archbishop of Iakovos Library of Ecclesiastical and Historical Sources, 11). Brookline, MA. 1986.

B. 'Irène-Eulogia.' V. Laurent, *EO* 29 (1930) 29-60. S. Salaville, Analysis of the *Homilies* by Theoleptus. *REB* 2 (1944) 119-25; 5 (1947) 101-15, 116-35.

ISAAC OF SYRIA

A. *The Ascetical Homilies of Saint Isaac the Syrian*. Edited by F. Panteleimon. Brookline, Mass., 1984. *Mar Isaacus Ninivita. De perfectione religiosa*. Edited by Paul Bedjan. Paris-Leipzig, 1909. English trans. by A.J. Wensinck. *Mystic Treatises by Isaac of Nineveh*. 2nd ed. Wiesbaden, 1967. 'Directions on Spiritual Traning.' Trans. E. Kadloubovsky and G.E.H. Palmer, in *Early Fathers from the Philokalia*. London (1954) 183-280.

B. Irénée Hausherr. *Les grands courants de la spiritualité orientale. OCP* 1 (1934) 114-38; *Penthos. La doctrine de la componction dans l'Orient chrétien. OrChrA* 132 (1944) 148, 161-70, 193-96. English trans. by Anselm Hufstader. *Penthos. The Doctrine of Compunction in the Christian East. CS* 53. Kalamazoo, 1982. E. Khalifé-Hachem, 'La prière pure et la prière spirituelle selon Isaac de Ninive.' *Mémorial G. Khouri-Sarkis*. Louvain 1969, 157-73.

ISAIAH. BYZANTINE MONK

A. J. Gouillard, 'Une compilation spirituelle du XII⁰ siècle. Le Livre II de l'abbé Isaïe.' *EO* 38 (1939) 72-90. Irénée Hausherr. 'Le *Métérikon* de l'abbé Isaïe.' *OCP* 12 (1946) 286-301.

ISAIAH. MONOPHYSITE AUTHOR

B. S. Vailhé,'Un Mystique monophysite: le moine Isaïe.' *EO* 9 (1906) 81-91.

ISAIAS (ESAIAS) OF SCETIS

B. L. Regnault, 'Isaïe de Scété ou de Gaza? Notes critiques en marge d'une introduction au probleme isaien.' *RAM* 46 (1970) 330-44.

ISIDORE OF PELUSIUM

A. *Apophthegmata*. PG 65: 221D-224B.

B. *De Isidori Pelusiotae Vita, scriptis et doctrina commentatio historica theologica*. Ed. by H.A. Niemeyer. PG 78: 102; 1647-74. *Isidoros ho pelousiotos*. Ed. by D.S. Balanos. Athens, 1922. G.J.M. Bartelinck, 'Observations stylistiques et linguistiques chez Isidore de Péluse.' *VC* 18 (1964) 163-80. P. Evieux, 'Isidore de Péluse. Etat des recherches.' *RSR* 64 (1976) 321-40. C.M. Fouskas, 'St. Isidore of Pelusium and the New Testament.' *Th* 37 (1966) 59-71, 453-72; 38 (1967) 74-94, 281-300; *Saint Isidore of Pelusium. His Life and His*

Works. Athens, 1970. M. Smith, 'An unpublished *Life* of St. Isidore of Pelusium,' in *Eucharisterion. Mélanges A.S. Alevisatos*. Athens, 1958, 429-38.

JAMES OF SARUG

B. Roberta C. Chesnut, *Three Monophysite Christologies: Severus of Antioch, Philoxenus of Mabbug and Jacob of Sarugh*. Oxford Theological Monographs. London: Oxford University Press, 1976. François Graffin, 'Jacques de Sarug.' *DSAM* 8 (fasc. LII-LIII). Paris, 1972, 56-60.

JEROME

A. *Vie de Paul de Thèbes et Vie de St. Hilarion*. Edited by P. de Labriolle. Paris, 1907. *Vita Hilarionis*. PL 32: 28-64.

B. P. Antin, 'St. Jérôme directeur mystique.' *RHS* 48 (1972) 25-30. E.P. Burke, 'St. Jerome as Spiritual Director,' in *A Monument to St. Jerome*. New York, 1952, 143-69. E. Coleiro, 'St. Jerome's *Lives* of the Hermits.' *VC* 11 (1957) 161-78. J.N.D. Kelley, *Jerome. His Life, Writings, and Controversies*. New York, 1975. F. Nau, 'St. Jérôme hagiographe.' *ROC* 5 (1900) 654-59. J. Plesch, *Die Originalität und literarische Form der Mönchsbiographien des hl. Hieronymus*. Munich, 1910. P. Winter, *Der literarische Character der 'Vita Hilarionis.'* Zittau, 1904.

JOHN THE ALMONER

A. *Leontios von Neapolis. Leben des heiligen Johannes des Barmherzigen Erzbishofs von Alexandria*. Edited by H. Gelzer. Freiburg-im-Breisgau, 1893. Leontius of Neapolis. *Vita Joh. Elimosinarii*. Trans. by Anastasius the Librarian. *Vitae Patrum*, PL 73: 337-84.
Three Byzantine Saints. Contemporary Biographies of St. Daniel the Stylite, St. Theodore of Sykeon and St. John the Almsgiver. Trans. from the Greek by Elizabeth Dawes and N.H. Baynes. Crestwood, N.Y.: St. Vladimir's Seminary Press, 1977.

B. H.T.F. Duckworth, *St. John the Almsgiver*. Oxford, 1901. H. Delehaye, 'Une vie inédite de St. Jean l'Aumônier.' *AnBoll* 45 (1927) 5-74. E. Lappa-Zizicas, 'Une épitomé de la Vie de St. Jean l'Aumônier par Jean et Sophronius.' *AnBoll* 88 (1970) 265-78.

JOHN OF APAMEA

A. *Jean le Solitaire (Pseudo-Jean de Lycopolis). Dialogue sur l'âme et les passions.* Trans. by Irénée Hausherr. *OrChrA* 120 (Rome, 1939).

B. S. Brock, 'John the Solitary on Prayer.' *JThS* N.S. 30 (1979) 84-10. P. Harb, 'Doctrine spirituelle de Jean le Solitaire (Jean d'Apamée).' *ParO* 2 (1971) 225-60. I. Hausherr, 'Un grand auteur spirituel retrouvé: Jean d'Apamée.' *OCP* 14 (Rome, 1948) 3-42.

JOHN CHRYSOSTOM

A. *Paraenesis ad Theodorum Lapsum.* PG 47; 300-8. 'Exhortation to the Fallen Theodore.' *A Select Library of the Nicene and Post-Nicene Fathers.* Series 1, vol. 9. Reprt. Grand Rapids, 1979.

B. J.-M. Leroux, 'S. Jean Chrysostome et le monachisme,' in Ch. Kannengieser, ed., *Jean Chrysostome et Augustin.* Actes du colloque de Chantilly,, 22-24 septembre 1974. Paris 1975 (Théol. histor., 35) 125-44. L. Schaepfer, *Das Leben des hl. Johannes Chrysostomus.* Düsseldorf, 1966.

JOHN CASSIAN

A. *Conferences.* Translated by Colm Luibheid. The Classics of Western Spirituality. New York: Paulist Press, 1985. *Conferences* and *Institutes*, Nicene and Post-Nicene Fathers series, XI [New complete translation by Boniface Ramsey OP, forthcoming in the CS series—ed.]

B. Owen Chadwick. *John Cassian.* Cambridge Univ. Pres, 1968. J.C. Guy, *Jean Cassien. Vie et doctrine spirituelle.* Paris, 1961.

JOHN CLIMACUS

A. *Klimax tou paradeisou. The Ladder of Divine Ascent.* Trans. by Lazarus Moore. Boston, Mass.: Holy Transfiguration Monastery, 1978.

B. S. Salaville, 'St. Jean Climaque.' *EO* 20 (1923) 400-54. A. Saudreau, 'La doctrine spirituelle de St. Jean Climaque.' *VS* 9 (1924) 352-70. P. Pourrat, *La spiritualité chrétienne* (Paris, 1947) 453-69.

JOHN COLOBOS

A. *Apophthegmata.* PG 65: 204E-220A.

B. 'Vie de Jean Kolobos.' Edited by E. Amélineau, in *Hist. monast.*, liv-lxiii, 316-413. E.A. Wallis-Budge, *The Book of the Saints of the Ethiopian Church* (Cambridge, 1928) vol. 1, 17-76; vol. 4, 1263-65. White, *Monasteries*, vol. 3, 222-23.

JOHN OF DAMASCUS

A. See BARLAAM AND JOASAPH.

B. A. Kallis, 'Handapparat zum Johannes-Damaskenos-Studium.' *OstKSt* 16 (1967) 200-13.

JOHN OF GAZA

A. See BARSANUPHIUS.

B. Lucien Regnault, 'Jean de Gaza.' *DSAM*, fasc. LIV-LV (1973) 536-38.

JOHN OF LYCOPOLIS

A. 'Un texte grec inédit attribué à Jean de Lycopolis.' Ed. by J. Muyldermans. *RSR* 41 (1953) 525-30; *id.*, 'A propos d'un texte grec attribué à Jean de Lycopolis.' *Ibid.*, 43 (1955) 395-401.

B. P. Devos, 'Fragments Coptes de l'*Historia Monachorum*' (*Vie* de S. Jean de Lycopolis). *AnBoll*, 87 (1969) 417-40. I.

Hausherr, 'Au origines de la mystique syrienne: Grégoire de Chypre ou Jean de Lycopolis?' *OCP* 4 (Rome, 1938) 497-520; 'Un grand auteur spirituel retrouvé: Jean d'Apamée.' *Ibid.* 14 (1948) 3-42. P. Peeters, ed. 'Une *Vie* de Saint Jean de Lycopolis.' *AnBoll* 54 (1936) 359-81. Rufinus. *Historia Monachorum* I. PL 31: 391-405. W. Strothmann, *Johannes von Apamea.* Patristische Texte und Studien II. Berlin, 1972.

JOHN MOSCHUS

A. *Leimonarion. Pratum spirituale.* PL 74: 121-241.
Le pré spirituel. Trans. by M.J. Rouet de Journel. *SCh* 12. Paris, 1946.

B. Ph. Pattenden,'The Text of the *Pratum spirituale.*' *JThS* 26 (1975) 38-54. S. Vailhé, 'Jean Mosch.' *EO* 5 (1901-1902) 107-116.

JOHN SABA

B. B.E. Colless, 'Le mystère de Jean Saba.' *OrChr* 12 (1967) 515-23; *id.*, 'The Mysticism of John Saba.' *OCP* 39 (1973) 83-101; 'La vie ascétique selon Jean de Dalyatha.' Actes du 29ᵉ Congrès intern. des Orientalistes. Cahier 5. *OrChr* (1975) 23-6.

JOHN OF THESSALONIKA

B. Martin Jugie, 'Le vie et les oeuvres de Jean de Thessalonique.' *EO* 21 (1922) 293-307; *id.*, 'Analyse du discours de Jean sur la Dormition de la Sainte Vierge.' *Ibid.*, 22 (1923) 385-97.

JOSEPH THE HYMNOGRAPHER

B. John the Deacon. *Vita Josephi.* PG 105: 940-976. Cfr *AnBoll* 65 (1947) 134-8. Theodore Pediasimos. *Theodori Pediasimi ejusque amicorum quae extant.* Edited by M. Treu. Postdam, 1899, 1-14.

Theophanes the Monk. *Vita Josephi*. Edited by Papadopoulos Kerameus, *Monumenta*. vol. 2, 1-14. G. da Costa-Louillet, 'Vie de S. Joseph l'Hymnographe.' *Byz B)* 27-27 (1955-1957) 812-23. E.I. Tomadakes, *Joseph ho Hymnographos. Bios kai ergon*. Athens, 1971. D. Stiernon, 'La vie et l'oevre de S. Joseph l'Hymnographe. A propos d'une publication récente.' *REB* 31 (1973) 243-66. C. Van de Vorst, 'Note sur St. Joseph l'Hymnographe.' *AnBoll* 38 (1920, 148-54.

JULITTA

B. H. Delehaye, *Les origines du culte des martyrs*. 1933, 167-8. S. Lenain de Tillemont, *Memoires pour servir à l'histoire des six premiers siècles*. vol. 5. Paris, 1913, 349-52.

LEONTIUS OF JERUSALEM

B. Theodore Goudeles, monachos. *Vita (Bios) Leontii*. Auctarium *BHG* n. 985. E.L. Branouses (Vranoussis) in *Ta hagiologika keimena tou hosiou Christodoulou. . . .* Athens 1966, 156-8. W. Hecht,'Der *Bios* des Patriarchen Leontius von Jerusalem als Quelle zur Geschichte Andronikos I. Komnenos.' *ByZ* 61 (1968) 40-3.

LEONTIUS OF NEAPOLIS

A. *Leontios von Neapolis. Leben des hl. Johannes des Barmherzigen Erzbischof von Alexandrien*. Edited by H. Gelzer. Freiburg-im-Breisgau, 1893. 'John the Almsgiver.' English trans. by Elizabeth Dawes and Norman H. Baynes in *Three Byzantine Saints*. Crestwood, New York, 1977, 199-270.
Vita S. Simeonis Sali. *BHG* n. 1677. Auctarium *BHG*, n. 1677b.
Vie de Syméon le Fou et Vie de Jean de Chypre. Edited by A. J. Festugière and L. Ryden. Institut français d'archéologie de Beyrouth. Biblioth. archéol. et historique 95. Paris, 1977.

B. H. Gelzer, 'Ein griechischer Volkschriftsteller des 7. Jahrhunderts.' *HZ* 61 (1889) 1-38. P. Viard, 'Léonce, évêque de Néapolis de Chypre.' *Cath* 7 (1972) 382ff.

MACARIUS THE GREAT

A. *Apophthegmata*. PG 65: 257C-281B.

B. 'Vie d'abba Macaire, père des moines de Scété.' Ed. E. Amélineau, *Hist. monast*, 46-117. A. Guillaumont, A. 'Le problème des deux Macaire dans les *Apophthegmata Patrum*.' *Ir*. 48 (1975) 41-59. H.G.L. White, *Monasteries*. vol. 2, 60-72, 118-20.

MACRINA THE YOUNGER

B. *Gregorii Nysseni opera*. Edited by Werner Jaeger. Leiden, 1960. 8/1:337-414.
Vie de sainte Macrine. Edited by P. Maraval. *SCh* 178. Paris, 1971. *The Life of St. Macrina*. Edited by W.K.L. Clarke. London, 1916. Translated by Kevin Corrigan. Saskatoon-Toronto: Peregrina Press, 1987. P.Th. Camelot, 'Macrine la jeune (4e S.).' *Cath*. 33 (1977) 126. Klöppe, M. 'Makrina die Jüngere, eine altchristliche Frauengestalt,' in *Frauen im Bannkreis Christi*. Maria Laach, 1964, 80-94. J.E. Pfister, 'A Biographical Note: The Brothers and Sisters of St. Gregory of Nyssa.' *VC* 18 (1964) 108-13.

MANUEL II PALEOLOGUS

A. *The Letters of Manuel II Paleologus*. Edited and trans. by G.T. Dennis. Corpus Fontium Historiae Byzantinae 8. *DOT* 4 (1977).

B. L. Petit, 'Manuel II Paléologue.' *DThC* 9 (Paris, 1926).

MARK THE ASCETIC

A. 'On the Spiritual Law: Two Hundred Texts.' Trans. by G.E.H. Palmer and E. Kadloubovsky. *The Philokalia*. vol. 1 (London, 1979) 110-24; 'On Those who Think that They are Made Righteous by Works: Two Hundred Texts.' *Ibid*., 125-46.

B. H. Chadwick, 'The Identity and Date of Mark the Monk.' *ECR* 4 (1972) 125-30. J. Kunze, *Marcus Eremita, ein*

neuer Zeuge für das Altkirchliche Taufbekenntnis. Leipzig, 1895.
Timothy Ware, 'The Sacrament of Baptism and the Ascetic
Life in the Teaching of Mark the Monk.' Studia Patristica
10. *TU* 107 (Berlin, 1970) 379-90.

MARY OF EGYPT

A. *Life.* PG 87 (3); 3693-3726. PL 72:671-90. Trans. B.
Ward, *The Harlots of the Desert.* CS 106 (1988) 35-56.

B. *Bios kai politeia Marias tes Aigyptias.* Edited by P. Longo.
Athens, 1962. F. Delmas, 'Remarques sur la vie de sainte
Marie l'Egyptienne.' *EO* 4 (1900-1901) 35-42; *id.*, 'Encore
sainte Marie l'Egyptienne.' *Ibid.*, 5 (1901-1902) 15-25.

MATRONA

B. PG 116: 920-954.
J. Anson, 'The Female Transvestite in Early Monasticism.
The Origin and Development of a Motif.' *Vi* 5 (1974) 1-32.
E. Patlagean, 'L'histoire de la femme déguisée en moine et
l'évolution de la saintete féminine à Byzance.' *StudMed.* III
17 (1976) 597-623.

MAXIMUS THE CONFESSOR

B. *The Life of our Holy Father Maximus the Confessor* (Based on
the life by his Disciple Anastasius). Trans. by Christopher
Birchall. Boston, 1982, 1-48.
S. Brock, 'An Early Syriac Life of Maximus the Confessor.'
AnBoll 91 (1973) 299-346. R. Devreese, 'La vie de S. Max-
ime le Confesseur et ses recensions.' *AnBoll* 46 (1928) 5-49.
M. Th. Didier, 'Les fondements dogmatiques de la spir-
itualité de st. Maxime le Confesseur.' *EO* 29 (1930) 296-313.
D.J. Geanakoplos, 'Some Aspects of the Influence of the
Byzantine Maximos the Confessor on the Theology of East
and West.' *ChH* 38 (1969) 150-63. Juan Miguel Garrigues,
Maxime le Confeseur. La charité, avenir divin de l'homme. Paris:
Beauchesne, 1976. W. Lackner,'Zu Quellen und Datierung

der Maximusvita (BHG 3/1234).' *AnBoll* 85 (1967) 285-316. E. Montmasson, 'Chronologie de la vie de s. Maxime le Confesseur (580-662).' *EO* 13 (1910) 149-54. Alain Riou, *Le monde et l'église selon Maxime le Confesseur.* Paris: Beauchesne, 1973. Lars Thunberg, *Microcosm and Mediator. The Theological Anthropology of Maximus the Confessor.* Lund, 1965. M. Viller, 'Aux sources de la spiritualité de St. Maxime le Confesseur.' *RAM* ll (1930) 156-84. W. Voelker, *Maximus Confessor als Meister des geistlichen Lebens.* Wiesbaden, 1965.

MAXIMUS AND DOMETIUS

B. 'Vie des saints Maxime et Domèce.' Ed. E. Amélineau, *Hist. monast.* 262-315. F. Nau, 'La légende de Maxime et Domèce.' *POr* 5, 750-66. White, *Monasteries.* vol. 2 (1932) 98-104.

MELANIA THE YOUNGER

A. *The Life of Melania the Younger.* Edited by Elizabeth A. Clark, Studies in Women and Religion 14. New York: Edwin Mellen Press, 1984. *Sanctae Melaniae Junioris Vita. The Life of Saint Melania the Younger.* Ed. and trans. by Th. C. Papazoilos. Diss. Catholic University of America, 1978. *Santa Melania Guiniore: Senatrice Romana.* Edited by M. Rampolla. Rome, 1905. *S.M. Iun. Acta graeca.* Edited by H. Delehaye. *AnBoll* 22 (1903) 5-50. *Vie de sainte Mélanie.* Edited by D. Gorce. *SCh* 90 (Paris, 1962). *Vita Sanctae Melaniae Iunioris.* Edited by Ch. de Smedt. *AnBoll* 8 (1889) 19-63. A. d'Alès, 'Les deux vies de sainte Mélanie la jeune.' *AnBoll* 25 (1906), 401-50; *id.*, 'Sainte Mélanie la jeune.' *Etudes* 108 (1906), 221-40. P. Th. Camelot, 'Mélanie la jeune (Sainte).' *Cath.* 37 (1979) 1109-10.

METHODIUS

B. *Vita Methodii.* PG 100: 1244-61. G. Da Costa-Louillet, 'Vie de S. Méthode (+ 847),' in Saints de Constantinople au VIIe, IXe, Xe siècles. *Byz(B)* 24

(1954) 453-61. Dobschütz, E. 'Methodios und die Studiten. Strömungen und Gegenströmungen in der Hagiographie des 9. Jahrhunderts.' *ByZ* 18 (1909) 41-10-5. Grumel, V. 'La politique religieuse du patriarche S. Méthode.' *EO* 34 (1935) 385-401. J. Pargoire, 'Saint Méthode de Constantinople.' *EO* 6 (1903) 126-31; *id.*, 'Saint Méthode et la persécution.' *Ibid.*, 183-91.

MICHEL ATTALIATES

A. *Typikon.* Edited by F. von Miklosisch and J. Mueller. *Acta.* vol. 5 (Vienna, 1887) 293-397.
Wald Nissen, *Die Diataxis des Michael Attaliates von 1077.* Jena, 1894.

MOSES

B. Paul Devos, 'Saint Jean Cassien et saint Moïse l'Ethiopien.' *AnBoll* 103 (1-2, 1985) 61-74. I.C. 'Moïse l'Ethiopien, moine de Scété.' *Cath.* 39 (1980) 477.

NICETAS STETHATOS

A. *Vie de Syméon le Nouveau Théologien.* Edited and trans. by Irénée Hausherr. *OrChrA* 12. n. 45 (Rome, 1928) xxxvii-li.

B. Basile Krivochéine, 'St. Syméon le nouveau théologien et Nicetas Stethatos. Histoire du texte des *Catechésès*,' in Akten des XI. Internationalen Byzantinistenkongresses (München, 1958). München, 1960, 273-77. V. Laurent, 'Un nouveau monument hagiographique: la *Vie* de Syméon le nouveau théologien.' *EO* 28 (1929) 433. W. Voelker, 'Nicetas Stethatos als mystischer Schriftsteller und sein Verhältnis zu Symeon dem Neuen Theologen,' in *Praxis und Theoria.* (Wiesbaden, 1974) 456-89.

NICODEMUS THE HAGIORITE

B. A. Argyriou, 'Nicodème l'Hagiorite (1749-1809).' *RSR* 50 (1976) 38-51.

NILUS OF ANCYRA

B. R. Browning, 'Le commentaire de saint Nil d'Ancyre sur le Cantique des Cantiques.' *REB* 24 (1966) 107-114. A. Cameron, 'The Authenticity of the Letters of St. Nilus of Ancyra.' *GrRBySt* 17 (1976) 181-96. F. Degenhardt, *Der hl. Nilus Sinaita. Sein Leben und seine Lehre vom Mönchtum.* Beiträge zur Geschichte des älten Mönchtums und des Benediktinerordens 6. Münster in Westph., 1915; *id., Neue Beitraege zur Nilusforschung.* Münster, 1918. H. Graef, 'St Nilus: a Spiritual Director of the fifth Century,' in *Life of the Spirit* (1949) 224-29, 272-79. K. Heussi, *Untersuchungen zu Nilus dem Asketen. TU* 42.2 (Leipzig, 1917); *Id., Das Nilusproblem.* Leipzig, 1921.

OLYMPIAS

B. Jean Chrysostome. *Lettres à Olympias.* Edited by Anne-Marie Malingrey. Trans. by R. Flacelière. *SCh* 28bis. Paris, 1970.

ORIGEN

B. S. Bettencourt, 'Doctrine ascetica Origenis.' *StA* 16 (1945) 85ff.

PACHOMIUS THE ELDER

A. *Pachomian Koinonia.* 3 volumes. *Life. Rules. Other Writings of St. Pachomius and his Disciples.* Trans. by Armand Veilleux. *CS* 45-47. Kalamazoo, Michigan, 1980, 1981, 1982. *The Life of Pachomius (Vita Prima Graeca).* Trans. by A.N. Athanassakis. Soc. of Bibl. Lit. Texts and Transl. 7. Early Christ. Lit. Series 2. Missoula: Scholars' Press, 1975.

B. Placide Deseille, 'L'Esprit du monachisme pachômiem,' in Coll. Spiritualité Orientale 2 (Bellefontaine, 1968) 1-120. Philip Rousseau, *Pachomius: The Making of a Community in Fourth-Century Egypt.* Berkeley: University of California Press, 1985.

PALLADIUS

A. *The Lausiac History*. Trans. by R.T. Meyers. *ACW* 34. Westminster, Maryl., 1975.

B. D.F. Buck, 'The Structure of the *Lausiac History*.' *Byz(B)* 46.1 (1977) 292-307. R.T. Meyer, 'Palladius and Early Christian Spirituality.' *Studia Patristica* 10. *TU* 107 (Berlin, 1970) 379-90; *id.*, 'Lectio Divina in Palladius.' *Kyriakon*. Festschrift J. Quasten II (Münster, 1970) 580-4. E. Preuschen, *Palladius und Rufinus. Ein Beitrag zur Quellenkunde des ältesten Mönchtums* (Giesen, 1897) 119-23. R.H. Rodgers, *An Introduction to Palladius*. Class. Stud. London. Bull. Suppl. 35. London, 1975.

PAPHNUTIUS KEPHALAS

B. J.-Cl. Guy, *Le centre monastique de Scété au IVe et au début du Ve siècle*. Dissert. Rome: Gregorian University, 1964.

PARASCEVA THE YOUNGER

B. *La passion de sainte Parascève par Jean d'Eubée*. Edited by F. Halkin in *Polychronion*. Festschrift F. Doelger (Heidelberg, 1966) 226-37. *Vita Stae Paraskevis*. Edited by A. Papadopoulos-Kerameus, *Analekta* (Saint Petersburg, 1891) 438-53.

PAUL OF LATROS

B. *Vita Pauli Iunioris*. Edited by H. Delehaye. *AnBoll* 11 (1892) 19-74, 136-81. Delehaye, *Mélanges* (Brussels, 1966) 84-116. R. Janin, *Les églises et les monastères des grands centres byzantins* (Paris, 1975) 218-40.

PAUL THE SIMPLE

A. *Apophthegmata*. PG 65: 381-85.
C. Butler, *Historia Lausiaca* 2. Texts and Studies VI.2. Cambridge (1904) 69-74.

PAUL OF THEBES

B. Jerome. *Vita Pauli*. Edited by Rosweyde. PL 73: 105ff. *The First Desert Hero. St. Jerome's Vita Pauli*. Trans. by I.S. Kozik. New York, 1968. F. Cavallera. 'Paul de Thèbes et Paul d'Oxyrhynque.' *RAM* 7 (1926) 302-5. J. De Decker, *Contribution à l'étude de Saint Paul de Thèbes*. Ghent, 1905. H. Delehaye, 'La personalité historique de Saint Paul de Thèbes.' *AnBoll* 44 (1926) 64-9.

PETER OF GALATA

B. Theodoret of Cyrus. *Vita Petri*, in *Historia Religiosa* 9. PG 82: 1377-88. English trans. by R.M. Price. *A History of the Monks of Syria. CS* 88. Kalamazoo: Cistercian Publications, 1987.

PETER THE IBERIAN

B. John Rufus (?). *Vita Petri Ib*. Edited by R. Raabe. Leipzig, 1895. E. Honigmann, *Pierre l'Ibérien et les écrits du Pseudo-Denys l'Aréopagite*. Brussels. Mémoires Acad. royale de Belgique. Classe de lettres. 47/3. 1952. Sikorski. *Die Lebensbeschreibungen Peters des Iberers*, in 92. Jahresbericht der Schlesischen Gesellschaft für Vaterländische Kultur. vol. 1.4 (Breslau, 1915) 1-17.

PHILOTHEOS OF BATOS

B. Irénée Hausherr. 'La méthode d'oraison hésychaste.' *Or-ChrA* 9.2 (Rome, 1927) 140-2.

PHILOTHEUS KOKKINOS

A. *Vita Greg. Palam.* PG 151: 551-656. *Vita St. Germ. Hagior.* (George Maroules of Thessalonika). Edited by P. Ioannou. *AnBoll* 70 (1952) 37-115. *BHG* 264. S.J. Kuruses, *Philotheos ho Kokkinos*. Athens, 1967.

PHILOXENES OF MABBUG

B. Roberta C. Chesnut, *Three Monophysite Christologies: Severus of Antioch, Philoxenus of Mabbug, and Jacob of Sarugh.* London: Oxford University Press, 1976. J. Gribomont, 'Les homélies ascétiques de Philox. de M. et l'écho du Messalianisme.' *OstKSt* 2 (1957) 351-66. A. de Halleux, *Philoxène de Mabbug. Sa vie, ses écrits, sa théologie.* Louvain, 1963. P. Harb, 'L'attitude de Philoxène de Mabbug à l'égard de la spiritualité "savante" d'Evagre le Pontique,' in *Mémorial Mgr Gabriel Khouri Sarkis* (Louvain, 1969) 135-55. I. Hausherr, 'Contemplation et sainteté. Une remarquable mise au point par Philox. de Mabb.' *RAM* 14 (1933) 171-95. E. Lemoine, 'La spiritualité de Philox. de Mabb.' *OstKSt* 2 (1957) 351-66.

PLATO OF SAKKOUDION

B. Theodore the Studite. *Parva Catechesis.* Edited by A. Mai. Scriptorum veterum nova collectio (Rome, 1835-1838) vol. 9, 80; 162-64. B. Hermann, *Verborgene Heilige des greichischen Ostens* (Kevelaer, 1931) 153-71.

B. Menthon, *L'Olympe de Bithynie* (Paris, 1935) 170-9. J. Pargoire, 'A quelle date l'higoumène S. Platon est-il mort?' *EO* 3 (1899) 4 (1901) 164ff.

POEMEN

A. *Apophthegmata.* PG 65: 317-68.

P. Resch, *La doctrine ascétique des premiers maîtres égyptiens.* Paris, 1921.

PROCOPIUS OF GAZA

B. K. Seitz, *Die Schule von Gaza.* (Heidelberg, 1892) 9ff.

ROMANUS THE MELODIST

A. *Kontakia of Romanos, Byzantine Melodist.* Edited by Marjorie Carpenter. 2 vols. Columbia: University of Missouri Press, 1970.

Romand le Melóde. Hymnes. Edited by José Grosdidier de Matons. Vol 1 (Paris, 1962), 2 (1965), 3 (1965), 4 (1967), 5 (1981). *SCh* 283.

B. C. de Boor, 'Die Lebenszeit des Dichters Romanos.' *ByZ* 9 (1900) 633-40. J. Grosdidier de Matons, *Romanos le Mélode et les origines de la poésie religieuse à Byzance.* Paris, 1977. Maas, P. 'Die Chronologie der Hymnen des Romanos.' *ByZ* 15 (1906) 1-44. K. Mitsakis, *The Language of Romanos the Melodist.* Byzantinisches Archiv 11. Berlin, 1967. Eva Katafygiote Topping, 'St. Romanos: Ikon of a Poet.' *GrOThR* 12 (1966) 92-111; 'The Apostle Peter, Justinian and Romanos the Melodos.' *BMGrSt* 2 (1976) 1-15. S. Vailhé, 'Saint Romain le Melode,' *EO* 5 (1902) 207-12. P. Van den Ven, 'Encore Romanos le Mélode.' *ByZ* 12 (1903) 153-56.

RUFINUS OF AQUILEA

A. *Historia Monachorum in Aegypto.* English trans. by Norman Russell. *The Lives of the Desert Fathers.* London: Mowbray, 1980. Kalamazoo, MI., *CS* 34, 1981.

B. J.F. Angerer, 'Mönchtum und Seelsorge. Widerspruch oder Vollendung? Dargestellt an der *Historia Monachorum*,' in *Studia Historico-Ecclesiastica.* Festgabe für Luchesius G. Spaetling. Biblioth. Pontif. Athenei Antoniani, 19. (Rome, 1977) 147-67.

SABAS THE ELDER

B. *Kyrillos von Skythopolis. Bios (Vita) Sabae.* Edited by E. Schwartz. TU 49.2 (Leipzig, 1939) 85-200.
P. De Meester, *Règlement des bienheureux et saints pères Sabas le Grand et Théodose le cénobiarque pour la vie des moines cénobites et celliotes.* Lille, 1939. S. Vailhé, 'Le monastère de st. Sabas.' *EO* 1 (1898-1899) 337ff.

SABAS OF VATOPEDI

B. Philotheos Kokkinos. *Bios (Vita) Sabae.* Edited by A. Papadopoulos-Kerameus. *Analekta.* vol. 5, 190-359.

SHENOUTE OF ATRIPE

A. *Oeuvres de Schenudi.* Ed. and trans. by C. Amélineau. 2 vols. Paris, 1907, 1914. *Sinuthii Archimandritae vita et opera omnia.* Ed. by J. Leipoldt. *CSCO* 41 (1906), 42 (1908), 73 (1913). *The Life of Shenoute* by Besa. Trans., with an Introduction by David N. Bell. CS 73. Kalamazoo: Cistercian Publications, 1986.
J. Leipoldt, *Shenute von Atripe und die Enstehung des national-aegyptischen Christentums. TU.* Neue Folge 10. 1 (1923).

B. E. Leuddeckens, 'Gottesdienstliche Gemeinschaften im Pharaonischen, Hellenistischen und Christlichen Aegypten.' *ZRGG* 20 (1968) 193-211.

STEPHEN OF NICOMEDIA

B. *Vie de Syméon le nouveau théologien.* Edited by Irénée Hausherr. *OrChr* 12 (Rome, 1928). Introduction 7, 'L'adversaire: Etienne de Nicomédie,' li-lvi.

STEPHEN THE YOUNGER

B. *Vita sancti Stephanis junioris monachi et martyris auctore Stephano diacono Constantinop.* PG 100:1067-1186. *The Life of Stephen the Younger by Stephen the Deacon.* Trans. by J. Gill. *OCP* 6 (1940) 114-39. J. Pargoire, 'Le Mont Saint-Auxence. Etude historique et topographique.' *ROC* 8 (1903) 251-66.
G.L. Huxley, 'On the *Vita* of St. Stephen the Younger.' *GRBySt* 18 (1977) 97-108.

SYMEON OF EMESA

B. *Vita S. Simeonis Sali. BHG* II, p. 256, nn. 1677-77b. Lev Gillet, 'Une forme d'ascèse russe: la "folie pour le Christ".' *RLM* 12 (1926-1927) 29-35. V. Rocheau, 'Saint Siméon Salos, ermite palestinien et prototype des "Fous-pour-le-Christ".' *PrOrChr* 28 (1978) 209-19.

SYMEON THE NEW THEOLOGIAN

B. *Vie de Syméon le nouveau théologien par Nicétas Stethatos.* Edited and trans. by Irénée Hausherr. *OrChr* 12. Rome, 1928, xxxviii-li. Hilda Graef, 'The Spiritual Director in the Thought of Symeon the New Theologian.' *Kyriakon.* Festschrift J. Quasten II (Münster: Aschendorff. 1970) 608-14. Irénée Hausherr. 'Un grand mystique byzantin. Saint Syméon le nouveau théologien.' *OrChr* 12 (Rome, 1928) 60ff. Basile Krivochéine, *Dans la lumière du Christ. Saint Syméon le nouveau théologien* (949-1022). *Vie-Spiritualité-Doctrine.* Collection Témoins de l'Eglise invisible 1. Chevetogne, 1980. Trans. by Anthony P. Gythiel. *In the Light of Christ. Saint Symeon the New Theologian. Life-Spirituality-Doctrine.* Crestwood, New York: St. Vladimir's Seminary Press, 1987 (See especially Part Two, chapter VI, 'Spiritual Direction and Fatherhood,' 91-101) D. Moosdorf, 'Symeon der Neue Theologe (+1022). Ein Mystiker der byzantinischen Kirche.' *EuA* 51 (1975) 458-67.

SYMEON THE STUDITE

B. *Syméon le nouveau théologien. Catéchèses.* vol 1. Edited by Basile Krivochéine and J. Paramelle. *SCh* 96 (Paris, 1963) 313-15, n. 4. I. Hausherr, *Vie de Syméon le nouveau théologien par Nicétas Stethatos.* Introd., xc.

SYMEON THE STYLITE THE ANCIENT

B. H.G. Bleisch, *Die Säule im Weltgeviert. Der Aufstieg Simeons des ersten Säulenheiligen.* Sophia 17. Trier, 1979. Hippolyte Delehaye, *Les saints stylites.* Subsidia Hagiographica 14. (Brussels, 1923) i-xxxiv. A.J. Festugière, *Antioche païenne et chrétienne* (Paris, 1959) 347-401, 403-506. H. Lietzmann, *Das Leben des hl. Symeon Stylites. TU* 32. 4 (Berlin, 1908) 1-18.

SYMEON THE STYLITE THE YOUNGER

B. H. Delehaye, *Les saints stylites,* lix-lxxxv, 223-7. Sergei Hackel, ed., *The Byzantine Saint.* London, 1981: cf Index. R.

Mouterde, 'Nouvelles images de Stylites.' *OCP* 13 (1947) 245-50.
La vie ancienne de S. Syméon le Jeune (521-592). Vol 2. Trans. and commentary by P. van den Ven. Subsidia Hagiographica 32. Brussels, 1970.

SYMEON OF THESSALONIKA

A. *Political-Historical Works of Symeon, Archbishop of Thessalonika* (1416/17-to 1429). Edited by D. Balfour. *WBSt* 13. Vienna, 1979. *Id.*, 'St. Symeon of Thessalonica: a Polemical Hesychast.' *Sob* 4. 1 (1982) 6-21.

SYNCLETICA

A. *Apophthegmata*. PG 65: 421-28.

B. *Vita Graeca*. BHG II, p.261, nn. 1694, 1694a.

THEOCTISTA OF LESBOS

B. Symeon Metaphrastes. *Menologion*. BHG II, 270, nn. 1725-26. H. Delehaye, 'Le vie de sainte Théoctiste de Lesbos.' *Byz(B)* 1 (1924) 191-200; 'Un groupe de récits "utiles a l'âme".' *Mélanges Bidez*. Brussels (1933-1934) 255-66.

THEOCTISTUS

B. Cyril of Scythopolis. *Vita S. Euthymii*. Edited by E. Schwartz. *TU* 49.2 (Leipzig, 1939) *passim*. F. Halkin, 'La passion de saint Théoctiste.' *AnBoll* 73 (1955) 56.

THEODORE THE STUDITE

A. *Epistolae*. PG 99: 904-1669. *Sermones*. PG 99: 688-901 *Studitisches Mönchtum. Theodoros Studites, Monastische Epigramme*. Edited by J. Leroy. Graz, 1969. *Theodoros Studites. Jamben auf verschiedene Gegenstaende*. Edited by P. Speck. Supplementa Byzantina 1. Berlin, 1968.

B. Pr. Dobroklonskij, *Theodor ispovednik i igumen Studijskij*. 2 vols. Odessa, 1913, 1914. A. Gardner, *Theodore of Studium*.

His Life and Times. London, 1905. I. Hausherr, 'S. Théo-
dore, l'homme et l'ascète.' *OrChr* VI (1926) 1-87. J. Leroy,
'La vie quotidienne du moine studite.' *Ir* 27 (1954) 21-50; *id.*,
'La réforme studite.' *OrChrA* 153 (Rome, 1958) 181-214; 'S.
Théodore le studite,' in Théologie de la vie monastique
(Paris, 1961) 423-36. H. Marin, *S. Théodore.* Paris, 1906. D.
Stiernon,'Notice sur S. Jean higoumène du monastère de
Kathara.' *REB* 28 (1970) 111-27.

THEODORE OF TABENNA

B. P. Ladeuze, *Etude sur le cénobitisme pakhômien.* Louvain,
1898. R. Steidle, 'Der heilige Abt Theodore von Tabennisi.
Zur 1600. Wiederkehr des Todesjahres (368-1968).' *EuA* 44
(1968) 91-103.

THEODORET OF CYRRHUS

A. *Théodoret de Cyr. Histoire des moines de Syrie. Histoire Phi-
lothée* I-XIII. Trans. and annotated by P. Canivet and Alice
Leroy-Molinghen. Vol I. *SCh* 234. Paris, 1977. *A History of
the Monks of Syria. The Religious History of Theodoret of Cyrrhus.*
Trans. with an introduction, by R.M. Price. Kalamazoo:
Cistercian Publications, 1985.

B. P. Canivet, *Contributions archéologiques à l'histoire des moines
de Syrie. A propos de l'Histoire Philothée de Théodoret* (444-
460). Studia Patristica XIII. 2= *TU* 116. *Id.*, *Le monachisme
syrien selon Théodoret de Cyr.* Théologie historique 42. Paris,
1977.

THEODOSIUS THE CENOBIARCH

B. *Der heilige Theodosius.* Edited by H. Usener. Leipzig,
1890. *BHG* 2nd ed., (1776). *Kyrillos von Skythopolis. Bioi (Vitae) of Euthymius the Great, . . . Theodosius the Cenobiarch.* Edited by E. Schwartz. *TU* 49.2. Leipzig, 1939. *BHG* 1777. S.
Vailhé, 'Répertoire alphabétique des monastères de Palestine.' *ROC* 4 (1899) 523-24; 5 (1900) 25, 286-80.

THEOLEPTUS OF PHILADELPHIA

B. *Nicephorus Choumnos. Panegyris Theolept.* Edited by J. Fr. Boissonade. *Anecdota graeca.* vol. 5 (Paris, 1833) 183-239. D.J. Constantelos, 'Mysticism and Social Involvement in the Later Byzantine Church: Theoleptus of Philadelphia—A Case Study.' *ByzSt* 6 (1979) 83-94. V. Laurent, 'Les crises religieuses à Byzance. Le schisme anti-arsénite du métropole de Philadelphie Théolepte.'. *REB* 18 (1960) 45-54. J. Meyendorff, *Introduction à l'étude de Grégoire Palamas.* Paris, 1959, 30-3, 49ff. J. Verpeaux, *Nicephore Choumnos: homme d'Etat et humaniste byzantin.* Paris, 1959, 60-5, 145-50.

THEOPHAN THE RECLUSE

A. Sergius Bolshakoff, *Russian Mystics.* CS 26. Kalamazoo, 1977, 298-300.

B. Bolshakoff, 196-221.
Igor Smolitsch, *Leben und Lehre der Starzen.* Vienna, 1934, 178-93.
Stanislas Tyszkiewicz, *Moralistes russes.* Rome, 1951, 110-27.

XANTHOPOULOS, IGNATIUS AND KALLISTOS

A. PG 145-147.

B. H.G. Beck, *Kirche und Literatur im byzantinischen Reich* (München, 1959) 784ff. J. Gouillard, in *EO* 37 (1938) 456-60.

ZACHARIAS RHETOR

A. *Vie de Sévère. POr* II. 1. Paris, 1907. *Vita Isaias monach.* Edited by E.W. Brooks. *CSCO.* series III. Scriptores syri. vol. 15. Paris, 1907. *Vita severi Antiocheni.* Trans. by F. Nau. *ROC* 4-5 (1899-1900).

B. E. Honigmann, *Patristic Studies* I. 4, a. *SteT* 173 (1953) 194-205. M.A. Kugener, 'Observations sur la vie de l'ascète Isaïe . . . par Zacharie le Scholastique.' *ByZ* 9 (1900) 64-70.

ZOSIMAS

B. S. Vailhé, 'S. Dorothée et st Zosime.' *EO* 4 (1901) 359-63.

SUBJECT INDEX

Entalteria grammata (written man-
date), 102, 336; *see:* Counsel
Enthusiasm, manifestation of, 40;
see: Delusion
Epikeia (benevolent application of
the rule), 192, 336
Epiklesis (invocation), 99
Epistle of Barnabas, 256, 346
Epitimesis (reproof of demons), 3;
see: Antirrhesis; Demon(s);
Diakrisis
Epitimion (pl., *-ia*, penance), xii,
69, 71, 103, 238, 306; *see:* Confession; *Exagoreusis; Penthos*
Evil, moral, the definition of, 253;
see: Philautia; Voluntas Propria
Exagoreusis (revelation, disclosure of
thoughts), xiii, xxi, 60, 63, 67,
83, 92, 101, 104, 105, 106, 107,
108, 109, 112, 151, 155, 157, 158,
159, 160, 162, 163, 164, 169, 170,
173, 174, 175, 176, 188, 189, 193,
197, 199, 205, 207, 213, 214,
223, 225, 230, 231, 233, 234,
236, 238, 240, 247, 249, 251,
260, 261, 264, 278, 279, 281,
282, 283, 285, 287, 337; *see:*
*Abba; Amma; Apophthegmata Pa-
trum;* Child, spiritual; Confession; Conscience; *Diakrisis;*
Direction, sp.; Director, sp.;
Disciple, sp.; Fatherhood, sp.;
Gerōn; Kardia; Logismos; Motherhood, sp.; Old Man; *Philautia;*
Voluntas propria

Fatherhood, spiritual, viiff., 51ff.,
123ff., 208, 240, 255, 262, 278,
305, 323, 341; the basic study
on, xxviii (n. 1); definition of,
vii, 149; sp. f. above natural fatherhood, 264; the centrality of
sp. f., ix; proceeds from, and

leads to, the Holy Trinity, 150;
sp. f. and apostolic succession,
vii, viii; the only *raison d'être* of
sp. f., 168; the analysis of, in Patristic sources, xiff.; the ministry
of, vii, xix, xxi, xxii; qualities
needed for, 51ff., 303; the duties
of, 123ff., 303; the efficacy of,
243ff.; the results of, 130; the ac-
quisition of, 255; sp. f., a fragile
reality, 240; continues after
death, 141; sp. f. in John
Climacus, xiff.; in Symeon the
New Theologian, xiff.; in St
Paul, viii, 12; sp. f. and sonship,
259; and the Holy Spirit, 324;
see: Abba; Amma; Apophthegmata
Patrum; Apostle; Child, spiritual; Daughter, sp.; Direction,
sp,.; Director, sp.; Disciple, sp.;
Generation, sp.; *Gerōn; Hypotagē;*
Motherhood, sp.; Old Man; Parents, sp.; Relationship, personal;
Sonship, sp.; Salvation
Fatwa (Arabic, legal advice), 9
First Ascetical Sermon, by St Basil,
232
Freedom, inner, 251, 252; fr. from
care, *see: Amerimnia*
Fruitfulness, spiritual, 243, 324

Generation (regeneration), spiritual, viii, 11, 26, 209, 264, 322;
see: Fatherhood, spiritual; Parents, sp.; *Rhēma*
Gerōn (spiritual father), vii, ix, x,
xiv, 4, 337, 342; (synonymous
terms: *Abbas,* q.v.; Old man,
q.v.; *Pater spiritualis,* 26, 29, 341;
Pneumatikos pater, 341; *Starets*
(pl., *Startsi*), vii, ix, xi, xxi, xvii,
xxvi, 58, 190, 337, 342; still oth-

Gnōsis (knowledge) (*cont.*)
 and the Holy Spirit, 84; *see: Idiōta; Philosophia*
Grace, sanctifying (*gratia gratum
 faciens*), 33; freely bestowed (*gr.
 gratis data*), 33

Hegumen (superior), 26, 61, 69,
 99, 103, 104, 108, 110, 111, 112,
 113, 114, 115, 129, 142, 146, 188,
 192, 193, 199, 203, 206, 208, 211,
 214, 216, 226, 229, 230, 233,
 234, 240, 278, 279, 284, 288,
 293, 295, 297, 301, 303, 304,
 313, 337
Heresies: Bogomils (Manicheism),
 187, 335; Donatism, xxii; Euchites (Messalianism), xxxi (n.
 73), 4, 41, 157, 160, 163, 338,
 366, 372, 392; Jansenism, 157;
 Montanism, 33, 34, 40, 41, 48
 (n. 19), 49 (n. 22), 339; Sabellianism, 342; Sarabaites, 177
Hēsychia (tranquillity, stillness, silence), 125, 179, 180, 337; *see:*
 Life, types of
Historia Monachorum, by Rufinus of
 Aquileia, 42, 118 (n. 28), 187,
 363, 366, 383, 393
Historia Religiosa, by Theodoret of
 Cyrrhus, 115 (n. 13), 273, 391,
 397
Holiness, definition of, 57; signs or
 marks of, 43, 187
Holy Spirit, baptism of, xix, 51;
 called 'the Father of the poor,'
 323; viewed as 'mother' by the
 Syrians, 323; *direct* inspiration
 by the Spirit, the essential qualification of the spiritual father,
 xvi; according to Symeon the
 New Theologian, a *direct experience* of the S., the one indispens-

able qualification for the
 spiritual father, xix, xx
Humility, 124, 125, 126, 128, 133,
 137, 138, 159, 191, 203, 246, 249,
 298, 301, 304
Hypotagē (obedience, submission),
 6, 127, 147, 164, 166, 175, 180,
 197–9, 203, 204, 207, 208, 214,
 216, 238, 246, 259, 304, 333; the
 classical definition of, 6, 147–8,
 204; the paradox of, 204; the virtue of, 246, 259; the perfection
 of, 207, 208; the limits of, 199,
 204; types of: administrative
 (formal) o., 258; ready, unmur-
 muring o. (*eupeitheia*), 203, 245;
 o. without discernment
 (*adiakritikos hypakoē*), 203, 204;
 true o., 214; unconditional o.,
 197, 203; 'blind o.,' 304, 333; o.
 and renunciation (*apotagē*) of the
 world, 207; o. and commanding
 well, 305; o., not the last word,
 208; *see: Apotagē; Diakrisis;* Disciple, spiritual; *Gerōn; Philautia;
 Voluntas propria*
Hypotyposis (Constitution, outline),
 229, 337; *H.* of St Athanasius,
 111; *H.* of the Monastery of John
 the Baptist, 108

Idiōta (unlettered man), 31, 84, 85,
 124, 337; *see: Gnōsis; Philosophia*
Isangelic (*eisaggelos*), the monastic
 life, 'equal to that of the angels,'
 298, 338

Kardia (heart), the movements of,
 157; the guarding of the h.
 (*custodia cordis*), 157, 225; knowledge of the h. (*kardiognōsis*), 32,
 92, 104, 338; openness of heart,
 155, 159, 170, 172, 175, 176, 226,

NÁMES INDEX

1. ANCIENT

2. MODERN

CISTERCIAN PUBLICATIONS INC.
Kalamazoo, Michigan

TITLES LISTING

CISTERCIAN TEXTS

THE WORKS OF BERNARD OF CLAIRVAUX

Apologia to Abbot William
Five Books on Consideration: Advice to a
  Pope
Grace and Free Choice
Homilies in Praise of the Blessed Virgin
  Mary
The Life and Death of Saint Malachy the
  Irishman
Parables
Sermons on the Song of Songs I-IV
Steps of Humility and Pride

THE WORKS OF WILLIAM OF SAINT THIERRY

The Enigma of Faith
Exposition on the Epistle to the Romans
The Golden Epistle
The Mirror of Faith
The Nature and Dignity of Love

THE WORKS OF AELRED OF RIEVAULX

Dialogue on the Soul
The Mirror of Charity
Spiritual Friendship
Treatises. I: On Jesus at the Age of Twelve,
  Rule for a Recluse, The Pastoral Prayer

THE WORKS OF JOHN OF FORD

Sermons on the Final Verses of the Song of
Songs I-VII

THE WORKS OF GILBERT OF HOYLAND

Sermons on the Songs of Songs I, II, III
Treatises, Sermons and Epistles

OTHER EARLY CISTERCIAN WRITERS

The Letters of Adam of Perseigne I
Baldwin of Ford: Spiritual Tractates
Guerric of Igny: Liturgical Sermons I-II
Idung of Prüfening: Cistercians and Cluniacs:
  The Case for Citeaux
Isaac of Stella: Sermons on the Christian Year
Serlo of Wilton & Serlo of Savigny
Stephen of Lexington: Letters from Ireland
Stephen of Sawley: Treatises

MONASTIC TEXTS

EASTERN CHRISTIAN TRADITION

Besa: The Life of Shenoute
Cyril of Scythopolis: Lives of the Monks of
  Palestine
Dorotheos of Gaza: Discourses
Evagrius Ponticus: Praktikos and Chapters
  on Prayer
The Harlots of the Desert
Iosif Volotsky: Monastic Rule
The Lives of the Desert Fathers
Menas of Nikiou: Isaac of Alexandra & St
  Macrobius
Pachomian Koinonia I-III
The Sayings of the Desert Fathers
Spiritual Direction in the Early Christian East
  (I. Hausherr)
The Syriac Fathers on Prayer and the Spiritual
  Life

WESTERN CHRISTIAN TRADITION

Anselm of Canterbury: Letters I-[II]
Bede: Commentary on the even Catholic
  Epistles
Bede: Commentary on Acts
Bede: Gospel Homilies
Gregory the Great: Forty Gospel Homilies
Guigo II the Carthusian: Ladder of Monks
  and Twelve Meditations
Peter of Celle: Selected Works
The Letters of Armand-Jean de Rance I-II
The Rule of the Master

CHRISTIAN SPIRITUALITY

Abba: Guides to Wholeness and Holiness
  East and West
Athirst for God: Spiritual Desire in Bernard
  of Clairvaux's Sermons on the Song of Songs
  (M. Casey)
Cistercian Way (A. Louf)
Fathers Talking (A. Squire)
Friendship and Community (B. McGuire)
From Cloister to Classroom
Herald of Unity: The Life of Maria Gabrielle
  Sagheddu (M. Driscoll)
Life of St Mary Magdalene... (D. Mycoff)
Rancé and the Trappist Legacy (A.J.
  Krailsheimer)
Roots of the Modern Christian Tradition
Russian Mystics (S. Bolshakoff)
Spirituality of Western Christendom
Spirituality of the Christian East
(T. Spidlék)

MONASTIC STUDIES

Community and Abbot in the Rule of St
Benedict I-II (Adalbert De Vogüé)
Consider Your Call: A Theology of the
Monastic Life (Daniel Rees et al.)
The Finances of the Cistercian Order in the
Fourteenth Century (Peter King)

Fountains Abbey and Its Benefactors
(Joan Wardrop)
The Hermit Monks of Grandmont
(Carole A. Hutchison)
In the Unity of the Holy Spirit
(Sighard Kleiner)
Monastic Practices (Charles Cummings)
The Occupation of Celtic Sites in Ireland by
the Canons Regular of St Augustine and the
Cistercians (Geraldine Carville)
The Rule of St Benedict: A Doctrinal and
Spiritual Commentary (Adalbert de Vogüé)
The Rule of St Benedict (Br. Pinocchio)
St Hugh of Lincoln (D. H. Farmer)
Serving God First (Sighard Kleiner)

CISTERCIAN STUDIES

A Second Look at Saint Bernard (Jean Leclercq)
Bernard of Clairvaux and the Cistercian
Spirit (Jean Leclercq)
Bernard of Clairvaux: Studies Presented to
Dom Jean Leclercq
Christ the Way: The Christology of Guerric
of Igny (John Morson)
Cistercian Sign Language
The Cistercian Spirit
The Cistercians in Denmark (Brian McGuire)
Eleventh-century Background of Citeaux
(Bede K. Lackner)
The Golden Chain: Theological Anthropology of
Isaac of Stella (Bernard McGinn)
Image and Likeness: The Augustinian
Spirituality of William of St Thierry   (David
N. Bell)
The Mystical Theology of St Bernard
(Étienne Gilson)
Nicholas Cotheret's Annals of Citeaux
(Louis J. Lekai)
William, Abbot of St Thierry
Women and St Bernard of Clairvaux
(Jean Leclercq)

MEDIEVAL RELIGIOUS WOMEN

Distant Echoes (Shank-Nichols)
Gertrud the Great of Helfta: Spiritual Exercises
(Gertrud J. Lewis-Jack Lewis)
Peace Weavers (Nichols-Shank)

STUDIES IN CISTERCIAN ART AND ARCHITECTURE
Meredith Parsons Lillich, editor

Studies I, II, III now available
Studies IV scheduled for 1991

THOMAS MERTON

The Climate of Monastic Prayer (T. Merton)
The Legacy of Thomas Merton (Patrick Hart)
The Message of Thomas Merton (Patrick Hart)
Solitude in the Writings of Thomas Merton
(Richard Cashen)
Thomas Merton Monk (Patrick Hart)
Thomas Merton Monk and Artist
(Victor Kramer)
Thomas Merton on St Bernard
Toward an Integrated Humanity
(M.Basil Pennington et al.)

CISTERCIAN LITURGICAL DOCUMENTS SERIES
Chrysogonus Waddell, ocso, editor

Cistercian Hymnal: Text & Commentary
(2 volumes)
Hymn Collection of the Abbey of the Paraclete
Molesme Summer-Season Breviary
(4 volumes)
Institutiones nostrae: The Paraclete Statutes
Old French Ordinary and Breviary of the
Abbey of the Paraclete: Text and
Commentary (5 volumes)

STUDIA PATRISTICA

Papers of the 1983 Oxford Patristics Conference
Edited by Elizabeth A. Livingstone

XVIII/1 Historica-Gnostica-Biblica
XVIII/2 Critica-Classica-Ascetica-Liturgica
XVIII/3 Second Century-Clement & Origen-
Cappodician Fathers
XVIII/4 available from Peeters, Leuven

TEXTS AND STUDIES
IN THE
MONASTIC TRADITION

North American customers may order these books
through booksellers or directly from the warehouse:

Cistercian Publications
St Joseph's Abbey
Spencer, Massachusetts 01562
(508) 885-7011

Editorial queries and advance book information
should be directed to the Editorial Offices:

Cistercian Publications
Institute of Cistercian Studies
Western Michigan University
Kalamazoo, Michigan 49008
(616) 387-5090

A complete catalogue of texts in translation and
studies on early, medieval, and modern monasticism
is available at no cost from Cistercian Publications.